D1104548

HARVARD EAST ASIAN MONOGRAPHS

92

*Studies in the Modernization of
The Republic of Korea: 1945–1975*

The Economic and Social Modernization of the Republic of Korea

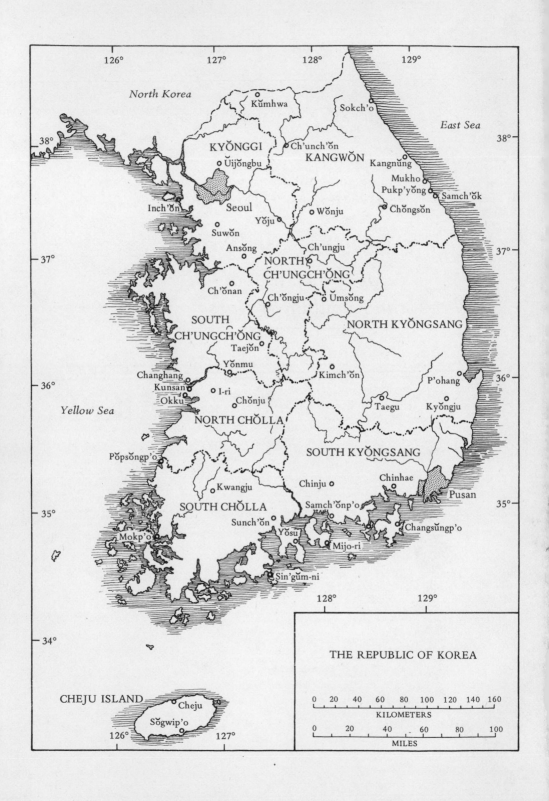

THE REPUBLIC OF KOREA

North Korea

East Sea

Kŭmhwa
Sokch'o

KYŎNGGI
Ch'unch'ŏn
KANGWŎN
Ŭijŏngbu
Kangnŭng
Mukho
Pukp'yŏng
Samch'ŏk
Inch'ŏn
Seoul
Wŏnju
Chŏngsŏn
Yŏju
Suwŏn
Ansŏng
Ch'ungju
NORTH
CH'UNGCH'ŎNG
Ch'ŏnan
Ch'ŏngju
Ŭmsŏng
NORTH KYŎNGSANG
SOUTH
CH'UNGCH'ŎNG
Taejŏn
Yŏnmu
Kimch'ŏn
P'ohang
Changhang
Kunsan
Okku
I-ri
Chŏnju
Taegu
Kyŏngju
Yellow Sea
NORTH CHŎLLA
SOUTH KYŎNGSANG
Pŏpsŏngp'o
Chinhae
Kwangju
Chinju
Pusan
Samch'ŏnp'o
SOUTH CHŎLLA
Changsŭngp'o
Sunch'ŏn
Yŏsu
Mijo-ri
Mokp'o
Sin'gŭm-ni

THE REPUBLIC OF KOREA

0 20 40 60 80 100 120 140 160
KILOMETERS

0 20 40 60 80 100
MILES

CHEJU ISLAND
Cheju
Sŏgwip'o

Studies in the Modernization of
The Republic of Korea: 1945–1975

The Economic and Social Modernization of the Republic of Korea

EDWARD S. MASON
MAHN JE KIM
DWIGHT H. PERKINS
KWANG SUK KIM
DAVID C. COLE
with
LEROY JONES
IL SAKONG
DONALD R. SNODGRASS
NOEL F. MCGINN

PUBLISHED BY
COUNCIL ON EAST ASIAN STUDIES
HARVARD UNIVERSITY

Distributed by
Harvard University Press
Cambridge, Massachusetts and London, England
1980

The Council on East Asian Studies at Harvard University publishes a monograph series
and, through the Fairbank Center for East Asian Research, administers research projects
designed to further scholarly understanding of
China, Japan, Korea, Vietnam, Inner Asia, and adjacent areas.

The Harvard Institute for International Development
is Harvard University's center for interdisciplinary research, teaching, and technical
assistance on the problems of modernization in less developed countries.

The Korea Development Institute
is an economic research center, supported in part by the Korean government,
that undertakes studies of the crucial development issues and prospects of Korea.

Library of Congress Cataloging in Publication Data

Main entry under title:
The Economic and social modernization of the
Republic of Korea.
(Studies in the modernization of the Republic of
Korea, 1945-1975) (Harvard East Asian monographs; 92)
Bibliography: p.
Includes index.
1. Korea—Economic conditions—1945-
2. Korea—Social conditions—1945-
I. Mason, Edward Sagendorph, 1899- II. Harvard University
Council on East Asian Studies. III. Series.
IV. Series: Harvard East Asian monographs; 92.
HC467.E26   330.9519'5043   80-21531
ISBN 0-674-23175-9

Foreword

This is one of the studies on the economic and social modernization of Korea undertaken jointly by the Harvard Institute
for International Development and the Korea Development
Institute. The undertaking has twin objectives; to examine the
elements underlying the remarkable growth of the Korean
economy and the distribution of the fruits of that growth,
together with the associated changes in society and government;
and to evaluate the importance of foreign economic assistance,
particularly American assistance, in promoting these changes.
The rapid rate of growth of the Korean economy, matched in
the less developed world (apart from the oil exporters) only by
similar rates of growth in the neighboring East Asian economies
of Taiwan, Hong Kong, and Singapore, has not escaped the
notice of economists and other observers. Indeed there has been
fairly extensive analysis of the Korean case. This analysis, has

been mainly limited to macroeconomic phenomena; to the behavior of monetary, fiscal, and foreign-exchange magnitudes and to the underlying policies affecting these magnitudes. But there are elements other than these that need to be taken into account to explain what has happened. The development of Korean entrepreneurship has been remarkable; Korea has an industrious and disciplined labor force; the contribution of agricultural development both to overall growth and to the distribution of income requires assessment; the level of literacy and the expansion of secondary and higher education have made their mark; and the combination and interdependence of government and private initiative and administration have been remarkably productive. These aspects together with the growth of urban areas, changes in the mortality and fertility of the population and in public health, are the primary objects of study. It is hoped that they will provide the building blocks from which an overall assessment of modernization in Korea can be constructed.

Economic assistance from the United States and, to a lesser extent, from other countries, has made a sizable but as yet unevaluated contribution to Korean development. A desire to have an assessment undertaken of this contribution, with whatever successes or failures have accompanied the U.S. involvement, was one of the motives for these studies, which have been financed in part by the U.S. Agency for International Development and, in part, by the Korea Development Institute. From 1945 to date, U.S. AID has contributed more than $6 billion to the Korean economy. There has also been a substantial fallout from the $7 billion of U.S. military assistance. Most of the economic assistance was contributed during the period before 1965, and most of it was in the form of grants. In later years the amount of economic assistance has declined rapidly and most of it, though concessional, has been in the form of loans. Currently, except for a minor trickle, U.S. economic assistance has ceased. The period of rapid economic growth in Korea has been since 1963, and in Korea, as well as in other countries receiving foreign assistance, it is a commonplace that it is the receiving country that is overwhelmingly responsible for what growth, or absence of growth, takes place. Nevertheless, economic assistance to Korea was exceptionally large, and whatever contribution was in fact made by outsiders needs to be assessed. One of the studies, *The Developmental Role of the Foreign Sector and Aid,* deals with foreign assistance in macroeconomic terms. The contribution of economic assistance to particular sectors is considered in the other studies.

All the studies in this series have involved American and Korean collaboration. For some studies the collaboration has been close; for others less so. All the American participants have spent some time in Korea in the course of their research, and a number of Korean participants have visited the United States. Only a few of the American participants have been able to read and speak Korean and, in consequence, the collaboration of their colleagues in making Korean materials available has been invaluable. This has truly been a joint enterprise.

The printed volumes in this series will include studies on the growth and structural transformation of the Korean economy, the foreign sector and aid, urbanization, rural development, the role of entrepreneurship, population policy and demographic transition, and education. Studies focusing on several other topics—the financial system, the fiscal system, labor economics and industrial relations, health and social development—will eventually be available either in printed or mimeographed form. The project will culminate in a final summary volume on the economic and social development of Korea.

Edward S. Mason

Edward S. Mason
Harvard Institute
for International Development

Mahn Je Kim

Mahn Je Kim
President,
Korea Development Institute

A Note on Romanization

In romanizing Korean, we have used the McCune-Reischauer system and have generally followed the stylistic guidelines set forth by the Library of Congress. In romanizing the names of Koreans in the McCune-Reischauer system, we have put a hyphen between the two personal names, the second of which has not been capitalized. For the names of historical or political figures, well-known place names, and the trade names of companies, we have tried to follow the most widely used romanization. For works written in Korean, the author's name appears in McCune-Reischauer romanization, sometimes followed by the author's preferred romanization if he or she has published in English. For works by Korean authors in English, the author's name is written as it appears in the original publication, sometimes followed by the author's name in McCune-Reischauer romanization, especially if the author has published in Korean also. In ordering the elements of persons' names, we have adopted a Western sequence—family name first in all alphabetized lists, but last elsewhere. This is a sequence used by some, but by no means all, Koreans who write in English. To avoid confusion, however, we have imposed an arbitrary consistency upon varying practices. Two notable exceptions occur in references to President Park Chung Hee, and Chang Myon, for whom the use of the family name first seems to be established by custom and preference. Commonly recurring Korean words such as si (city) have not been italicized. Korean words in the plural are not followed by the letter "s." Finally, complete information on authors' names or companies' trade names was not always available; in these cases we have simply tried to be as accurate as possible.

Contents

Contents

Contents

Contents

Contents

Tables

Tables

Figures

Abbreviations

BOK	Bank of Korea
CRIK	Civil Relief in Korea
DDE	domestic demand expansion
DPM	Deputy Prime Minister (head of the Economic Planning Board)
DRP	Democratic Republican Party
EE	export expansion
ECA	Economic Cooperation Administration
EPB	Economic Planning Board
FOA	Foreign Operations Administration
GARIOA	Government Appropriations for Relief in Occupied Areas
GDP	gross domestic product
GNP	gross national product
IBRD	International Bank for Reconstruction and Development
ICOR	incremental capital-output ratio
IMF	International Monetary Fund
IO	input-output
IS	import substitution
KCAC	Korean Civil Assistance Command
KDI	Korea Development Institute
KIST	Korea Institute of Science and Technology
KOTRA	Korean Trade Promotion Corporation
KSIC	Korean Standard Industrial Classification
LDC	less-developed country
MAF	Ministry of Agriculture and Forestry
MPC	Military Payment Certificate
NACF	National Agricultural Cooperative Federation

ODA	Official Development Assistance
OEC	Office of the Economic Coordinator
ORB	Overall Resource Budget(s)
PL 480	Public Law 480
PPP	purchasing-power-parity
SITC	Standard International Trade Classification
TC	technological change
UNCACK	United Nations Civil Assistance Command in Korea
UNKRA	United Nations Korea Reconstruction Agency
USAID	United States Agency of International Development
USAMGIK	United States Army Military Government in Korea

Preface

The years since 1963 in South Korea have witnessed both a remarkable economic growth and a course of political development that has moved away from democratic practices and,
particularly since 1972, toward a rather severe repression of
civil liberties. These lines of development could hardly fail to
have provoked conflicting assessments of the modernization
process in Korea and divergent judgments on where this process
may lead. Those primarily interested in economic analysis have
sought to explain a growth of national income which, in terms
of annual rates and duration, has had few precedents in economic history; a growth, moreover, that has been accompanied
by a relatively equitable distribution of income. Others, primarily interested in political processes, have seen much to
criticize in the way the government of Park Chung Hee maintained itself in power and curtailed the liberty of the citizenry.
What the relation has been between President Park's use of

authority and the rate of economic growth is an interesting question but one that may well be susceptible to different answers in the short run and the long run. In the short run, for example, a period covering the years 1963 to date, we have reasons for believing that a government able to maintain political stability (law and order if you will), undertake economic policies that a more democratic government would find it difficult or impossible to do, and implement these policies through a disciplined and well-organized bureaucracy, has been a significant factor in explaining Korea's growth. Whether the increase achieved in standards of living was worth the limitation of public participation and of civil liberties imposed on the population is a different question and one that is sure to provoke different answers.

An evaluation of the relation between political and economic development is also likely to be influenced by the time horizon within which this evaluation takes place. The relatively short period in which economic growth in South Korea has been encompassed has seen changes in the character of economic forces and social institutions that can hardly fail, over time, to have significant political effects. As the Korean economy has become more complex, it has become more difficult to direct from a central locus of power. Other power centers are emerging, and an institutional development is taking place that inevitably moves society toward a more pluralistic pattern. There may also be other changes with political consequences. The division of the culturally homogeneous Korean population into the highly antagonistic regimes of the north and south, with the south still fearful of incursions from the north, has been an important determinant of the character of government. Very few South Koreans care to risk a replay of a war that cost more than a million lives and tremendous property damage, and the risks have, at least to date, appeared to be less with a strong government backed by a powerful army. If tension between north and south should lessen, the political forces that now support the existing regime might lessen too and the dominant role now played by the armed forces lessen with them. The possible effects of socio-economic and military-security developments on politics and government in South Korea are interesting questions, but they are highly speculative and no discussion of them can be expected in this study.

Our task is more modest. It has two objectives: to examine the elements underlying the remarkable growth of the Korean economy and the distribution of the fruits of that growth, together with associated changes in society and government; and to evaluate the importance of foreign economic assistance, particularly American assistance, in promoting these changes. Economic growth in Korea has not escaped the notice of economists and, indeed, there have been a number of analyses of the Korean case. These analyses, however, have been mainly focused on macroeconomic phenomena; the behavior of monetary, fiscal, and foreign exchange magnitudes and the underlying policies affecting these magnitudes. But there are elements other than those that need to be taken into account. The development of Korean entrepreneurship has been remarkable; Korea has an industrious and disciplined labor force; the contribution of agricultural development both to overall growth and to the distribution of income requires assessment; the level of literacy and the expansion of secondary and higher education have made their mark; and the combination and interdependence of government and private initiative and administration has been remarkably productive. These aspects, together with the expansion of urban areas, changes in the mortality and fertility of the population and in public health, are examined in their relation to economic development.

Economic assistance from the United States and, to a lesser extent, from other countries, has made a sizable but as yet unevaluated contribution to Korean development. A desire to have an assessment undertaken of this contribution, with whatever successes or failures have accompanied the U.S. involvement, was one of the motives for this, and the underlying studies that have accompanied it. They have been financed in part by the U.S. Agency for International Development and, in part, by the Korea Development Institute. From 1945 to date, the United States government has contributed more than $6 billion in economic assistance to the Korean economy. There has also been a substantial economic fallout from the $7 billion of U.S. military assistance. Most of the economic assistance was contributed before 1965, and most of it was in the form of grants. In later years the amount of economic assistance has declined rapidly, and the larger part, though concessional, has taken the form of loans. Currently, except for a minor trickle, U.S. economic assistance has ceased. The period of rapid growth in Korea began after 1963 when U.S. economic assistance was already on the decline; and, in Korea, as well as in other countries receiving assistance, it is a commonplace that the receiving country is overwhelmingly responsible for what growth, or absence of growth, takes place. Nevertheless, economic assistance to Korea was exceptionally large, and whatever contribution was in fact made by outsiders needs to be evaluated.

The chapters in this volume have been mainly based on a series of underlying studies and, indeed, they are to be regarded, in the main, as a summary of the results of those studies. All have been the product of collaboration between American and Korean authors and have or will be issued by the Council on East Asian Studies at Harvard or the Korea Development Institute in Seoul. They cover the following subjects:

Growth and Macro Changes in the Structure of National Product

The Foreign Sector and Foreign Aid

Government and Entrepreneurship in Economic Development

Industrial Case Studies

Development of the Financial System

Development of the Fiscal System

Rural Development

Urbanization and Urban Problems

Education and the Modernization of Korea

Health and Economic and Social Development

Although the primary focus of this summary volume is on the period 1945 through 1975, no study of Korean development can neglect the 1200 years of Korea's existence as an independent and united country or the influence of the period of Japanese penetration followed by 35 years of colonial rule. The fact that the countries deriving from the great East Asian culture have been in the forefront of rapid economic development says something important about the conditions of Korea's growth. And it was Japan that disturbed the isolation and traditionalism of the "Hermit Kingdom" and, while drastically exploiting the Korean population, yet gave Koreans their first experience of modern management and technology. Rapid economic growth began only in 1963, but the Korean "miracle" was not devoid of historical antecedents.

Although the writing of this volume has been a joint effort in the sense that the contributors of individual chapters have had to meet the criticism and objections of their colleagues, it may be of some interest to note the primary responsibility for first drafts. Edward S. Mason is the author of Chapters 1, 2, 8, and 13. In writing Chapter 8 he was joined by Leroy Jones and Il SaKong, the authors of the underlying study entitled *Government, Business, and Entrepreneurship in Economic Development: The Korean Case.* Chapter 8 is essentially a summary of that study. Dwight H. Perkins is responsible for Chapters 3, 7, and 12. Chapter 7 is largely a summary of the underlying study *Rural Development* by Perkins and a number of collaborators. David C. Cole is the author of Chapters 6, 9, and 11, which draw heavily on the studies of the foreign sector and foreign aid, the development of the fiscal system, and the development of the financial system, and the studies on urbanization and demographic transition. Kwang Suk Kim is the author of Chapters 4 and 5, which owe much to the study by him and Michael Roemer called *Growth and Structural Transformation.*

Donald R. Snodgrass drafted the chapter on Education based on *Education and Development in Korea*, which he coauthored with Noel F. McGinn, Shin-Bok Kim, Yung Bong Kim and Quee-Young Kim. Mahn Je Kim made his contribution in the discussion of future prospects which concludes the final Chapter 13.

The assassination of President Park on October 26, 1979 found this manuscript ready for the press and the underlying studies either published or in course of publication. This event which may have large consequences for the political and economic future of the Republic of Korea does not, however, appear to call for changes in this volume or in the associated studies. What we have attempted is to set forth the historical record of a period, 1945 to 1975, with an analysis of the consequences of American assistance and the sources of economic growth. The death of President Park, who was the principal leader of Korean development, may or may not mark the end of an era in some significant sense but it does not alter the historical record. In Chapter 2 and Chapter 13 we shall have something to say about the character of President Park's legacy.

ONE

Introduction

The main theme of this study is the economic, social, and administrative modernization of South Korea. If modernization means an approach toward the institutions, values, and procedures of Western Europe and North America, Korea, in common with most of the countries of the Third World, presents a sharp contrast between development in the social and economic areas and development in the political sphere. What we have to say about political change in developing countries and in Korea is contained in Chapter 2.

There can be no question of the success of modernization and development in Korea in terms of changes in the economy, in social institutions, and in government administration. In these areas the increasing division of labor, differentiation of roles, and specification of function that Fred W. Riggs holds to be characteristic of the development process is everywhere evident. [1]

It has produced in Korea, at least since 1963, a rate of growth of national income remarkable by any standard, a growth, moreover, from which all elements in the society, rural and urban, have benefited. This growth has been accompanied by all the social changes we have learned to expect in a modernizing society—decline in the percentage of the rural population, rapid urbanization, increased geographical and social mobility of the population, formation of professional and other interest groups, and the acquisition of attitudes and habits of thought of an industrializing community. It has also been accompanied by an increasing capacity of the government to govern, to formulate policies favorable to development, and to put these policies into practice by effective administration.

The success of Korea's economic development has not failed to capture the attention of economists around the world. By now there is a large literature on this "success" story and the supposed reasons for success.[2] This literature in the main stresses changes in macroeconomic magnitudes and the macroeconomic policies to which these changes are attributed. Indeed, according to certain interpretations, rapid economic growth of Korea is to be principally accounted for by these macroeconomic policies, the implication being that if other less-developed countries want to accelerate development all they need do is adopt similar measures. We do not believe this is so. There is much more to Korean economic development than sensible monetary, fiscal, and foreign exchange policies. A large part of this study is devoted to an examination of what these underlying forces are.

A second, and secondary, theme of this study is the contribution to Korean development of the United States economic assistance program. American economic assistance to Korea has been large, over $6 billion from 1945 to date. In the period before 1965, this assistance was almost entirely in the form of grants; since then it has been mainly loans, and by now has been reduced to a trickle. During the war and immediate post-war period, it is hardly too much to say that American economic assistance and the economic fallout from military assistance kept

Korea alive. But how much such assistance contributed to Korean development is a subject that has not yet been assessed, and the desire for such an assessment was the chief motivation in USAID's financial contribution to this study. This contribution to development was not limited to financial assistance but included, at various periods, close collaboration between United States and Korean officials on developmental policies. The relation between American assistance and Korean development is discussed, in general terms, in Chapter 6. The contribution in particular areas such as rural development, education, and public health is covered in later chapters.

Although the United States was by far the largest supplier of economic assistance, it was not the only one. Smaller contributions were made available from the United Nations and, as a result of a "normalization" of Japanese-Korean relations in 1965, from Japan. Beginning in the 1960s, the inflow of foreign private investment became significant, bringing with it effective access to modern technology. Private loan financing was even more significant. At all stages of Korean development since the war, foreign savings have accounted for a large fraction of Korean investment. The relation of foreign private investment and the importation of technology to Korean development are discussed in Chapter 6.

Before an analysis of Korean modernization since 1945, it is necessary to assess two prior influences that had strong impact on Korean development—the heritage of East Asian civilization and the effects of the Japanese occupation. Chapter 3 presents a broad-brush treatment of these influences. It is a remarkable fact that wherever the Confucian influence has been strong (including China itself, Korea, to a certain extent Japan, Taiwan, Hong Kong, Singapore, and Chinese elements in Indonesia, Malaysia, and Thailand), modern economic development has prospered. The similarities to the Protestant and Puritan interpretation of capitalism are obvious. The second major influence, touched on in Chapter 3, is that of Japanese culture and organization. Japan occupied Korea from 1910 to 1945, but

Japanese influence had been growing ever since the "opening up" of Korea in 1876. Although the Japanese exploited Korea for their own purposes, they left a heritage of land management, governmental organization, and the beginnings of industrialization that had a lasting influence.

The years from 1945 to 1953 are dealt with more cursorily both because of data limitations, and because they were accompanied by such turmoil and disruption that no orderly movement toward development is discernible. These years included the division of Korea between north and south, the disorderly and unfocused period of U.S. Military Government, the political struggles that brought the Syngman Rhee regime to power, the Korean War that left over a million people dead and destroyed at least a quarter of Korea's fixed capital, and the very large influx of population from the north and from Japan. The years immediately after World War II were primarily devoted to installing and gaining experience for Koreans in the key economic and political positions formerly held by Japanese. These efforts were beginning to bear fruit in increased production and stability when the Korean War erupted. While the three-year war caused extreme destruction and suffering, it also established South Korea as a viable political entity with a clear sense of national identity.

The systematic analysis of Korean economic and social modernization really begins in 1953 with the end of the Korean War, when continuous statistical series became available, and when both the Korean government and foreign supporters turned their attention to reconstruction and development. Recent Korean development has been described as export-led growth and, to a large extent, that is correct. But in the 1950s, industrialization in Korea leaned heavily on import substitution, and it was not until 1961 that exports began to grow strongly. Since then, the rate of expansion of exports has been phenomenal, averaging 30–40 percent a year in real terms, exceeding in almost every year the very high rate of growth of national income. But the meaning of "export-led growth" needs to be interpreted. It would be possible, at least for a period of time, to promote a rapid expansion of exports at the expense of the rest of the economy through subsidies, differential tax advantages, preferential access to credit, and to imports and other measures. Although exports could grow, the domestic economy, hampered by high costs inflicted through export policies, might well stagnate. There are well-documented examples of this in other countries where a dollar earned in foreign exchange through exports has been exorbitantly expensive in terms of domestic resources. There have even been cases in which the net earnings in foreign exchange via exports have been negative. Under these circumstances one cannot speak of export-led growth (but, rather, of export-led stagnation).

In order that an expansion of exports may lead to growth, not only must exports be competitive in world markets, but at home the prices of inputs for domestic and export production must not be too far out of balance. Under these circumstances the goods and services that are exported will be those in which a country has, in fact, a comparative advantage and not those that are made competitive on world markets through extensive subsidization. If, then, the export sector grows more rapidly than the rest of the economy, one can speak correctly of export-led growth in the sense that this sector is contributing an increasing share of value added to the economy. But if the economy as a whole is growing rapidly, there is more to this growth than the contribution of the export sector. All, or most, sectors of the economy must be experiencing an increase in productivity. If an explanation of this is to be found, it will lie beyond the expansion of exports in areas in which influences affecting the whole of the economy are at work.

The influence of foreign trade policies on Korean exports and the rate of growth of the economy has been carefully studied by a number of competent analysts. In general, they conclude that, although the incentive structure steered resources toward export industries, "the low average incentive rates and the relatively small dispersion in South Korea are presumptive evidence that

Korean development has been efficient."[3] The allocation of factors has not been very different, at least since 1965, than it would have been under a free-trade regime. Korean manufactured exports have been labor-intensive and manufactured imports capital-intensive which is what would be expected if the forces of comparative advantage were allowed to work. The same underlying factors that have made Korean exports competitive in world markets have led to a steady growth of productivity in the rest of the economy. Changes in the structure of the economy under the influence of export-oriented growth are examined in Chapters 4 and 5.

If the expansion of exports has been accompanied by an increase in productivity in the domestic economy, it is fair to assume that, although the export sector is the leading growth sector, it is not the only growth sector. It is necessary, therefore, to inquire why factor inputs have been increasingly productive in the economy as a whole as well as in the export sector. An efficient allocation of resources explains much but not all. The emergence of a group of competent entrepreneurs, the availability of an industrious and disciplined labor force, a literate and well-trained working population, an unusually effective cooperation of government and business, the development of a supportive financial system for mobilizing capital, and improved management of land and other agricultural inputs have their contribution to make to increased productivity not only in the export but in the domestic sectors of the economy. Later chapters are concerned with an examination of these and other aspects of economic and social development.

Chapter 4 charts the tempo of economic growth and examines the changes, in macroeconomic dimensions, of the structure of national product from 1910 to date. Although the Japanese colonial administration shaped the development of the Korean economy primarily in the interests of Japan, it supervised, particularly in the later years, a rapid growth of national output and significant changes in the structure of production. Most of the heavy industry was located north of the 38th parallel together with a preponderance of power facilities. South Korea inherited light manufactures, predominantly cotton textiles, and the richest agricultural lands. The division of Korea had serious economic as well as political consequences.

The feeble beginnings of development, first under the aegis of U.S. Military Government and then, from 1948, under Korea's first elected government, were shattered by the Korean War. The period from 1953 to 1960 was one of slow recovery assisted by massive grant aid from the United States. The highly personal and dictatorial regime of Syngman Rhee espoused industrialization as its main strategy of development, and behind a complex barrier of tariffs, quantitative restrictions, and exchange controls, amenable to corruption and the growth of individual fortunes, a certain amount of investment in import replacing manufactures did occur. Nevertheless the slowness of recovery led officials in Washington to wonder whether Korea was not, in fact, a "basket case," destined to repose indefinitely on the U.S. doorstep.

There can be few examples in economic history of the rapidity with which the Korean economy changed from relative stagnation to buoyant growth. In the space of three years from 1960 to 1963, the country experienced a political revolution, a military coup, two years of rather fumbling military government, and emerged with an elected regime supported by the armed forces, which, because of, or despite, an increasingly authoritarian posture, has maintained political stability and fostered a highly successful set of developmental politics ever since. Chapter 4 goes on to trace the character of aggregate and sectoral economic growth in Korea and to compare this growth pattern with "normal" accomplishments in less-developed countries and with those of other rapidly growing economies in East Asia.

The most striking feature of Korean economic growth has been the rapid increase in output in manufacture and mining together with the ancillary services of transportation, communications, construction, and power. In 1954, at the end of the war, Korea was still a predominantly agrarian economy in which manufacture and construction accounted for only 11 percent of GNP. By 1976 this percentage had increased to 37 percent, and Korea was already an industrialized society whose exports of manufactures and overseas construction activities were permeating markets around the world. Changes in the industrial structure and the sources of change are the subject of Chapter 5. The most rapidly growing sector of manufactured output was production for export. Manufactured exports accounted for 15 percent of total export goods and services in 1955, 38 percent in 1963, and 70 percent in 1973. In that year, 24 percent of all manufactured output was exported.

By the end of the 1950s, most of the easily available opportunities for import substitution in non-durable consumers goods had been exploited, and in the early 1960s, Korea turned toward the promotion of manufactured exports. The years of decisive policy changes were 1964–1967 when the wǒn was devalued by 50 percent to a unitary floating rate, interest rates on bank deposits and some loans were more than doubled, trade was liberalized, tax reforms introduced, and a series of incentives was offered to exporters. This policy direction has, with minor modifications, been carried on to the present. The First Five-Year Economic Development Plan, 1962 to 1966, established as its primary target export-oriented industrialization and growth, and this objective has dominated all subsequent plans including the fourth, introduced at the beginning of 1977.

Rapid industrial growth has brought with it significant changes in the structure of manufactures. The early leaders, including food-processing industries and textiles, have given way to clothing and apparel, consumer electronics, and more complex producer goods, in particular chemicals, petroleum products, machinery, and transportation equipment. There has as yet, however, been little change in the capital-output ratio due largely to a remarkable increase in the rate of capital utilization. Assuming a 24-hour basis, capacity utilization increased on certain measures from 13 percent in 1962 to 27 percent in 1971. Nevertheless, Korea is definitely moving away from the highly labor-intensive output that marked earlier stages of growth towards a more sophisticated, capital-intensive structure of manufacture.

Chapter 4 also attempts an econometric analysis of the sources of growth, approaching the problem both from an analysis of factor inputs and an analysis of changes in the structure of demand. During the period of rapid growth since 1962, the capital stock is estimated to have grown at approximately 8.3 percent a year for the economy as a whole (10.4 percent in manufactures) and labor inputs, in terms of hours worked, at 4.6 percent for the economy (10.7 in manufactures). But the inherent quality of capital stock can be improved by economies of scale, reallocation from less to more productive uses, increase in the rate of utilization, and technological changes embodied in capital equipment. Labor quality can be increased by education and on-the-job training. Some estimates of the value of "residual" inputs, that is, output not explained by quantitative changes in labor and capital, run as high as 40 percent in Korea.

The chapter concludes with some comparisons of industrial growth in Korea with that in other countries. Since 1960, Korea has had a substantially more rapid growth than Japan had for a similarly extended period in the first half of the twentieth century. And, among Third World non-oil exporting countries, only Taiwan and Singapore are comparable.

In 1945, most of the people of Korea were farmers working tiny plots of land as tenants. In 1975, a majority lived in cities or held non-agricultural jobs in the countryside. Those who remained in agriculture were overwhelmingly cultivators of their own land. The major external forces that brought about these changes were the explosively rapid expansion of industrialization and the growth of foreign trade. But within agriculture there were also significant developments that not only produced a respectable growth of farm output but yielded a more than respectable increase in farm incomes and standards of rural living. How these came about is the subject of Chapter 7.

Korean farmers have been highly skilled for centuries. During the period of Japanese occupation, an extension service was established, agricultural credit was provided, and farm output grew. But there was a rising level of tenancy as Korean farmers lost their land to Japanese and Korean landlords, and rural incomes, in fact, fell. Korean agriculture was well organized from the point of view of Japanese interests. In the 1920s and 1930s, although rice production fell slightly, exports to Japan more than doubled. The educational system that the Japanese encouraged in urban areas did not penetrate far into the country-side. The main inheritance from the Japanese in agriculture in 1945 was an impoverished, hard-working mass of tenant farmers.

By any standard, the land tenure system that Korea inherited from the Japanese was an oppressive one. At the beginning of World War II, nearly 60 percent of all cultivated land in what is now South Korea was owned by landlords. The U.S. Military Government had no difficulty in coming to a decision to expropriate and distribute Japanese-held land. But it required action by the newly elected Korean government in 1949 to purchase and to redistribute large Korean-owned estates. Although these estates were purchased, the terms of sale were such that expropriation rather than compensation was the more accurate description. As a result of these two acts of land redistribution, the number of tenants fell to 5–7 percent of the total number of cultivators, and the amount of rented land fell from 60 percent to 15 percent of the total cultivated area. In fine, Korea achieved with independence a relative equality of agricultural assets and incomes not to be found in most of the less-developed world. In part because the size of agricultural holdings was limited by law to 3 chŏngbo (approximately 3 hectares), a relatively equitable distribution of agricultural assets and incomes has continued to characterize Korean farming.

From the end of Japanese occupation to the beginning of the Korean War, farm output increased rapidly, recovering from the low levels to which it had sunk toward the end of World War II. War inevitably reduced output but, from 1952 to 1954, agricultural production again increased rapidly. From 1954 to 1975, the trend rate of growth of agricultural value added was about

3.5 percent per annum. Although this fell far short, in the 1960s, of rates of growth attained in industry, it is a respectable figure as compared with rates of growth in other less-developed countries. Since there was little if any change in the farm labor force from 1955 to 1975, Korean agriculture was able to channel its surplus labor into urban and industrial employment. By the middle of the 1960s, if not before, Korea had ceased to be a surplus-labor economy. Indeed, in the late 1960s and 1970s, the shortage of farm labor was leading to a rapid mechanization of agricultural activities.

Since both the farm labor force and the quantity of available land remained relatively constant from the beginning of independence to the present, the sources of growth of agricultural output must be sought elsewhere. The major sources were increased use of fertilizers, improvements in plant varieties, a shift away from grain production to more valuable cash crops and livestock, the improving quality of farming and farm management, and, in recent years, mechanization. After the program of land distribution had been accomplished, the role of government in rural development was, at least until the late 1960s, marginal. Indeed, the government's price policy, aimed at checking urban inflation by keeping the price of rice low, a policy that was abetted by easy imports of Public Law 480 grain from the United States, seriously dampened farm incentives. The Rhee regime's neglect of agriculture was nearly complete. Although this situation improved in the 1960s with an expansion of agricultural credit facilities, an improvement in price incentives, and a strengthening of the bureaucracy concerned with agricultural services, it was not until 1968 and the years thereafter that government reversed its agricultural policies.

Evidence of a growing disparity between rural and urban incomes led to a number of steps designed to improve agriculture's terms of trade, among them the adoption of a two-tier price system for rice and barley, involving government procurement at a relatively high price from farmers and sale at relatively low prices to urban consumers. The election of 1971, which appears to have indicated to President Park that he might be losing his rural constituency, led to other measures including the Saemaul Undong (New Community Movement). The stated purpose of Saemaul is to upgrade the quality of rural life by promoting cooperation, self-help, and a transformation of traditional rural attitudes. Although the program has probably been stronger in rhetoric than action, it has managed to have an influence on many Korea villages. Saemaul has been accompanied by an extensive program of construction of farm access roads which has made it easier to get crops to markets. Although government has developed an active program of agricultural promotion, it is the growing urban market for fruits and vegetables that has had a larger influence on increasing farm incomes. This rapidly expanding urban market has made it possible for farmers to shift their production toward higher value per hectare crops. Another important aspect of the government's new agricultural policy has been a revitalization of the bureaucratic agencies serving Korean farms, with a definite diminution of corruption. This is of importance because the Korean farm services, as all other aspects of Korean government, are highly centralized and bureaucratic. Historically there has always been a high degree of centralization of government services, and this was reinforced during Japanese rule. There is little popular participation either in the choice of local officials or in the formulation of farm policies they implement. The Office of Rural Development is attached to the Ministry of Agriculture and Fisheries, but it controls its 10,000 extension workers from its quasi-independent headquarters. The National Agricultural Cooperative Federation is also a centrally directed bureaucracy, and local members have little voice in determining policies or the manner of operations. If agricultural services are to be provided by centralized bureaucracies, it is a matter of considerable importance that the bureaucrats be not only professionally competent but relatively uncorrupt and also responsive to farm interests. Apparently there has been considerable progress in this direction since the introduction of Saemaul.

The income of the typical Korean farmer has increased substantially more than the rate of increase in value of agricultural output, since land distribution has made him an owner entitled to the full product of his efforts rather than a tenant paying half his output to a landlord. He has also benefited from the extension of educational facilities to the countryside and the provision by government of additional rural services. Farm incomes, however, still fall substantially short of urban incomes, though the disparity has been reduced since 1968, and there are fairly wide differences in farm incomes in different regions of the country. Still, as compared with urban-rural income differences in most other less-developed countries, the Korean situation must be given high marks on grounds of equity.

The period, during the 1950s, of massive U.S. economic assistance on a grant basis was a period of recovery followed by sluggish growth. The Korean economy really "took off" only after U.S. assistance had fallen to about half its 1950s level and grants had been converted to concessional loans. This does not mean, of course, that foreign aid had little to do with subsequent Korean development. In a number of respects it helped lay the foundation in the 1950s for the spectacular successes of the 1960s and 1970s. The influence of U.S. assistance on educational expansion, land distribution and land management, the development of an import-saving industrialization, and the improvement of transportation facilities is examined in the various chapters dealing with sectoral development. The extent of Korean dependence on U.S. assistance inevitably generated a certain amount of friction between the Rhee government and American representatives. President Rhee was adept at maximizing aid flows through skillful mismanagement of foreign exchange policy and domestic inflation. Washington could not make up its mind whether its primary objective was to keep the Korean economy afloat for security reasons, or whether economic development was also an important desideratum. Similarly, Washington debated whether the aid level should be targeted on the internal fiscal deficit or the external balance of payments deficit without fully appreciating their interdependence. In the course of time, relations became more productive, a process facilitated by the departure of Syngman Rhee and a shift in the orientation of U.S. assistance to a predominant emphasis on development. By the middle of the 1960s, U.S. participation in the shaping of development policy was welcome and effective.

The first half of the decade of the 1960s was a period of transition from heavy dependence on U.S. assistance toward Korean economic independence. The grant element of aid continued to decline, and by 1965 the USAID program had been converted mainly to concessional long-term loans. Although foreign savings continued to account for most of Korean investment, the share of imports financed by USAID fell from 87 percent in 1960 to 32 percent in 1965. The fact that American economic assistance had been provided mainly in the form of grants meant that Korea entered its period of rapid growth with a very low burden of foreign debt. External debt stood at $301 million in 1965, $176 million public, and the rest private. By this time, Korea had become credit-worthy for foreign borrowing and proceeded to take full advantage of this position. Total foreign indebtedness tripled between 1965 and 1967 and had increased 10 times by 1971. By 1975, public external debt stood at $3,125 million, and private debt, mainly government guaranteed, at $3,571 million. Since debt-service payments absorbed 30 percent of foreign exchange earnings in 1971, doubts were expressed regarding the soundness of Korean expansion, but the extremely rapid growth of Korean exports after 1972 brought this debt-service ratio down to an easily manageable level of 12.7 percent by 1975. Thus, while recent economic growth in Korea has been heavily dependent on the inflow of foreign resources, both private and public, the U.S. assistance program and continuing U.S. political and economic support have contributed greatly to Korea's external borrowing capability.

It can be argued, however, that, although foreign assistance was necessary to keep Korea alive in the years immediately following the war, it was, during the last years of the Rhee regime, tending to become counter-productive. Rhee used this massive grant assistance as a protection against the necessity of policy changes that would have made the economy more productive and self-supporting and against normalization of relations with Japan. Although USAID officials stormed and fumed and relations between Korea and the United States steadily worsened, fears of what might happen in South Korea if economic and military assistance was reduced always stayed the American hand. As in so many recorded instances in USAID relationships, it was the weaker power that held the whip hand. It was only after a new and more effective government had come into power and had been convinced that the volume of U.S. assistance was going to be sharply curtailed, that steps were taken making it possible for foreign economic assistance again to make a positive contribution.

Chapter 6 undertakes a survey and an evaluation of American economic assistance to Korean development. Total economic assistance from the United States, as indicated above, has been very large, over $6 billion from 1945 to 1976, and, until 1960, it was provided entirely in the form of grants. In addition, the direct and indirect economic consequences of American military spending in Korea have been sizable. An assessment, however, of the contribution of this assistance to Korean development is not an easy matter.

From 1945 until the end of the war in 1953, over $1 billion was provided by a bewildering complex of United States and United Nations agencies with most of the U.N. contribution coming from the United States. Of necessity, this contribution was almost entirely in the form of relief supplies enabling the country, with difficulty, to hold its head above water. From 1953 to 1960, American economic assistance averaged about 10 percent of Korean GNP; it financed over three-quarters of imports; it accounted for nearly the whole of savings and investment; and it generated more than half of the government's revenues. The high point was in 1957 when the United States provided $382.9 million in economic assistance. After that U.S. aid levels began to decline and the eventual realization by the Korean government that a decline was inevitable had a good deal to do with the ensuing shift in government policies away from import replacement and toward export promotion. Most of American economic assistance took the form of general commodity imports, and it was only after 1957 that project aid directed to specific development activities accounted for more than 25 percent of total U.S. assistance.

Chapter 8 deals with a highly important element in Korea's growth, but one not very extensively explored previously, the relations of government and business. Students of the Japanese growth "miracle" have frequently attributed importance to the close cooperation of government and business in that country, and, to emphasize the closeness, have referred to "Japan, Incorporated." The term is, in fact, much more applicable in Korea, but in Korea there is little doubt that the chief party in the corporation is government. This may come as a surprise to those who have been accustomed to think of Korea as a free-enterprise economy. It *is* free in the sense that private enterprise has flourished, and the role of market considerations looms large in the formulation of both private and public economic policy. But there is no denying that it is government that establishes the framework within which firms operate, sets the rules, and exercises a close oversight of performance.

Economic planning is taken seriously in Korea, and the Economic Planning Board, headed by the Deputy Prime Minister, in addition to assuming the chief responsibility of formulating medium-term plans, exercises the budgetary function that in other countries belongs to the Ministry of Finance. Many less-developed countries formulate five-year plans but in many, perhaps most, of them there is a substantial hiatus between what is included in the plan and what, in fact, gets done. In Korea attention focuses strongly on plan implementation, and the annual review procedures permit not only an adaptation of planning to changing circumstances but a close supervision of the performance of public and private operating units. The government has permitted, indeed encouraged, the technical participation of foreigners in the formulation of all its five-year plans. On the occasion of the First Five-Year Plan, in 1962, and the Second Five-Year Plan, in 1966, foreign experts were, perhaps, the senior partners. Although this is no longer so, the assistance of experts from abroad is still welcomed and, in the shaping of the Fourth Five-Year Plan which went into effect in 1977, a number of consultants, primarily from The World Bank, participated.

It is difficult for outsiders—and only less so for domestic observers—to know with any precision how, in any government, important policy decisions tend to get made. It is, perhaps, less difficult in this case than in most others. In Korea there is no doubt that the leadership has a strong commitment to economic development and that the President and a relatively small number of senior officials participated actively in all policy decisions. Institutions are structured to facilitate this participation, and there is ample testimony that President Park and his economic secretariat in the Blue House (the executive mansion) were fully engaged in the process. Organized business groups are regularly consulted on matters affecting the private sector, but it is evident that such groups exercise nowhere near the influence that their counterparts do in Japan. Gunnar Myrdal, in his studies on Southern Asia has drawn a useful distinction between "hard" and "soft" states.[4] A soft state is characterized by a lack of social discipline, an unwillingness on the part of the population to accept obligations, and an unwillingness on the part of government to enforce them. By these tests Korea is indubitably a hard state, and the evidence lies clearly in the effectiveness with which public policy decisions are implemented.

Although Korea is a government-directed economy, its private enterprises are managed by a highly competent group of entrepreneurs. The rise of this group is remarkable since, during the colonial regime, almost all the executive positions in both public and private enterprise were occupied by Japanese. An extensive questionnaire has elicited a good deal of information concerning the family backgrounds, religious affiliations, education, and work experience of Korea's business leaders. A considerable number were immigrants from the north, and the Christian community has contributed more than its share, but the unusual degree of social mobility generated by the collapse of the traditional society, the chaos of war and revolution, and the extraordinarily rapid spread of educational opportunities seems to have opened the door, at least for small business, to many elements. On the whole, however, as indicated in Chapter 8, the business elite has sprung from the preindustrial elite—large landowners, the bureaucracy, and professional groups.

Industrialization in Korea has been accompanied by the growth of a sizable number of large-scale private enterprises and extensive family fortunes. What are characterized as the zaibatsu in Japan are known as the *chaebŏl* in Korea, comprising perhaps a few dozen leading families. The *chaebŏl* are by no means as significant in the business community of Korea as were the zaibatsu before World War II in Japan, and government exercises a considerably greater control of their activities. Nor is economic concentration, by any measure, as high in Korea as in a number of other less-developed countries. Still, there is a rapidly growing group of large fortunes and extensive industrial holdings. The Korean government puts very little check on the accumulation of these fortunes, providing they are reinvested in productive activities judged by the planners to have high priority. In recent years, the government has attempted to convert these family holdings into public corporations through enforced sale of equity interests. So far, success in these efforts has been limited.

Although private ownership has been predominant in the industrialization of Korea, public ownership has also played a large role. Indeed, the share of public ownership in industrial assets in Korea, usually considered a private enterprise economy, is fully as large as that of public ownership of industrial assets in India, with its "socialist pattern of society." Public enterprise has been particularly important in the development of the fertilizer industry, iron and steel, chemicals, and other branches of heavy industry. It has been effectively used as one of the chief instruments of government in its direction of the course of economic development.

Perhaps the chief public instrument in shaping the direction of private industrialization has been government control of access to domestic credit and foreign borrowing. In 1962, the Minister of Finance gained legal as well as de facto control over the central bank and monetary policy and since then has seen to it that access to bank credit was given to borrowers willing to follow the developmental priorities of the government. At about the same period, Korean enterprises wishing to borrow abroad and seeking the necessary government guarantee were required to obtain the approval of the Economic Planning Board. The capital structure of Korean corporations with their extraordinarily low equity and very large debt components, which was an outgrowth of governmental financial policies, helped to make control over access to domestic and foreign credit an unusually powerful instrument. In 1970, debt accounted for 82.5 percent of the liabilities of Korean industrial corporations as compared with 67.5 percent in Japan and 35 percent in the United States.

Chapter 9 undertakes a survey of the development of the fiscal and financial systems in Korea. This involves an examination of the changing relations between the fiscal and financial activities of government and the behavior of private financial markets.

The confusion, inflation, and governmental disarray resulting from partition, military occupation, and withdrawal of the Japanese, destroyed the fairly well developed financial and fiscal system inherited from the Japanese and left South Korea with a largely non-functioning set of banking institutions, a hyperactive unorganized money market, and a fiscal system heavily dependent on counterpart funds generated by American economic assistance. In the latter half of the 1940s and throughout the 1950s, nearly 50 percent of Korean government revenues came from aid-generated counterpart funds. The needs of private borrowers were supplied in large part by the unorganized, so-called "curb market," with rates of return and costs of capital varying widely among financial transactions. Domestic savings were very low, and over 80 percent of the low level of investment was accounted for by foreign assistance. In the late 1950s, strong anti-inflation policies resulted in some rise in government revenues and financial savings, but these fell back to very low levels in the first half of the 1960s as a result of erratic government policies and renewed inflation.

In the mid-1960s, the Korean government, with foreign advice and encouragement, initiated both fiscal and financial reforms that greatly increased the resource mobilizing capabilities of these two sets of institutions. At the same time, the government encouraged and facilitated the inflow of private foreign credit to finance industrial investment. As a result of these measures, the supply of domestic and foreign savings was sufficient to sustain high rates of domestic investment that were an essential part of accelerated growth of the economy. In Chapter 9 we discuss the institutional and policy changes that brought about this remarkable expansion of finance, and show how the government saw to it that the foreign and domestic financial resources as well as the fiscal system were directed towards priority objectives.

Chapters 10 and 11 are concerned with a number of elements affecting human resource development and the quality of life in Korea—population growth, the delivery of health services, social security, the spread of educational opportunities, and urbanization. These chapters constitute the principal treatment in this study of social development in Korea.

Korea is one of the three most densely populated countries in the world, the other two being Bangladesh and Taiwan. In 1975, there were 338 people per square kilometer; the population density in Japan in the same year was 294 per square kilometer. With a crude birth rate in 1961 of 41 per thousand and a population growing at the rate of nearly 3 percent a year, a Malthusian solution seemed to be not far off. Since then there has been a remarkable decline in the crude birth rate to 24 per thousand in 1974. This was among the most rapid declines in birth rates ever recorded anywhere. A determined government program of family planning combined with changes in economic opportunities, in social structure, and attitudes toward family size helped to bring this about. Korea still faces a serious problem of pressure of population on limited space, but it no longer seems an insoluable problem.

The high degree of cultural homogeneity and the absence of strong class barriers has meant that little resistance was offered to the diffusion of low-fertility values or to the spread of contraceptive methods. Between 1965 and 1975, desired family size declined as rapidly for young women in rural as in urban areas. Both urbanization and the increasing labor participation rate by women have been closely associated with an increase in age at marriage and with a decline in marital fertility. The increase in education, particularly of women, has undoubtedly contributed to this decline in fertility. So also has the rising cost of child care as the number of years at school has expanded. Despite the sharp decrease in the birth rate, the low average age of the Korean population will mean a relatively slow decline in the rate of population growth from its present value of about 2 percent per year. It seems probable that South Korea will enter the new century with a population of 54 or 55 million as compared with the 1975 figure of approximately 35 million.

Social services have been relatively neglected in Korea. Low government expenditures on health care and social insurance released budgetary resources for investment in economic infrastructure and have no doubt contributed to some extent to the rapid growth of national income but at some cost to the quality of life. This is not to say that health care has not significantly improved during the last three decades. The number of qualified physicians has quadrupled, while the population has doubled. The death rate has fallen from 15 per thousand in 1960 to 9 per thousand in 1970. Growth in per capita incomes has permitted a significant increase in private expenditures on sanitation and health care, not to mention a greatly improved diet. Nevertheless, there is still a considerable amount of preventable disease in Korea, and the expansion of health-care facilities has been conspicuously slow in reaching rural areas. A substantial increase in public expenditure on health and other social services is contemplated in the Fourth Five-Year Plan, 1977–1981.

To date, these expenditures have been meager. In 1973, public expenditures on social insurance, public health, public assistance and welfare, and veterans relief constituted only 0.97 percent of GNP. Similar expenditures amounted to 1.2 percent in Taiwan, nearly 3 percent in Malaysia, and 5.3 percent in Japan, with many developed countries spending more than 10 percent of GNP. The Confucian ethic, which places on a son the responsibility for his parents' welfare, is no longer adequate in a society that is becoming rapidly urbanized and in which the nuclear family is replacing and, in most areas, has replaced the extended family. The enactment of the National Welfare Pension Law on December 1, 1973, still to be put into effect, will, when implemented, represent a first step toward the development of a comprehensive social security program in Korea, and the Fourth Five-Year Plan promises more. As the leading authority on social security in Korea has put it, "The question is not whether Korea can afford a more comprehensive social security program but whether it can afford any longer not to make a beginning."[5]

In the expansion of educational facilities and opportunities, Korea has been as advanced as any developing country, but with an unusually heavy reliance on private initiative and financial support. Most serious studies of Korean development contrast the poverty of natural resource endowment with the richness of Korea's human resource endowment and find, in the latter, a significant element in their explanation of rapid economic growth. How did this rich human resource endowment come into being? Was it the product of a centuries-old cultural environment, or was it the product of an extraordinarily rapid expansion of educational opportunities oriented toward the promotion of economic growth in the period since 1900 or since 1945? The answer would seem to involve some of each.

Educational facilities in Korea expanded very rapidly after the Korean War with large inputs of U.S. assistance. By 1960, 59 percent of the student age group was enrolled in primary schools, as compared with 22 percent in other countries with similar per capita incomes. Between 1960 and 1972, Korea achieved universal primary enrollment; secondary enrollment also increased rapidly and, although university enrollments have not yet reached the levels attained in Taiwan and the Philippines, they are high as compared with most other countries with similar per capita incomes. The literacy rate in Korea had reached 88 percent by 1970.

This development has been influenced by the two countries most closely associated with Korea, Japan and the United States, but even more by the insatiable demand for education of the Korean people. The inheritance from the Japanese included large-size classes, a heavy emphasis on academic—rather than vocational—studies, moral education, deep respect for the authority of the teacher (without which large classes would be unmanageable), and a government-managed system of examinations for entrance to high school and university. Korean schools are, in the Japanese tradition, rigidly controlled, and the examination system plays a very important part in the selection that governs entrance into preferred positions in Korean society.

The American contribution, after an initial unsuccessful effort under the occupation government to inject more democratic content into the educational system, was thereafter directed more to the provision of physical facilities, although the U.S. educational example had some influence on educational pattern. The United States supported coeducation, which was fully implemented only in the primary grades, and attempted to promote female education at all levels. It also attempted to loosen some of the rigidities inherited from the Japanese, but even today the pattern of student as passive participant is prevalent in Korean schools.

The private contribution to the expansion of educational facilities in Korea is unique in the experience of less-developed countries, or even developed ones. Although primary education is assumed to be free, families in fact make large contributions in books and materials. The percentage of the private contribution to the total costs of education, even in public schools, rises with the grade level. In recent years, unmet social demands for education have resulted in a large private educational system at the secondary and tertiary levels. Currently there are more students in private universities than in public. Although numerous secondary schools and universities are privately financed, government maintains a tight control over their size and curriculum. As with other public services in Korea, administration of the school system is highly centralized.

In comparison with other less-developed countries, access to education is relatively equally distributed in Korea. Furthermore, equality of access has improved over time. Although there are still some severe inequalities—access to the better schools in Seoul is easier for those who live in the capital than those in the countryside, men are more likely to become educated than women, children of educated parents are three times more likely to reach the university than children whose parents have low levels of education—still, as compared with other countries at similar income levels, the Korean educational system must be judged to have made a substantial contribution to equality of opportunity.

Migration to the city has been a characteristic of the third quarter of the twentieth century around the world, but particularly in less-developed countries. In no country has urbanization been as rapid as in Korea. In the United States and Western Europe, the proportion of the population living in urban areas grew at about 1 percent per annum from 1950 to 1975 and at, perhaps, 1.5 percent during the most active period of growth in the nineteenth century. In most less-developed countries the rate was between 2 and 3 percent from 1950 to 1975. In Korea, urbanization, defined as the rate of growth of the percentage of population in cities of over 50,000, was at the astounding figure of 4.1 percent.

In most of the Third World, urbanization has been accompanied by a long series of economic and social plagues—unemployment, slum housing and crowding, inadequate sanitary facilities, lack of transportation, and various types of pollution. Korean cities have managed to escape much of this though not all. The extremely rapid growth of industry has managed to keep unemployment low. Urban unemployment has steadily declined over the last decade, and in 1975 was down to 6.6 percent of the urban labor force. The national average was 4 percent. Urban transportation, which is mainly by bus—though Seoul has a short subway system—has pretty well kept pace with demand. Although urban housing is inadequate, it does not suffer from comparison with urban housing in other countries of similar per capita income. In 1960, housing in Korea provided 6.6 square meters per person as against 18.6 in Japan. The figure of 2.3 persons per room was not out of line with other countries with approximately equal per capita incomes. Owner occupancy was 69 percent in 1970 as against 63 percent in the United States and 58 percent in Japan. Still, the housing situation in Korea cannot be considered satisfactory. The average age of the available stock is old and, over the last decade, the stock has been increasing at only 1 percent a year. Only 15 percent of new housing has been provided by public construction, and this percentage would need to be considerably increased if the housing situation is not to deteriorate.

Public opinion in Korea has only recently become familiar with the problems of pollution and, as in most other less-developed countries, not much has been done about it. Air quality levels in Seoul, a city of 7 million surrounded by mountains, are definitely lower than in American and Japanese cities. The Han River, flowing through Seoul, is heavily polluted. Until recently, government expenditures on water and sewage facilities have been small. The high priority given to economic growth has hitherto precluded adequate attention to matters of this sort. These observations, however, must be considered in relation to the urban situation in other less-developed countries. Despite the speed of urbanization, the most serious difficulties that have affected large cities in other LDCs have been avoided, and the authors of our special study on urbanization have heralded "Korean urbanization" as "a great success story during the third quarter of the twentieth century."

Chapter 12 raises, and attempts to answer, the question "Who has benefited from Korean growth?" The answer involves more than an examination of statistics, such as they are, on income distribution. How equal, or unequal, is access to various levels of education? How are public health services distributed to various elements of the population? What has been done to ease the burdens of the seriously disadvantaged through various types of social security measures? Are these various elements of the population "ill housed, ill fed, and ill clothed"? On the other hand, is there a rapidly growing group of large fortunes?

During the early years of independence, the situation in Korea could be described as a relatively equal distribution of poverty. Per capita incomes were in the neighborhood of $70 in 1953, and there were few, if any, large fortunes. The large land holdings had been distributed; both agricultural assets and agricultural incomes were relatively equal, and Korea was a predominantly agricultural economy. Ninety percent of the industrial capital, prior to independence, had been in the hands of the Japanese, and the dislocation and destruction accompanying independence and war had prevented anything like an orderly transfer to Korean private hands. Although a few large fortunes were made during the Rhee regime, chiefly through exploitation of foreign exchange and import policies, Korea, at the end of the period before the commencement of rapid growth, was one of the most egalitarian economies outside the central planning group. The Gini ratio (according to which zero measures perfect equality) was in the low .30s.

Although statistics on income distribution are better in Korea than in most less-developed countries, there is some doubt whether the trend since 1960 has been toward greater equality, less equality, or little change. There is, however, no doubt that, for the period 1970 to 1975, the level of inequality in the size distribution of income is less than in most other low-income countries and comparable to levels in some industrialized countries. A survey in 1970 indicated that the lowest 40 percent of the income receivers received 18 percent of total income, and the top 20 percent received 45 percent of total income.

The distribution of income *within* the rural sector has remained relatively equal throughout the whole period. In 1974 the poorest 40 percent received 17 percent of farm income; the richest 10 percent received 25 percent. The Gini ratio was in the low .30s. If one excludes large fortunes, the distribution of earnings within the urban sector of the Korean economy has also maintained a low level of inequality, and, although there has been a rapid increase in large incomes and fortunes in Korea, the percentage of increase accruing to the wealthy group is probably still less than in most LDCs.

In sum, despite the many uncertainties concerning the statistics, it is clear that all four of these forms of income inequality (in the national distribution, between the rural and urban sectors, and within each of these sectors) were low by international standards on the eve of the period of rapid growth in 1963–1964. What has happened since is less clear, but at least they have not worsened dramatically. This in itself makes Korea outstanding among low-income countries, especially, perhaps, among those that have experienced significant economic growth.

When one moves outside the area of income statistics to consider other elements of the question "Who benefited from Korean development?" one encounters a mixed bag. There is no doubt that, with respect to educational opportunities, Korea presents a more equitable pattern than exists in all but a very few less-developed countries. Primary education has been relatively accessible from early on and is now universal. A high percentage of the relevant age cohort attend secondary schools, and university enrollments are large. Furthermore, partly as a result of American influence, the education of women has expanded rapidly. On the other hand, in the areas of public health and social security the Korean record is not particularly good. The access of the rural population to public health facilities has been less than adequate, and the condition of the aged poor and other disadvantaged elements of the population has been neglected in favor of a single-minded pursuit of economic growth. These deficiencies are in process of being remedied, but to date more dependence has been placed on the traditional recourse to assistance from extended families than a rapidly industrializing society can tolerate.

Chapter 13 attempts an assessment of the sources of Korean growth and has a word to say about future prospects. Any such attempt must go back a certain way to consider the developmental potentialities of the Korean culture and to evaluate the consequences of the Japanese occupation. It is a striking fact that all the areas in which the Confucian ethic has penetrated have shown, during this century, a remarkable capacity for economic growth, and Korea is no exception. We must conclude that a basic reason for development is that the country is occupied by Koreans. What this means in terms of self-discipline, work attitudes, desire for education and family advancement, and adaptability to change, is in certain respects similar to the values and attitudes brought by Protestantism to the emergence of early capitalism.

The Japanese occupation was conceived and carried through in the interests of Japan. Nonetheless, it left a residue that has inevitably influenced the course of Korean development. What the Japanese brought to Korea was access to modern technology and management. Managerial practices were changed in agriculture, industry, transportation, and government. Although the Japanese managed in their own interest, they managed well, and the lessons they taught were not forgotten by Koreans.

Independence, military government, separation from the north, war, and the influx of 4 million refugees and returnees from the north and from Japan combined to destroy much of traditional authority, create a mobile population, and open the way to new men. Existing class barriers were broken down and, along with them, obstacles to upward movement. There were no unassimilated ethnic groups, and the cultural homogeneity of the Korean population facilitated the easy mobility of ideas and new techniques and practices.

Massive foreign assistance, mainly from the United States, helped Korean society to survive the ravages of war and begin the process of recovery. Although the availability of this assistance permitted the Rhee Government in the late 1950s to avoid taking steps that would have facilitated economic growth, a change of regime opened the way to a more fruitful collaboration. By the time grant aid had ceased in the mid-1960s, a revitalized Korean economy was able to approach the capital markets of the world with a burden of debt service low enough to assure its credit-worthiness. Korean development has been accompanied and stimulated by an unusually large inflow of foreign capital.

These, plus a rapidly expanding educational system, were the major factors that made available to Korea at the beginning of its rapid development: a disciplined and literate labor force augmented by a continuous influx of additional workers made surplus by increases in agricultural productivity; a ready access to investible funds from abroad and from increasing domestic savings; a rapidly expanding stock of energetic and ambitious entrepreneurs; and relatively easy access to foreign technologies. This combination of inputs, however, would not have produced Korea's phenomenal growth rate without political stability with power in the hands of a government committed to economic development and capable of formulating and implementing the policies needed to accomplish this objective. Whatever one thinks of the political record of the Park regime, its competence in the economic area can hardly be questioned.

TWO

Modernization in the Third World

and in Korea

Modernization was a term much in use a few years ago. It has, however, somewhat fallen out of favor for reasons that are easy to understand. As commonly interpreted, modernization implies an approach toward the institutions, structures, and values of Western society. "Historically, modernization," according to S. M. Eisenstadt, "is the process of change toward those types of social, economic and political systems that have developed in Western Europe and North America from the seventeenth century to the nineteenth and have then spread to other European countries and in the nineteenth and twentieth centuries to the South American, Asian and African continents."[1] While the less-developed countries of the Third World have indeed appeared to be on a course towards "Europeanization" in some respects, particularly those concerned with economic growth, in other respects no such movement is discernible.

Particularly notable is the lack of progress toward the political institutions, structures, and values of Western Europe.

THE THIRD WORLD

Political movement has, if anything, been in the opposite direction both in the "new states" of Asia and Africa and the older states of Latin America. The democratic institutions and political institutions carefully provided by the British Raj for colonies emerging into independence have almost everywhere given place to authoritarian regimes controlled by the military, carefully disciplined one-party systems, or, as in Uganda, by particularly repressive dictatorships. India has been, apart from Mrs. Gandhi's lapse into "disciplined democracy," a notable exception. Of the twelve sizable states of South America, all but two, Venezuela and Colombia, are, or have recently been, under the control of military governments, and democracy in Colombia appears to be in a rather shaky condition. In Southern Asia, Sri Lanka (Ceylon) and Malaysia have some claim to be called democracies, but in Malaysia, a peaceful transfer of power, which is one of the primary indicators of democracy, can only take place within one ethnic group. For the rest of the Third World, participation in political decision-making appears to be concentrating in fewer and fewer hands.

Economists, in analyzing the growth process in less-developed countries, have frequently found it useful to rely on the concept of dualism. A distinction is drawn between the modern sector employing advanced, capital-intensive technologies, occupied by market-oriented enterprises, and motivated by Western values, and the traditional sector of peasant agriculture and small-scale cottage industry, employing labor-using techniques, producing for local consumption, and with relatively static wants and patterns of consumption. Economic growth, defined as an increase in per capita incomes, has been accompanied by an expansion of the modern and a contraction of the traditional sector; with increased urbanization, a marked change in the structure of output and employment, increasing literacy, and a decrease in production for domestic use. The employment consequences of modernization have tended to lag behind economic growth in many countries, and relative disparities of income have frequently increased. Nevertheless, in the economic area, modernization in the sense of movement toward the values and institutions of the West, has a certain validity. There has been something like a linear, irreversible progression, marked by increase in per capita incomes, urbanization, industrialization, increased literacy, communications, social mobility, and other indexes.

The political sphere in less-developed countries is at least as subject to a dualistic interpretation as the economic sphere, and here there is little evidence of an expansion of the modern sector and a contraction of the traditional. If, with Bernard Crick,[2] we define politics as "the activity by which different interests within a given unit of rule are conciliated by giving them a share in power in proportion to their importance to the welfare and the survival of the whole community," politics in most less-developed countries is usually limited to a relatively small element of the population, an elite that shows few signs of encouraging a broader participation. Facing this "modern" political sector that commands all the levers of power is a "traditional," and usually politically inert and apathetic peasantry, and an urban population whose tendencies to political opposition are often firmly held in check by measures that may be more or less repressive. Whether, in the course of time, there will develop from these authoritarian regimes a style of government more closely resembling the societies of the West is unclear. But as things now stand, modernization in the sense of Westernization has, in the political sphere, by and large eluded the Third World.

Why this is so has been the subject of much speculation by political scientists. Cultural relativism is often brought forward as one significant influence. As Lucien W. Pye puts it, "constitutional democracy is a peculiarly Western institution and few questions relating to contemporary public affairs are more puzzling and more fundamentally disturbing than that of whether western political forces and ideals are appropriate or even relevant for the new states of Africa and Asia."[3] Indeed conditions under which democratic institutions and practices developed in Western Europe and North America were very different from those now confronting the new states of Asia and Africa.

Whether one accepts a Marxian interpretation of political development, emphasizing the structure of the economy as the determinant of the locus of political power, or espouses a more pluralistic interpretation, there is general agreement that in the West political change has been closely interwoven with social and economic change. As George Unwin noted, "The main feature of British history since the seventeenth century has been the remoulding of a State by a powerful Society."[4] Although the relations between social and political change have varied among Western countries, in general it can be said that the rise of democratic institutions has been shaped by powerful social forces.

These social forces, the institutions that intermediate between the state and the citizen in a pluralistic society, have been absent in most of the Third World and, consequently, for these and other reasons, political development has followed a different course. The more or less autocratic authority of colonial regimes has been transferred to the more or less autocratic authority of domestic elites who claimed legitimacy not on the basis of a consent of the governed ascertained through a democratic process but on the basis of an assumed identity of interest arising out of common nationhood. Nationalism has been a powerful cement holding many of these societies together and legitimizing, at least to some extent, existing regimes. Where this source of legitimacy has worn thin, political power has been sustained by denying opportunities to any plausible opposition.

A sizable number of governments in the Third World are military regimes. Where societies are under ostensibly civilian control as they were in Iran and Korea, the influence of the military was, nevertheless, very much in evidence. During the last decade, military expenditures have grown more rapidly in less-developed than in developed countries.[5] And expenditures on paramilitary forces, which include all internal security forces except local police, have grown much more rapidly. As Morris Janowitz observes,

> The period since 1965 has seen increases in coercive practices in the developing nations—both in the new nations and in Latin America. The trends since 1965 also have revealed increased political regime stability, although there are, of course, important exceptions. My assessment is that coercive practices have not only become more frequent and widespread but have also emerged as more effective instruments to consolidate and maintain regime stability. The political elites—and that includes those recruited from the military— have built institutions through which to exercise their power more effectively.[6]

Whether or not the difference in the course of political development in the Third World from that in the Western democracies is an indication of cultural relativism, it certainly tarnishes the usual concept of modernization. The growth of democracy in the West occurred in a social environment in which government was not expected to undertake the tasks that have been asked of governments in the new states. *The Wealth of Nations* indeed required that government limit its role to the maintenance of law and order and the protection of the state against foreign encroachment. The decisions determining the use of resources and the distribution of income were made in the market place with government, though by no means an impartial referee, holding the ring. The division of labor, as Adam Smith pointed out, is determined by the extent of the market and, as markets expanded in the industrial revolution, the increasing subdivision of activities and complexity of economic and social interdependence led to the creation of a myriad of new organizations, associations, and interest groups in which government, though playing a facilitating role, was not actively engaged as a participant. It was not until late in the nineteenth century that an expansion of the franchise led to political demands that brought government as an active participant into decisions affecting economic welfare. This was, moreover, a slow development. Social welfare legislation, the growth of trade unions into powerful interest groups, extensive government regulation of business practices have largely been twentieth-century phenomena. Political democracy in the West, then, emerged and grew strong during a period when government decision-making played a relatively minor role in the socio-economic development process.

The "mixed" economies of the contemporary Western world assign quite a different role to government. Although the extent of intervention into economic decision-making varies substantially among Western countries, governments everywhere establish public enterprises, proliferate controls over private firms, transfer incomes through taxation and subsidies, intervene in labor-management relations, and attempt to play a guiding role in determining the use of resources. This transformation of an essentially market-determined economic development process into one in which government plays an increasingly important part confronts democratic politics with a set of issues quite different from those attending its early Western development. When, and if, critical decisions affecting the use of resources and the distribution of income become political issues will democratic institutions and procedures be able to stand the strain? The Scandinavian countries, particularly Sweden, have gone very far in this direction with no visible impairment of political democracy. The Western world has, to date, been greatly assisted in its reconciliation of increased government intervention with the maintenance of democratic procedures by the unusually rapid growth of national incomes in the period since World War II. More could be given to some groups without taking away from others. If the West is now confronted with a period of much less rapid growth, the problem of maintaining democratic procedures will inevitably become more difficult. The world has not yet witnessed a country in which a socialist structure of the economy has been successfully combined with political democracy.

The central point is that Western democratic institutions and practices developed in a socio-economic milieu very different from that confronting governments of the new states and even those of the older states in Latin America. In market-dominated economies an expansion of the franchise could take place and the institutions of representative government take shape without affecting, except slowly and over time, the process of socio-economic development. The tasks confronting government were not very serious. This was certainly not true of the governments of the new states, nor has it been true in the less-developed world in general. Freed from the incubus of colonialism, populations demanded, if not the millennium, a reasonable facsimile thereof. People talked of how long it might take to attain the per capita incomes of Western countries; would it be ten years, twenty years, or thirty? Obviously this task could not be left to private enterprise, which, where it existed, was largely foreign, or to market forces. What was required, in the common view, was expansion of public enterprise, a planning of resource use for the long-run, and in the short-run immediate benefits via minimum wages, social security, old age pensions, and all the paraphernalia of the Western welfare state. These were some of the demands that impinged on governments. Governments that could not meet these requirements were either overthrown or maintained themselves in power by increasingly repressive internal security measures.

The usual form of overturn was by military coup and, since World War II, experts have counted some 125 military coups in the Third World.[7] The new governments, whether military or civilian, rapidly discovered that, if they were to maintain themselves in power, they had to find a means of suppressing potential opposition. Hence the rarity of transfers of power by peaceful means from one political entity to another. Of the 47 members of the Organization of African States only 3 have multi-party systems. There are 2 such states in South America and 2 or 3 in Asia. Not only have such transfers of power been limited in number, but it appears to be true that the rate of transfer via military coup is lessening. The tightening of internal security measures appears to be producing a greater political stability. It tends to be, of course, a political stability of a particular type very far removed from the political stability of most Western democracies. Whether a political stability maintained by repressive measures can long endure in societies in which rapid economic development and social differentiation are taking place remains to be seen. The period since 1945 has not been long enough to permit an answer to that question.

Authoritarian regimes, no matter how stable politically, have not, of course, guaranteed economic growth in the countries they administer. Here the record is mixed, ranging all the way from the debacles presided over by Nkrumah in Ghana and Sukarno in Indonesia to the very rapid growth rates achieved under authoritarian regimes in Brazil, Korea, and Taiwan. Furthermore, the record of the few less-developed countries that have been able to maintain democratic governments is a mixed one. Venezuela, aided by oil revenues, has been able to sustain a respectable economic growth rate and so has the ethnically oriented democratic regime in Malaysia. At the other end of the income scale are Sri Lanka and India, where growth has been, at best, sluggish.

Although most of the countries of the Third World are authoritarian to some considerable degree, there are, of course, differences. In analyzing the political aspects of development, it is necessary to consider how the values, objectives, practices, and procedures of the governing elites influence the inputs, policies, incentives, and organizations relevant to economic growth. The ability to stay in power is not necessarily identical with the ability to govern, and the ability to govern does not necessarily assure that a primary objective of government is economic development. Economic modernization, particularly in the early stages of development, requires transformations that are injurious to certain groups, though they may be advantageous to others. An increase in the rate of savings may demand unpopular increases in the level of taxation. A redistribution of agricultural land or changes in land tenure will meet with opposition from vested interests. Changes of this sort are difficult to bring about under any system of government, but they are particularly difficult in a full-fledged democracy. Significant changes in land tenure in South America, for example, have only been undertaken by authoritarian military regimes. If we can assume that a primary objective of government is the promotion of economic growth, and also that government is well advised with respect to the measures needed to promote growth, authoritarian government capable of maintaining political stability has certain advantages over a democratic regime at least for a period of time. When the oil crisis struck Korea in 1974, to cite a small example, the government, in order to check consumption, quadrupled the price of gasoline overnight. This obviously desirable measure would have been difficult to carry out in a political democracy. In general, it is probably true to say that an authoritarian government possesses greater flexibility in adjusting policies and practice to changed circumstances. How long an authoritarian regime will be able to maintain itself in power, and what combination of concession and repression will be found most useful in assuring political stability will obviously vary greatly among different countries.

Authoritarian regimes frequently attempt to adorn themselves with the trappings and verbiage of democracy. Consequently, one encounters such terms as "guided democracies," "disciplined democracies," "directed democracies," "people's democracies," "Arab democracies," "African democracies," and what not. Everyone is entitled to his own definition, and so are we. If political modernization means an approach toward the parliamentary democracies of the West, the process should presumably have the following characteristics: the possibility of a peaceful transfer of power from one civilian group to another; the organization of constituents for voting purposes into two or more political parties that have a breadth of membership and life expectancy beyond that of a "faction"; the existence of a sufficient degree of freedom of speech and the press, freedom of assembly, and other civil liberties necessary to the organization and functioning of effective political parties aspiring to power. One could add other features, for example, an independent judiciary, but those mentioned above are critical. Obviously they are interdependent. A peaceful civilian transfer of power cannot take place unless there are two or more well-organized political groups or parties. And such alternative claimants to power cannot flourish unless there is freedom of organization and propaganda.

Some authoritarian regimes in the Third World exhibit some of the indexes of democracy and some of those labeled democracies have certain authoritarian characteristics. Mexico has only one effective political party, but peaceful transfer of power takes place between different interests in that party, and political propaganda is relatively free. Until the Shah decided in 1975 that one was enough, Iran had two political parties, though both were relatively tame creatures of the court. Governments in countries that can rightly be called democratic find it necessary on occasion to curtail press freedom and in other ways stifle political opposition. There are substantial differences among countries in the extent and severity of political repression. But a view of the less-developed world in the large would indicate that, if modernization means progress toward the institutions, structures, and values of the West, there is a large gap between economic and political development. In the political area, for the last two decades, movement has, on the whole, been in the direction of authoritarianism.

The fact, however, that political development in the Third World has not moved in the direction of parliamentary democracy does not mean that there has been any lessening in the ability to govern; quite the contrary. In many, if not most, less-developed countries economic development has been accompanied by a strengthening of the administrative structures and processes through which public policies are formulated and put into effect. The division of labor, the specialization of function, which Riggs characterizes as the essence of modernization, is as evident in public administration as it is in economic organization and the development of social institutions.[8] It would be difficult to deny that the industrial societies of Communist Europe are modern, even though political control is highly centralized. Similarly, the modernization process in the Third World need not move and certainly as yet has not moved clearly in the direction of political democracy.

KOREA

Korea presents in some ways a typical—one might almost say classical—example of the divergence of Western-type economic and political development. During the years after Liberation in 1945, the Korean economy suffered through a period of fumbling by the U.S. Military Government, a division of the country into north and south in which most of the heavy industry was inherited by the north, and a devastating war in which, perhaps, a quarter of the wealth of South Korea was destroyed, together with the loss of over a million lives. Recovery from these catastrophes was slow and, during the period 1953 to the early 1960s, the economy was kept alive largely by massive economic and military assistance from the United States. This period, it is true, witnessed a large expansion of education and other changes that helped lay the groundwork for later rapid development. The growth of national income was, however, slow; indeed so slow that USAID administrators in Washington began to wonder whether South Korea would ever become independent of U.S. support. But economic prospects began to improve rapidly in the early 1960s. From 1963 to 1976, Korean GNP increased at a rate of about 10 percent per year, one of the most rapid growth rates experienced anywhere in the world. During this period, foreign economic assistance continually declined and, to all intents and purposes, the U.S. economic assistance program was phased out in 1975. This rapid growth was accompanied by all the changes, other than political, that are usually attributed to modernizing economies: decline in the share of agricultural employment and income; rapid industrialization, urbanization, and improved communications; increased literacy and social services; and the rest. The values and motivations, moreover, that sociologists say characterize the modern man, were increasingly evident—"individuals who can keep fixed schedules, observe abstract rules, make judgements on the basis of objective evidence, and follow authority legitimated not by traditional and religious sanctions but by technical competence."[9] From the social and economic point of view, modernization in Korea seems well underway.

Political development in Korea, however, has, in many respects, not moved toward the "institutions, values, and structures" of Western society. In terms of ability to govern, there has, indeed, been a strengthening of administrative services and a development of procedures and lines of authority, within a politically stable regime, that permits and facilitates the formation and implementation of public policies. But, if we agree with Pye that "the great problem today in nation building is that of relating the administrative and authoritative structures of government to political forces within traditional societies,"[10] we should have to conclude that Korea has not made much progress. Indeed movement, as in so many less-developed countries, has been in the opposite direction.

How this has come about merits a brief review. The capitulation of the Japanese on August 15, 1945, left Korea in chaos. The 70,000 Japanese administrators who had governed Korea disappeared rapidly, and by the spring of 1946 all were gone. A casually arranged agreement separated the areas of Russian and American occupation at the 38th parallel. The forces of the Soviet Union had begun to enter North Korea on August 12, before the final capitulation, and were soon busy organizing a political regime under their chosen representatives. The commander of the U.S. Military Government forces, General John R. Hodge, arrived on September 7. Uninformed about Korean affairs and with little direction from either General MacArthur in Tokyo or the State Department in Washington, Hodge found himself beset by the claims and clamor of dozens of Korean factions. It had been determined at the tri-power conference in Cairo, almost as an afterthought, that a trusteeship should be established for Korea for a period of undetermined length, with the Soviet Union and the United States as trustees. General Hodge's central task, therefore, was to negotiate the terms of this trusteeship with the North Korean representatives and their Soviet backers. The immediate problem was to find dependable representatives for South Korea.

The return to Korea of the grand old man of Korean independence, Syngman Rhee, had been delayed by State Department objections to his strong anti-Soviet position, and he arrived in Seoul on October 19. He proceeded to justify the State Department fears and to annoy General Hodge considerably by a speech on October 20 attacking the Soviet Union, the division of Korea, and the proposal of trusteeship. Obviously Rhee was an inappropriate candidate for negotiations with North Korean representatives. Nevertheless, as negotiations dragged on inconclusively and the desire of the United States for disengagement in Korea increased, official attitudes toward Rhee began to change. Despairing of agreement with the Soviet Union on a unified Korea, the United States asked the U.N. General Assembly to undertake the supervision of an election of a Korean National Assembly. Since the Soviets refused to cooperate, the election was held only in the south on May 10, 1948. The Rhee faction was overwhelmingly successful in this election, and on July 20 the Assembly elected Rhee as the first President of Korea.

The gradual withdrawal of U.S. forces, if it did not provoke invasion from the north, left South Korea in no position to defend itself. The bloody war that followed, beginning June 25, 1950, and lasting nearly three years, had numerous consequences for later political development. It eliminated the remnants of organized Communist activity in South Korea, and considerably diminished, to say the least, sympathy for

Communist institutions and practices. The leftist opposition to government, which continued and on occasion grew strong, no longer flaunted the Communist label. It considerably strengthened the image of Rhee as the father of his country, particularly in the countryside, and made it difficult for opposing political figures to become popularly known. It brought the United States permanently on the Korean scene and created a center of influence that not only the Rhee Government but other governments have had to deal with. And it left the greatly expanded armed forces by far the strongest organization in Korea.

Although the war increased Rhee's prestige in the countryside, it did not relieve him of opposition in the Assembly. The Constitution of 1948 had given the Assembly the authority to elect the President. When it became clear in 1952 that the Assembly would not reelect him, Rhee, with substantial help from the Martial Law Commander, bulldozed through an amendment to the Constitution transferring the selection process to the electorate. In the ensuing election there were four opponents, none well known to the electorate, and Rhee had no difficulty in capturing well over two-thirds of the vote cast. Rhee's highhanded treatment of the Assembly drew rebukes from U.N. Secretary General Trygve Lie, President Truman, and the heads of state of Canada, Australia, and Great Britain, with no noticeable effect. Another constitutional amendment in 1958 consolidated power by transferring to the central government the authority to appoint local officials who, under the Constitution of 1948, had been subject to local electorates.

Rhee faced reelection for another four-year term in 1956, and this time he confronted opposition from well-organized political parties. His principal opponent was Cho Pong-am, a former Communist who had broken with the party in 1946, but who now organized a frankly leftist Progressive Party along Marxian lines. Cho Pong-am managed to get 2,164,000 votes as against Rhee's 5,046,000 in a relatively free election. Cho was arrested in 1958 and charged with espionage activities, found guilty, and shot. His party collapsed. Reflecting on this episode, a Korean historian has remarked: "The tragic end of Cho Pong-am and his Progressive Party made it unequivocally clear that a serious leftist movement could not be openly promoted in South Korea without falling victim to violent suppression by the Government."[11]

When elections came round again in 1960, Rhee was not about to yield to any hankering for the democratic process. Opposition to him and the Liberal Party had grown mightily in the universities, in the cities, among intellectuals, and journalists, and he was confronted by a well-organized Democratic Party. His police and internal security forces did what they could to curb "malcontents," but it was obvious that, if Rhee was to continue in power, the election would have to be stolen. The plans for this became so well known and the ensuing results were so discordant with what a fair election should have produced that a revolt led by students, but provoking wide participation, brought about the resignation of Rhee on April 27. He was then 85 years of age and, despite the fact that he was anathema to a large part of the population and had lost the support of the United States, Koreans "recalled enough of his former services to cheer him as he reluctantly abdicated."[12]

Despite the existence of certain trappings of democracy, the Rhee regime was indubitably an authoritarian government, but it was a personal authoritarianism based on an astute manipulation of political factions, as well as suppression of outright opposition, as contrasted with the later authoritarianism of President Park, who built up and governed with a highly developed bureaucracy.[13] Rhee was very little an administrator and very much a politician as contrasted with Park, who had shown himself to be a very effective administrator but to whom politics and politicians were anathema. Although Rhee had no hesitation in declaring martial law and using the army to put down regional revolts, he did not regard the armed forces as an integral part of government as President Park did. Rhee was inflexible, unwilling to accept criticism, and obsessed with his own infallibility. His was very much a personal government strengthened by constitutional changes in 1958 that gave the President power to appoint provincial governors and the chief officials of major cities. The Park regime was even more centralized but has shown itself to be highly flexible, at least with respect to economic policy, and, in keeping with a well-ordered bureaucracy, top-level decisions involve participation by concerned senior officials, informed by competent technical advice.

The overturn of the Rhee Government brought to power a regime that might properly be called democratic. It lasted for approximately one year. An interim government introduced constitutional amendments that greatly weakened the office of the President, increased the power of the Assembly, and attempted to introduce responsible cabinet government under a Prime Minister. Provision was made for the local elections of provincial governors and mayors of municipalities. Elections on July 29 gave clear majorities to the Democratic Party in both houses, and Chang Myon was elected Premier. He faced monumental difficulties. The violence of the preceding months had been directed largely against the police and Rhee's security forces, and consequently the Chang Myon Government found itself without the instruments to control vandalism, thuggery, and a rapidly mounting wave of crime. The Democratic Party, which had come in with large majorities, was so badly divided that Chang Myon's control was seriously undermined. The United States, which had tried in vain to persuade Rhee to introduce economic reforms, was more successful with Chang Myon, but these measures, though serving economic needs, were politically unpalatable, and their enactment further fueled popular dissatisfaction with the Chang Myon Government. This dissatisfaction was fanned by the press which reflected the complete fractionization of Korean political opinion. Whether the Chang Myon regime, given time, could have survived and laid the basis for further democratic development is impossible to say. The regime was overturned by a military coup in May 1961. Its requiem was pronounced by a sympathetic observer:

Even as it was, the system had its staunch supporters. Yet few will deny that the "democracy" of those days encouraged and widened splits, aggravating the power free-for-all and projected an image of weakness and hesitation where chaotic conditions demanded strength and resolution. In these areas it raised questions concerning democracy in Korea that have got to be answered. Cohesion by democracy might not be impossible, but its demands are stern.[14]

Until 1961 the armed forces in Korea had maintained a position of relative political neutrality. And, indeed, the May coup was undertaken by a very small group of men led by some 250 officers. The mastermind was Chong-p'il Kim, Director of the Korean Central Intelligence Agency and nephew-in-law of General Park Chung Hee, but it was Park himself as chairman of a council of some 30 colonels and brigadier generals who governed Korea, assisted by a greatly enlarged Korean CIA. Although there was some dissension among the leaders of the coup, law and order were reestablished, and a series of necessary economic reforms, discussed in later chapters, was undertaken. It became evident early that the promotion of economic growth was to be the primary objective of the military regime, and that economic growth was regarded as the chief factor that would legitimize the new government. As General Park said in 1963, "Economic resurgence is an integral part of a nationalistic vision of a more independent Korea to come—more independent of the United States aid and control and, as an economically stronger and independent entity, more able to deal with North Korea."[15]

There was no organized opposition to the military regime but, on the other hand, there was little popular support. It became evident to the ruling military junta that lasting control would need to be based on a broader foundation. Washington, moreover, had made it clear that further economic and military assistance would be forthcoming only to a civilian government.

A new constitution was drafted in advance of elections, establishing a strong presidential system with a unicameral legislature of 175 members to be elected through proportional representation. The Constitution gave the President the power to appoint and dismiss the Prime Minister and Cabinet without the advice or consent of the Legislature. It also reestablished the strong control over local governments that had existed in the latter days of the Rhee regime. The mayors of Seoul and Pusan, the nine provincial governors, and the heads of various administrative agencies were to be appointed by the President. County heads were to be appointed by the President on the recommendation of provincial governors, and ward chiefs by the President on the recommendation of mayors. Certainly government in Korea under this constitution, which, in this respect, has remained unchanged to the present, is one of the most centralized in the non-Communist world.

A governmental party, the Democratic Republican Party, was formed under the leadership of Park Chung Hee, presenting its candidates for the Presidency and the Assembly in the elections of October and November 1963. Although opposition candidates received 53 percent of the vote, the opposition was so badly splintered that Park was elected President, and the Democratic Republican Party controlled 110 of the 175 Assembly seats. Lagging economic growth and mounting inflation in the two years following the military coup led Park to expand the civilian component in his cabinet and higher bureaucracy with an eye to a better management of economic affairs. A tightening of fiscal and monetary controls in 1963 forced a cutback in the military junta's over-optimistic goals, and the targets of the First Five-Year Plan, 1962–1966, were officially lowered in 1964. At the same time, the stage was set for the stabilization programs of 1963 and 1966 which were basically dictated by the U.S. government as conditions for release of U.S. assistance. The stabilization programs and the reestablishment of a Joint U.S.-Korean Economic Cooperation Committee contributed to more effective marshaling of Korean economic resources and increased influence of U.S. officials in the formulation of Korean economic policies.

The response of the Korean economy to the stabilization measures was basically positive, and the growing confidence in government led Park, with U.S. encouragement, to set in motion an operation that was to prove a severe test of the stability of his regime. Early in 1964, Chong-p'il Kim, chairman of the government party, was authorized to enter into secret negotiations for the normalization of relations with Japan. When the terms of the ensuing agreement became known and, as a result of that agreement, Japanese investments began to be undertaken in Korea, widespread protests were mounted, particularly in the universities. Opposition was on a sufficiently broad scale to test the legitimacy of the Park Government. Park responded with a series of severe measures. Martial law was declared, a number of colleges and universities were closed, and several hundred of the opponents of the regime were arrested.

The normalization of relations with Japan in late 1965 represented a large step forward both in Korea's economic development and in the stability of the Park Government. Japanese reparations of $500 million and the inflow of private investment and technology from Japan accelerated an economic growth already set in motion. The Park regime emerged from the political crisis far more confident of its ability to manage the opposition. Foreign observers on the spot described these events as a major turning point.[16]

The years following the normalization of relations with Japan saw the growth of a civil-military bureaucracy, the development of the politico-economic strategy, and the process of executive decision-making that characterized the Park regime throughout. Although the top Cabinet posts in the economic area have generally been held by civilians, and the technical posts in the bureaucracy are entirely civilian, personnel from the armed forces are present in large numbers both in government posts and in the nationalized enterprises. A student of the Korean military establishment noted in 1970 that,

> of all officers of the general level who had retired from the armed forces since the beginning of the First Republic (1948–1960), and who were still living in 1968, more than half were actively employed in government. Of the eight surviving four star generals, all were in

government, including the President and the Prime Minister. In 1968, former generals alone (excluding military men of other ranks) made up half the Cabinet, one fifth of the National Assembly, two-fifths of all ambassadorial appointments, and two-thirds of the heads of state-run firms (which play a major role in the economy). In addition other military men were prominent in the government party, on the presidential staff, in the higher bureaucracy and in the economic planning board. Although the military men employed in the government were no longer on active duty, it would not be inaccurate to characterize the government as being heavily dominated by military personnel.[17]

Although there is a good deal of criticism among intellectuals, at least sotto voce, of the incompetence of retired generals, particularly as directors of the state-owned enterprises, the training in administration received in the course of military service has produced a large number of highly competent government executives. The Korean bureaucracy, in comparison with bureaucracies in most other less-developed countries, deserves high marks. This is despite a salary scale that inevitably invites a certain amount of corruption. As a student of the Korean Civil Service observed, "Although government service does not enjoy the social prestige of the old Confucian tradition it still ranks at top priority in careers."[18]

The influence of the military on Korean development is by no means limited to their contribution to government bureaucracy. Armed forces of over 600,000 draw men from every village and discharge them back into civilian life at the rate of 200,000 a year. In 1970, there were over 2,000,000 who had received military training and, in addition, there were 2,270,000 men, two-fifths of all those between the ages of 18 and 40, in the militia. "During their stint in the army, men learn to handle and operate modern equipment, to drive vehicles, and to relate to new ways and new forms of organization. Furthermore, they come into contact with urban life. They become geographically mobile."[19] There is little doubt that military training and the presence of large numbers of former military personnel have contributed not only to the economic development of Korea but, in all probability, to the political stability of a disciplined society.

The years after 1965 also saw the development of a politico-economic strategy. Economic growth became the primary objective to government and political stability was considered to be indispensible to growth. Political stability was to be achieved by infrequent changes in top government positions, by imposing limitations on civil liberties, and by assuring strong military backing to government policies. If necessary, universities, the usual breeding grounds of dissent, would be shut down and the intellectual community kept under close surveillance. The government's security forces were deemed adequate to this task, with the army in the background available if necessary.

The formulation of economic and other public policies came to be a matter for the President and a few top officials, advised when necessary, by representatives of affected economic groups. There developed during the years of the Park administration a unique relationship between government and business, a relationship in which, although private enterprise provided the principal operating units, government was clearly in the driver's seat. The influence of the Economic Planning Board and the other economic ministries continually increased, and the direction of economic development was guided and controlled by checks and incentives administered by those ministries. The President and his top advisers were at the center of policy-making, and President Park, in fact, maintained extraordinarily close touch with all aspects of the economy. As one authority described the system, it was "elite-authoritarian rule" and it "was consistent with Korean tradition." [20]

Consistent or not, it successfully maintained political stability and economic growth. In the 1967 presidential election, unlike 1963, when anti-militarism and criticism of the coup were stressed by the opposition, the themes emphasized by both sides centered on the government's economic policies. Running on the basis of the solid administrative and economic achievements of his first term, President Park sought victory by appealing to the development potential in the Second Five-Year Plan. In campaign speeches, Park and Chong-p'il Kim, Chairman of the Democratic Republican Party, reiterated the theme "construction first and distribution later." By construction, they meant industrialization, and industrialization was equated with modernization.

The opposition candidate, Po-sŏn Yun, criticized the Park regime for its failure to achieve justice in the distribution of wealth. The rich were getting richer, he said, and the poor poorer, and the gains of big business were made possible only by ignoring the claims of the masses. The influx of capital and technology from Japan was denounced as well as the loss of provincial and local autonomy. The opposition was prepared to argue for a reduction in the rate of growth if necessary to achieve a more equitable distribution of income and a greater emphasis on social welfare. A return to democracy, it was claimed, could serve as the foundation on which the unification of Korea could be achieved. To this the government party replied that South Korea might be able to acquire sufficient strength by the end of the Second Five-Year Plan to open effective negotiation with the north, but, until such time, it would be wise to shelve the issue of reunification.[21]

A landslide victory for Park in 1967 set the seal of majority approval on the achievements of the previous six years and established economic growth as the preferred objective of government in Korea. President Park not only increased his share of the vote, but the Democratic Republican Party (DRP) raised its representation in the Assembly from 110 to 130 seats. While the presidential election was generally conceded to have been honest and represented a high water mark of popular support for President Park, there were many charges of irregularities in the Assembly elections held one month later, for which both the DRP and the President were held responsible. This Assembly election marked the beginning of a trend away from fair and open elections.

The Constitution of 1962 had limited the holding of presidential power to two terms. In 1969, however, a plebiscite ratified a constitutional change increasing the number of permitted terms to three. On this occasion, President Park promised that, if elected in 1970, he would step down in 1975. In this plebiscite, Park received only 67.5 percent of the vote, and only 77.1 percent of the eligible voters voted. This was by far the poorest showing in any plebiscite the government had attempted from the beginning of the Park regime to date. Furthermore, the plebiscite deeply divided the Democratic Republican Party and alienated the supporters of its founder, Chong-p'il Kim, one of the prime contenders to succeed President Park. On the other side, the major opposition party, the New Democratic Party, was united behind a candidate Tae-jung Kim. Kim had a number of popular issues at hand: the questionable modification of the Constitution to permit a third term, the suppression of opposition by the security police, particularly on university campuses, curtailment of freedom of speech and the press, and lack of progress in the desired unification of Korea.

Although Kim carried Seoul, Park won the election with 45 percent of the vote cast by 80 percent of the electorate. The opposition was divided among a number of parties, and even the New Democratic Party was rent by factionalism. As a knowledgeable observer commented, "President Park undoubtedly profited from the image of the New Democratic Party as a fractionalized instrument incapable of running a stable government . . . The voting reflected a strong desire for strength and stability in the face of anxieties brought about by the recent reduction in American force levels in South Korea."[22]

In 1972, the Park regime proposed a new Yusin (Yushin, revitalizing reforms) Constitution which, in effect, left the President's continuation in office at his own discretion. The new Constitution gave the President sweeping new powers to rule by emergency decree. It also gave him the power to dissolve the National Assembly, and the authority to prepare a slate of representatives making up one-third of its membership. The

Constitution also declared that neither court actions nor objections could be raised against the special declarations issued by the President and the extraordinary measures taken thereunder. The new Constitution was submitted to a popular referendum and was approved by a 91 percent vote of 92 percent of the registered voters.

This affirmative vote for strong—not to say repressive—government, coming as it did shortly after the end of a period of martial law, may have been influenced by the developments in Vietnam. Widespread doubt existed in Korea as to the willingness of the United States to support its allies in East Asia, and this emphasized the necessity of rallying around a strong leader.

Since then, Korea has received reassurance of continued American support, the danger from the north has receded, and the Korean economy has regained its rapid rate of growth. There is, however, not much evidence of a diminution in the strictness of government control. After 1972, President Park made full use of his emergency powers, and the political opposition was kept firmly in check by a long series of prohibitions against criticism of the government and other types of political action. Criticism of, and attempts to amend, the Constitution were easily discouraged. When dangers from the north seemed to threaten, President Park resorted to plebiscites designed to reaffirm the legitimacy of his government. On such an occasion in February 1975, 80 percent voted, and the regime was supported by 73.3 percent of those voting.

The fact that 25 percent of the votes were negative, and 20 percent of the registered voters abstained from voting suggests that there was still substantial opposition to the government of Korea. The opposition is centered mainly in the cities and in the universities and other intellectual communities. The size of these communities will inevitably increase. So long, however, as rapid economic development continues, which is an important factor conferring legitimacy, the opposition is unlikely in the near future to be able to mount an effective attack even if the repression of civil liberties is substantially lessened. Whether the maintenance of political stability requires measures as repressive as those that have been pursued in recent years in Korea, and whether the value of a political stability of this sort does or does not outweigh the costs are important questions, but they are not questions that will be dealt with in this study.

In any case it is clear that, if modernization means an approach toward the institutions, values, and structures of the West, political developments in Korea have not moved in this direction. This does not mean that government has had no role to play in the modernization of the rest of Korean society; quite the reverse. Government has, in fact, had a pervasive influence on the use of economic resources and the distribution of income in Korea, an influence that is elaborated in the following chapters. But the administrative and authoritative structures of government have not been closely related to the democratic political aspirations that continue to exist in Korea. Nor has such a relationship been cemented in many less-developed countries. Concerning the failure of democracy in Korea, it may be well to consider the advice of a contributor to the *Far Eastern Economic Review:* "It is important to keep a sense of proportion and recognize that no matter how authoritarian Park's administration may be, it is personification of perfect democracy compared with the Byzantine power-play in hermetically sealed Pyongyang."[24]

CONCLUSION

Modernization in the societies of the Third World has not, in general, led in the direction of political democracy, and Korea is no exception. The form that authoritarian government has taken in Korea, however, has been powerfully shaped by local circumstances. The invasion from the north in 1950 and the possibility of renewed invasion is considered sufficient justification for maintaining the fifth largest standing army in the world. The size of the armed forces, the government positions offered to retired officers, the sizable fraction of the population that has experienced military service, and the equally large fraction held in readiness for future military service have given a pronounced cast to the society. Korean society has also been deeply influenced by the two countries with which it has been in close contact—Japan during the thirty-five years of colonial rule and during the period since 1965 when the transfer of capital and technology has been large; and the United States, whose economic and military assistance has been vital to the continued existence of Korea. Trade relations with Japan and the United States still account for over one-half of Korea's exports and imports, though this percentage will probably decline over time. Large numbers of Korean students were educated in Japan during the colonial period and even larger numbers in the United States since 1945. The United States and Korea are linked with a defense treaty, and Japan is at least as interested in the defensibility of South Korea as is the United States. President Park, like Syngman Rhee before him, exhibited an extraordinary ability to pursue an independent course withstanding pressures from countries on which Korea is heavily dependent. No one can doubt the political independence of Korea. Nevertheless, the society has been permeated by outside influences to an extent that would be hard to match in the Third World. Some of these influences have tended to favor democratic values and procedures. As Korea develops economically and socially in close interrelationship with outside influences, the divergence of the present course of political development from the current of social change will inevitably become more pronounced. Whether this will, in time, lead to significant political change in the direction of democratic procedures and institutions must be left to the future.

A second respect in which authoritarian government in Korea differs from that in most other less-developed countries is in the heavy emphasis placed on economic growth as a national objective. Not only has the increase in national income since 1963 been remarkable, but all elements of the population, though not in the same measure, have shared this prosperity.

The governing elite has clearly considered political stability to be essential to economic growth and has justified whatever repression of political opposition seemed necessary to maintain stability in terms of economic growth and the maintenance of an effective defense posture against political aggression from the north. As long as the possibility of aggression seemed real to a majority of the population and as long as continued growth assured increased real incomes to both rural and urban communities, the legitimacy of the Park Government in Korea was widely accepted.

———————

Since this was first written, dramatic events have overtaken Korea. The assassination of President Park by the head of the Korean CIA on October 26, 1979, was as unforseen as its consequences are imponderable. This action followed serious political disturbance in Korea occasioned principally by the dismissal from the Legislative Assembly of the head of the New Democratic Party and the resignation of his followers. The disturbance was severely repressed but it is unknown at this date—and it may never be known—the extent to which the assassination was influenced by the political disturbance or the methods used to repress it. Western friends of Korea now see an opportunity for the establishment of a fundamentally democratic state. This may happen, but it must be emphasized that there is no democratic tradition in the Republic of Korea and that the attempt at democratic government following the resignation of Syngman Rhee in 1960 was as inept as it was short-lived. Perhaps the best that can be hoped for is a regime less repressive than President Park's and far more decentralized, a regime that, over time, by encouraging local government and permitting a wider participation in decision-making, will develop the constituencies and the experience needed for full-fledged democracy. But, given the continuing threat from the north, any signs of indecision and weakness by a more democratic regime would probably again elicit a demand for strong direction. Only if the posture of the north changes, due to internal developments or external pressures, does it seem likely that democratization can be pursued in a more permissive and secure environment.

THREE

The Historical Foundations
of Modern Economic Growth

Korean economic development during the two decades ending in 1975 did not spring suddenly from nowhere. To foreigners familiar only with pictures of devastation during the Korean War, Korea may well have appeared both "poor and blank," a nation with little left of its past and facing a bleak future. In fact, Korea was and is a nation with a rich heritage based on over twelve hundred years as a single, unified, and (most of the time) independent state. Where the great majority of today's developing countries were formed by colonial powers who amalgamated various tribes and principalities (Nigeria, India, and Indonesia being among the many examples) or by Spanish and Portuguese colonization (Latin America), Korea was unified by its own Silla dynasty rulers in the seventh century A.D., and Korean rulers continued to govern from then on with only brief interruptions during the height of first Mongol and, in the twentieth century, Japanese military power. The Korean people spoke one language, were of one race, and all shared a single culture.

Although Korea's pre-modern experience differed from that of many developing nations, that experience was not unique. Korea, like Japan and Vietnam, was part of a broader East Asian culture centering on China. Concern here is not with porcelains or landscape painting, but with those elements of the East Asian experience that have a direct bearing on economic development. Confucianism, the state philosophy of Korea as well as of China, for example, places great emphasis on the benefits of education. At the village level, the dominant characteristic of all of East Asia was the large number of people scraping an existence out of a very small amount of land, an existence that was made possible only by achieving very high yields, by pre-modern standards, per unit of arable acreage. These peasant farmers were capable not only of supporting themselves, but also an aristocracy of landlords and officials, together with a commercial network designed to supply the cities where a part of this aristocracy lived.

As Korea's own leadership began to lose its vitality in the nineteenth century, the alien but dynamic force of Western and later Japanese imperialism had begun to sweep across East Asia. By 1910, overcome by superior power, Korea was formally annexed into the Japanese Empire. The next thirty-five years under Japanese rule constitute only a brief interlude in the broad sweep of Korean history, but the changes introduced in that period were profound nonetheless. Nationalistic Koreans (a term that describes the great majority of the population) stress the negative side of the Japanese colonial experience, and there is little doubt that most Koreans suffered real deprivation under Japanese rule. But even the casual visitor to Korea today will notice the continuing influence of the Japanese mode of bureaucratic control of the economy, and there are many other less obvious parts of the experience of Japanese rule that have helped shape developments over the three post-1945 decades.

Finally and tragically, the modernization of Korea was shaped profoundly and indelibly by a casual decision made in February 1945 at Yalta to have Soviet and American troops divide the acceptance of the surrender of Japanese troops at the 38th parallel.

There are, therefore, three basic parts to Korea's historical foundations that had a profound bearing on the shape of Korean development since 1945: the centuries of unity and independence within the broader East Asian experience, Japanese colonialism, and the division of the nation into two parts. Each will be taken up in turn.

THE ECONOMIC AND SOCIAL STRUCTURE OF TRADITIONAL KOREA

A key feature of modern economic growth is a rise in per capita income. Because pre-modern societies experienced small increases in per capita income or none at all, there has been a tendency to lump all these societies together under the term "traditional" or "backward." But such a procedure ignores profound changes that were occurring in some pre-modern societies, notably in East Asia, but not in others. In Tokugawa Japan (1600–1868), for example, there was not only a political unification of the country, but a steady rise in commerce, in urbanization, levels of literacy, and agricultural productivity.[1] Around 1700 Japan was one of the most urbanized and literate nations in the world. Many of the same developments occurred in pre-modern China as well, only at an even earlier date. China had several cities with a population of a million or more a thousand years ago, and perhaps one-third of the adult males were literate.[2] Tens, perhaps even hundreds of thousands, had the equivalent of nearly twenty years and more of formal education and tutoring. And Chinese grain output between the fourteenth and nineteenth centuries was able to rise sufficiently to keep fed a population that had increased sixfold.[3]

Without such large numbers of literate people, it is difficult to see how either Japan or China could have moved so rapidly toward universal primary education, in the late nineteenth century in the former case and after 1949 in the latter. Lacking a highly educated core, there would have been few who could have been sent abroad to acquire the technical training essential to the operation of modern industry. Pre-modern commercial development also stood these countries in good stead. Europeans and Americans were able by force of arms to attain the right to live and trade in East Asia in accordance with their own laws, but they never were able to displace significant numbers of Chinese or Japanese traders. Foreigners never had much of a role in the domestic commerce of these two nations, and their role in foreign trade diminished rapidly as over time they lost their one advantage, greater knowledge of European and American markets. Trade in many of the nations in Southeast Asia and Africa, in contrast, was largely in the hands of either Europeans or other alien groups (Chinese in Southeast Asia, Indians and Lebanese in Africa, and so on). Experience in running one's own political affairs, however badly, was also of great importance. The governmental institutions that eventually arose were, for better or worse, solidly grounded in the political realities of these two nations, not in theories of politics developed in England or France. In China's case, nearly a century of chaos preceded the rise of a government capable of dealing with the challenge of the modern world, but that still gave China advantages over nations whose people played little role in the creation of the governmental institutions that were presented to them on achieving independence in the late 1940s, 1950s and 1960s.

Korea in a number of basic ways was a part of this greater East Asian experience, but with significant differences. To begin with, Korea by the early twentieth century already had a large population eking out an existence on a small amount of arable land. In Korea, as in China and Japan, during periods of comparative peace and stability, the number of births usually exceeded the number of deaths, and the population rose. The rate of rise was not high, less than 0.5 percent per year (see Table 1), but over a period of centuries such a small rate of increase can have a profound impact. And Korea had the

TABLE 1 Population Growth in Pre-Modern East Asia

Country	Period	Annual Rate of Increase in Population (%)
Korea	1397–1917	–0.55
	1917–1949	1.79
China	1393–1913	0.32–0.36
	1913–1953	0.76
Japan	1665–1872	0.32
	1872–1940	1.09

Sources: Korea: Table 2. The minus indicates that the 1397 figure is probably an underestimate and hence that the estimated growth rate is a bit too high.
China: Dwight H. Perkins, *Agricultural Development in China, 1368–1968* (Chicago, 1969), p. 216.
Japan: The 1665–1872 figures are derived from data in Sekiyama Naotarō, *Kinsei nihon no jinko kōzō* (Tokyo, 1969), pp. 123–127. The pre-1732 figures (for 1665) were derived by assuming that total Japanese population grew at the same rate as that in 6 han for which data are available.
The 1872–1940 growth rate is based on data in Kazushi Okawa, *The Growth Rate of the Japanese Economy Since 1878* (Tokyo, Kinokuniya Bookstore, Co., 1957), pp. 140–141.

necessary long periods of comparative peace. The Korean people suffered enormously during the Mongol invasions of the peninsula in the thirteenth century, and the population probably fell substantially in that period as it did in China. There was also a briefer but very destructive invasion by the Japanese under Hideyoshi in the 1590s which presumably also had a negative demographic impact. But there were no other periods of comparable devastation during the long period of Yi dynasty rule from the fourteenth century to 1910, and Korea's population appears to have risen seven to eightfold (see Table 2). The area of arable land also increased but by only twofold or less over the same period.[4] By the time of the first Japanese land survey in 1918, Koreans on the average had only 0.12 hectares (about

TABLE 2 Population Growth in Korea, 1397–1970

Year	*(1)* Families	*(2)* Reported Persons	*(3)* Estimate of Total Population
1397	180,247	370,365	990,000+
1423	196,975	n.a.	1,080,000+
1669	1,313,652	5,018,744	7,225,000+
1750	1,783,044	7,328,867	9,810,000+
1917	–	–	16,969,000
1925	–	–	19,016,000
1935	–	–	21,891,000 (north plus south)
1949	–	–	29,907,000
1970	–	–	45,325,000

Notes: 1397–1750: These figures were all taken from the Korean historical records. The Korean population data for the pre-twentieth century periods have not yet been worked over systematically to determine when real efforts were made to update the population registers, the degree of consistency between the population data and historical events, etc. Until such a study is made, these figures must be used with great caution. The principle used in selecting population data for this table was to pick years when population peaked. After 1750, for example, the records indicate that population declined, but it is more likely that this decline reflects a lack of attention to the registers than an actual reduction in population. The number of people reported per family is clearly too low for a rural Asian country presumably because of a failure to register such individuals as children. Hence column (3) was derived by multiplying the number of families by 5.5. The "+" indicates that there is probably still some underreporting (of the number of families, etc.)

1917–1935: Himeno Minoru, *Chōsen keizai zuhyō* (Keijō, 1940), p. 27. Estimates of population by the Japanese go back to 1910, but the very high growth rate between 1910 and 1917 (3.5% a year) suggests that there was a great deal of underreporting in the years before 1917.

1949–1970: BOK, *Economic Statistics Yearbook, 1976* (Seoul, 1976), p. 6.

one-third of an acre) of arable land per capita. In the entire world at that time, only Japan had less cultivated acreage per capita.

The other side of the coin of a limited land endowment was a relatively high crop yield per hectare. After 1600 the introduction of rice transplanting led to the double-cropping of rice and barley in the southern provinces. Cotton was introduced from China in the fourteenth century (it did not reach Japan until the sixteenth century). The European discovery of America led to the spread of potatoes, corn, tobacco, and peanuts to Asia, although only tobacco and sweet potatoes appear to have had a major impact on Korea. There was also a gradual development of irrigation systems but, during the last century of the Yi dynasty, these were neglected and most fell into disuse.[5] Even though most land depended on rainfall, however, Korea by the early twentieth century had evolved a complex and, by pre-modern standards, an advanced agricultural technology.

By the latter part of the Yi dynasty, Korea had also acquired a land tenure system that was in key respects "modern" and a rural labor force that was largely "free." Korean society was made up of essentially three classes: the aristocracy or *yangban*, commoners, and the "lowborn" who were mainly serfs or slaves. Entrance into the aristocracy was less restricted than in the case of Japan, but more so than in China. In China, in principle at least, anyone who passed the three degree examinations could enter into the highest reaches of the bureaucracy. In Korea, for the most part, only those who were by birth *yangban* could take the examinations. At the other end of the scale, serfs or slaves could be bought and sold by their masters. In actual practice, however, the boundary between serfs and commoners was not always clearly drawn. Slaves sometimes owned land, and the obligations of a commoner to his landlord or government official often went well beyond the payment of rent and taxes. There was also considerable movement by families through the generations from commoner to slave status and back again.

Two of the main social trends of the Yi dynasty were the gradual decline in size of the slave class and the consolidation of private (as contrasted with government) ownership of land. Korean kings, like those in many other countries, rewarded their supporters and high officials with grants of land. In Korea some of these awards were permanent gifts that could be inherited, while others went with an office and had to be surrendered at the time of leaving that office. At a theoretical level, there was much talk of instituting the Chinese equal-fields system whereby all land was the possession of the king or state and was parcelled out to able-bodied male adults, but this system never came much closer to reality in Korea than it did in China.[6] By the latter part of the Yi dynasty, in fact, most land was privately owned and freely bought and sold.

The gradual disappearance of slavery appears to have coincided with the filling up of the country with people. Owners of large estates no longer had to worry about finding and keeping a labor force to till their land. There was little uncultivated land in distant corners of the nation to which a peasant could flee in an effort to escape debts and other obligations to his lord. Given an adequate supply of labor, it was simpler and generally more productive to rent the land to free labor. Whether the peasants themselves were better off under this arrangement is an open question. Land records studied for half a dozen villages in the eighteenth century[7] indicate that land ownership was highly concentrated in the hands of a few well-to-do families. A precise estimate of the level of tenancy for the whole nation in the eighteenth century is not possible. We know from Japanese surveys that in the 1910s 40 percent of all farm families rented all the land they cultivated, while only 20 percent owned all the land they tilled.[8] It is unlikely that the situation was much different in the eighteenth century.

At the top of the social pyramid were the high officials of the government and the royal family. Power in the Yi dynasty, for the most part, was concentrated in Seoul. There were no pockets of power in the provinces capable of standing up to the center.[9] But the concentration of power in Seoul did not mean that the king was omnipotent. During the early part of the dynasty, vigorous kings did assert something approaching absolutism in practice as well as theory. But by the latter half of the dynasty, Korean kings were hemmed in by a powerful bureaucracy vigorous in the preservation of its prerogatives and its perquisites.

A second force limiting Korean absolutism, one connected with the first, was the weak financial position of the government, particularly in the latter half of the nineteenth century when funding limitations greatly weakened its ability to respond to the challenges of that period. Much of the history of the last decades of the dynasty, in fact, involved desperate efforts by the Taewŏngun and King Kojong to find additional sources of funding or to restore the vitality of older sources.[10] Land was resurveyed, palace estate and academy lands were confiscated, commercial transit taxes were imposed, and yet the government still had to resort to debasing the coinage to obtain financing. Of all land tax revenue collected, only about 20 to 30 percent made it to Seoul.[11] The remainder was retained to defray expenses at the local level. No one has yet attempted to estimate the percentage of gross domestic product at the disposal of the Korean government (central and local), but all indications are that the result would be much closer to the under 2 percent of China's financially weak government than to the 25 percent of late Tokugawa Japan or the 12 percent of early Meiji Japan.[12]

A lack of funds in the hands of the government did not mean a similar lack of resources in the hands of the elite. As the land ownership data indicate, wealth and income were very unequally distributed. A portion of the *yangban* elite continued to live in the countryside, but large numbers also moved to the cities. In fact, it was the existence of the court, the bureaucracy, and the decision of many of the elite not in active government service to live in these centers of power that created the cities of Korea (and also China and Japan) in the first place. East Asian cities were not the consequence of the development of commerce, often in opposition to the landed aristocracy, as they were in Europe. East Asian cities were instead the very creatures of the aristocracy and its government. Bureaucrats and other aristocrats lived there with their families and large numbers of servants. Their urban location in turn created the need for a commercial and transport system to supply them with food, fuel, and other material.

In Ch'ing China, this situation led to the growth of a number of urban centers with a population of over a million people. In Tokugawa Japan the requirement that the very numerous military class, the samurai, live in cities led to the development of an even greater number of large cities relative to the size of Japan's population at that time (see Table 3). Korea with roughly one-third the population of Japan (and perhaps one-thirtieth that of China) in the eighteenth and nineteenth centuries was not capable of supporting a city of a million or more, particularly when that city largely took from the countryside while returning little in exchange. Seoul appears to have had about 200,000 people, not only in the early twentieth century, but in previous centuries as well. No other city in Korea had even 100,000 people in this period. But as a percentage of the total population, Korea's urban centers were comparable in size to those of China (Table 3) even if there was little likelihood of a traveler's mistaking Seoul for the grandeur of Peking or Edo.

As already indicated, the existence of a substantial urban population (by pre-modern standards) created the need for a commercial network. In a real sense there were two interconnected commercial networks in Korea. Villagers traded among themselves and took their produce to nearby market towns to trade it for the goods of their neighbors. Most of these markets were periodic, that is, they met every fifth day with pedlars traveling from one market to another on a rotating basis.[13] Settled merchants could also be found, but usually only in the larger towns that doubled as administrative as well as marketing centers.

The other marketing system was connected with the supply of Seoul and the other cities. The government played a large but declining role in this trade. Much grain, for example, came from government estates and many of the handicraft manufactures came from government-sponsored craftsmen. In the seventeenth and eighteenth centuries, however, the gradual expansion of private commerce made the government's role increasingly superfluous. The rise of a money economy best symbolizes the increasing sophistication of Korean commerce. Until the seventeenth century, Korea had no real currency, using cloth and grain as rather poor substitutes.[14] In the late seventeenth and

TABLE 3 Urbanization in Pre-Modern East Asia

	Over 3,000		Population in Cities of Over 30,000		Over 100,000	
	1,000s	% of Total Population	1,000s	% of Total Population	1,000s	% of Total Population
KOREA						
1911	675	4.8	453	3.2	279	2.0
1921	860	4.9	540	3.1	262	1.5
CHINA						
Early 19th century	20,500	5.1	12,000	3.0	10,000±	2.5±
1900–1910	—ᵃ	—ᵃ	—ᵃ	—ᵃ	14,600	3.4
1938	—ᵃ	—ᵃ	—ᵃ	—ᵃ	24,600	4.9
JAPAN						
Early 19th century	5,100	17.0	2,800	9.3	1,800+	6.0+

Sources: Korea: Government General of Chosen, *Annual Report on Reforms and Progress in Chosen (1921–1922)* (Keijo, 1923), p. 261. China: The early 19th century estimates are those of Gilbert Rozman, *Urban Networks in Ch'ing China and Tokugawa Japan* (Princeton, 1973), p. 102. Rozman does not present estimates for cities above 100,000, only for above 30,000 and above 300,000, hence the ± after the figure. The 1900–1910 and 1938 estimates are from Perkins, *Agricultural Development in China*, p. 155.
Japan: Rozman, p. 102.

Note: ᵃestimates not available.

early eighteenth centuries, however, Korea finally succeeded in establishing a copper coinage patterned on that of China, although coins circulated mostly in the cities, and to a much lesser degree in the countryside. The development of a money economy led to the commutation of rents from grain to money and may also have been a cause of the decline of government handicrafts.

Foreign trade was a government monopoly throughout most of the Yi dynasty and was carried out within the tribute format. Embassies were sent by Korea to China and received by Korea from Japan. But in comparison to the gross domestic product of Korea, the size of this foreign trade was miniscule and, given the way it was carried out more for political than economic purposes, it is likely that the governments involved lost money from the trade.[15]

Although much research, particularly of a quantitative nature, remains to be done on Korean traditional commerce, two tentative conclusions appear possible. First, Korean commerce in the eighteenth and nineteenth centuries was considerably more developed than in earlier periods. Second, commerce still lagged behind, perhaps far behind, comparable developments in China and Japan. By the eighteenth and nineteenth centuries, for example, both China and Japan had banking systems capable of transferring funds all over their respective nations without having to move actual currency (except where imbalances persisted). In contrast, in Korea in the late nineteenth century, one foreign traveler, for example, had to carry all the cash she needed along with her, no mean trick when it took six men or one pony to carry copper cash worth only U.S. $50.[16] A traveling Korean government official could avoid this nuisance by drawing on local government resources, but merchants could not profitably rely on the government in this way. Nor was there anything comparable in Korea to cities such as Osaka or the cities of the lower Yangtze River which were major handicraft manufacturing and commercial centers more than they were political cities long before the opening of foreign trade with Europe and

America. Perhaps this impressionistic evidence reflects only the comparatively greater size of Japan and China but, in the absence of evidence to the contrary, Korea at the time of the arrival of the West appears to have been something of a commercial backwater in comparison to its East Asian neighbors, but far more developed commercially and in the size of its urban centers than many of today's developing nations were in the nineteenth century.

In many ways, the most important part of modern Korea's East Asian heritage was the Confucian emphasis on education. Education in Korea, to begin with, was, as in China, the major route to government office. Without two decades or so of training in the Confucian classics a non-military man had little hope of obtaining the great prestige and substantial material rewards of a government position. Unlike China, however, it was mainly the hereditary aristocracy, the *yangban*, who were eligible for the examinations and hence for government office. But there were a great many *yangban* so this restriction was not as limiting as at first it might appear. In six villages in the early eighteenth century, for example, *yangban* families made up from 17 to 32 percent of the landholding families.[17]

Training of the elite was in classical Chinese, since that was the language of written communication at the court. Teaching was carried out by private tutors and in schools. Since classical Chinese is an unusually difficult language, it is unlikely that many Koreans outside of a tiny elite truly mastered the language, but hundreds of thousands of others apparently picked up enough Chinese characters to be able to read routine documents. Some idea of the extent of formal training can be obtained from estimates of the school population in 1911 and 1921. In the latter year, for which data are probably more complete, there were over 500,000 Korean students in school, with nearly 300,000 in traditional schools.[18] The 300,000 figure may not be a bad guide to the level of the school-attending population in the nineteenth century.

But Chinese was not the only written language available to

Koreans. Unlike China, Korea was blessed with an excellent phonetic alphabet of its own, Han'gǔl, invented by the Yi dynasty King Sejong in the fifteenth century. There were no doubt many motives for learning to read and write Han'gǔl, but one major motive was that it greatly facilitated commercial transactions beyond those of the village market variety. Unfortunately we have only the vaguest knowledge of the extent of literacy in Han'gǔl. Japanese surveys of rural literacy in the 1930s, for example, measured those who had literacy in something more than Han'gǔl (that is, in either Japanese or Chinese characters). By the 1930s, these surveys indicate that less than 20 percent of rural families were without a member literate in terms of this higher standard (out of a total family size of five or six people).[19] If the remaining 80 percent of the rural families had one or several members literate in more than Han'gǔl, it is likely that a substantial majority of the rural male population could at least read Han'gǔl. There are no comparable surveys for the nineteenth century, but we do have Isabella Bishop's statement that "a great many men of the lower orders on the river were able to read their own script."[20]

The final part of the Korean traditional heritage bearing directly on later economic and social transformation was the extreme isolation of the nation. China traded with the West for centuries, and Japan had the annual calls of the Dutch at Nagasaki, but, except for occasional shipwrecked sailors, Korea had no direct contact with European peoples or commerce. What little the Koreans knew about the West was obtained through their residents in Peking as filtered through Chinese eyes. When it came to managing relations with distant English, American, or French "barbarians," that was a job the Koreans were content to leave to the Chinese. Korea, after all, was a suzerain state within the greater Chinese world order, and it was the job of the Chinese Emperor, not the Korean King, to maintain that order. It was a world view that was to prove disastrous for Korea.

Much of South and Southeast Asia had fallen under colonial

rule, direct or indirect, in the sixteenth and seventeenth centuries. Western industrial and military might had not reached a point where it could challenge China until the first Opium War in 1839–1842, but, when the challenge came, China was quickly humiliated and forced to accept trade, missionaries, and other foreign residents from the West. The arrival of Commodore Perry's black ships were all that was required for Japan to agree to terms similar to those of China in 1854. Improbable as it may seem to an outsider, Korea, with one-third Japan's population and with a military that was even weaker in relative terms, chose force to resist French and American incursions as late as 1866 and 1871.

When Korea was finally "opened up" to the West in 1876, it was dangerously late. Japan had already begun the political and economic transformation that was to turn that nation into a Western-style imperialist power by the end of the century. If Korea's government had had the resources, the imagination, and the vigor to introduce a rapid and broad-based modernization program immediately, Korea's independence might not have fallen prey to the times. But simply to state these conditions is to realize how hopelessly unrealistic it was to expect Korea's government to meet them. The financial resources of that government were extremely weak, and it was led from the King on down by men thoroughly schooled in Confucianism but almost totally ignorant of the nature of the transformation of economy and society occurring in the West and just beginning in Japan.[21] Even if these men had understood the challenge better, it is doubtful that they would have moved more quickly to meet it, since effective resistance required a fundamental alteration of the things they valued most, the Confucian system itself.

For thirty-four more years, Korea managed a semblance of independent government. The source of Korean independence, however, was not its own internal strength but the indifference of most of the West to this remote peninsula and the rivalry for control between the nearby Russians and Japanese. When the Russian fleet sank to the bottom of the Straits of Tsushima in

1905, Korea's fate was sealed. Only the formality of annexation remained to be completed in 1910. From that time on, Koreans' knowledge of industrialization and the modern societies of the West was received through the filter of Japanese experience. And Korea itself was to be ruled for thirty-five years by a nation that was not only militarily strong but was right next door and possessed a considerable "surplus" population of its own. Colonial rule was not something remote and indirect, but very direct, profound, and traumatic in its impact.

Although the next three and a half decades in Korea were to be dominated by Japan, the point of this discussion has been to show that Japanese colonialism was built upon a substantial Korean traditional base. Korea not only had a millenia and more of independence but, during the centuries when Koreans ruled themselves, their society changed in many fundamental ways. By the nineteenth century, serfdom or slavery had nearly disappeared from the countryside. The landlordism that remained may not have represented any improvement from the point of view of a more equal income distribution, but contractual relations between landlords and tenants were more conducive to increases in the productivity of paddy land than the relations of master and slave. As Korea's population rose during the centuries of comparative peace and the man-land ratio increased because the opening up of new land could not keep pace, crop yields rose substantially, and the cropping system became complex even by modern standards.

Built upon this agricultural base was an advanced culture, including a number of substantial cities and the commercial network needed to supply them. If Korea appears to have been behind both China and Japan in the level of its urbanization and commercial development, it was nevertheless more "advanced" in both respects than most other currently developing countries were in their pre-colonial periods. In the field of education, Korea may even have surpassed its larger Chinese and Japanese neighbors, at least in the area of mass education, although the data available do not really allow precise comparisons of levels of literacy. All we can say is that the invention of the Korean phonetic alphabet put reading within closer reach of the Korean peasant than of his Chinese counterpart, and that there is some evidence that he took advantage of this opportunity.

Finally, Korea was in every sense a single, unified nation; not a region of different principalities, languages, and races pulled together for the convenience of colonial administration. Nationalism may be a creation of the West and of industrialization, but Koreans long ago knew that they were one people, however faction-ridden the court or however much the people of Kyŏngsang province might not like those of Chŏlla province.

THE IMPACT OF JAPANESE COLONIALISM

The period of Japanese rule of Korea, which began formally in 1910 but in most respects five years earlier, was both bitter and short—lasting only thirty-five (or forty) years and ending with Japan's surrender to the Allied Forces in 1945. And yet, although the period of Japanese rule was brief, its impact on Korea was profound.

When writing about the 1910–1945 period, most Koreans see only the dark side of that experience. Vigorous Korean political and military resistance to Japanese rule was met by equally vigorous and ultimately successful Japanese military and police action to suppress that resistance. The Japanese, moreover, were not content with an end to most armed resistance and took further steps to wipe out Korea's national and cultural identity. Koreans were never accepted as the equals of the Japanese, but all Koreans were forced to take Japanese names, and schools had to teach in the Japanese language. Even on the playground, Korean children were expected to speak to each other in Japanese. If these policies had continued in effect for a century or two, Japan's goal of wiping out Korea's separate identity might have succeeded. In the actual situation, the most important impact of this effort was to reinforce both Korean nationalism and Korean hatred of the Japanese. Antipathy toward the Japanese was so deep that it continued to shape Korean policies, including the key area of Korean-Japanese economic relations, throughout the 1950s and into the 1960s.

This study, however, is concerned with what explains Korea's rapid economic growth in recent years and, from that perspective, Japanese colonial rule cannot be seen as an unrelieved disaster. It is true that, during the period of colonial rule, not only did Japanese residents in Korea fare much better than Koreans, but many Koreans experienced an absolute, not just a relative, decline in their standard of living. And yet, for all the hardships imposed on the Korean people, Japanese colonial rule laid some of the key foundations for Korea's later entrance into modern economic growth.

ECONOMIC GROWTH, 1910–1945

Because the Japanese Government General made a major effort to collect and record reasonably reliable economic data, there is ample evidence that economic growth in Korea between 1910 and 1940 was substantial. Manufacturing in particular averaged an annual growth rate of over 10 percent a year throughout the three decades (Table 4). Agricultural output also rose, although there are different estimates of agricultural growth rates in this period, and the average growth rate varies considerably, depending on which years are used for the beginning and end of the period. The data in Table 4, for example, suggest a growth rate of 2 percent between 1919–1921 and 1939–1941, whereas Sung Hwan Ban's estimates suggest a growth rate over roughly that same period of only 1.6 percent.[22] Even with the lower agricultural growth rate, thanks to the rapid rise in manufacturing, gross material product in Korea rose nearly 4 percent a year, and GNP probably grew at a similar rate. Since Korea's population during this same period grew at only 1.6 percent a year, thanks in part to large out-migration of Koreans to Manchuria

TABLE 4 Net Value of Commodity-Product, 1910–1941

Period	Agriculture, Forestry, & Fisheries	Mining & Manufacturing	Total
	(million yen at 1929–1931 prices)		
1910–1912	473	41	514
1919–1921	621	133	754
1929–1931	756	225	981
1939–1941	923	600	1,523
	(annual growth rate in %)		
1910–1912– 1939–1941	2.3	9.7	3.8

Source: Sang-Chul Suh, *Growth and Structural Changes in the Korean Economy, 1910–1940* (Cambridge, Mass., 1978).

and Japan, per capita commodity-product increased at an average rate of about 2 percent a year. Such figures seem modest in comparison with the rates achieved by Korea in the 1960s and 1970s, but Japan itself in this earlier period was doing no better,[23] and Japan was one of the world's most rapidly growing nations at that time.

But was there something artificial about this growth that reduces its significance for what happened after 1945? A point often made is that Korean economic growth in the colonial period was carried out by Japanese and was intended to serve the economic needs of Japan, not those of Korea. The implication is that when the Japanese were withdrawn in 1945, the economic fruits of their efforts in Korea left with them.

There is more than a little truth to this argument. In 1940, for example, Japanese accounted for 94 percent of the authorized capital of manufacturing establishments in Korea, and such key sectors as metals, chemicals, and gas and electrical appliances were almost wholly Japanese. Korean firms, where they existed, were much smaller and financially weaker than those of the Japanese. There were over 1,600 Korean technicians in these industries (in 1944), but this number was only 19 percent of all technicians in Korean manufacturing and construction. The other 81 percent were Japanese, and this percentage rose to 89 percent in such high technology industries as metals and chemicals. [24]

One measure of the artificiality of much Korean economic growth at this time is what happened when the Japanese left. By 1947 or 1948, the number of manufacturing and construction establishments in South Korea had fallen from 10,065 (in 1943) to 4,500; employment in these sectors declined 41 percent, and manufacturing output was only 15 percent of the level achieved in 1939. [25] Part of the problem, of course, was the division of Korea at the 38th parallel, together with highly unstable political conditions in the late 1940s, but the other source of the problem was the withdrawal of Japanese technicians and managers, and the loss of Japanese markets. Subsequently, much of the physical capital that the Japanese did leave behind was destroyed by the Korean War. Even by the late 1950s after massive injections of American assistance, Korean per capita income was only U.S. $135–140 (in 1970 prices) or only slightly above the per capita income of India today. The conclusion seems almost inescapable that little of importance was left over from the Japanese period.

Concentration on ownership and physical capital, however, can be misleading. Between 1910 and 1945 large numbers of Koreans gained experience in factories, in other modern institutions, and with life in modern urban centers. As the data in Table 5 indicate, for example, there was a considerable expansion in the size of the Korean factory labor force. Where in 1912 only 12,000 Koreans worked in factories in Korea, by 1940 their number had risen to nearly 300,000. When expressed as a percentage of a total population of 23.5 million (in 1940), these factory labor force figures are not large, but the point is that Korea began its independence with a substantial cadre of experienced workers. Many other nations in Africa and Southeast Asia which achieved independence in the late 1940s and the 1950s were not in a comparable position.

77

TABLE 5 The Factory Labor Force, 1912–1940
(numbers of workers)

	Textiles		Food Processing		Other		Total	
	Koreans	Japanese[a]	Koreans	Japanese[a]	Koreans	Japanese[a]	Koreans	Japanese[a]
Men								
1912	587	72	9,109	991	2,392	1,222	12,088	2,285
1920	5,422	515	16,853	2,064	23,502	6,301	45,777	8,880
1928	22,188	1,236	29,866	2,164	34,713	8,005	86,767	11,405
Women								
1929	6,372	14,735	25,411	6,129	30,394	6,070	62,177	26,934
1935	9,942	24,646	39,939	8,940	68,943	15,078	118,824	48,664
1940	19,640	43,560	30,716	11,075	162,568	27,412	212,924	82,047

Source: With minor exceptions these data are for factories with 5 or more employees. The original data are from *Chōsen Sōtokufu tōkei nenpō* as reported in Gary Saxonhouse, "Labor in Korea's Development Process" (unpublished paper).

Note: [a]Includes other non-Koreans.

Factory employment in Korea, however, is only part of the story. The percentage of Koreans living in cities rose steadily throughout the colonial period (see Table 6). Of comparable, if not greater, importance was the large number of Koreans who emigrated to cities in Japan. By 1940, there were more Koreans in the great commercial city of Osaka than there were in any city of Korea other than Seoul or Pyŏngyang. Overall by 1945, there were some 1.9 to 2.0 million Koreans in Japan,[26] a large number of whom were repatriated to Korea when Japan surrendered. In addition, by 1940 there were well over a million Koreans in Manchuria many of them residing and working in the cities of that Japanese-held territory.

From a welfare point of view, this large migration of Koreans to other parts of the Japanese Empire presented a mixed picture. The Koreans who migrated to Japan received higher wages than in Korea, and they were subject to less police surveillance, but it was the depressed state of rural Korea that led them to migrate. From a growth perspective, however, there is little doubt that residence in cities, often with employment in the modern sector, was a positive contribution to the stock of human capital available for post-independence economic development. It is not always very clear just what it is about urban life that makes people who have experienced it more valuable contributors to modern economic growth than people straight off the farm, but there is little doubt that they do make a greater contribution.

Japanese colonial rule also added to the stock of human capital in the more conventional sense by expanding the modern educational system. As pointed out above, the educational base of traditional Korea was much stronger than that of many other pre-modern societies. Modernization of this system began before 1910 largely under Christian missionary auspices. After 1910 the Japanese expanded modern primary-level education vigorously as a major element in their program to integrate Korea into the Japanese Empire. The number of "common" (that is, modern primary) schools expanded from only 306 in 1911 to

TABLE 6 Urbanization During the Colonial Period
(1,000s)

	1910		1926		1935		1941	
	Person	*%*	*Person*	*%*	*Person*	*%*	*Person*	*%*
Total population	12,934	100.0	19,103	100.0	21,891	100.0	24,703	100.0
Urban areas								
Over 100,000	341	2.6	527	2.8	863	3.9	2,428	9.8
Over 50,000	596	4.6	658	3.4	1,325	6.1	3,163	12.8
Over 20,000	752	5.8	1,378[a]	7.2	1,908	8.7	4,672	18.9

Sources: Chapter by John Sloboda in Edwin S. Mills and Byung-Nak Song, *Urbanization and Urban Problems, Studies in the Modernization of the Republic of Korea: 1945–1975* (Cambridge, Mass., 1979), p. 58. Chōsen Sōtokufu tōkei nenpō, *1910, 1926, 1935, 1941.*

Note: [a]Including myŏn (townships), which have population over 20,000.

715 in 1921 and to 2,600 by 1937, in effect, one common school for each of the 2,493 myŏn (townships).[27] By 1937, there were over 900,000 pupils in the common schools, and by 1945 this figure had risen to well above one million (see Table 7). In 1921, by contrast, there were only 157,000 pupils in the common schools, but at that time there were still 293,000 enrolled in traditional schools so that the total primary school enrollment, even at that early date, was nearly half that in 1937.[28] Thus, something like a quarter of Korea's total population had received at least several years of formal schooling at the time Korea regained its independence in 1945.

The educational pyramid narrowed rapidly towards the higher grades, but Korean enrollments did not disappear altogether, as they did under some colonial regimes (for example, the Dutch East Indies or the Belgian Congo). By the 1930s and 1940s, there were tens of thousands of Koreans in high schools, and thousands more were attending universities in either Korea or Japan, despite severe discrimination against Koreans admitted to Japanese universities including Keijō Imperial (now Seoul National) University in Seoul. Thus, when the Korean educational system began to develop rapidly in the late 1940s and 1950s, there was a large if inadequate number of qualified people to draw on to teach in and to administer the expanded system. Furthermore, institutions such as the public Seoul National and the private Yonsei and Korea universities could draw on a long tradition of excellence, one they have maintained to this day.

Institutional development in the Japanese period was not confined to education. The finances of the government were separated from those of the Korean Imperial Household and established on modern principles. The Japanese also introduced a modern monetary system to replace the chaotic system that existed at the end of the Yi dynasty. A railroad connected Pusan and Seoul with Manchuria and Europe. In the rural areas, the Japanese established a high-quality extension service designed to increase Korea's ability to supply Japan's demand for inexpensive rice.

TABLE 7 School Enrollment in 1945

	Number of Enrollments 1945
Primary schools	1,366,024
Middle schools	n.a.
Academic high schools	50,343
Vocational high schools	33,171
Higher educational institutions	7,819

Source: Ministry of Education, *Statistical Yearbooks of Education* as given in Noel F. McGinn, et al., *Education and Development in Korea,* Studies in the Modernization of the Republic of Korea: 1945–1975 (Cambridge, Mass., 1980) p. 5.

Not all these institutional innovations survived the transition to independence. The usual measures of financial development suggest that Korea's monetary and banking system reverted to a level similar to that at the beginning of Japanese rule.[29] A negative reaction to the authoritarian methods of the rural extension system led in the late 1940s to the near total destruction of that service. Removal of control over forest areas led to the general deforestation of Korean hillsides after decades of Japanese efforts to build up those forests. But even where the destruction of these modern institutions seemed most complete, something of value was retained. In the late 1950s and 1960s, for example, the rural extension system was rebuilt on the old foundations and in the same location (in the city of Suwŏn). Experience with chemical fertilizers and improved plant varieties introduced in the 1930s did not disappear during the extension service's temporary hiatus. Similarly, the Bank of Korea was built on the base of the old Bank of Chōsen as were other special banks for agriculture and industry.

TRADE AND INCOME DISTRIBUTION

In one important area, however, the Japanese colonial legacy left Korea with a fundamental structural imbalance. As already pointed out, Korea was seen by the Japanese as a source of cheap rice. Korea was also seen as a place to which Japan's surplus population could emigrate, although Manchuria was seen as more valuable in this regard. To achieve both ends, one of Japan's first major efforts in Korea was to conduct a thorough land survey and to follow that survey with the takeover of all land in the public domain—namely crown lands, temple lands, and the like.

Even more serious and partly as a result of the land survey was the gradual but steady conversion of farmer-owned-and-tilled land into landlord-owned-and-tenant-tilled land. Over a twenty-year period, the number of farm families who owned no land at all rose from 38 percent to 55 percent of the total (see Table 8). About 17 percent of the land farmed by tenants was owned by Japanese landlords,[30] but the remainder was owned by Korean landlords. The central point, however, is not the nationality of the major landowners, but the fact that a rising proportion of the rural population was being reduced to a bare subsistence level. No precise data on income distribution in rural Korea are available, but in 1937 half the farm families in what is now South Korea farmed less than half a hectare of land, and much or, in some cases, all of that land was owned by landlords who received half the main crop or about a quarter of total household income. This large "surplus" of rural poor not surprisingly had a depressing effect on urban wages as well. Between 1910 and 1944, money wages regularly lagged behind the rise in wholesale prices (except briefly during the 1930s). By the end of the period in 1944, the money-wage index had risen by 262 percent, but wholesale prices had risen by 315 percent implying some decline in real wages.[31] Not only was the distribution of income becoming more unequal, but there is some, though not conclusive, evidence that the income of half or more of the

TABLE 8 Owner-Tenant Distribution Before 1945
(%)

	1918	1922	1926	1930	1934	1937
Farm Families Who Are:						
Owners	22.3	22.9	22.6	20.9	19.2	19.2
Part-owners	39.6	36.1	33.2	31.7	25.5	25.7
Tenants	38.1	41.0	44.2	47.4	55.3	55.1
Total	100.0	100.0	100.0	100.0	100.0	100.0
Land Share Farmed by:						
Owners	49.6	49.4	49.3	44.5	42.8	42.5
Tenants	50.4	50.6	50.7	55.5	57.2	57.5
Total	100.0	100.0	100.0	100.0	100.0	100.0

Source: Himeno Minoru, *Chōsen keizai zuhyō*, pp. 163 and 168.

population was declining in absolute terms despite a steady rise in average national product per capita.

The problem of income inequality itself was dealt with decisively in the years after 1945 through land reform and the unintended side effects of the Korean War. But the pattern of trade relationships that supported the inequality under the Japanese created a problem in terms of the structure of the economy that was not so readily dealt with. Rising farm output together with increasing tenancy had both been important elements in turning Korea into a major exporter of rice and other agricultural products. Throughout most of the 1920s and 1930s, foodstuffs accounted for 60 percent and more of Korean exports, most of which were destined for Japan. From 1925 through 1939, an average of 40 percent of Korea's total rice crop was exported to Japan.[32] Korea's foreign trade sector, therefore, was built on a foundation of inequality that collapsed when land was redistributed and farmers started consuming most of their own rice instead of giving it to landlords who then sold it to Japan. In the late 1940s and again in the 1950s, there was a widespread belief that South Korean self-sufficiency could only be achieved by reconstituting this colonial trading pattern based on agricultural exports. It was not until the 1960s that Korea finally succeeded in developing manufactured exports as an alternative source of earnings with which to pay for needed imports. Until then Korea handled its foreign-exchange shortage to some degree by eliminating many "non-essential" imports, and covered the remainder with foreign aid and United Nations Forces payments.

This discussion of the Japanese colonial period would be remiss if it did not conclude with some mention of the political impact of Japanese rule. For thirty-five crucial years, Korea was ruled almost exclusively by Japanese. Koreans gained comparatively little experience in the management of the political affairs of their own country. When Koreans finally regained control over their own affairs in 1948, they had numerous foreign political models they could attempt to emulate, but their only direct experience was with the discredited system of the Yi dynasty and with the autocratic rule of the hated Japanese. In a very real sense, therefore, the political instability that characterized the late 1940s and most of the 1950s until the military coup of 1961 was also partly the heritage of Japanese colonialism. At a crucial point in Korean history, Koreans had been deprived of the opportunity to develop effective political institutions of their own. And without effective political institutions, sustained modern economic growth was also an impossibility.

THE DIVISION OF THE NATION

If the Japanese colonial heritage was a mixture of positive and negative elements from the point of view of economic growth, the division of the country at the 38th parallel in 1945 was an unmitigated disaster.

The most immediate impact of the partition was that an economy that had been built as an integrated whole was split in two. The south retained nearly two-thirds of the population and about half of the arable land, but more than two-thirds of the paddy acreage (Table 9). The north kept most of the mines and about half of all manufacturing output (Table 10). Of more immediate importance than the overall share of manufacturing was that most of the peninsula's electricity was produced in the north (Table 11).

It is not easy to assess the overall impact of this division of the economy. The immediate impact was considerable disruption in the manufacturing sector and a lesser amount in agriculture. Agricultural output did fall, but partition of the country was not the primary reason. The long-term impact of the division at the 38th parallel is difficult to appraise, because it is not easy to put a value on the physical capital—the manufacturing and mining plant and equipment—left behind by the Japanese. As already pointed out, much of this physical capital was unutilized or

TABLE 9 Comparison of Land and Population Between
South and North Korea at the Time of Partition

	South	North	All Korea	Share of the South in All Korea (%)
Total land (km^2)	108,366[a]	118,366	226,732	47.8
Population, 1944 (1000 persons)	17,041	8,859	25,900	65.8
Population density (persons per km^2)	158	75	114	
Arable land, 1939 (km^2)	22,300	24,175	46,475	48.1
Rice paddies	(13,293)	(5,684)	(18,977)	(70.0)
Dry fields	(9,007)	(18,491)	(27,498)	(32.8)
Arable land to total (%)	20.6	20.4	20.5	
Per capita arable land (m^2)	1,309	2,729	1,791	

Sources: Kwang Suk Kim and Michael Roemer, *Growth and Structural Transformation,* Studies in the Modernization of the Republic of Korea, 1945–1975 (Cambridge, Mass., 1979), p. 22. Compiled from the data given in BOK, *Annual Economic Review of Korea, 1948,* III, 17–25.

Note: [a]The exact area of land for South Korea was 93,634 km^2 at the time of partition. But since population and arable land statistics are available only by provincial breakdown, we used the land size of the provinces that were mostly included in South Korea.

underutilized after the Japanese left. Furthermore, a high percentage of plant and equipment in both the north and the south was destroyed during the Korean War. What was left of this industrial heritage, therefore, was the pool of trained workers and technicians, and many of these presumably fled south immediately after partition or during the Korean War.

The one clear advantage enjoyed by the north was its retention of most of the best mines, but even this was a mixed blessing. To this day, North Korea continues to rely to a significant degree on the products of its mines in order to earn foreign exchange. South Korea, on the other hand, faced with an almost total loss of its traditional exports, was forced by circumstances

TABLE 10 Net Commodity-Product in South and North Korea,
1939–1940 Averages
(million K¥ at 1936 market prices)

	South	*North*	*All Korea*	*Share of the south in all Korea (%)*
Agriculture	496.3 (59.9)	333.3 (46.8)	829.6	59.8
Forestry	65.8 (7.9)	58.7 (8.2)	124.5	52.9
Fishery	80.2 (9.7)	46.8 (6.5)	127.0	63.1
Mining	28.9 (3.5)	90.6 (12.7)	119.5	24.2
Manufacturing	157.9 (19.0)	183.7 (25.8)	341.6	46.2
TOTAL	829.1 (100.0)	713.1 (100.0)	1,542.2	53.8
Population (1,000s)	15,627	7,920	23,547	66.4
Per capita net commodity-product (K¥)	53.1	90.0	–	–

Source: Sang-Chul Suh, *Growth and Structural Changes*, pp. 137–139.

to develop manufactured exports with results that are now well
known throughout the world.

The real impact of partition, however, did not lie in the direct
effect caused by the disruption of established economic links
between the north and the south. These effects were either
temporary or were only one of many sources of difficulties in
the late 1940s. The most important impact of the division of
Korea, on the economy as well as on the society as a whole, was
the Korean War itself and the continuing military confrontation
that has existed on the Korean peninsula ever since. The war was
enormously destructive of lives and property in both the
north and the south. In addition, continuing north-south
hostility has led to large military budgets which have diverted
5 percent of the GNP of the south and perhaps 15–20 percent

TABLE 11 Comparison of Manufacturing Production
Between South and North Korea, 1939[a]

(current million yen)

	South		North		All Korea	Share of the South in All Korea (%)
Textiles	171.0	(24.1)	30.4	(3.9)	201.4	84.9
Metal	13.6	(1.9)	122.5	(15.5)	136.1	10.0
Machinery	38.4	(5.4)	14.8	(1.9)	53.2	72.2
Ceramics	12.1	(1.7)	31.2	(4.0)	43.3	27.9
Chemicals	91.2	(12.9)	410.6	(52.0)	501.8	18.2
Wood products	13.7	(1.9)	7.4	(0.9)	21.1	64.9
Printing & publishing	17.2	(2.4)	2.2	(0.3)	19.4	89.0
Processed foods	213.6	(30.1)	114.8	(14.5)	328.4	65.1
Gas & elec. products	11.1	(1.6)	19.4	(2.5)	30.5	36.4
Miscellaneous	127.5	(18.0)	35.8	(4.5)	163.3	78.1
Total	709.4	(100.0)	789.1	(100.0)	1,498.5	47.4

Sources: Zenkoku Keizai Chōsa Kikan Rengōkai, *Chōsen Keizai Nenpō* (Seoul, 1942). Kim and Roemer, p. 24.

Note: [a]The breakdown of manufacturing production between South and North Korea was based on the production data by province. The breakdown between the south and the north will not therefore be exact because the 38th parallel did not match the provincial boundaries.

of the GNP of the north to what in economic terms are mostly unproductive uses. It is the constant threat of renewed civil war, therefore, that is the real legacy of that decision to divide the country made so casually more than three decades ago.

CONCLUSION

There were, it is clear, many parts to the Korean historical heritage, and many of these had and continue to have an impact on economic growth. Korea's long unified history and its homogeneous population have largely removed the kind of ethnic differences that play such a large part in the economies of so many other developing nations. Even Korea's class structure with its rigid barriers between *yangban*, commoner, and serf had begun to erode during the latter part of the Yi dynasty, were further undermined by Japanese colonial rule, and received the *coup de grace* from independence, land reform, and the Korean War.

Long years of comparative stability also led to a gradual rise in the size of Korea's population, a rise that was accelerated by public health measures during Japan's thirty-five-year rule. Food output managed to keep up with population—first by slow improvements in traditional technique and later by modern improvements introduced through the Japanese-created extension service. By the 1940s Korea had a very sophisticated agricultural system capable of supporting a large number of people on a very limited amount of land.

Confucianism gave to Korea a deep sense of the importance of education, which resulted in Korea's having a more educated population than most nations in the nineteenth century outside of Europe and North America. Koreans were also blessed by the invention of an excellent phonetic spelling of their language, Han'gŭl, which brought elementary education within easier reach of the great majority of people. By building on this base, the Japanese, together with private sources, modernized and expanded the primary school system. Much less, but still something, was accomplished with the higher levels of the school system despite considerable discrimination against Koreans in those higher levels.

There was also a negative side to the Korean heritage. The very harshness of Japanese rule left a considerable reserve of enmity between the two nations that continues to poison relations. While some Koreans received training in modern industry either in Korea itself or in Japan, Japanese discrimination held this acquisition of experience well below what could have been accomplished, given the amount of industrialization that occured under Japanese rule.

Perhaps the most serious negative features of Japanese colonial rule were the continued isolation of Koreans from experience in the international arena and from experience in running their own country. The former undoubtedly contributed to the casualness with which Korea was treated by the Allied powers during World War II which led to the tragic partitioning of the country. The latter accounts in part at least for the political instability that plagued Korea in the late 1940s and 1950s.

There have, of course, been dramatic changes in Korea since 1945, changes that have taken Korea a long way from its traditional and colonial heritage. Even the casual observer, however, can see that important elements of that heritage continue to set the context in which change and modernization are occurring.

FOUR

Economic Development in Macroeconomic Terms,

1953–1976

Political events have repeatedly interrupted the growth of Korea's economy. This was never truer than in the period 1945–1953. During these years, the economy was disrupted first by the collapse of the Japanese Greater East Asia Co-Prosperity Sphere and later by the arbitrary division of the peninsula into Soviet and American zones of occupation. The ensuing civil war destroyed much of the urban housing and industry in Korea and devastated the countryside. When the Armistice was signed in 1953, the level of production of the Korean economy was far below what it had been during the early 1940s. The GNP for 1953 amounted to 48.8 billion wŏn at current prices, or U.S. $2,715 million at 1970 constant prices; per capita GNP was $134 at 1970 constant prices. Unfortunately it is not possible to compare directly this magnitude with figures for earlier years, since reliable national accounts data are not available for the period prior to 1953. However, a comparison of net commodity-product data from 1939/40 and 1953 indicates that output in all sectors of the economy declined significantly.

In 1953 South Korea possessed a backward rural economy in which agriculture, forestry, and fishing accounted for 47 percent of GNP and manufacturing for less than 9 percent.[1] Total fixed investment amounted to only 7 percent of GNP, barely enough to cover the depreciation on the existing capital stock. Yet 90 percent of even this modest figure had to be financed out of foreign savings. Similarly, Korea's large balance-of-payments deficits were covered by foreign assistance, mainly war relief and reconstruction aid from the United States and the United Nations.

During the first years of the post-war period, the Korean government necessarily gave priority to the reconstruction of the infrastructure and factories that had been destroyed in the fighting. The more urgent programs of repairing war damage were completed by the middle of 1957. Thereafter, the government increasingly shifted its emphasis to stabilizing prices. Nevertheless, a substantial portion of the available resources continued to be allocated to national defense. This policy was not unique to the early post-war years, and defense spending has continued to account for over 4 percent of GNP under all succeeding governments.

Many of the post-war reconstruction and stabilization programs were financed with aid from the United States and the United Nations.[2] Throughout the 1950s, large quantities of aid-financed food, medicines, machinery, and raw materials arrived in Korea. Between 1953–1960, the assistance provided by the United Nations amounted to $120 million, while that provided by the United States totaled $1,745 million, including $156 million worth of Public Law 480 food.[3] Over 70 percent of Korea's imports were financed by foreign grants during this period. Foreign assistance was also important for reconstruction activities, where the "counterpart funds" generated by the sales of grant-aid dollars provided a non-inflationary source of domestic currency financing for investment. Furthermore, almost half of all general government expenditures were financed out of these "counterpart funds."

Despite large inflows of foreign assistance, economic performance during the period of reconstruction failed to meet the expectations of either the Korean people or the aid donors. Inflation was a persistent problem. The annual rate of increase in the wholesale price index dropped from 531 percent in 1951 to 25–28 percent in 1953–1954, but it rose again to 82 percent in 1955. In order to remedy this situation, the government accepted the advice of the U.S. Aid Mission and, in the latter half of 1957, adopted strict measures to stabilize prices. The first target of the new measures was the elimination of the large government deficits which had been the major source of monetary expansion. Through fiscal restraint, the government was able to reduce the rate of growth of the money supply from 62 percent in 1955 to 29 percent in 1956, and further to 20 percent in 1957. Despite some relaxation of monetary policy, relative price stability continued to be maintained during the next few years, although this was as much a consequence of two successive bumper harvests in 1957 and 1958, which made possible a sharp reduction in grain prices, as of deliberate government policy. Economic growth, as in prior years, continued to be assigned secondary importance.

ECONOMIC POLICY CHANGES

During the 1950s, no serious effort was made to increase domestic savings, since Korean policy-makers believed that postwar incomes were still too low to permit the extensive mobilization of private savings. Instead, the government directed its strategy towards maximizing foreign assistance to overcome the scarcity of domestic resources. Furthermore, interest rates on the organized financial markets were also controlled in order to accelerate private long-term investment by keeping the cost of investors' capital low, since it was generally felt that aggregate domestic savings were not very responsive to changes in interest rates.

Industrial policy was inward-looking. The official foreign exchange rate remained overvalued throughout the 1950s, despite large periodic devaluations. In addition, the government used both high tariffs and various quantitative restrictions to protect domestic industry. These measures encouraged some import substitution, primarily in the consumer goods industries. The government also made some minor attempts to promote exports, and although exports grew, they remained at miniscule levels. In essence, the government emphasized reconstruction and price stabilization more than growth during the post-war 1950s. However, growth was not entirely overlooked, and it remained a secondary objective of policy throughout the period. With the collapse of the Syngman Rhee Government in 1960 and the installation of a military government, economic policy clearly shifted from reconstruction and stabilization to a program of rapid industrialization based on exports.

This shift of policy reflected the changed circumstances confronting the economy. By 1960, post-war reconstruction and the early stage of import substitution were complete. Imports of nondurable consumer goods and the intermediate goods used in their manufacture could now be replaced by domestic production. Economic growth continued to lag, however, and, in the early 1960s, unemployment and inflation began to rise again. At the same time, the U.S. government announced that assistance would be terminated in the near future. Consequently, expanding exports seemed the soundest way of replacing the impending loss of foreign exchange, as well as of creating employment in the major urban centers.

The new growth strategy played a large role in the first formal plan ever adopted by the Korean government: the First Five-Year Economic Development Plan 1962–1966. The First Five-Year Plan called for a 7.1 percent annual real growth rate, a pace thought sufficient to allow the creation of a firm economic base for industrialization and self-sustaining growth. In view of the poor growth performance of previous years, the plan's targets seemed ambitious. Thus, it came as a great surprise to everyone when these goals were exceeded.

In deciding to adopt a new growth strategy, the government also committed itself to a variety of economic reforms. In 1961 the exchange rate was revalued, and in 1962 the government undertook the reform of exchange controls, the national currency, the budget, and tax collections. Although some of these measures were ineffective or even counterproductive to economic growth, they clearly demonstrated the government's intent to rely on domestic resources to industrialize.

During the next several years, the government continued to lend its full support to the export-oriented growth strategy. In May 1964, the wŏn was devalued by almost 50 percent, from 130 to 255 wŏn per dollar and, in March 1965, a unitary floating exchange rate system was adopted. Shortly thereafter, the government doubled the interest rates on bank deposits and loans. This was done in order to increase voluntary private savings and discourage the unproductive use of bank credit. These changes made possible a significantly higher ratio of investment to national income. In 1967, additional measures to liberalize imports and lower tariffs were introduced.[4] The government also took steps to increase tax revenues and stabilize consumer prices. Much of the price stabilization program was carried out at the expense of farmers, who were forced to accept the government's policy of low grain prices. Consequently, agriculture development was neglected, and the government made little effort to increase investment in this sector.

This basic strategy of export-oriented industrialization was continued under the subsequent Second (1967–1971), Third (1972–1976), and Fourth (1977–1981) Five-Year Economic Plans. Nevertheless, specific policies were modified to take into account changing economic circumstances. One important modification was the reversal of the government's traditional view of agriculture. Beginning in 1969, the government shifted to a policy of high grain prices and initiated the Saemaul Undong (New Community Movement) which hoped to improve the farm village environment and increase agricultural production and income (see Chapter 9). Another important modification, which was not justified on economic grounds, was the return in the early 1970s to the low interest rate policy of the pre-reform period.

GROWTH AND STRUCTURAL CHANGE IN NATIONAL PRODUCT

The results of the Korean government's decision to change to an export growth strategy are well known. The annual growth rate of GNP at 1970 constant prices accelerated from a modest 4.1 percent during the period from 1953–1955 to 1960–1962 to 9.6 percent in the 1962–1976 period. In terms of GNP per capita, the acceleration was even more impressive. The annual rate of growth rose from 1.7 percent during the first period to 7.2 percent during the second.

The dramatic shift from the indifferent growth record of the 1950s to rapid progress in the 1960s and 1970s is shown in Table 12. The peak rate of GNP growth in the 1953–1962 period, 7.7 percent in 1957, was approximately the minimum rate for the 1962–1976 period. Furthermore, non-agricultural output, particularly industrial output, clearly dominated growth. While the average growth rate of value added in the primary sector recorded only a small upward shift after 1960–1962, the increase in the average growth rate of industrial value added was very sharp—from just over 10 percent per year in the period prior to 1960–1962 to 18 percent afterwards. Within the industrial sector, manufacturing, predictably, accounted for the preponderate share of growth. The services sector, buoyed by the strong performance of industry, also registered strong gains, its average annual growth rate rising from 4 to 9 percent between the periods.

TABLE 12 Annual Growth Rate of GNP by
Industrial Origin, 1953–1976
(based on 1970 constant price data)
(%)

| Year | Primary | Industry | | Services | GNP | (Commodity |
		Total	(Manufacturing)			Export)
1954	6.7	20.0	(18.7)	2.5	5.5	(−36.0)
1955	2.7	17.1	(22.8)	5.7	5.4	(−27.9)
1956	−5.8	13.3	(17.3)	4.0	0.4	(42.1)
1957	9.4	11.8	(8.3)	5.8	7.7	(1.5)
1958	6.1	8.1	(9.1)	3.5	5.2	(−20.3)
1959	−0.9	11.3	(9.2)	7.5	3.9	(11.3)
1960	−0.5	6.7	(8.2)	2.8	1.9	(54.1)
1961	11.8	4.6	(3.1)	−1.1	4.8	(22.7)
1962	−5.0	14.0	(13.2)	8.9	3.1	(30.0)
1963	7.9	11.4	(17.3)	7.4	8.8	(53.9)
1964	15.3	12.6	(6.5)	3.0	8.6	(36.7)
1965	−1.6	20.4	(20.0)	9.9	6.1	(47.0)
1966	10.5	18.7	(17.1)	12.6	12.4	(44.5)
1967	−4.4	21.4	(22.8)	13.8	7.8	(32.7)
1968	2.3	29.5	(27.0)	15.4	12.6	(45.8)
1969	12.0	25.5	(21.4)	14.6	15.0	(36.9)
1970	−0.4	15.5	(18.4)	8.9	7.9	(33.8)
1971	3.2	14.1	(17.7)	8.9	9.2	(27.5)
1972	1.6	12.5	(15.7)	5.8	7.0	(46.9)
1973	4.2	29.0	(30.9)	14.7	16.7	(58.4)
1974	5.8	14.8	(17.5)	4.9	8.7	(5.7)
1975	7.3	12.9	(12.9)	5.8	8.3	(19.8)
1976	8.7	23.7	(26.1)	11.1	15.5	(39.8)
Average 1953–1955 to 1960–1962	2.5	10.8	(11.1)	4.3	4.1	(7.6)
Average 1960–1962 to 1974–1976	4.5	17.9	(18.4)	9.4	9.6	(36.8)

Source: BOK, *Economic Statistics Yearbook 1977*, pp. 262–263.
    BOK, *National Income in Korea, 1975,* pp. 146–147.
Note: See Table 13 for the composition of the primary, industry and service sectors.

These large differences in sectoral growth rates during the 1960s and 1970s profoundly affected the structure of production in Korea. In terms of current prices, the share of the industrial sector, including manufacturing, construction, and utilities, doubled from 18 percent of GNP in 1960–1962 to 35 percent by the mid-1970s (see Table 13). Manufacturing, which accounted for only 11 percent of GNP in the early 1960s, contributed 29 percent by the mid-1970s. In contrast, the share of the primary sector (including agriculture and mining) fell sharply from over 45 percent in 1962 to 26 percent in 1976. The services sector maintained its share at around 40 percent of GNP throughout the period.

Total fixed investment also expanded rapidly after the early 1960s (see Table 14). However, the distribution of investment by sector provides little insight into the reasons for the acceleration of growth and structural change in the economy. For instance, the primary sector's share of total fixed investment fell slightly from 12 percent in the 1954–1960 period to 10 percent during the 1961–1975 period. However, this was only a fraction of a rapidly growing total, and it in itself cannot fully explain the decline of the primary sector's share of value added. The investment share of the leading sector, manufacturing, also declined from 24 percent during the 1954–1960 period to 22 percent during 1961–1975, while the utilities' share of investment rose slightly from 28 percent to 31 percent. Over half of all investment continued to be allocated to the services sector throughout both periods. [5]

If the manufacturing share of investment did not rise, but its share of GNP rose substantially, then the incremental capital-output ratio (ICOR) for manufacturing must have declined during 1961–1975 and, conversely, increased for the primary sector. The ICORs were calculated by first summing the investment over the two periods, 1954–1960 and 1961–1975, and then by dividing by the incremental value added based on the terminal averages for 1953–1955, 1960–1962, and 1976; in other words, a time lag of one year was assumed. These

TABLE 13 Share of GNP by Industrial Origin, 1953–1976
(share in percent based on current price data)

	1953–1955	1960–1962	1974–1976
Agriculture, forestry, and fisheries	44.1	37.9	25.0
Mining & quarrying	1.1	2.0	1.2
Primary total	45.2	39.9	26.2
Manufacturing	10.5	13.8	28.8
Construction	2.6	3.3	4.6
Utilities	0.5	1.1	1.3
Industry total	13.6	18.2	34.7
Transportation, storage, & communication	2.0	4.7	5.6
Wholesale and retail trade	12.7	12.0	17.5
Banking, insurance, & real estate	0.7	1.6	2.4
Ownership of dwellings	10.6	5.8	1.8
Public administration & defense	6.2	7.2	4.6
Other services	7.8	9.7	8.4
Service total	40.0	41.0	40.3
Rest of the world	1.1	0.8	–1.2
Gross national product	100.0	100.0	100.0
Memo item: Social overhead (Utilities plus transportation)	2.5	5.2	5.8

Sources: BOK, *National Income in Korea, 1975*, pp. 144–145.
BOK, *Economic Statistics Yearbook, 1977*, p. 261.

calculations show that the ICOR for the primary sector rose by 79 percent from 0.86 to 1.54, while for manufacturing it fell by 49 percent from 2.59 to 1.33. The ICOR for services also increased somewhat from 3.39 to 4.00. Nevertheless, for the economy as a whole, the ICOR remained virtually constant, averaging 2.4 during 1961–1975.

A number of recent studies lend support to these figures. For instance, Young Chin Kim and Jene K. Kwon[6] found in their

TABLE 14 Fixed Investment by Industrial Origin
(1970 constant market prices)

	Primary	Industry *(Manufacturing)*		Services	Domestic Gross Fixed Investment
A. Total Investment (billion wŏn)					
1954–1960	70	168	(140)	349	586
1961–1975	734	2,320	(1,611)	4,329	7,383
1954–1975	804	2,488	(1,751)	4,678	7,969
B. Share of investment (%)					
1954–1960	11.9	28.7	(23.9)	59.6	100.0
1961–1975	9.9	31.4	(21.8)	58.6	100.0
1954–1975	10.1	31.2	(22.0)	58.7	100.0
C. Incremental capital-output ratio[a]					
1953–55 to 1960–62	0.86	2.37	(2.59)	3.39	2.30
1960–62 to 1974–76	1.54	1.56	(1.33)	4.00	2.42
1953–55 to 1974–76	1.37	1.59	(1.37)	3.84	2.36

Sources: BOK, *National Income in Korea, 1975*, pp. 148–161. BOK, *Economic Statistics Yearbook, 1977*, pp. 266–267.
  Note: [a]Total investment for 1954–1960, 1961–1975, or 1954–1975 divided by the increase in valued added at factor cost for 1953–55 to 1960–62, 1961–63 to 1976, or 1953–55 to 1976.

1973 study of the Korean manufacturing industry that the rate of capacity utilization in manufacturing roughly doubled from 1962 to 1971, the decade of greatest growth. Another study published in 1976 on the factor supply and intensity of trade in Korea by Wontack Hong[7] concluded that there was a 3.7-fold increase of the net-manufacturing capital stock from 1961 to 1974. Both of these findings are consistent with the 9-fold increase of the net manufacturing capital stock from 1961 to 1962 to 1973–1975 and the 9 percent fall in the manufacturing ICOR. Thus the observed fall in the ICOR can largely be explained by the doubling of capacity utilization, which implies that there were only minor improvements in efficiency from investment in less capital-intensive technologies and from sectoral shifts in manufacturing investment towards labor-intensive industries.

The growth pattern of the leading sector, manufacturing, and the commodity composition of trade also reveal important aspects of the structural change which has occurred during the past twenty-four years. As might be expected in a rapidly growing and diversifying economy, the more complex producer goods industries—the heavy and chemical industries—substantially increased their share of manufacturing value added, from 23 percent in 1953–1955 to 29 percent in 1960–1962 and further to 42 percent in 1974–1976. Conversely, the share of light industries shrank during the period, although manufacturers of certain products were able to hold on to their shares of GNP because of the expansion of both domestic and export demand. Finally, shifts in the commodity composition of trade, especially of exports, also contributed to the structural change in national product. Manufactured exports (SITC 5–8), which had accounted for only 17 percent of exports in 1960–1962, increased to comprise 85 percent of a much larger volume of exports (33 percent of GNP) by 1974–1976. There was no correspondingly dramatic change in the structure of commodity imports.

THE DOMESTIC RESOURCE GAP AND
INFLOWS OF FOREIGN CAPITAL

Exports were the real engine of growth in Korea. Export growth surpassed the growth rates of all other national expenditure aggregates during the post-war period. Because exports of goods and services started out from a very small base, their growth rate was relatively higher than that of the other expenditure aggregates, even during the 1950s. Nevertheless, until the 1960s, exports were still a very minor fraction of GNP. Thereafter, the rate of export growth increased to 29 percent annually, and by 1974–1976, exports totaled 30 percent of GNP (see Table 15). In contrast, imports of goods and non-factor services grew much more slowly, remaining at about 10 percent of GNP in the 1950s. After 1960–1962, however, the average annual growth rate of imports increased to 17 percent, thus lifting the level of imports to 30 percent of GNP by 1974–1976. Because the growth of imports was not as rapid as that of exports, export earnings, which were able to finance less than 30 percent of imports in the 1950s, rose to exceed imports by 1974–1976. This is the best indication of the significant improvement that took place in Korea's balance of payments between 1960–1962 and 1974–1976.

Another important improvement that occurred during this period was the nation's increasing ability to finance investment out of its own resources. Prior to the First Five-Year Plan, gross domestic investment was an unimpressive 10 percent of GNP, 70 percent of it financed by foreign savings. However, investment began to grow rapidly after 1962 and reached 27 percent of GNP in 1974–1976. The increase in the volume of investment was accompanied by a corresponding rise in the proportion of investment financed out of domestic resources, from 30 percent in 1960–1962 to 100 percent in 1974–1976. This was made possible by the rapid growth of domestic savings, which expanded from only 3 percent of GNP in the early 1960s to 27 percent by 1974–1976. Alternatively, the rapid growth of

TABLE 15 Expenditure on National Product, 1953–1976
(1970 market prices)

	Annual Average (bil. wŏn)			*Share of GNP*		
	1953–55	*1960–62*	*1974–76*	*1953–55*	*1960–62*	*1974–76*
Private consumption[a]	714	979	2,696	.801	.830	.636
Government consumption	150	165	417	.168	.139	.098
Investment	100	112	1,152	.112	.095	.272
(Fixed investment)	(63)	(111)	(1,073)	(.070)	(.094)	(.253)
Exports of goods & non-factor services	13	36	1,289	.015	.031	.304
Imports of goods & non-factor services	97	122	1,242	.108	.103	.293
Gross domestic product[b]	881	1,171	4,278	.988	.993	1.010
Net factor income	10	8	-43	.011	.007	-.010
Gross national product[b]	891	1,179	4,236	1.000	1.000	1.000
Memo item:						
Foreign saving[c]	74	78	-4	.083	.066	-.001
Domestic saving[d]	26	34	1,156	.029	.029	.273

TABLE 15 (continued)

	Annual Growth Rate (%)			Marginal Ratio to GNP		
	1953–55 to 1960–62	1960–62 to 1974–76	1953–55 to 1974–76	1953–55 to 1960–62	1960–62 to 1974–76	1953–55 to 1974–76
Private consumption[a]	4.6	7.5	6.5	.920	.562	.593
Government consumption	1.4	6.8	5.0	.052	.082	.080
Investment	1.6	18.1	12.3	.042	.340	.314
(Fixed investment)	(8.4)	(17.6)	(14.4)	(.167)	(.315)	(.302)
Exports of goods & non-factor services	15.6	29.1	24.5	.080	.410	.381
Imports of goods & non-factor services	3.2	17.3	12.9	.087	.366	.342
Gross domestic product[b]	4.1	9.7	7.8	–	–	–
Net factor income	–	–	–	–.007	–.011	.010
Gross national product[b]	4.1	9.6	7.7	1.000	1.000	1.000
Memo item:						
Foreign saving[c]	0.8	–	–	.013	–.025	–.023
Domestic saving[d]	3.9	31.1	19.8	.028	.367	.338

Sources: Bank of Korea, *National Income in Korea, 1975,* pp. 142–143.
Bank of Korea, *Final Estimate of Gross National Product for 1976* (August 1977).
Kim and Roemer, p. 47.

Notes: [a]Includes statistical discrepancy, which increases consumption by 0.9% in 1960–1962 and reduces it by 2.4% in 1973–1975. No discrepancy was measured in 1953–1955.
[b]Totals may not add, due to averaging, rounding, and the exclusion of statistical discrepancy.
[c]Imports of goods and non-factor services less exports of goods, non-factor services, and net factor income.
[d]Gross investment less foreign saving.

domestic savings can be demonstrated by comparing the marginal rates of savings in the two periods. The marginal rate of savings, which was equivalent to the average rate of savings during the period from 1953–1955 to 1960–1962, jumped to 37 percent or much higher than the average rate during the latter period.

The preceding statistics on the balance of payments and investment financing in Korea are based on 1970 constant-price data. Thus, to some extent they fail to reflect the significant changes which took place in relative prices during the period, particularly at the time of the world resource crisis. Nevertheless, the figures do indicate what would have happened if there had been neither a resource crisis nor a change in relative prices. In actuality, the world resource crisis (1973–1974) worsened Korea's terms of trade, since the prices of imports rose much faster than those of exports. Consequently, Korea's balance of payments at current prices ran a large deficit, particularly during 1974–1975 when the shortfall exceeded 10 percent of GNP. Even in 1976, when the economy had largely recovered from the oil crisis, the balance-of-payments deficit was still about 3 percent of GNP.

The domestic savings rate measured at current prices is also lower than that based on 1970 constant prices. Nevertheless, even in terms of current price data, the growth of domestic savings since the early 1960s has been rapid. As shown in Table 16, the gross domestic savings to GNP ratio at current prices declined from about 7 percent in 1953–1955 to 3 percent in 1960–1962 but thereafter increased continuously to 16 percent in 1967–1969 and further to 19 percent in 1974–1976. If changes in grain inventories are excluded,[8] the domestic savings rate remained almost constant at about 4 percent until the early 1960s but grew rapidly thereafter.

In regard to the sectoral patterns of savings, business firms not only made the largest contribution to domestic savings but also steadily increased their savings ratio to GNP. The government sector actually dissaved until the early 1960s, but subsequently it rapidly increased its savings rate to about 5–6 percent of GNP.

TABLE 16 Trends in Domestic Savings Rates, 1953–1976
(in percent of GNP, based on current price data)

	1953–1955	1960–1962	1967–1969	1974–1976
Gross domestic savings rate	6.9	3.0	15.7	18.7
Gross domestic savings rate, net of change in grain inventories	4.1	3.6	15.7	15.9
Government	–2.5	–1.7	5.5	5.0
Business firms	5.0	6.7	7.9	10.1
Households[a]	1.7	–1.4	2.4	0.7

Source: BOK, *National Income in Korea, 1975,* pp. 150–151, 180–181, 186–187; and *Final Estimate of Gross National Product for 1976*, (August 1977).

Note: [a]All changes in grain inventories are subtracted from household saving.

This change is reflected in the steady rise in the national taxes as a percentage of GNP and in the growth of the fiscal surplus of the general government sector during the period. The national tax burden, including local government taxes, rose from only 6 percent of GNP in 1953–1955 to 10 percent in the early 1960s and further to 17 percent during 1974–1976. As a result, current revenues surpassed current expenditures beginning in the mid-1960s. Similarly, household savings (excluding changes in grain inventories), which were negative in the early 1960s, became positive and increased steadily after the interest rate reform of 1965. Due to the slow growth of real disposable income and the high rate of inflation following the recent world oil crisis, however, the propensity of the household sector to save has again declined significantly. Nevertheless, the expansion of domestic savings allowed the share of foreign savings in investment financing at current prices to be brought down from 75 percent in 1960–1962 to about 30 percent in 1974–1976. If the unusual years of the oil crisis (1974–1975) are excluded, the relative decline of foreign savings is more dramatic: from 75 percent in the early 1960s to 10 percent by 1976. This decline in the importance of foreign savings was also accompanied by a switch in the sources of foreign borrowing. From the mid-1950s, to the early 1960s foreign grant aid, especially U.S. assistance, financed the bulk of imports. The other sources of foreign capital, such as private transfers and short-term and long-term capital inflows, were relatively unimportant during this period. However, by 1974–1976, foreign grant aid had become negligible, and other forms of external financing, such as long-term loans, met the entire requirement for foreign savings.

THE GROWTH OF EMPLOYMENT

A labor force survey has been conducted regularly by the Korean government since 1953. However, due to a change in 1962 of survey methods and the statistical definition of the labor force and employment, the survey results for earlier years are not comparable with those for later years. Consequently, the discussion will be limited to labor force data from the period 1963–1976. Nevertheless, it should be mentioned that the survey results from 1957–1962 show a 4 percent growth in total employment per year. Furthermore, the data indicate that the structure of employment did not change appreciably during this period, since the average annual growth rate of non-agricultural employment, including employment in manufacturing, was similar to that of agricultural employment. [9]

The improved labor force and employment statistics for later years indicate that in 1963 a little over 60 percent of the total labor force was still engaged in agriculture and fishing (see Table 17). Employment in the farm sector accounted for 63 percent of the total employment in the country but included a fairly large amount of disguised unemployment or underemployment. Unemployment in the cities was also high—about 16 percent of the urban labor force was without work in 1963. These problems were further complicated by the rapid growth of the labor force. Although the annual rate of population increase gradually declined after 1963, the working-age population expanded

TABLE 17 Growth of Farm and Non-Farm Labor Force
and Employment, 1963–1976
(millions of persons, except as otherwise noted)

	1963	1976	*Average annual growth rate (%)*
Total population	26.99	35.86	2.2
Population, 14 years old & over	15.09	22.55	3.1
Labor force—total	8.34	13.06	3.5
Farm	5.09	5.91	1.2
Non-farm	3.25	7.15	6.3
Labor force participation rate (%)	55.30	57.90	0.4
Employment—total	7.66	12.56	3.9
Farm	4.94	5.86	1.3
Non-farm	2.72	6.70	7.2
Unemployment rate (%)	8.20	3.90	–
Farm	2.90	1.00	–
Non-farm	16.40	6.30	–

Source: EPB, *Annual Report on the Economically Active Population, 1976*; and *Monthly Statistics of Korea*, July 1977.

quickly as the large number of children born in the immediate post-Korean War period reached maturity. While the total population grew at an average annual rate of 2.2 percent during 1963–1976, the annual rate of increase of the population over 14 years of age was 3.1 percent. The labor force expanded at an even more rapid rate, reflecting the gradual increase in percentage of the female population holding jobs.

The growth of manufacturing in the early 1960s provided employment opportunities not only for the existing pool of unemployed but also for the increasing numbers newly joining the labor force. Employment in the non-farm sector expanded at an average annual rate of 7 percent during 1963–1976, while farm employment rose by a little over 1 percent per year. Total employment grew 3.9 percent per year. Conversely, the unemployment rate in the urban sector declined sharply from 16.4 percent to 6.3 percent between 1963 and 1976, while the national unemployment rate fell from 8.2 percent to around 4 percent.

The structure of employment also underwent a dramatic transition. For instance, the portion of the labor force employed in agriculture shrank from 63 percent in 1963 to 45 percent in 1976, while the percentage employed in manufacturing almost tripled to 21 percent (see Table 18). During the same period, total labor productivity measured in terms of average value added per worker increased nearly 6 percent annually. Labor productivity gains by individual sector did not vary greatly, ranging from 3.5 percent a year in agriculture, forestry, and fishing to 6.5 percent in manufacturing. Thus after 1963, the manufacturing sector was able to maintain its share of investment, expand its share of the labor force, and substantially increase labor productivity in achieving a rapid growth of output.

INFLATION AND RELATIVE PRICE CHANGES

Throughout the entire post-Korean War period, Korea has experienced rates of inflation that would be considered high by all but Latin American standards: 16 percent per year on the basis of the implicit GNP deflator, or 14 percent using both the wholesale price index and the Seoul consumer price index (see Table 19). When the post-war period is divided into the sub-periods, as in the preceding analysis of real variables, there is little difference between the average annual rates of inflation in each period. If the period is broken down into smaller sub-periods, however, significant fluctuations in the annual rate of inflation appear. For instance, the average annual rate of increase in the GNP deflator fell from 36 percent during the immediate post-Korean War period 1953–1957 to about 4 percent in 1957–1960. The rate of inflation rose again to 22 percent during the early 1960s but declined to 12.5 percent during the nine years of rapid growth from 1964 to 1973. The impact of the world resource crisis, however, returned the rate of domestic inflation

TABLE 18 Employment and Labor Productivity by Sector, 1963–1976

	Employment (1,000 persons)			Value Added per Worker (1,000 wŏn, 1970 prices)[b]		
	1963[a]	1976[a]	Growth (% p.a.)	1963	1976	Growth (% p.a.)
Agriculture, forestry & fishing	4,837 (63.1)	5,601 (44.6)	1.1	110	173	3.5
Mining	57 (0.7)	65 (0.5)	1.0	349	677	5.2
Manufacturing	610 (8.0)	2,678 (21.3)	12.1	217	494	6.5
Construction	193 (2.6)	529 (4.2)	8.1	196	437	4.6
Social overhead & services	1,965 (25.6)	3,683 (29.3)	5.0	256	444	4.3
TOTAL	7,662 (100.0)	12,556 (100.0)	3.9	160	335	5.8

Source: EPB, *Annual Report of the Economically Active Population, 1976.*
BOK, *Economic Statistics Yearbook, 1977.*

Notes: [a]Figures in parentheses indicate percentages.
[b]Value added from BOK, *Economic Statistics Yearbook, 1977,* pp. 266–267, divided by the number of employed.

TABLE 19 Inflation Rates
(percent per year)

Period		GNP Deflator	Wholesale Price Index	Seoul Consumer Price Index
From	To			
1953–1955	1974–1976	16.7	14.9	14.4
1953–1955	1960–1962	16.8	15.6	14.8
1960–1962	1974–1976	16.7	14.5	14.2
1953	1957	36.0	37.4	36.6
1957	1960	3.8	2.0	3.1
1960	1964	22.2	19.1	15.8
1964	1973	12.5	8.7	10.8
1973	1976	22.2	26.3	21.7

Source: BOK, Economic Statistics Yearbook, various years.

to the 22 percent level of the early 1960s in 1974–1976. The wholesale price index and the Seoul consumer index recorded a similar pattern of fluctuation over the period.

Using annual data, Kwang Suk Kim[10] has made an econometric investigation of the sources of inflation in Korea for the period 1955–1972. According to the study, the major reasons for inflation during the period were: 1) the fact that money supply expansion exceeded the demand for real money (which is determined by the real growth rate of total available resources); 2) an increase in the rate of turnover of demand deposits (which were used as a proxy for a price acceleration variable); and 3) an increase in grain prices. The study also found that changes in both the official exchange rate and real wages were statistically insignificant in explaining inflation during the period. However, the study concluded that the high rate of price increase after 1972 resulted largely from the world oil crisis and the ensuing worldwide inflation.

The post-war history of Korean inflation has witnessed significant changes in relative prices which have, in turn, influenced income distribution, savings, investment, exports, and employment creation. Real wages in manufacturing remained stable until the mid-1960s and thereafter rose rapidly to double by the mid-1970s. Similarly, the farmers' terms of trade fluctuated with the trends in grain prices but, beginning in the late 1960s, improved continuously. This improvement in farm income was, nevertheless, somewhat lower than the rise in real urban wages.

Real interest rates on bank deposits and loans were negative in 1963–1964, years of high inflation. However, due to the interest rate reforms of 1965 and relative price stability during the next seven years, real interest rates rose to between 10 and 15 percent. Subsequently, lower bank rates and rising inflation again reduced real interest rates and brought them into negative territory by 1974. The index of investment costs, which measures the combined effect of changes in real interest rates and the relative prices of capital goods, also peaked in the mid-1960s and then fell steadily. Consequently, the ratio of wage costs to capital costs, which remained roughly constant until 1968, moved sharply upward as wages rose and investors' costs fell. By the mid-1970s, the wage-rental ratio stood at almost four times its 1968 value, an indication of how rapidly the incentive to substitute capital for labor was growing. Even if the 6 percent annual labor productivity increase which was mentioned earlier was applied to the period from 1969 to 1975, and no productivity increases were assumed from capital (which contradicts the observed facts), the adjusted wage-rental ratio would have more than doubled.

The purchasing-power-parity effective exchange rates for both exports and imports, which take into account the official exchange rate, duties, subsidies, and other price and non-price incentives and disincentives, have remained fairly constant since the early 1960s. Thus, successive devaluations, tariff and subsidy adjustments, and domestic price rises have combined to maintain a fairly constant level of incentives to export or import-substitute. Producers have responded, apparently, not to the increasing profitability of exports, but to a trade regime that seems to promise the stability of unit profits.

Although the purchasing-power-parity effective exchange rates remained constant during more than a decade of rapid growth, Korea's net barter terms of trade—the export-unit-value index divided by the import-unit-value index—rose steadily until 1972. Thereafter, they deteriorated sharply as a result of the world resource crisis. In 1976, however, there was again an upturn in the terms of trade, which resulted from the decline in the rates of increase of the international prices of crude oil and other raw materials.

SOURCES OF GROWTH:
FACTORS OF PRODUCTION

Past attempts to measure the respective contribution to output growth of individual factors of production have a short but intense history, as indicated by M. Ishaq Nadiri's survey.[11] These attempts are generally based on the concept that a production function can be specified for an entire economy or for a specific sector, just as for a single industrial plant. Unfortunately, there are major theoretical and statistical problems in choosing a specific production function for an entire economy. Nevertheless, much can be learned from applying a generalized production function, roughly estimating its parameters, and thus trying to account for the sources of growth.

A generalized production function simply indicates that the output of an economy or a sector is a function of the capital and labor used and time—a proxy for technological change. After some mathematical manipulation, the growth-accounting equation can be derived as:

$$g(Q) = \alpha g(L) + \beta g(K) + T,$$

where $g(X)$ is the annual growth rate of any variable, X; Q is the value added; L is the labor employed in producing Q; and K is the capital stock; α and β are, under competitive equilibrium conditions, the value-added shares of labor and capital, respectively; and T is the residual growth not explained by the growth of labor and capital inputs.[12] With constant returns to scale assured, the income shares will sum to unity. Any number of explicit factors of production can be added to the above equation. This general formulation, however, assumes that the economy is competitive and in equilibrium.

This kind of growth accounting requires data from at least two points in time on the capital stock, employment, and value added. Table 20 presents the average annual growth rates for various aggregates of output, capital, and labor for 1963–1973

TABLE 20 Average Annual Growth Rates of Output and
Factor Inputs for 1963–1973
(based on 1970 constant prices)

	Whole Economy	*Non-Agriculture*	*Mining & Manufacturing*
Output			
a) GDP at factor cost	9.9	13.0	18.4
b) GDP net of ownership of dwellings	10.1	13.4	–
Capital			
a) All (including land)	6.9	–	–
b) Reproducible	8.3	8.0	11.0
c) Reproducible, except dwellings	11.5	11.6	–
d) Utilized capital	n.a.	n.a.	19.8
Labor			
a) Employees	3.8	7.6	10.6
b) Hours worked	4.6	7.7	10.7
c) Human capital per worker[a]	2.2	2.2	2.2

Source: Kim and Roemer, p. 86.

Note: [a]Indicates the average annual growth rate of human capital per worker for 1960–1971 as estimated by Chang Young Jeong, "Rates of Return on Investment in Education: The Case of Korea" (Seoul, 1974).

which are used as the basis for growth accounting. Output and labor-force growth have already been discussed in the preceding sections. The capital stock for the whole economy, including privately owned land, grew at an average annual rate of 6.9 percent during 1963–1973, and the reproducible capital stock at 8.3 percent a year, or, if dwellings are excluded, at 11.5 percent. The growth rates of capital in mining and manufacturing grew almost as rapidly, if land and dwellings are excluded. However, if the most conservative estimate of increased utilization from Young Chin Kim and Jene K. Kwon cited earlier is accepted, capital services in mining and manufacturing grew by almost 20 percent a year, or slightly faster than output.

The sources-of-growth estimates based on these data are summarized in Table 21, together with the factor shares used to approximate output elasticities in the sources-of-growth equation. For the economy as a whole, as well as for the non-agricultural sector, the minimum contribution of capital to growth is 27 percent. However, if land and dwellings are excluded, increases of capital contributed 37 percent of the growth of the whole economy and 32 percent of the growth of the non-agricultural sector. The growth of the labor force accounted for about one-fourth of the total growth in the economy, but for 33 percent in the non-agricultural sector. The maxima, which include the 2.2 percent growth of human capital per worker, range from 44 to 47 percent. The unexplained residual is about 50 percent for the entire economy, but could be as low as 19 percent of total growth if land and dwellings are excluded from the capital stock and the educational quality of the labor force is included. For the non-agricultural sector, the residual ranges from 21 to 40 percent.[13]

The results for mining and manufacturing are quite different, because of the higher factor growth rates and the substantially greater weight given to capital. At least 45 percent of the annual growth of value added in this sector can be explained by increases in the reproducible capital stock. When rising capacity utilization is also taken into account, however, this share becomes 81 percent. Since the labor share of factor inputs in manufacturing is only one-quarter of the total, the growth of the manufacturing labor force, although rapid, was responsible for only about 15 to 18 percent of output growth. In the absence of any allowance for utilization or education, the residual is 40 percent. But if both utilization and education are included, the residual almost disappears, and all growth appears to be accounted for by changes in factor supplies and the accompanying improvements in quality.

So far, only labor, capital and, in a rough way, land have been

TABLE 21 Estimated Sources of Growth by Factor, 1963–1973
(%)

Output measure		Share of Growth Attributable to			Capital & Labor Shares Applied
		Capital	Labor	Residual	
GDP at factor cost	(a)	27	23	50	39 : 61
	(b)	37	44	19	32 : 68
Non-agricultural GDP	(a)	27	33	40	44 : 56
	(b)	32	47	21	37 : 63
Mining and manufacturing	(a)	45	15	40	75 : 25
	(b)	81	18	1	75 : 25

Source: Kim and Roemer, p. 90.

Notes: (a) Estimates for GDP are based on the growth rates of the entire capital stock (including land and dwellings) and employment, and on those of the entire reproducible capital stock and employment for both non-agricultural GDP and value added in mining and manufacturing.

(b) Estimates are based on the growth rates of all capital and the reproducible capital stock (excluding land and dwellings), the growth rates of hours worked and human capital per worker in the cases of GDP and non-agricultural GDP. For mining and manufacturing, the growth rates of utilized capital, hours worked, and human capital per worker were used.

considered factors of production. The development literature centering around "two-gap" models is based on the assumption that imports are essential to certain developing economies and therefore constitute another factor of production. Korea, with its heavy trade dependence and poor raw material base, would qualify as a country that depends on imports as a factor of production. In order to incorporate imports in the sources-of-growth analysis, it is necessary to convert measures of output from GDP to total available resources. These can be defined as GDP plus imports of goods and other non-factor services. Total available resources grew by 11.7 percent a year from 1963 to 1973, while imports of goods and non-factor services grew almost 20 percent annually.

When the average import share (18 percent for 1963–1973) and the adjusted capital and labor shares were used as estimates of output elasticities with respect to imports, capital, and labor supplies, the three factors were discovered to be equally responsible for economy-wide output growth in all calculations. If land and dwellings are excluded from the capital stock, and education is included in the labor supply, the relative contribution of the factors would be 26 percent for capital, 32 percent for labor, 31 percent for imports, and 11 percent for the residuals. This estimate, however, involves some double-counting, since imports also include capital goods which are already counted in the capital stock estimates. If an adjustment is made for this double-counting by eliminating imports of machinery and transport equipment both from imports and total available resources, the relative factor contributions to the 11 percent growth rate of adjusted, total available resources were: 29 percent for capital, 36 percent for labor, 22 percent for imports, and 13 percent for the residuals.[14]

COMPARISONS WITH OTHER COUNTRIES

Korea has achieved a real average GNP growth rate of 7.5 percent a year in the period since 1953 and 9.6 percent since 1960. This rapid growth record has been matched by only a few countries over a similar length of time. The World Bank, which gives Korea's per capita GNP growth rate as 7.3 percent from 1960 to 1974, reports that annual growth rates were higher than 6.5 percent only for Libya, Japan, Saudi Arabia, Singapore, Greece, Hong Kong, Iran, and Taiwan.[15] Thus, among Third World non-petroleum-exporting countries, only Singapore, Hong Kong, and Taiwan have growth records roughly matching those of Korea.

In what manner have Korea's patterns of accumulation (savings and investment) and allocation (primary and industry shares of output, exports, imports, and so on) during the period of rapid growth been distinct from those of a "normally" developing economy with a similar population and level of income? This question may be answered partially by comparing Korea's development patterns with the "normal" patterns predicted by Chenery and Syrquin.[16] Chenery and Syrquin analyzed cross-section and time-series data for 101 countries between 1950 to 1970. They attempted to explain patterns of accumulation (savings, investment, government revenue), allocation (private and government consumption, primary sector and industrial shares of production), and trade (imports and primary and manufactured exports) by regressing the shares of each of these variables on several explanatory variables. The explanatory variables consisted of GDP per capita, population, the share of foreign capital inflows in GDP, a dummy variable for different time periods and, in some regressions, the GDP shares of primary, manufactured, and services exports.

In Table 22, Korean development patterns are compared with two different standards from Chenery-Syrquin: 1) a sample of all large countries, defined as those with populations of over 15 million in 1960 (when Korea had 25 million); and 2) a sample

TABLE 22 Korean Development, 1953–1974, Compared with Chenery-Syrquin Regression Means[a]

	1953–1955 Average			1960–1962 Average			1972–1974 Average		
		Predicted by			Predicted by			Predicted by	
	Korea Actual	Large Country Pattern[b]	Exogenous Trade Variables[c]	Korea Actual	Large Country Pattern[b]	Exogenous Trade Variables[c]	Korea Actual	Large Country Pattern[b]	Exogenous Trade Variables[c]
Korea Parameters									
Population (millions)	21.3			25.7			33.2		
GDP (factor cost) per capita (1964 US $)	74.3			80.4			175.4		
Net resource inflow[d] (share GDP)	.100			.084			.036		
Comparisons (Share of GDP)									
Saving	.020	.043	.041	.023	.073	.062	.228	.165	.207
Investment	.113	.142	.127	.096	.156	.130	.258	.200	.211
Private consumption	.810	.728	.836	.836	.793	.805	.672	.716	.683
Government consumption	.170	.136	.130	.141	.119	.127	.100	.119	.111
Government revenue	.138	.108	.128	.144	.111	.130	.180	.151	.185
Primary production	.513	.522	.418	.467	.510	.405	.273	.354	.266
Industry production[e]	.078	.155	.172	.121	.155	.180	.305	.235	.294
Exports	.015	.072	—	.031	.083	—	.260	.107	—
Primary exports	.007	.054	—	.009	.056	—	.037	.053	—
Manufactured exports	.000	.017	—	.002	.017	—	.206	.025	—
Imports	.110	.177	—	.104	.172	—	.292	.147	—

Source: Kim and Roemer, p. 129.

Notes: [a]Chenery and Syrquin, *Patterns of Development, 1950–1970.*

[b]Chenery-Syrquin, Tables 55 (p. 200) and 59 (p. 204); using $T_1 = 1$ for 1953–1955, $T_3 = 1$ for 1960–1962, and $T_4 = 1$, an approximation, for 1972–1974.

[c]Chenery-Syrquin, Table 514 (p. 210), using regressions containing F (net resource inflow); in these regressions, exports of primary products, manufactures, and services are each treated as exogenous variables.

[d]Defined as imports of goods and non-factor services *less* exports of goods and non-factor services.

[e]Includes manufacturing and construction.

of all countries in which the GDP shares of primary, manufactured, and services exports were added to the explanatory
variables. Korea's GNP per capita was then converted into 1964
dollars, using the 1964 exchange rate in order to be consistent
with the original study.

According to these comparisons, Korea performed poorly in
terms of development indicators for a country with its characteristics during the 1953–1962 period, but improved its position
sufficiently to exceed the expected norms by the early 1970s.
Korea's performance in saving, investing, industrializing, and
exporting differs significantly from the cross-country averages in
both periods. On the basis of this evidence, changes in government policies and other factors appear to have been successful,
not only in stimulating fast growth, but also in achieving levels
of investment, savings, industrial output, and exports well above
the average for a country of Korea's income level.

It is also interesting to compare the patterns of Korean growth
since the Korean War with those of its two near neighbors,
Japan and Taiwan, with whom Korea shares a common cultural
heritage. In structural terms, Korea can be compared to Japan
before its build-up for World War II. Korean income per capita
was lower in the mid-1970s than Japan's income was in the late
1930s, but both its growth rate and efficiency in using capital
were significantly higher. A higher agricultural share for Korea
in the mid-1970s would seem to indicate a structurally less
advanced economy, but Korea's industrial share of output is
similar to Japan's prior to the late 1930s. There is, of course,
nothing in the Korean industrial structure to match the wartime
output of Japan.

Although structural comparisons with post-war Japan are not
entirely valid, Korea's income per capita in the mid-1970s was
about the same as Japan's in the early 1950s and, if current
growth rates continue, would match Japan's early 1960s income
by the mid-1980s. However, Korea has both a much greater
export share of GDP and a lower savings rate than Japan had in
the early 1950s. Nevertheless, Korean growth has been substan-

tial, in part because it has imported a relatively larger amount of foreign capital, and in part because it has used its lower volume of savings more efficiently than Japan did.

Korean growth and structural change have closely paralleled Taiwan's. Korean income in 1972–1974 was equivalent to Taiwan's in 1964–1966 and, at similar income levels, the two countries have almost identical agricultural and industrial shares of GDP. Taiwan's dependence on trade, however, was somewhat greater than Korea's, probably reflecting the smaller size of Taiwan's population. At similar income levels, Korea's savings rate is slightly lower than the rates of Taiwan, or Japan in 1950. The lower savings rate in Korea may be due to the fact that Korean development was accompanied by considerable price increases, while development in Japan and Taiwan was achieved without much inflation. To compensate for the lower rate of savings, Korea has relied relatively more on net foreign resource inflows than her two neighbors did.

CONCLUSION

The reconstruction of Korea's war-torn and aid-dependent economic base began in 1953. Despite massive inflows of foreign assistance, however, economic growth during the post-Korean War reconstruction period was disappointing. In the early 1960s, the pace of growth began to accelerate, a process which has continued to the present. This continuous progress since the early 1960s has substantially altered the structure of national product and employment and the patterns of national expenditure and trade.

The basic change from an inward-looking, import-substituting industrialization strategy to an outward-looking one which took place in the early 1960s is in large part responsible for the remarkable growth and structural change in later years. This viewpoint is supported by the phenomenal growth of commodity exports, which has averaged more than 35 percent a year in real terms since the early 1960s, thereby surpassing the real growth rate of GNP.

Today the important question is whether this export-oriented growth will continue in the future. Assuming that the economy is managed competently in the next decade, will world markets continue to demand the manufactured exports on which further growth and development are universally assumed to depend? Korea is no longer a minor supplier of export commodities but is a major factor in world markets capable of arousing protectionist sentiment in the United States and in other industrialized countries. In addition, the cost of imported energy with which to fuel the continued growth of manufacturing has risen precipitously, while energy conservation programs in the industrial world threaten to slow down the growth of the export markets which are most critical to Korean expansion.

Fortunately, none of these fears materialized during the recent oil crisis and ensuing world recession. Rather, Korea was able to maintain its historic growth rate of 9 percent throughout 1974 and 1975, and actually increased this rate to 16 percent in 1976. Although the oil crisis initially enlarged the balance-of-payments' deficit, it also opened up new opportunities to Korea. Foreign-exchange earnings from construction contracts in the Middle East grew rapidly after 1976. Thus, Korea enjoyed a surplus in its transactions with the Middle Eastern countries in 1977, as well as overall balance in its foreign accounts for the first time in modern history. Furthermore, the rate of inflation fell to around 10 percent in 1976–1977, consistent with Korea's experience during the 1960s and another indication that the structural changes traced in this study were bearing fruit.

Nevertheless, inflation has always been the weak point of Korea's development policy, and numerous attempts to stabilize the price level have failed. This is due mainly to the government's preference for growth rather than stability and to its failure adequately to manage domestic demand. In view of the government's growth policy and the present goals of fiscal and monetary management, it is doubtful whether this trend can be turned around in the near future.

FIVE

Industrialization and Foreign Trade

Korea's economic development since the end of the Korean War can be characterized as a process of industrialization. Economic growth has been led by the rapid development of the non-agricultural sectors, particularly the manufacturing industries. Consequently, substantial changes have taken place in the structure of national production. The relative share of the manufacturing sector in gross domestic product has risen, while that of the primary sector has declined. There has also been a substantial shift in the composition of industrial output towards more sophisticated manufactured products.

Foreign trade has played the leading role in the process of industrialization in Korea, both because of the country's lack of important natural resources and the relatively small size of the domestic market.

THE EVOLUTION OF INCENTIVE POLICIES

The evolution of Korea's industrial incentive policies from the end of Korean War to 1977 is a story of continuous, although sometimes halting, movement towards an open economy. For convenience, however, the historical development of incentive policies in the post-war period is divided into three phases. The first phase lasts from the end of the Korean War to 1960 and is characterized by easy import substitution. The second phase encompasses the years 1961–1965 and marks the transition to an export-oriented policy. The third phase begins in 1966 and is the period in which the export-oriented industrialization strategy became institutionalized.

THE FIRST PHASE, 1953–1960

During the years from 1953 to 1960, the major objectives of economic policy were to reconstruct the infrastructure and industrial facilities that had been destroyed by the war and to stabilize prices. The high rate of domestic inflation brought about a situation in which the official foreign exchange rate, despite large periodic devaluations, consistently overvalued the wŏn. Although the government permitted this situation to continue, it also undertook various ad hoc measures to alleviate the excessive demand for imports and to offset disincentives to exporters. The result was the emergence of a complicated system of multiple exchange rates.

In order to restrict trade quantitatively, the import and export licensing system was administered on the basis of a semi-annual trade program that designated items eligible for import. In addition, basic tariff rates, first enacted in 1949 and later modified in 1957, were imposed on imports. These rates varied according to the type of commodity, ranging from zero to more than 100 percent.[1] The simple average of the differential tariffs was about 40 percent.

The government attempted to counteract the export disincentive effects of currency overvaluation. A foreign exchange deposit system was adopted so that export earnings might be used to purchase imports or be sold at the market exchange rate. Between 1951 and 1955, a preferential export system was also instituted which granted successful exporters of specified commodities import rights to popular items. In addition, direct subsidies were given to exporters of certain minerals in 1955. Finally, the export credit system, which had been established prior to 1953, was kept in operation, although it set up interest rates that were much lower than the rate on ordinary bank loans.

On balance, industrial policy during the 1950s remained inward-looking, although some measures were taken to counteract disincentives to export. Consequently, exports grew slowly and fluctuated according to the demand for and supply of a few primary commodities. On the other hand, high tariffs and a variety of quantitative trade restrictions encouraged substitution, particularly in the consumer-goods industries.

THE SECOND PHASE, 1961–1965

The first major step to alter the direction of policy took place when the Chang Myon Government attempted to unify the exchange rate and reduce the degree of wŏn overvaluation. In January and February 1961, the Chang Myon Government twice devalued the wŏn, actions which together changed the exchange rate from 65 wŏn to 130 wŏn per U.S. dollar. However, this initial attempt to unify the exchange rate was doomed to failure by the expansionary policy of the Park Military Government. In the early 1960s, the government discontinued its financial stabilization program and adopted a fairly expansionary policy. Although this policy helped to activate the sluggish economy, it sharply accelerated the rate of domestic inflation and made even the devalued nominal exchange rate quite unrealistic by the end of 1962. In order to mitigate again the effects of currency overvaluation, the government introduced in 1963 a full-scale export-import link system under which the volume of non-aid imports was limited to the amount of export earnings. Quantitative controls over imports were also substantially tightened in that year. The result was a return to the multiple exchange rate system, since the market premium rates on export dollars rose rapidly from about 25 percent of the official exchange rate in early 1963 to 50 percent by April 1964.

A more significant step in the transition to an export-oriented policy was the exchange rate reform of 1964–1965. In May 1964, the government devalued the official exchange rate from 130 wŏn to 256 wŏn per dollar. This 1964 devaluation, although proportionately large, actually only restored the real exchange rate to the 1961 level. Because the government coupled this reform with fiscal and monetary restraint, however, it succeeded in unifying the exchange rate and, beginning in March 1965, the wŏn was allowed to float. Unlike the 1961 situation, the government made serious efforts to increase tax collections through administrative improvement and tax rate reform in 1965. Furthermore, in September 1965, the interest rates on both bank savings deposits and loans were raised sharply.

Quantitative controls over imports were gradually eased as the trade balance improved after the exchange rate reform of 1964. However, the basic tariff rates, as revised in 1957, continued to be imposed on imports, with only minor adjustments. In addition to these regular tariffs, special tariffs were established to absorb the differential between landed cost and domestic price for a wide range of import items. The special tariffs were first adopted in 1961, but they were substantially raised after the 1964 devaluation. Thus, despite the fact that quantitative controls were significantly liberalized, the average legal tariff on imports increased.

Export incentives were continuously expanded during the period 1961–1965, an indication of the government's commitment to growth through export-oriented industrialization. Before the 1964 reform, when the official exchange rate was considered unfavorable to export promotion, the government even granted direct subsidies to certain commodity exports. The adoption of an export-import link system in 1963 further increased the returns to exporters by giving them the right to use the full amount of their export earnings for imports or sales at the market exchange rate. However, these two export promotion measures were abolished after the 1964 exchange rate reform. Subsequently, the export-import system was reintroduced on a very limited scale to promote exports of certain selected new commodities.

Among the other export incentives provided during this period were included: 1) tariff exemptions on imports of raw materials for export production (since 1959); 2) domestic indirect tax exemptions on both intermediate imports used for export production and export sales (since 1961); 3) direct tax reductions on income earned from exports and other foreign exchange earning activities (since 1961); 4) a preferential export credit (since 1950); 5) a system linking import business to export performance (since 1957); 6) wastage allowance subsidies (since 1965); 7) tariff and tax exemptions for domestic suppliers of intermediate goods used in export production (since 1961).[2] Of these incentives, #1, #2, and #7 merely served to offset the disincentive effects on exports that the trade regime would otherwise have created. In other words, these measures merely enabled Korean producers to purchase intermediate goods for export production at world-market prices.

In addition to these measures, a government export-targeting system was established in 1962 to further strengthen the drive for export expansion. The Korean Trade Promotion Corporation (KOTRA) was also created in 1964 to support overseas market development. Thus by 1964–1965, the system of export incentives that was to be in effect during the following decade had been largely established.

Although government policy had clearly shifted toward exporting, import substitution was not neglected and, in fact, was pushed on a selective basis. On the other hand, because U.S. aid continued to decline both absolutely and relatively, the government started to solicit foreign loans and direct foreign investment.

THE THIRD PHASE, 1966–1977

It is difficult to demarcate the specific years in which Korea's transition to export-oriented policy was actually completed. As already mentioned, the system of export incentives that remains in effect today was generally established by 1965. In fact, there has not been a significant increase in the level of effective subsidy since 1965, although some modifications have been made in the system to reflect changing economic conditions. Consequently, the export-oriented policy that had been adopted in prior years continued to be maintained.

In contrast to earlier years, between 1965 and 1973 the government was able to maintain relative price stability. Nevertheless, inflation in Korea rose more rapidly than in the industrialized countries throughout 1965–1977. Although a unitary, floating exchange rate system had been nominally adopted by the government, and there had been some initial floating in 1965, the exchange rate continued to be adjusted through government intervention. Thus in order to maintain the purchasing-power-parity (ppp)-adjusted, real exchange rate constant, the government abruptly devalued the currency several times during the period from 1966 to 1977.[3] When the exchange rate became overvalued between these devaluations, the government further increased indirect export subsidies and tightened import controls to counteract the currency overvaluation.

As rapid increases in both exports and foreign-capital inflows substantially improved Korea's balance of payments during 1966–1967, the government began to increase the degree of import liberalization. In 1967 the previous positive-list approach to trade controls was abandoned in favor of a negative-list approach. Thereafter, however, further liberalization was sporadic and short-lived, a situation largely due to adverse trends in the balance of payments and the increasing debt-service burden. After the oil crisis, however, the balance-of-payments situation improved greatly. By 1977, the increase in foreign exchange reserves was making the management of domestic demand difficult, and the government shifted its attention to liberalizing imports.

The government also undertook three major reforms to lower tariff barriers generally. The first reform was made effective in early 1968. During the next several years, the special tariffs on scarce imports, which had been imposed in addition to regular tariffs since 1964, were completely abolished. Furthermore, the system of outright tariff exemptions for imports of intermediate goods used in export production was changed to a drawback system. Under this system, exporters were required to pay tariffs on imports but were refunded these payments when exports were actually shipped out. The final reform in 1977 reduced the degree of tariff escalation between raw materials and finished products.

Although the level of subsidies implicit in the system of incentives increased very little, several new export-incentive schemes were introduced during the period, and some existing programs abolished. For instance, accelerated depreciation was granted for the fixed assets of export industries effective from 1966. Beginning in 1967, discounts on railway freight and electricity rates of 20 to 30 percent were given to exporters for whom utility charges occupied a large share in total production or export costs. Between 1967 and 1971, exporters who developed new export markets were granted monopoly rights to export in those markets, while in the early 1970s some preference was given to exporters in the allocation of import-quota items. On the other hand, the system of direct tax reductions for income from foreign exchange earning activities was completely abolished in 1973. The many adjustments of export incentives did not basically change the system during this period. Within the established framework, the government was able flexibly to adjust the level of implicit subsidies by increasing or decreasing wastage allowances and preferential loans for exports.

Although emphasis had been placed on export-oriented

industrialization, import substitution in selected major industries was also promoted by means of tax concessions and the allocation of preferential credits. The import-substituting industries promoted included shipbuilding, iron and steel, machinery, and petrochemicals, although some of these, particularly shipbuilding, have recently become new export industries. Consequently, the machinery industry is now promoted not only for import substitution but also for export expansion. In addition to assisting these major industries, the government has provided both tax and credit incentives for coal mining and the livestock industry, while still controlling the prices of their products to consumers.

EFFECTIVE EXCHANGE RATES
FOR EXPORTS AND IMPORTS

The quantitative effects of many of the policy changes that took place during the post-war period are reflected in the purchasing-power-parity-adjusted, effective exchange rates for exports and imports. As shown in Table 23, the estimated nominal effective exchange rates for exports and imports were converted into PPP-adjusted, effective exchange rates by correcting for changes in domestic prices and in the prices of Korea's major trading partners. Due to the limited data for the years prior to 1958, the effective rates are estimated only for the period 1958–1976.

The effective exchange rate for exports includes exchange premiums resulting from multiple exchange rates (1958–1961 and 1963–1964), direct subsidy payments (1961–1964 only), direct tax reductions, and interest rate subsidies, all per dollar of exports. This export rate, however, excludes indirect tax and tariff exemptions per dollar of exports, because they do not constitute "genuine" export subsidies. These exemptions permit exporters to purchase their tradable inputs and sell their output at world-market prices, but do not increase their profit margins

132

TABLE 23 Nominal and Purchasing-Power-Parity (PPP)-Adjusted Effective Exchange Rates, 1958–1976
(wŏn per U.S. dollar)

	Nominal Exchange Rate			Wholesale Price Index (1965=100)		PPP-Adjusted Exchange Rate		
	Official Rate	Effective Rate[a]		Korea	Major Trade Partners[b]	Official Rate	Effective Rate	
		Exports	Imports				Exports	Imports
1958	50.0	115.2	64.4	39.9	96.8	121.4	279.6	156.6
1959	50.0	136.0	82.8	40.8	97.5	119.5	324.9	197.9
1960	62.5	147.6	100.2	45.2	98.0	135.6	320.1	217.4
1961	127.5	150.6	147.0	51.2	98.4	244.9	289.3	282.2
1962	130.0	141.7	146.4	56.0	97.7	226.7	247.1	255.5
1963	130.0	177.5	148.1	67.5	98.4	189.5	258.8	215.9
1964	214.3	263.7	247.0	90.9	98.6	232.5	286.1	268.0
1965	265.4	275.3	293.1	100.0	100.0	265.4	275.3	293.1
1966	271.3	283.8	296.4	108.8	102.8	256.4	268.2	280.4
1967	270.7	290.7	296.2	115.8	103.9	242.8	260.8	265.4
1968	276.6	294.8	302.5	125.2	105.5	233.2	248.5	255.0
1969	288.2	306.6	312.7	133.7	108.7	234.3	249.3	254.5
1970	310.7	331.5	336.4	145.9	112.7	239.9	255.9	260.0
1971	347.7	370.5	369.5	158.5	115.5	253.5	270.1	269.7
1972	391.8	404.3	415.2	180.7	126.8	275.0	283.1	290.2
1973	398.3	407.0	417.7	193.3	155.6	320.6	327.6	332.5
1974	407.0	415.6	425.5	274.7	188.4	279.2	285.1	288.1
1975	485.0	497.9	509.9	347.4	197.0	275.0	282.3	286.6
1976	485.0	493.7	516.6	389.2	207.2	258.2	262.8	272.5

Source: Larry E. Westphal and Kwang Suk Kim, "Industrial Policy and Development in Korea," World Bank Staff Working Paper No. 263, 1977, pp. 1, 13, 17, and Ministry of Finance.

Notes: [a]The effective exchange rate for exports includes exchange premiums resulting from multiple exchange rates, direct cash subsidies, direct tax reductions, and interest rate subsidies per dollar of exports, but it excludes indirect tax and tariff exemptions. The effective rate for imports includes actual tariffs and tariff equivalent barriers per dollar of imports.
[b]An average of the wholesale price indexes of the U.S. and Japan, weighted by Korea's annual trade volume with the respective countries.

on export sales.[4] On the other hand, the effective exchange rate for imports is the weighted average of the official exchange rate and the free market rates as applied to export earnings, and it includes actual tariff collections as well as other tariff-equivalent barriers per dollar of imports.

It should be noted that the estimated effective exchange rates are partially incomplete in the sense that they do not incorporate all subsidies or tariff-equivalent barriers. Because of the lack of consistency in the time-series data, the estimated rate for exports excludes subsidies implicit in excessive wastage allowances for export production, accelerated depreciation allowances, discounts on the price of overhead inputs, as well as the effects of the limited export-import link system in use after 1964. Westphal and Kim estimated that in 1968, the subsidy implicit in the wastage allowance alone was equivalent to 2.4 percent of total commodity exports, although subsidies resulting from other measures were much smaller in relative terms.

The effective rate for imports, furthermore, does not reflect the impact of quantitative restrictions on imports. Consequently, the rate does not really show changes in the degree of domestic protection over time. This is even truer after 1964 when the heavy quantitative restrictions on imports, which characterized the years 1958–1964, were significantly lessened.

Despite these limitations, the nominal and PPP-adjusted (real), effective exchange rates give some indication of the effects of changes in trade regimes over the period 1958–1976. An important point to note is that the real, effective exchange rate for exports was already high even before the exchange rate reform of 1964, and was not significantly increased by that reform. Nevertheless, the 1964 reform substantially reduced the gap between the official and the effective exchange rates, largely by replacing the market premium on foreign exchange with official devaluation of the currency. Although the real exchange rates for exports in the late 1950s and early 1960s were relatively high, export growth was quite modest compared with later periods. One possible explanation for this low export growth is the limited supply capacity of domestic industry during the 1950s. However, a more likely cause is the fact that export incentives during the period were quite unstable, the government depending largely upon ad hoc administrative measures to bring non-aid imports into line with foreign exchange earnings.

After the 1964 reform, export incentives became increasingly institutionalized as the official exchange rate was adjusted to a more realistic level and additional non-discriminatory export incentives were established for all exporters. In response, exports increased rapidly. Although the real effective exchange rate for exports fluctuated slightly during 1964–1976, the real level of export incentives seems to have remained roughly constant because of the flexible adjustment of wastage allowance subsidies which could not be incorporated into the estimates. On the other hand, the real, effective exchange rate for imports, which had been much lower than the rate for exports, rose to roughly equal the export rate by 1964 and generally moved parallel with it thereafter.

In summary, the industrial policy changes that took place in the first half of the 1960s did not clearly result in a significant increase in the measurable incentive to export. They did, however, gradually replace a complicated, largely ad hoc system of incentives based on multiple exchange rates (including those resulting from the export-import link system) and direct cash subsidies with a simplified and more stable system. Consequently, the reforms may be credited with having laid the foundations for continued rapid export growth by assuring stable profit margins for exporters.[5]

PATTERNS OF EXPORT EXPANSION

The evolution of industrial and trade policy is well reflected in the growth performance of Korean exports. Commodity exports in the 1950s were not only small in value but also fluctuated annually depending upon the supply and the demand for a small number of primary commodities. For instance, due to the high export demand for tungsten in 1953, Korea's commodity exports amounted to about $40 million, a level not regained until 1961. Rapid export expansion first began from a very small base in the early 1960s and has continued ever since, despite the expansion of that base. Between 1960 and 1965, the nominal value of commodity exports increased from $33 million to $175 million, or an average annual growth rate of 40 percent. During the following twelve years, exports grew by about 40 percent annually. Even discounting for the rise in world prices, the export volume increased by 38 percent and 34 percent annually during 1960–1965 and 1965–1977, respectively. Thus the nominal value of exports in 1977 reached $10 billion, equivalent to about one percent of the world's exports.

The rapid growth of exports was accompanied by a substantial change in the commodity composition of exports. As shown in Table 24, Korean exports in the 1950s and early 1960s were mostly primary products, such as tungsten, iron ore, raw silk, agar-agar, fish, and rice. Manufactured exports accounted for only a small fraction of total exports until the early 1960s. Since 1962, manufactured exports have increased much more rapidly than exports of primary products, comprising almost 90 percent of total exports in 1976. Major Korean exports in 1976 included such manufactured goods as clothing, electrical machinery, textile yarns and fabrics, footwear, plywood, transport equipment (mainly ships), and iron and steel sheets.

The expansion of manufactured exports necessitated a corresponding increase of imports for export production. The direct import content of exports, which had been negligible until 1963, increased rapidly to about 47 percent by 1968. Thereafter, the import content of exports remained stable, ranging roughly from 37 to 50 percent.[6] Consequently, the annual growth rate of net exports was not much different from the growth rate of gross exports during 1963–1976.

Accompanying the structural change in export commodities was a significant diversification of export markets. In 1965,

TABLE 24 Exports by Commodity Group and
         Major Commodities
         (percent of total exports)

SITC Group and Commodities	1954	1960	1965	1976
0. Food & Live Animals	12.1	29.6	16.1	6.6
Fish & fish preparations	2.9	8.3	10.2	4.1
Rice	0.0	11.5	1.9	0.0
Dried laver (seaweed)	0.0	3.9	1.9	0.0
1. Beverages & Tobacco	0.1	1.4	0.5	1.0
2. Crude Materials except Fuel	76.7	48.2	21.2	2.5
Raw silk	15.8	3.0	3.9	0.2
Iron ore & concentrates	39.5	7.5	3.9	0.0
Tungsten ore & concentrates		14.3	3.6	0.3
Ginseng	0.4	0.3	1.1	0.3
Agar-agar	5.7	2.8	1.3	0.1
3–5. Mineral Fuels; Animal & Vegetable Oils & Fats; and Chemicals	0.0	5.3	1.3	3.4
6. Manufactured Goods Classified Chiefly by Material	4.6	12.0	37.9	30.3
Plywood	0.0	0.1	10.3	4.4
Textile yarn	0.0	0.0	1.3	3.3
Textile fabrics	0.0	7.4	12.8	8.1
Sheets of iron & steel	0.0	0.0	5.8	2.1
7. Machinery & Transport Equipment	0.3	0.3	3.1	16.6
Electrical machinery	0.0	0.0	1.1	10.4
Transport equipment	0.0	0.0	0.6	4.4
8. Misc. Manufactures	0.2	0.3	19.7	39.2
Clothing	0.0	0.0	11.8	23.9
Footwear	0.0	0.0	2.4	5.2
Wigs & false beards	0.0	0.0	1.3	0.9
9. Unclassifiable	0.2	3.0	0.1	0.3
Total Exports	100.0	100.0	100.0	100.0
($ millions)	(24)	(33)	(175)	(7,715)

Source: BOK, *Economic Statistics Yearbook, 1964, 1968,* and *1977.*

about 60 percent of Korean exports went to two rich countries, the United States and Japan. By 1976, this percentage had declined slightly to 55 percent, as sales to Europe, the Middle East, and other areas outside Asia expanded. In particular, Korean exports to Middle Eastern countries, which had accounted for a mere 1 percent of total exports in 1970, sharply increased after the world oil crisis to reach 9 percent by 1976. Korean exports to Asian countries other than Japan declined substantially in relative terms between 1965 and 1976. The diversification of export markets can also be measured by the number of countries to which Korea exported. Until the early 1960s, Korea exported to only 19 countries versus 175 in 1976 (see Table 25).

The continuous expansion of exports through the diversification of commodities and markets could not have been possible without the drastic expansion of overseas marketing activities. The Korean Trade Promotion Corporation, which was established by the government in 1964 to conduct overseas marketing activities for Korean exports, has continuously expanded its overseas network. By 1977, KOTRA maintained branches in nearly 80 important business centers throughout the non-Communist world. In addition, the government encouraged private traders to establish overseas marketing branches by providing tax concessions and financing on favorable terms. As a result, of a total of about 3,000 registered trading firms, nearly 450 maintained more than one foreign branch in 1977, while the number of companies with at least 10 overseas branches reached 12.

It appears that the diversification of export commodities and markets was largely a consequence of the Korean effort to penetrate important foreign markets. In this regard the Korean contacts with American and Japanese firms developed in connection with imports of aid-financed commodities in the 1950s were helpful in initially starting marketing activities. Foreign direct and joint investments in Korea have always been relatively small compared with annual gross investment and annual gross

TABLE 25 Exports by Destination
(percent of total exports)

	1954	*1960*	*1965*	*1970*	*1976*
United States	56.3	11.1	35.2	47.3	32.3
Japan	32.9	61.5	25.1	28.1	23.4
Other Asia	9.6	11.3	23.3	8.8	8.6
Europe	1.1	13.1	12.2	9.1	17.5
Middle East	0.0	0.0	0.6	1.0	9.1
Rest of the world	0.1	3.0	3.6	5.7	9.1
Total	100.0	100.0	100.0	100.0	100.0
($ Millions)	(24)	(33)	(175)	(835)	(7,715)
Total number of countries to which Korea exported	5	19	24	126	175

Source: BOK, *Economic Statistics Yearbook*, various years.

inflows of foreign capital. Thus foreign investors have not been the major promoters of Korean export markets. Rather, resident branches of foreign trading companies, particularly the large Japanese "general trading companies" have played a large role in exploring export markets, since they have been able to take advantage of their own overseas contacts for trade activities.

In any case, the extensive expansion of exports has led to a significant acceleration of GNP growth since the early 1960s. Because exports increased more rapidly than GNP, the share of gross exports in GNP rose from about 2 percent in the early 1960s to 30 percent by the mid-1970s. If the import content of Korean exports is excluded and only net exports are regarded, the net exports to GNP ratio grew from about 5 percent to 15 percent between 1963 and 1976.[7]

THE GROWTH OF IMPORTS

During the period of post-Korean War reconstruction, the level of merchandise imports was largely determined by the availability of foreign assistance. Since Korea's foreign exchange earning capacity was extremely limited, about two-thirds of imports were financed by foreign assistance, mainly U.S. aid.[8] Consequently, total merchandise imports did not increase between 1953 and 1960 but fluctuated annually according to the volume of aid financing. In 1960, imports still amounted to only $343 million, or about the same nominal level as in 1953. Because the level of imports remained almost constant, the ratio of imports to GNP at 1970 constant prices gradually declined from 13 percent in 1953 to 9 percent in 1960, implying that significant progress was made in import substitution.[9]

During the following five years, the nominal value of imports increased at an annual average rate of 6 percent. This growth, which occurred in spite of a reduction in foreign assistance, was made possible by both higher export earnings and disbursements of new foreign loans. Whereas in 1960, U.S. assistance had financed about 68 percent of total imports, it accounted for only 30 percent of them in 1965. Conversely, the share of imports financed out of Korea's own foreign exchange earnings rose from 28 percent to more than 50 percent. Foreign loans, which first began to arrive in 1962, financed less than 10 percent of imports until the mid-1960s.

From 1965 to 1976, the rate of import growth substantially accelerated. The nominal value of imports increased at an average annual rate of 31 percent to reach $8.8 billion by 1976. Even if rising import prices are discounted, the import volume increased 23 percent annually. Thus the imports to GNP ratio rose from 15 percent to 35 percent during 1965–1976.[10] This significant development can be explained by several factors. First, the rapid expansion of exports during this period not only extended the availability of financial resources for imports but also necessitated a corresponding increase of imports for export production. Second, the share of imports financed by U.S. foreign assistance declined and disappeared altogether by 1972, while other sources of external finance, such as foreign loans, direct investment, and Properties and Claims funds from Japan, more than replaced declining U.S. assistance. Third, invisible exports increased more rapidly than invisible imports. Finally, the rapid export-oriented industrialization and growth created an ever increasing demand for imports, while import liberalization and an improved foreign exchange position made possible the expansion of imports.

Although commodity imports increased significantly from 1960 to 1976, they grew less rapidly than exports. As a result, the trade balance improved greatly during the period, despite the adverse impact of the international oil crisis in 1973 and the ensuing recession. Commodity exports, equivalent to a mere 11 percent of commodity imports in 1960, rose steadily to about 85 percent of commodity imports in 1973. During 1974–1975, however, the trade deficit again grew to nearly $2 billion a year, and the ratio of exports to imports declined to about 67 percent, due mainly to the sharp deterioration in Korea's net barter terms of trade caused by the world oil crisis. With the trend towards recovery in the economies of Western industrialized countries, export growth and a modest improvement in the terms of trade again raised the exports to imports ratio to over 90 percent by 1976.

Along with the rapid growth of imports, there was some change in the commodity composition of imports (see Table 26). Although the large number of unclassifiable items in the earlier years (1955–1960) makes it difficult to discern trends in the commodity composition of imports, imports of crude materials appear to have grown rapidly in relative terms. On the other hand, imports of manufactures (except chemicals and machinery) fell between 1955 and 1960, reflecting increased domestic production of these manufactures in the 1950s. The unusually low share of machinery and transport equipment in 1960 was probably due to sluggish investment activity in that

TABLE 26 Commodity Composition of Imports
(percent of total imports)

	1955	1960	1965	1976
Food and beverages (0 & 1)[a]	6.8	9.2	13.7	7.5
Crude materials (2 & 4)	9.4	20.7	24.6	18.5
Mineral fuels (3)	12.7	6.7	6.7	19.9
Chemicals (4)	17.5	22.2	22.3	9.9
Manufactures (6 & 8)	18.5	15.4	16.8	16.9
Machinery and transport equipment (7)	16.8	11.7	15.8	27.2
Unclassifiables (9)	18.3	14.1	0.1	0.1
TOTAL	100.0	100.0	100.0	100.0
($ million)	(341)	(344)	(463)	(8,774)

Source: BOK, *Economic Statistics Yearbook 1965, 1968,* and *1977.*

Note: [a]The figures in parentheses indicate SITC group numbers.

year. With the exception of this unusual phenomenon, there was no significant change in the structure of imports between 1960 and 1965. However, the relative shares of both foods and beverages and chemicals declined sharply during 1965–1976, while the share of fuels, mainly crude oil, rose from about 7 percent to 20 percent of total imports. Imports of machinery and transport equipment also increased significantly in relative terms during the period.

THE PATTERN OF INDUSTRIALIZATION

The rapid expansion of exports which began in the early 1960s significantly accelerated the growth of real GNP. Economic growth was led by the industrial sector, particularly by manufacturing. For instance, the growth rate of value added in manufacturing, which had averaged a little over 10 percent a year during 1953–1962, rose to 18 percent during 1962–1976, while the growth rate of GNP increased from about 4 percent to

10 percent during the two periods. As a result, the GNP share of manufacturing at current domestic prices rose from 14 percent in the early 1960s to 29 percent by the mid-1970s.

This structural change in industrial output is also revealed in a time series study of Korean input-output (IO) data deflated to 1968 constant world prices.[11] Deflating to constant world prices compensates for possible domestic price distortions arising from tariffs, domestic indirect taxes, and quantitative import restrictions, although it does not remove the effects of price distortions on real input-output flows. According to the constant world price IO data, manufacturing production rose from about 25 percent of total domestic production in 1955 to 56 percent in 1975. Manufactured exports, which had accounted for a little over 10 percent of total exports of goods and services in 1955, rose to 38 percent of exports in 1963 and nearly 80 percent by 1975. Conversely, the share of manufactured goods in total imports declined from 97 percent to 72 percent during the same period.

The extent to which industrialization is linked to exports is indicated by the rapid increase in manufactured exports as a percentage of total production. Manufactured exports constituted only 4 percent of total manufacturing production through 1963, but thereafter rose rapidly to reach 22 percent by 1975. In contrast, manufactured imports, which had accounted for nearly 40 percent of domestic demand (domestic production plus imports less exports) in 1955, declined to 20 percent in 1963 and then gradually recovered to about 22 percent by 1975. Overall, Korea's exports of goods and services were less than 4 percent of total national production through 1963, but rose to make up 16 percent of it by 1975. Finally, imports as a percentage of total domestic demand remained almost constant at 12–13 percent during 1955–1963, but thereafter gradually increased to about 17 percent by 1975.

The pattern of industrialization can also be discussed in terms of structural changes in production, trade, and domestic demand within the manufacturing sector. Table 27 shows that

TABLE 27 Structure of Manufacturing Production, Trade and Demand by Major Sector, 1955–1975 (based on 1968 constant world-price data)

	Processed Food	Textiles	Finished Consumer Goods	Intermediate Products	Mach. & Transp. Equip.	Manufacturing Total
1. Production (%)						
1955	37.7	18.3	20.0	19.2	4.8	100.0
1963	30.5	13.8	18.3	29.9	7.5	100.0
1970	25.6	10.0	21.2	35.2	8.0	100.0
1975	18.4	13.8	17.8	34.8	15.5	100.0
2. Exports (%)						
1955	38.4	29.4	14.4	13.8	4.0	100.0
1963	27.6	20.2	13.4	34.1	4.7	100.0
1970	8.1	12.6	45.8	25.7	7.8	100.0
1975	5.2	14.3	32.9	22.6	25.0	100.0
3. Export ratio (2/1, %)						
1955	1.3	2.1	0.9	0.9	1.1	1.3
1963	3.7	6.0	3.0	4.7	2.6	4.1
1970	4.4	17.6	30.3	10.2	13.8	14.0
1975	6.3	23.2	41.3	14.7	36.2	22.4

TABLE 27 (continued)

	Processed Food	Textiles	Finished Consumer Goods	Intermediate Products	Mach. & Transp. Equip.	Manufacturing Total
4. Imports (%)[a]						
1955	9.9	16.6	8.2	47.0	18.3	100.0
1963	6.5	6.8	2.0	52.7	32.0	100.0
1970	5.7	7.2	4.0	39.2	43.9	100.0
1975	4.3	5.1	6.6	36.8	47.2	100.0
5. Domestic demand (1-2+4,%)						
1955	26.9	17.6	15.5	30.0	10.0	100.0
1963	25.8	12.2	15.2	34.3	12.5	100.0
1970	23.4	9.1	14.2	37.3	15.9	100.0
1975	18.3	11.8	12.0	37.7	20.3	100.0
6. Import ratio (4/5,%)						
1955	14.3	36.5	20.5	60.6	70.8	38.7
1963	5.1	11.3	2.7	30.9	51.5	20.1
1970	5.4	17.7	6.2	23.3	61.1	22.2
1975	5.2	9.4	12.0	21.4	50.9	21.9

Source: Input-output data deflated into 1968 constant world prices. See Kwang Suk Kim, "Sources of Industrial Growth and Structural Change in Korea," KDI Working Paper 7703, 1977.

Note: [a]Excludes natural-resources-intensive, non-competitive imports.

the relative importance of "early industries" such as food processing and textiles in total manufacturing production, exports, imports, and demand consistently declined during the years 1955–1975, while that of intermediate products and machinery gained considerably. The share of finished consumer goods in total production remained almost unchanged between 1955 and 1975. The share of finished consumer goods in exports also remained roughly 13 percent until 1963, after which it grew to 33 percent by 1975. Since finished consumer goods as a percentage of domestic demand declined over the period 1955–1975, the industry was able to maintain its relative share of production only by exporting a greater proportion of its output. That is, exports of finished consumer goods, which had amounted to less than 3 percent of production until 1963, rose sharply to 41 percent of it by 1975, a higher figure than for any other manufacturing industry.

The production and export shares of the machinery industry also increased from 1955 to 1963, while machinery imports as a percentage of domestic demand declined substantially. Nevertheless in 1975, Korea still relied on imports to satisfy over 50 percent of the domestic demand for machinery and transport equipment, although about 36 percent of domestic production was exported. This indicates that Korea was able to export some relatively simple machinery, but still imported more sophisticated machinery. Another point to note is that the production share of intermediate products rose rapidly between 1955 and 1963 but did not increase much thereafter. This pattern of change is reflected in the ratio of intermediate product imports to domestic demand, a measure which provides some firsthand information regarding the relative contribution of export expansion and import substitution to industrial growth.

It is instructive to compare the Korean structure of manufacturing at current domestic prices with the results predicted by the Chenery and Taylor regressions[12] for a country with similar characteristics. The Chenery and Taylor regressions are based on cross-country data covering 50 countries for the period 1950 to 1963. The authors treat value added per capita for 12 manufacturing sectors as a logarithmic function of income per capita, population, and the respective shares of primary and manufactured exports in GNP.

The results of this comparison for three periods (1953–1955, 1960–1962 and 1972–1974) are shown in Table 28. It can be seen that Korean manufacturing as a whole followed a slightly different pattern than that noted in the previous comparison with Chenery-Syrquin norms (see Chapter 4). In 1953–1955, the Korean manufacturing industry's share of GNP was only slightly below the norm, by 1960–1962 it exceeded the norm, and by 1972–1974 Korean manufacturing was almost twice the GNP share predicted by the Chenery-Taylor regressions. Even when the manufacturing share of GDP at factor cost is used, the pattern does not change significantly, although Korean manufacturing does tend to look somewhat less developed, particularly in the 1953–1955 period.[13]

In 1953–1955, Korean manufacturing lagged substantially behind the predicted GNP shares in only two sectors—food and chemicals. In textiles, Korea was more developed than the typical country. Other sectors were about as developed as those in nations of similar size and income. By 1960–1962, Korea had drawn even with the Chenery-Taylor regression expectations in food and chemicals, and had substantially exceeded the norm in textiles and clothing, even before these industries became leading exporters. By 1972–1974, Korean output was well above the norm in several sectors: food, textiles, clothing, paper products, chemicals, non-metallic minerals, and metal products, The last three sectors demonstrate the degree of progress in the import substitution of key producer goods, convincing evidence that Korea has been able to break out of the import-substitution dead end typical of many developing countries and move towards a modern, integrated manufacturing structure producing both intermediate and capital goods.

TABLE 28 Korean Industrial Structure, 1953–1974, Compared with Chenery-Taylor Norms

Industry	Manufacturing Value Added–Percent of GNP[b]					
	1953–1955[a]		*1960–1962*[a]		*1972–1974*[a]	
	Chenery-Taylor	*Korea*[a]	*Chenery-Taylor*	*Korea*[a]	*Chenery-Taylor*	*Korea*[a]
1. Food, beverages & tobacco	4.2	3.1	4.0	4.2	3.7	6.5
2. Textiles	0.9	1.4	1.0	2.1	2.1	4.1
3. Leather products	0.2	0.1	0.2	0.1	0.2	0.5
4. Clothing & footwear	0.2	0.4	0.3	0.9	0.8	3.6
5. Wood products	0.4	0.4	0.4	0.4	0.8	0.7
6. Paper & paper products	0.1	–	0.1	0.2	0.3	0.6
7. Printing & publishing	0.2	0.3	0.2	0.5	0.6	0.5
8. Rubber products	0.1	0.1	0.2	0.2	0.4	0.4
9. Chemical & petroleum coal products	0.6	0.3	0.7	0.7	0.8	4.5
10. Non-metallic mineral products	0.2	0.2	0.3	0.4	0.8	1.2
11. Basic metals	0.1	–	0.2	0.2	0.8	0.8
12. Metal products	0.5	0.5	0.5	0.4	1.6	4.1
Total share GNP[a]	7.7	7.0	8.1	10.3	12.9	28.2
Memo item: Manufacturing share of GDP at factor cost		5.9		9.4		25.0

Sources: (Korean data) BOK, *National Income in Korea, 1975*, pp. 198–199. Kim and Roemer, p. 134.
Note: [a]Total for Korea may not add due to rounding and omission of "miscellaneous" industry.

SOURCES OF INDUSTRIALIZATION

In Chapter 4, the sources of Korea's economic growth are discussed in terms of changes in the amount and productivity of broadly defined primary factors: labor (including education), capital, and imports. This section attempts to discuss the degree to which domestic demand, exports, import substitution, and technological change have each contributed to the growth of industrial output. The analytical framework used here is based on Syrquin's method,[14] which represents a recent modification of the pioneering work of Chenery, Shishido, and Watanabe.[15] Both methods start from a basic demand-supply balance and attempt to attribute changes in the structure of production to various demand and supply conditions. Although Syrquin's method is able to measure changes in the structure of production as either deviations from proportional growth or as absolute change, the present method uses only measurements based on absolute change, or the first-difference method.

The analysis of the sources of industrialization is based on four input-output tables for 1955, 1963, 1970, and 1975. In order to make the four tables consistent, import data were first reclassified. Because non-competitive imports become competitive once Korea starts to produce them, the list of competitive and non-competitive imports changes in each IO table. All non-competitive imports, except those natural resource-intensive imports which cannot be replaced by domestic production in the foreseeable future, were consolidated with competitive imports. Furthermore, the scrap data for the 1970 and 1973 tables were adjusted to make them consistent with their treatment in tables for earlier years. Finally, "business consumption," which is classified as part of value added in the Korean IO table, was reclassified as part of intermediate input.[16] The four IO tables were then deflated into 1968 constant world prices in order to eliminate the effects of domestic price distortions arising from tariffs, domestic indirect taxes, and quantitative restrictions on imports.

Structural changes in production, trade, and domestic demand based on these constant world-price IO data have been briefly examined in the preceding section. The sources of industrial growth for the period 1955–1975 are decomposed, and the results summarized in Table 29. Although the decompositions are made for three time intervals (1955–1963, 1963–1970, and 1970–1975), the results for the last two periods were linked to give a single estimate for the years from 1963 to 1975. This was necessary, not only to simplify the discussion, but also to allow examination of the effects of the policy shift in the early 1960s. It should also be noted that the table presents both direct and total measures of the sources of growth. Differences should be taken to reflect the backward-linkage effects of direct change in various autonomous factors on the expansion of output.

As shown in Table 29, the relative sizes of both the direct and total contributions of various autonomous factors to aggregate output growth for the whole economy varied considerably from 1955–1963 to 1963–1975. The direct contribution of export expansion (EE), for instance, was about 6 percent of total national output growth in the earlier period, but it increased to 19 percent in the later period, while at the same time the direct contribution of import substitution (IS) declined from 5 percent to nearly zero. Similarly, the total contribution of EE increased sharply from around 9 percent in 1955–1963 to 32 percent in 1963–1975, while the total IS contribution declined from 17 percent to a mere 4 percent. Both the direct and the total contributions of domestic demand expansion (DDE) declined between the two periods. The contribution of technological change (TC), or more specifically changes in IO coefficients, however, remained almost unchanged.

The increase in manufacturing output over the period 1955–1975 was much greater than the increases in other sectoral outputs. The growth of manufacturing output was mainly attributable to DDE and IS in the earlier period, and to DDE and EE in the later period. Thus, DDE was the most important factor for the growth of manufacturing output in both periods. Trade effects, on the other hand, shifted greatly between the two periods. For instance, the total IS contribution, which explained about 35 percent of the increase in manufacturing output in 1953–1963, declined to 7 percent in 1963–1975. In contrast, the total EE contribution expanded from around 9 percent to 39 percent.

When the sources of growth by major industry within the manufacturing sector are examined, it appears that DDE also contributed greatly to the growth of certain individual industries during the two periods, while the trade effects were again reversed in all major industries. Although the total IS contribution to the growth of individual industries' outputs generally declined to negligible or negative levels during 1963–1975, the total IS contributions to the growth of the intermediate products and machinery industries were 16 percent and 10 percent, respectively, or higher than in any other major industry. On the other hand, the IS contributions to the growth of the textiles and finished consumer goods industries were negligible or negative, while the EE contribution was over 50 percent, or again higher than in any other industry.

Output in the primary sector grew more slowly than the overall GNP throughout both periods. What growth took place was mainly due to the expansion of domestic demand, while EE and IS played a smaller, but increasingly important, role in the expansion of output. The total contribution of EE rose from 8 percent to 29 percent between the two periods, while that of IS rose from negative 16 percent to negative 15 percent.

These results support the conclusion that import substitution was much more important to Korea's industrialization during the period 1955–1963 than export growth, a situation which reversed itself during the later period. This conclusion partially corroborates the hypothesis that the policy changes in the first half of the 1960s were quite effective in altering the pattern of industrialization. In any case, when all periods are combined, it is clear that export expansion contributed substantially more to growth than import substitution, since the

TABLE 29 Sources of Industrial Output Growth, 1955–1975
(Syrquin's Method–First Difference)

| | Domestic Demand Expansion | | Export Expansion | | Import Substitution | | Technological Change | Total Output Increase (billion wŏn) |
	Direct (%)	Total (%)	Direct (%)	Total (%)	Direct (%)	Total (%)	Total (%)	
1955–1963								
1. Agriculture	126.0	93.2	3.3	7.0	-29.3	-22.4	22.2	102.7
2. Mining	93.3	57.9	14.4	19.3	-7.7	40.5	-17.7	12.3
Primary total	122.5	89.4	4.5	8.4	-27.0	-15.7	17.9	115.0
3. Food processing	77.2	65.1	6.2	7.8	16.6	15.4	11.7	61.4
4. Textiles	36.2	68.7	10.8	20.0	53.0	102.1	-90.8	25.5
5. Finished consumer goods	79.9	70.0	4.7	6.0	15.4	17.4	6.6	41.4
6. Intermediate products	64.8	48.8	6.0	7.9	29.2	37.5	5.8	90.3
7. Machinery & transport equipment	73.1	41.1	3.1	6.4	23.8	34.0	18.5	22.6
Manufacturing total	68.3	57.9	6.1	8.7	25.6	34.9	1.5	241.2
8. Social overhead & services	102.6	102.3	5.4	11.4	-8.0	8.6	-22.3	96.0
Total	89.4	75.4	5.5	9.2	5.1	16.5	-1.0	452.2

TABLE 29 (continued)

	Domestic Demand Expansion		Export Expansion		Import Substitution		Technological Change	Total Output Increase
	Direct (%)	Total (%)	Direct (%)	Total (%)	Direct (%)	Total (%)	Total (%)	(billion wŏn)
1963–1975								
1. Agriculture	111.6	123.3	12.8	28.5	−24.4	−16.8	−35.0	349.5
2. Mining	119.9	98.1	5.0	32.8	−24.9	−0.2	−30.7	41.7
Primary total	112.4	120.6	12.0	28.9	−24.4	−15.0	−34.5	391.2
3. Food processing	94.0	88.2	6.9	11.7	0.9	−0.2	0.3	553.0
4. Textiles	71.4	32.1	25.3	56.9	3.3	2.1	8.9	454.3
5. Finished consumer goods	56.2	50.6	46.7	52.5	−2.9	−2.0	−1.1	578.0
6. Intermediate products	74.4	46.8	15.7	34.4	9.9	15.6	3.2	1,156.3
7. Machinery & transport equipment	56.5	41.5	38.1	45.9	5.4	9.8	2.8	541.7
Manufacturing total	71.1	51.5	24.7	38.8	4.2	7.0	2.7	3,283.3
8. Social overhead & services	92.5	80.6	8.4	19.5	−0.9	1.9	−2.0	1,772.7
Total	81.0	66.0	18.5	31.8	0.5	3.7	−1.5	5,447.2

Note: Calculated from 1968 constant world-price IO data for 1955, 1963, 1970, and 1975. All estimates are arithmetic averages of estimates derived from Laspeyres and Paasche indexes.

expansion of output after 1963 was overwhelmingly larger than in the earlier period.

NOMINAL AND EFFECTIVE
PROTECTION RATES

An assumption common to many static analyses of trade and development is that inefficient resource allocation results from any substantial deviation of the exchange rate from the unified equilibrium rate, from large variations in effective tariffs, and from quantitative import controls. Accordingly, the world market prices of tradable commodities are held to reflect the true opportunity costs of production of those commodities. Thus the tariffs, quantitative controls, and other policies that cause domestic prices to deviate significantly from world-market prices lead to inefficiencies.

A simple measure of the divergence between domestic and world-market prices is the legal tariff rate. In Korea, however, the legal tariff rate is generally not a good measure of such divergence for three reasons. First, some tariffs are prohibitive, because they are redundantly high. Second, widespread exemptions and reductions of tariff levies are frequently granted. Third, much of Korean industry is export-oriented, even though the domestic market is still largely protected by tariffs and non-tariff restrictions. To examine the divergence between domestic and world-market prices, therefore, it is necessary to compare domestic prices directly with world-market prices. The divergence, or the excess of a commodity's domestic price over its world-market price, is called the rate of nominal protection to distinguish it from the legal tariff rate.

Neither the legal tariff nor the nominal protection rates provide a very good measure of the resource-diverting effects of tariffs and quantitative restrictions. A much better measure is the rate of effective protection, which takes into account the fact that intermediate goods, as well as primary factors, are required for production. The effective protection rate measures the excess of domestic value added due to protection over the value added in world-market prices. In the usual measure of effective protection, however, subsidies in the form of income tax reductions and preferential low interest loans for specific activities are not taken into account. The effective rate of protection, which consolidates the effects of these subsidies, is generally called the effective rate of subsidy.

A study by Westphal and Kim provides estimates of nominal protection rates, effective protection rates, and subsidy rates for 150 tradable sectors in 1968. Table 30 summarizes the Westphal-Kim estimates by major industrial group, showing that the structure of Korean protection was unusual in a number of ways. First, the nominal rates of protection, which were derived from direct price comparisons, are substantially lower than the legal tariff rates, indicating considerable tariff redundancy. Tariff redundancy is particularly great in manufacturing, where the average rate of nominal protection was only 11 percent, and the legal tariff rate was 59 percent. Tariff redundancy within manufacturing was relatively lower in such heavy industries as transport equipment, machinery, and consumer durables.

Second, the average levels of effective protection and subsidies were relatively low in Korea compared with other countries, reflecting the fact that the exchange rate in 1968 was not significantly overvalued. Although the effective rates varied by industrial group, the average level of effective protection for exports of all tradable commodities was 0.3 percent, while that for domestic sales reached 9 percent. When account is taken of preferential tax and credit subsidies, the average level of effective subsidies for exports of all tradable goods rose to 6.5 percent, but that for domestic sales remained almost unchanged.

Third, domestic sales of primary sector output were given a greater average level of protection (or subsidization) than domestic sales of manufacturing output. The average rate of effective protection placed on domestic sales of primary products was 17 percent, while that placed on manufactured goods was

TABLE 30 Nominal and Effective Protection by Industry Group, 1968
(%)

Industry Group	Average Legal Tariffs	Average Nominal Protection	Effective Protection[a]		Effective Subsidy[a]	
			Exports	Domestic Sales	Exports	Domestic Sales
Agriculture, forestry, & fishing	36.0	16.6	-15.3	17.9	-9.4	21.7
Mining	9.0	6.9	-0.9	3.5	2.7	4.5
Primary production -Total	34.1	15.9	-7.0	17.1	-2.4	20.7
Processed food	56.7	2.7	-2.2	-14.2	1.8	-19.6
Beverage & tobacco	135.4	2.1	-1.7	-15.5	12.6	-20.8
Construction materials	30.5	3.7	-3.9	-8.8	4.4	-12.9
Intermediate products (I)	31.0	2.4	18.6	-18.8	26.0	-21.9
Intermediate products (II)	53.4	19.1	-0.2	17.4	11.6	13.1
Nondurable consumer goods	67.9	8.6	-1.4	-8.0	4.1	-15.7
Consumer durables	78.4	30.7	-3.0	39.8	1.5	23.6
Machinery	49.1	27.9	-4.6	29.5	1.9	21.0
Transport equipment	61.8	54.3	-13.1	83.2	-5.6	80.8
Manufacturing - Total	58.8	10.7	2.2	-1.1	8.9	-6.5
All industries	49.4	12.6	0.3	9.0	6.5	8.6

Source: Westphal and Kwang Suk Kim, pp. 3, 9, 10.

Note: [a]Based on the Corden measure.

a negative 1 percent. This difference is also observable in terms of effective subsidies.

Finally, exports, on average, were given higher effective protection and subsidies than domestic sales of manufactured products. For instance, the average rate of effective subsidy for total manufactured exports was about 9 percent, compared with an average of negative 6.5 percent on manufactured products sold domestically. Some heavy manufacturing industries, however, such as transport equipment, machinery, consumer durables, and intermediate products (II), received higher protection and subsidies on domestic sales than on exports.

It is clear from the above discussion that the average levels of Korea's effective protection and subsidies for 1968 were relatively low, indicating the absence of either excessive profitability or substantial inefficiencies. The structure of protection was consistent with the nation's export-oriented industrialization strategy in the sense that higher incentives were generally given to exports than to domestic sales of manufactured products.

These observations are based on the estimated structure of protection for 1968, when the system of incentives for export-oriented industrialization was already well-established. Since that year, further modifications have been made in the system. In order to illustrate changes in the structure of protection after 1968, the estimated nominal rates of protection for selected years from 1955 to 1975 are summarized in Table 31. Although it is not possible to compare the structure of effective protection and subsidies between 1968 and 1975, the data presented in the table indicate that the average nominal rates of protection for all major industries declined between 1968 and 1975 and became negative in half of the six major industries listed in the table by 1975. The decrease in the average level of nominal protection is attributable partly to the realistic adjustment of the exchange rates in December 1974 and partly to the increased government control of major commodity prices after 1973. Because of this low level of nominal protection, the nominal value of Korean exports was able to rise 14 percent in 1975,

TABLE 31 Estimated Nominal Rates of Protection by Major
Industrial Group for Selected Years
(%)

	1955	1963	1968	1970	1975
1. Primary production	67.5	25.3	15.1	25.1	46.8
2. Processed food & tobacco	92.0	16.5	1.3	−4.7	−17.6
3. Textiles	134.1	11.1	23.7	16.1	4.5
4. Finished consumer goods	91.9	13.7	11.3	0.8	−19.9
5. Intermediate goods	181.7	16.5	9.1	1.7	−3.8
6. Machinery & transport equipment	183.7	31.6	41.1	47.6	13.3
2–6 Total manufacturing	125.4	16.1	11.1	4.0	−6.7
1–6 All tradable commodities	92.7	20.7	12.9	10.9	3.7

Source: Kwang Suk Kim, "Sources of Industrial Growth," p. 77.

despite the worldwide recession. In any case, the data presented
in the table support the conclusion that the average level of
protection for all tradable products declined from 1955 to 1975.
The decline is indicative of the gradual improvement in Korea's
industrial efficiency.

FACTOR UTILIZATION AND EFFICIENCY

Korea's industrialization strategy clearly shifted from import
substitution to export promotion in the early 1960s. It would,
therefore, be quite interesting to compare the patterns of factor
use under the two different strategies of industrialization. However, due to the lack of reliable statistics for the earlier period,
this section will discuss only the allocation and utilization of
primary factors under the export-oriented industrialization
strategy.

In the early 1960s, Korea had the typical characteristics of a
labor surplus economy as defined by A. Lewis, G. R. Ranis, and
J. H. Fei.[17] It can, therefore, be safely assumed that Korea's
comparative advantage, at least during the 1960s, lay in labor-

intensive as opposed to capital-intensive activities. Although a country's comparative advantage is determined, not only by the factor endowment, but also by many other conditions, the allocative efficiency of export-oriented industrialization can be assessed, at least partially, in terms of the factor intensity of trade.

There are two sets of estimates of the factor intensity of trade summarized in Table 32. However, the two are not directly comparable for a number of reasons.[18] First, the estimates by Westphal and Kim are based entirely on factor input coefficients for 1968. Thus the intra-sectoral composition of production and the underlying factor input coefficients by sectors are held fixed over the period 1960–1968. In contrast, Wontack Hong's estimates are based on separate input-output coefficients for each year and thus take into account both changes in the output mix and in the factor intensity within each sector. Second, Westphal and Kim's estimates are in terms of 1965 world prices, while Hong's data are in 1970 domestic prices. Finally, the commodity categories used by the two sets of estimates are not directly comparable.

According to the Westphal and Kim estimates, the direct, as well as the total (direct plus indirect) labor intensity of manufactured exports, was substantially greater than that of imports over the period from 1960 to 1968. In the primary sector, however, the labor intensity of exports was substantially lower than that of imports. This reflects the fact that Korea's natural resource endowment has led to exports of relatively capital-intensive mining production and to imports of highly labor-intensive agricultural products.

Hong's estimates, which cover a longer period, also indicate that the direct and total labor intensities of exports were generally greater than those of competitive imports through 1968. But the labor intensity of exports declined rapidly after 1968 and roughly matched that of competitive imports by 1970. By 1975, the direct, as well as the total labor intensity of exports, actually had fallen below that of competitive imports.

TABLE 32 Factor Intensity of Production by Commodity
Category, 1960–1973

	Estimates of Labor/Capital Ratio by Westphal and Kim[a]			
	1960	*1963*	*1966*	*1968*
Direct Factor Requirements				
Primary				
Domestic output	16.60	17.20	17.08	17.16
Exports	8.19	6.89	6.15	5.69
Imports	16.58	15.91	16.13	15.48
Manufacturing				
Domestic output	2.97	2.89	2.67	2.64
Exports	2.72	3.02	3.24	3.55
Imports	2.09	1.93	1.98	2.33
Total Factor Requirements				
Primary				
Final demand less imports	11.46	11.79	12.10	12.61
Exports	6.55	5.75	5.13	4.81
Imports	11.99	11.50	11.90	11.30
Manufacturing				
Final demand less imports	5.43	5.41	5.03	5.14
Exports	3.74	3.71	4.09	4.29
Imports	2.77	2.40	2.40	2.74

	Estimates of Labor/Capital Ratio by Hong[b]					
	1963	*1966*	*1968*	*1970*	*1973*	*1975*
Direct Factor Requirements						
Exports	1.73	1.29	1.16	0.93	0.58	0.35
Competitive imports	1.44	0.72	1.02	0.96	0.64	0.58
Total Factor Requirements						
Exports	1.40	1.00	0.87	0.68	0.47	0.32
Competitive imports	1.06	0.63	0.68	0.64	0.38	0.36

Notes: [a]Man-years per million wŏn of capital in 1965 constant prices. See Westphal
and Kwang Suk Kim, pp. 4–47.

[b]Man-years per thousand dollars of capital in 1970 constant prices. Hong's estimates
of the capital/labor ratio were converted into a labor/capital ratio to facilitate
comparison with the results of Westphal and Kim. See Wontack Hong, *Factor Supply
and Factor Intensity of Trade in Korea* (Seoul, 1975), pp. 2, 41, 42.

Hong has also separately estimated the factor intensity of non-competitive imports, excluding natural resource-intensive imports, using U.S. and Japanese factor input coefficients. Estimates of the factor intensity of non-competitive imports based on foreign input coefficients can not be compared directly with those based on domestic coefficients. Nevertheless, they seem to indicate that non-competitive imports were substantially more capital-intensive than both exports and competitive imports.[19] When both competitive and non-competitive imports are taken together, they appear to be more capital intensive than exports, since the non-competitive imports have accounted for 20–30 percent of total imports in recent years.

Despite these differences, the two estimates show that Korea exported relatively labor-intensive goods and imported capital-intensive goods. Thus, they support the conclusion that the export-oriented strategy resulted in an efficient allocation of primary factors in line with the nation's comparative advantage. It is also clear that export-oriented industrialization was accompanied by a rapid increase in employment. According to a study by David C. Cole and Larry Westphal,[20] direct employment in manufacturing production for export rose from about 3 percent of total manufacturing employment in 1960 to 19 percent by 1970. If the indirect employment generated by exports is included, more than one-quarter of manufacturing employment and nearly 10 percent of total employment in 1970 were attributable to exports. The same study estimates that export expansion was responsible for 38 percent of the increase in manufacturing employment and 33 percent of the increase in total employment between 1960 and 1970. A more recent study by Hong[21] indicates that the direct and indirect employment generated by manufactured exports rose from 25 percent of total manufacturing employment to 30 percent between 1970 and 1975. Hong's estimate of the total employment generated by all exports, although slightly lower than the estimate of Cole and Westphal, indicates that it rose from a mere 1 percent of total employment in 1960 to 11 percent by 1975.

Although export expansion has contributed greatly to increase employment since the early 1960s, Hong's estimates show a rapid decline in the labor-capital ratio of exports after 1968. This decline in the labor intensity of export production can be attributed to the sharp rise in Korea's wage-rental ratio.[22] Korea's real wage rate increased rapidly after the mid-1960s. Although Korean labor union pressure on wages has been negligible, the average wage for industrial workers has risen greatly, reflecting gains in labor productivity. On the other hand, a gradual reduction in the average interest rate on bank loans since 1968, as well as the acceleration of price inflation in recent years, has continuously lowered the cost of capital, while the growing inflows of foreign loans since the mid-1960s have further loosened the constraints on borrowing for Korean industries.

Thus, if the wage-rental ratio had not increased at a rapid rate, Korea's industrial employment would probably have expanded even more swiftly than it did. This might have been desirable in view of the current 4 percent unemployment rate. It is, however, questionable whether the high rates of growth in GNP and exports could have been attained continuously if Korea had prevented the accumulation of capital simply to maximize employment growth. Because developed countries have increasingly restricted imports of labor-intensive goods through tariffs and other barriers in recent years, the diversification of Korean exports into capital-intensive items has helped to maintain the momentum of the export-oriented industrialization strategy.

The rapid rise in the wage-rental ratio has accelerated the process of capital accumulation in Korea and encouraged the substitution of capital for labor in industrial production. However, this trend has not resulted in a significant waste of resources. Although the capital-labor ratio has risen since the late 1960s, the utilization of capital by industry has also grown, as indicated by the continuous increase in the value added/capital ratio for manufacturing during 1960–1973. The value added/labor ratio in manufacturing also increased greatly during the period,[23] implying a significant rise in total factor productivity.

CONCLUSION

The main orientation of Korea's industrial and trade policy shifted in the first half of the 1960s from import substitution to export promotion. This transition to an export-oriented policy provided the important precondition for sustained, rapid growth in Korea during the following period. The dramatic growth of exports was led by the manufacturing sector and was accompanied by the diversification of both export commodities and markets. Although imports have also expanded greatly since the early 1960s, the more rapid growth of exports has gradually improved Korea's trade balance.

Along with the expansion of exports, dramatic growth and structural changes have taken place in production, trade, and domestic demand. The entire pattern of change can be characterized as export-oriented industrialization. Accordingly, the major sources of Korea's industrialization changed between 1955–1963 and 1963–1973 in a manner which was consistent with this shift of policy. Nevertheless, the relative contribution of domestic demand expansion to industrial growth remained quite important throughout both periods. In regard to the trade effects, however, the dominant source of industrialization clearly shifted from import substitution during 1955–1963 to export expansion during the later period.

There are indications that export-oriented industrialization since the early 1960s has resulted in a relatively efficient allocation of resources, as indicated by relatively low levels of effective protection and subsidization. Given the assumption that Korea has a comparative advantage in labor-intensive activities, the higher labor-intensity of exports relative to imports is indicative of the relatively efficient use of primary factors. It should, however, be noted that the labor-intensity of Korean exports has been declining since the late 1960s. This drop is a consequence of both the accumulation of capital and the rise in the wage-rental ratio in recent years. In some ways, this process of capital deepening has actually been accelerated by the protectionist policies of developed countries that restrict imports of labor-intensive goods more heavily than those of capital-intensive goods.

Anne O. Krueger has suggested that Korea was able to make a smooth transition to an export-oriented policy in the early 1960s because import substitution had not yet progressed to the development of high-cost intermediate and capital goods industries.[24] In other words, if import substitution in the 1960s had already reached the stage where most imports of intermediate and capital goods were replaced by domestic production, pressures from domestic industry might have prevented duty-free imports of low-cost intermediate and capital goods for export production. Under such circumstances, Korean exporters would have encountered great difficulty in producing export goods efficiently enough to be competitive in world markets.

Korea has recently begun to promote the construction of heavy and chemical industries in order further to replace imports of capital goods, as well as of intermediate goods. Although the government's announced intention is to promote selected skill-intensive heavy and chemical industries in which Korea enjoys a comparative advantage, business investment in capital-intensive industries may still increase greatly due to the recent large rise in the wage-rental ratio. It is evident that, when the domestic heavy and chemical industries start to produce replacements for imports of intermediate and capital goods, there will be increasing pressure placed on export industries to use domestically supplied goods. It is, therefore, likely that future progress of export-oriented industrialization will largely depend upon the efficiency of the new heavy industries. This is even more certain now that Korea has reached the stage where heavy industrial exports must be promoted to sustain the momentum of export-oriented industrialization.

SIX

Foreign Assistance and Korean Development

Over the past three decades, Korea has been one of the largest recipients of foreign aid in the world. The United States alone supplied $12.6 billion in economic and military assistance between 1946 and 1976, the international financial institutions an additional $1.9 billion, and Japan approximately $1 billion. The total of over $15 billion for a country with a population of 25 million at the mid-point of 1960 gives a per capita assistance figure of $600 for the three decades. With the exception of South Vietnam and Israel, no other major country has received such a high level of per capita assistance.

In this chapter we shall review this assistance record in terms of its magnitude, composition, and administration and try to assess its contribution to Korea's development. Such an assessment is inevitably speculative, because it is not possible to know with certainty what would have happened if there had been no external assistance. It seems clear that South Korea would not have survived as an independent political entity for the decade after 1945 without massive foreign assistance. The picture thereafter is more complicated. The post-Korean War decade was one in which foreign assistance was large, while South Korea's economic growth was relatively modest. This was followed by a third decade in which those relationships were reversed. A simple correlation of aid and economic growth for these three decades would show an inverse relation. But what were the lagged effects of aid that was used to build infrastructure and provide training, and to what extent did the aid release domestic resources for investment, or even for consumption and survival, so the human resources necessary for Korea's development were available and could be mobilized subsequently? Was the foreign assistance really necessary, or could substantial amounts of savings have been squeezed out of the impoverished population in the post-Korean War years, and could the large gap between imports and exports have been narrowed significantly? Or could Korea have obtained comparable amounts of external financing from other sources or in forms that would have been more productive? Our review is intended to shed some light on these questions.

Because the United States was the source of well over 90 percent of the foreign assistance to South Korea during the critical years before 1965, our analysis will focus heavily on the U.S. programs. Japanese aid, much of which the Koreans considered to be a form of reparations, became significant after the signing of the peace agreement in 1965, but commercial loans from Japan since that time have been much more important than loan or grant assistance from the Japanese government. The World Bank, the Asian Development Bank, and other aid donors have also become more active in Korea since the late 1960s, so that by the end of 1975 their loans amounted to 20 percent of Korea's total external public debt. Foreign investment and commercial lending have both assumed increasing importance over the past decade and have largely replaced aid as the major form of external financing.

An important dimension of the foreign assistance programs that will be discussed in this chapter is the negotiating that occurs between donor and recipient about the broader economic and political context of which the assistance is a part. In Korea this has been an extremely important factor because of the multiple forms and layers of interdependence and interaction between the United States and the Korean governments. U.S. occupation of South Korea from 1945 to 1948, support of South Korean independence from 1948 through 1953, control over all military forces in Korea under the United Nations Command, and supply of most of Korea's military and economic assistance all meant that the various arms of the U.S. government became intimately involved in Korean affairs. At the same time, the U.S. government was supposedly attempting to foster, and the Korean government was desperately trying to achieve, a degree of autonomy and independence that would give it some claim to legitimacy in the eyes of its own people and of the world.

There were periods when Korean and American officials had similar and compatible views as to the objectives and appropriate forms of U.S. assistance. There were other times when the disagreements were profound and often exposed to public view. Then there were some critical turning points when a change in the substance, or form, or even the perception of the assistance precipitated a convergence or divergence of views and actions of the two governments which, in turn, had significant implications for Korean development and U.S.-Korean relations.

THE EARLY AID PROGRAMS, 1945–1953[1]

The American aid program to Korea began in September 1945 under the United States Army Military Government in Korea

(USAMGIK). American occupation officials had three stated objectives: to fulfill the promises that had been made at the Cairo and Potsdam Conferences to establish a free and independent Korea; to make Korea strong enough to be a factor of stability in Asia; and to build up the new Republic as a display window of democracy for other Asian peoples to see and emulate.[2] One factor clouded these objectives, and that was the continuing division of Korea and the inevitable question as to whether these objectives were to be applied to a unified or divided Korea. Until late 1947, the implicit assumption of all American policy toward Korea was that reunification would take place; thereafter there was growing awareness that the south had to be prepared to stand on its own.[3]

The American aid program began with a de facto set of short-run objectives. The relief program which accompanied the U.S. Military Government (1945–1948) was the GARIOA (Government Appropriations for Relief in Occupied Areas) aid program. This emergency program targeted three basic aims: 1) prevention of starvation and disease; 2) boosting of agricultural output; and 3) massive provision of imported commodities to overcome the pervasive shortages of most types of consumer goods. Of the more than $500 million in economic aid sent by the United States to Korea under GARIOA, most was in the form of food, fertilizer, clothing, fuel, and other commodities, with only 14 percent going to reconstruction efforts. The major medium-term priority was to raise agricultural production, especially rice, as rapidly as possible so as to make South Korea a net exporter of foodstuffs. More than half a million metric tons of fertilizer were imported into Korea under the Army program before mid-1948, making possible the highest levels of application of commercial fertilizer to Korean soil in its history and improving supply conditions so dramatically as to make agricultural self-sufficiency a prediction for the 1950s.[4]

Major rehabilitation programs were not considered feasible at this point for a number of reasons: the U.S. Congress was reluctant to provide more funds; the Korean question was still being debated in the U.N.; and the belief was held by many Americans (including Lt. General Albert C. Wedemeyer, sent to Korea to review the economic and military situation in 1947 by President Truman) that, because Korea would eventually be reunited, America had no real stake in a costly and taxing program aimed at economic development of a South Korea that might shortly be reunited with its northern half. The GARIOA program was therefore predicated on the notion that it was neither feasible nor desirable to attempt to make South Korea self-sustaining. The alternative to such an unambiguous relief effort was, to Wedemeyer's mind, a risky "experiment in industrialization without resources" which would better be avoided. [5]

Although the primary objective of the Military Government was short-term (the prevention of starvation, disease, and unrest), certain actions were taken that had longer-term consequences. The American authorities were confronted with the problem of what to do with Japanese-owned land and other properties. Political reasons argued for an early distribution of land, but action was delayed until the New Korea Company, Ltd., established by the U.S. Military Government, had acquired the information needed for a land distribution program. In March 1948 a National Land Administration was established, and land sales began. By September, some 487,621 acres had been sold to 502,072 tenants. This represented more than 96 percent of agricultural land formerly owned by the Japanese. This distribution was followed by provisions in the new Korean Constitution, adopted in 1948, providing for distribution of large Korean landholdings. After some delay, these provisions were put into effect in 1949. Thus a very large land distribution program had been accomplished before the beginning of the Korean War. It was, without doubt, the most significant accomplishment of U.S. Military Government. The details of this land distribution program and its consequences are discussed in Chapter 7.

Efforts on the part of the U.S. Military Government to divest Japanese properties other than land were less successful. When

TABLE 33 Commodity Composition of GARIOA Imports, 1945–1949 ($1,000s and %)

Commodity	1945		1946		1947		1948		1949[b]	
	$1,000s	%	$1,000s	%	$1,000s	%	$1,000s	%	$1,000s	%
Foodstuffs	3,604	73	21,551	43.5	77,574	44.2	67,698	37.7	4,887	5.2
Agricultural supplies			6,983	14.1	31,394	17.9	38,609	21.5	43,481	46.9
Unprocessed materials			113	0.2	3,809	2.2	8,093	45.0	11,844	12.8
Petroleum and fuel	1,330	27	12,224	24.7	14,221	8.1	25,510	14.2	9,711	10.5
Medical supplies			134	0.3	2,096	1.2	3,321	1.8	2,369	2.6
Clothing and textiles			1,863	3.7	26,680	15.2	5,627	3.1	–	–
Reconstruction[a]			4,994	10.1	17,696	10.1	26,856	15.0	20,172	21.7
Miscellaneous			1,683	3.4	1,911	1.1	3,878	2.0	239	0.3
Total	4,934		49,545		175,381		179,592		92,703	

Sources: BOK, *Economic Review, 1955*, p. 314 for 1945–1948; and *Monthly Statistical Review*, February 1952 for 1949. The categories listed for 1949 do not correspond precisely to those for 1948. Their allocation in the 1945–1948 classification is indicated in Note b.

Notes: [a]"Reconstruction" includes the following categories: automotive, building materials, chemicals, and dye stuffs, communications, educational support, fishing industry supplies, highway construction equipment, mining industry, office supplies, power and light, and railroad.

[b]1949 categories of aid goods, when differently classified, were allocated as follows: fertilizer is the only item in agricultural supplies; in "unprocessed materials" are raw cotton, spinning raw materials, crossties, bamboo, lumber and raw materials and semi-finished products; reconstruction includes chemicals, hides and skins, pulp and paper, cement; salt, iron and steel, machines and equipment, motor vehicle equipment, transport equipment, and rubber products.

a Korean government came into being in 1948, these properties were transferred to the new Republic. "Despite an effort in 1949 to persuade landlords dispossessed in the land reform to purchase Japanese enterprises, almost all of them remained in government hands until after the end of the Korean war."[6]

Education was a second area in which the efforts of the U.S. Military Government had longer-term consequences. Although the Japanese had operated the Korean educational system as a vehicle of "Japanization" with strong regimentation of Korean youth, primary and secondary educational facilities, as we saw in Chapter 3, were greatly expanded during the period of colonial rule. With the exodus of the Japanese, the U.S. Military Government was faced with the problem of attempting to expand educational facilities while changing the character of instruction. There were grave shortages of educational supplies and physical facilities as well as of qualified instructors and administrators. During the period of U.S. Military Government, primary school attendance nearly doubled and secondary school attendance tripled. Vigorous teacher training programs were introduced, and the Americans encouraged the admission of women and attempted to introduce local control of education through popularly elected school boards. As we note in Chapter 10, many of the U.S. Military Government innovations in the field did not survive. Coeducation was not extended beyond the primary school, and universal primary education was not attained until the late 1950s. Local control of education was abandoned in favor of governance by a strong central ministry. Still there is little doubt that the educational activities undertaken during the period of U.S. Military Government contributed to development potential in later years.

While the land reform and education programs of the U.S. Military Government were departures from the essentially short-run maintenance focus of U.S. assistance efforts in Korea, there were other evidences of concern for the longer-term needs of the country. The U.S. State Department put forward an economic rehabilitation plan for South Korea as early as March

1947 which was intended to provide half a billion dollars for development objectives, but subsequently withdrew it for lack of Congressional support. When, in 1948, plans were made to terminate the U.S. Military Government and establish a Korean government, the State Department again began to plan for a more positive aid program that would make the new republic less dependent on foreign aid for its long-run survival. Before agreement was eventually reached that a Korean aid program be included under the aegis of the Economic Cooperation Administration (which was already conducting the Marshall Plan in Europe) in January 1949, the ECA administrator demanded and received assurances that the Congressional aid package would produce "a real recovery program with emphasis on capital development that would result in decreasing Korea's need for extraordinary outside assistance."[7]

An assessment in 1948 concluded that the U.S. Military Government had accomplished its limited economic objectives fairly successfully. Starvation and disease had been prevented, some repair work and maintenance had begun, and some significant technical assistance programs had been started. But agricultural and industrial production were still well below prewar levels, and much of the existing physical plant and equipment was barely usable.[8] The content of the aid was changed accordingly to give greater emphasis to production inputs and less to relief supplies. A prime example of this was the large inflow of aid-financed fertilizer which contributed significantly to a 25 percent increase in grain production.

In December 1948, shortly before the ECA took responsibility for the American aid program to Korea, the first government-to-government pact between the two nations was signed. Called the ROK-US Agreement on Aid, the pact was similar to ECA agreements with Western European countries and outlined the quid pro quo the United States expected in exchange for provision of aid. It required the Korean government to follow certain stable economic policies aimed at strengthening the economy, notably balancing the budget, regulating foreign exchange, effectively disposing of the formerly Japanese-owned properties (by then vested in the Korean government) and establishing a "counterpart fund" in the Bank of Chosun (the existing Central Bank) into which the Korean government promised to deposit the wŏn equivalent of the dollar cost of all United States aid made available to South Korea on a grant basis and to use those funds only for purposes mutually agreed upon with the United States government (including the financing of local expenditures involved in carrying out the American aid program).[9] These stipulations were intended as safeguards to ensure that the aid funds would not be misused. The terms of the agreement suggested an implicit lack of confidence on the part of the Americans in the Korean government's ability to handle its economic affairs responsibly. While this skepticism was not without some justification in view of the government's apparent failure either to control its deficit spending or to check inflation, the agreement provided fertile ground for subsequent donor-recipient friction. Paul W. Kuznets has observed, "These terms were regarded unfavorably by the Korean Government, which felt that it knew its own needs best and did not welcome the sort of interference in domestic politics called for by the agreement."[10]

By mid-1949, the ECA had drawn up a three-year recovery program explicitly aimed at development—Paul Hoffman, the ECA administrator at the time, argued for the program before Congress by pointing out that "continuation of a mere relief program would necessarily result in the progressive pauperization of the people of South Korea."[11] The proposed aid program focused on three basic areas of capital investment necessary to attain a viable Korea: development of coal, expansion of thermal power generating facilities, and construction of fertilizer plants, in that priority order. The strategy revolved around building up indigenous coal resources as a means of boosting power-generating capacity, and then creating and operating fertilizer plants which could provide enough nitrogenous fertilizer to make South Korea a net exporter of foodstuff by early 1953. This program optimistically envisaged that official United States aid would be eliminated by fiscal year 1952–1953, under the expectation that by then the balance-of-payments deficit could and would be financed by private foreign investment and international credit institutions.[12] Despite its relatively modest budget request ($350 million of aid over the three-year period ending in 1952), the aid program encountered strong opposition in the Congress and the first third of the appropriation (in the form of aid bill HR 5330) failed to pass by one vote, "an expression of a (Congressional) feeling that further help for Korea would be useless."[13] Despite the fact that the bill was later recast, amended, and successfully passed so as to authorize $110 million of the $150 million originally requested for FY 1950, the failure of the complete aid package had a number of repercussions. The ECA was forced not only to pare down its total program, but also to operate again on a short-run basis and make substantial cutbacks in the capital development and investment phase of the program. The failure of the bill further signaled both the North and South Koreans that American support for the south was flagging—several observers have branded the vote on HR 5330 (rather than the famous Dean Acheson speech at the National Press Club a few days later) as the expression of American sentiment which provided an impetus for the North Korean decision to invade later in the year.

The South Koreans, Paul Kuznets suggests, were at the same time "understandably disturbed by the inconsistency of an American policy that first assisted the creation of a democratic government in Korea and then proved reluctant to give it economic support."[14] On the other hand, the Americans were growing increasingly disgruntled by what they considered Korean government laxity in instituting stabilization policies. American concern at the Korean government's apparent unwillingness to check inflation prompted an ECA-inspired, imperious *aide-mémoire* from Secretary of State Acheson to the Korean government in April 1950 which threatened to re-examine the entire aid program and to consider the possibility of reducing future aid should the Korean government fail to adopt effective counter-inflationary measures.[15] Remedial actions that had actually been taken prior to the American protest led to a significant reduction in the money supply within the six months preceding the North Korean invasion. This marked the beginning of often acrimonious donor-recipient conflict over stabilization policy.

When the North Koreans launched their invasion on June 25, 1950, all hopes of a recovery program had to be set aside. The ECA readjusted its procurement program for wartime effectiveness, canceling authorizations for commodities such as cotton and fertilizer, and once again focused attention on relief first and development second. A military-run relief and assistance program was organized under the U.N. flag, and civil relief programs initiated, most notably the CRIK (Civil Relief in Korea) program. While theoretically a U.N. endeavor, wartime relief in fact came almost entirely from the United States, which contributed $429 million of the $457 million in relief goods provided under the CRIK heading. CRIK relief was administered by a military unit known as the United Nations Civil Assistance Command, Korea (UNCACK) which was later renamed the Korean Civil Assistance Command (KCAC) when its functions were taken over completely by the U.S. Army. During the actual hostilities, UNCACK, headquartered in Pusan, was the operative agency and proved remarkably successful in preventing the outbreak of massive starvation or epidemics of the kind endemic to refugee populations.

A second organization, the United Nations Korea Reconstruction Agency (UNKRA) was created in December 1950 by the General Assembly to deal with Korea's rehabilitation and reconstruction problems. Unlike UNCACK, UNKRA's mission was not relief but to "lay the economic foundations for the political unification and independence of the country." Unfortunately, UNKRA was created with two presumptions in mind: first, that hostilities would cease in the near future, and second, that the end of hostilities would leave Korea once again a unified nation.

UNKRA was thus mandated to repair devastation, to begin provision of relief and rehabilitation supplies, transport, and services for Korean industry, and to relieve suffering. The funds for UNKRA were to come from the voluntary subscriptions of U.N. member nations, of which the United States had pledged to provide no more than 66 percent. This attempt at "multi-nationalization of aid," however, quickly fell apart. The uncertainties surrounding the unification made it difficult for UNKRA to organize a feasible program; individual rehabilitation projects had little interconnection with one another, and the funding, originally intended to come from a variety of nations, came almost entirely from the United States.[16] Anne Krueger notes that, because the other nations' pledges of support to Korea fell far below the level which would have been necessary for the entire American aid contribution to be spent, it became inevitable that the aid effort should revert to an essentially bilateral relationship between Korea and America.[17]

The amounts of economic assistance to Korea from various sources between the end of World War II and the end of the Korean War are shown in Table 34. All but a small fraction of the UNKRA assistance came from the United States. The average per capita aid figure for the eight years 1946–1953 was about $5 per annum, which was roughly equal to 10 percent of per capita income in the prices of that time. This aid plus foreign-exchange earnings from the sale of goods and services to the U.S. and United Nation forces in Korea financed practically the total of Korea's imports, since regular commercial exports were negligible during this period.

Because the foreign exchange earned from sales within Korea constituted such a large fraction of the foreign exchange over which the Korean government had unilateral control, the exchange rate between the dollar and the wŏn for such transactions became a major source of controversy between the U.S. and Korean governments and a distorting influence on the Korean economy for the succeeding decade.[18]

Immediately after the fighting started the Korean government

TABLE 34 Economic Assistance to Korea, 1945–1953
(millions of U.S. dollars)

	GARIOA	ECA	CRIK	UNKRA	TOTAL
1945	4.9				4.9
1946	49.9				49.9
1947	175.4				175.4
1948	179.6				179.6
1949	92.7	23.8			116.5
1950		49.3	9.4		58.7
1951		32.0	74.4	0.1	106.5
1952		3.8	155.2	2.0	161.0
1953		0.2	158.8	29.6	188.4
	502.5	109.1	397.8	31.7	1,040.9

Source: BOK, *Economic Statistics Yearbook,* various years.

turned over a large wŏn "advance" to the U.N. Command with
the understanding that the terms of repayment in U.S. dollars
would be negotiated subsequently. Further advances followed
throughout the war. During the early months of the fighting
when all attention was focused on survival, no one worried about
repaying these advances, but by mid-1951, when the fighting
stabilized near the ultimate armistice line, the issue surfaced.
The Korean government insisted that repayment should be at
the official exchange rate at the time of the advances—a rate
which had become grossly overvalued due to the wartime inflation. The U.S. government demanded that repayment be at a
"reasonable" rate at the time of repayment and refused to make
any payment pending such an agreement. The debate continued
for months and was ultimately resolved by a series of unsatisfactory compromises. In the meantime, inflationary pressures
continued, and the Korean government's foreign exchange
reserves diminished.

This same issue carried over to the setting of the exchange rate
for depositing funds into the counterpart account. The Korean

government was obsessed with the idea of gaining more foreign exchange for a given outlay of wŏn, while the U.S. government was equally obsessed with the reluctance to turn over more dollars to the Korean government which might dispose of them in ways that the United States could not control. Both sides lost sight of the harmful consequences of the uncertainty and price distortions resulting from the controversy.[19]

As fighting moved south to the Pusan perimeter and then north, devastation of the South Korean economy was severe. Over a million lives were lost and, perhaps, one-quarter of the fixed capital destroyed. The average unweighted production index of major commodities (excluding tungsten) which had stood at 250 in 1949, fell to 184 in 1950, and 124 in 1951.[20] The disruption of the economy occurred primarily during the first year of the war. During the last two years, military action took place within a 10-mile strip of land. This relatively static front permitted substantial economic recovery, and the index of commodity production had reached 277 by 1953.

As the stalemated war dragged on into 1952 and 1953, the army managers of the U.S. aid program continued their preoccupation with relief rather than reconstruction. The Rhee Government grew increasingly restive and uncooperative with this approach. As John P. Lewis noted,

> By the end of 1952 neither side had come close to deciding what the reconstruction efforts for consumption and other goods should be or to canvassing systematically the investment requirements for reaching such objectives, or to analyzing the undertaking's feasibility in such terms as transport, power and manpower availabilities, and needed anti-inflationary and other supporting policies. Lacking such unilateral planning, no joint ROK-UN agreement had been reached on the general scope and design of the reconstruction effort.[21]

The choice between reconstruction with multilateral support or a predominantly bilateral U.S.-Korean effort was explicitly presented by the two planning missions which arrived in Korea in 1952–1953. The first was an UNKRA-sponsored economic advisory team from the Washington-based consulting firm of Robert R. Nathan; the second was a U.S. Presidential mission sent under the leadership of Henry J. Tasca. The Nathan group engaged in a year-long study of the Korean economy and recommended that South Korea seek to develop by exploiting comparative advantage and export opportunities in the areas of agriculture and minerals, in effect drawing up a five-year plan by which Korea would develop raw material exports to pay for manufactured imports.[22] The Nathan Plan suffered from the fact that its terms of reference called for a program to achieve the unrealistic goal of Korean self-sufficiency within five years. The means proposed by the Nathan Plan for achieving this objective were unrealistic, and the basic development strategy that it recommended was subsequently proven inappropriate.[23]

The Tasca mission, on the other hand, engaged in a six-week evaluation of the entire gamut of Korea's economic problems while at the same time attempting to repair diplomatic relations with the ROK government and to analyze administrative failures in the aid program to date. The Tasca mission made quantitative recommendations as to the size of U.S. aid appropriations in the future, but also tended to be overly optimistic about the potentialities of the Korean economy.

The Tasca report was used as a programming document by the new Eisenhower Administration for its Korea aid program and as a result its official impact was considerable, both in the long and short-term. The mission advocated a "unilateral" U.S. aid program to Korea in place of a multilateral U.N. program, suggesting that the U.N. turn over all responsibility for economic activities in Korea (including UNKRA) to the United States. The United States chose to act on this recommendation, first establishing the Office of the Economic Coordinator (OEC) in Seoul under the U.N. Command to oversee and coordinate the various aid programs, and eventually replacing the OEC with a unilateral U.S. Aid Mission. Upon the recommendation of the Tasca mission, a new aid agency was created in July 1953 to act as the ascendant agency in dealing with Korea's economic and defense effort. Called the Foreign Operations Administration (FOA), the new agency was created to deal with the reality of a divided Korea with a need for its own defense forces. Its creation was the final recognition that the United States was assuming the large burden of military and economic assistance to Korea.

During the period 1945 through 1953, American economic assistance to South Korea totaled nearly $1.2 billion. What was there to show for it? Most, but by no means all, of this economic assistance was in the form of straight relief supplies, foodstuffs, clothing, medical supplies, and the like. But also included were large supplies of fertilizer essential to farm crops, considerable amounts of petroleum products and unprocessed materials and, in the period just before the war, substantial quantities of "reconstruction" supplies. Despite the disturbed conditions existing in South Korea, some progress had been made by 1950 in setting the Korean economy on its feet. The war destroyed all that. During the war period, almost all economic assistance was in the form of relief supplies. Still, by 1953, although much reconstruction remained to be undertaken, the output of agricultural and manufacturing production had returned to the admittedly low level of 1949. Perhaps the most that can be said is that American economic assistance kept the South Korean economy in existence during this period, with standards of living, though low, no lower than in many other less-developed countries. In addition, the U.S. Military Government had carried through a successful land distribution program and had made a strong beginning in reestablishing educational facilities. American influence was less successful in disposal of other types of Japanese property, and most of this task was left to be undertaken by the Korean government after the war. Aid relationships are at best difficult, and perhaps it was inevitable, with the United States in such a dominant position, that dealings between the U.S. aid authorities and the Korean government, once it had been established, did not always run smoothly. Koreans complained of intervention in what they considered their domestic affairs; President Rhee wanted much more assistance in support of reconstruction than the United States was prepared to give; and the issues of inflation and the foreign exchange rate were particularly abrasive. These questions continued to be central to aid relationships in the 1950s.

POST-WAR FOREIGN ASSISTANCE

The war, as we noted earlier, served to concentrate the faculties of the American government with respect to policy toward South Korea. From 1953 on, the United States recognized a responsibility for economic and military assistance, and Korea became, in a sense, a client state. From 1953 through 1962, economic assistance amounted to roughly $2 billion and military assistance to roughly $1 billion. It was a period of relatively slow growth, despite massive assistance, with GNP in real terms increasing at an annual rate of 4.2 percent. At the end of the period, USAID officials were wondering audibly whether South Korea was to remain indefinitely a pensioner of the United States. Since South Korea's remarkable economic growth can be dated from 1963, the decade prior to this seems to represent a logical time period in which to discuss the quantity and character of U.S. assistance, the reasons why it had, apparently, so small an impact on Korean development, and the transition, early in the 1960s, to the changes in policy and structure that introduced the subsequent expansion.

The availability of national accounting statistics from 1953 makes it possible to assess the role of foreign assistance in a more quantitative framework than is possible for the previous years. But there is still a problem in arriving at an appropriate measure of foreign assistance, because Korean statistics have tended to understate the magnitude by omitting military assistance, loan-financed economic assistance, some portions of the PL 480 agricultural commodities, and Japanese grant aid. The United States, on the other hand, publishes comprehensive statistics on obligations or payments for U.S. fiscal years, but these seldom bear any resemblance to the Korean statistics, which are on a calendar year arrivals basis. Thus, it is not easy to relate aid flows to concurrent national accounts magnitudes in Korea.

MILITARY ASSISTANCE

The major omission in the Korean trade, aid, and national accounting statistics is any indication of military assistance. This results in a significant understatement of Korean imports, of resources absorbed by the Korean government, and of financial resources transferred into Korea from abroad. The only indicator of the magnitude of such assistance is from the U.S. government which reports that, for the 30 years from 1946 through 1976, total military assistance of $6.8 billion exceeded total economic assistance of $5.7 billion by nearly 20 percent (see Table 35).

TABLE 35 Summary of Economic and Military Assistance to South Korea from the United States ($ million for U.S. fiscal years)

	1946–52	1953–61	1962–69	1970–76	Total
Economic assistance	666.8	2,579.2	1,658.2	963.6	5,745.4
Military assistance	12.3	1,560.7	2,501.3	2,797.4	6,847.3
TOTAL	679.1	4,139.9	4,159.5	3,761.0	12,592.7

Source: U.S. Government, Agency for International Development, "U.S. Overseas Loans and Grants and Assistance from International Organizations," Washington D.C., July 1, 1945–September 30, 1976.

Even these figures are probably understated, because the very small amount of military assistance between 1946 and 1952 obviously does not cover the massive amounts of military equipment supplied to Korea during the Korean War. Subsequent figures are subject to all the problems of valuing military supplies which are sometimes valued at cost and sometimes reflect reduced prices of surplus stocks, but similar problems exist too for economic assistance.

While the remainder of the discussion will focus on economic assistance and its contribution to the modernization of the Korean economy, it is useful to keep in mind that, since the end of the Korean War in 1953, Korea has received nearly $7 billion of military assistance from the United States, and that the level of military assistance has been rising, at least in nominal if not in real terms, while the level of economic assistance has been diminishing since the end of the 1950s in both nominal and real terms.

The military assistance programs have made a significant contribution to the training of Korean military personnel in organization, management, and technical skills. After leaving military service, many enlisted men have gone to work in industrial and service occupations, and many officers have moved into senior management positions, especially in the government-owned enterprises. In addition, military units, with equipment supplied by the military assistance program, have undertaken the construction of roads, bridges, and other infrastructure, especially in areas that were important for the support of military operations near the demilitarized zone. None of these activities is included in the national investment or construction figures or adequately identified in the military assistance statistics.

In addition to these direct effects, there were other indirect effects of both military assistance and military activity. Since construction of roads, bridges, and other installations built for military use were undertaken to a significant extent by both Korean private firms and military units, the beginning of what has become a very large and efficient construction industry dates from the pre-war and war periods. The employment of Korean firms to construct port facilities and other military installations in Vietnam not only added to the expansion of the industry but gave these firms foreign experience on which they have capitalized successfully in recent years in the Middle East and elsewhere. U.S. support for Korean troops stationed in Vietnam and local procurement for U.S. troop support in Korea provided significant opportunities for foreign exchange earnings. Such earnings in no way constituted a part of military assistance since equivalent services were rendered, but they helped to pay for imports needed for Korean development. In the period before 1962, imports paid for from these sources of foreign exchange earnings were larger than those paid for by regular export earnings.

If we assume that the maintenance of a large and fully equipped army was necessary to the independence of South Korea after 1953, U.S. military assistance relieved the Korean budget of a major part of military expenditures. During the 1960s and early 1970s, defense expenditures varied between 22 and 32 percent of the Korean national budget and amounted to 4–4.5 percent of GNP. This has risen to 6–6.5 percent of GNP in recent years and may well persist at this high rate. Compared with military expenditures in most other less-developed countries, this is high, but it falls far short of what is reported to be the 15–20 percent of GNP expended in North Korea on the military.[24] It is impossible to place a figure on the contribution of U.S. military assistance to Korean development but, if we assume that the forces maintained in South Korea were no larger than necessary to deter attack from the north, the contribution was significant.

ECONOMIC ASSISTANCE

The contribution of foreign assistance to a country's development is generally assessed in two main dimensions: as a supplement to domestic savings which makes possible a higher rate of capital formation; and as a supplement to imports that permits a higher rate of production from the existing capacity. Thus, in assessing the relative magnitudes of foreign assistance, it is useful to relate them to the rate of investment and of imports. This is done in Table 36 which shows the ratios of imports,

TABLE 36 Ratios of Aid Imports and Net Foreign Saving to
GNP, Total Imports, and Fixed Capital Formation
(%)

	1953–62	*1963–64*	*1965–74*
Ratios to GNP of:			
Total imports	11.7	15.1	26.7
Fixed capital formation	10.5	12.7	22.7
Foreign savings	9.1	9.6	9.5
Aid imports	8.1	6.5	4.4
Ratios to Total Imports of:			
Foreign savings	78	64	36
Aid imports	69	41	17
Ratios to Fixed Capital Formation of:			
Foreign savings	88	75	42
Aid imports	77	51	20

Source: Derived from Tables 43 and 44.

fixed capital formation, foreign savings, and aid financed imports
to GNP, and then shows the ratios of foreign saving and aid
imports to total imports and to fixed capital formation.[25]

The post-war decade was a period during which foreign
assistance played a major role in the Korean economy. It
financed nearly 70 percent of total imports from 1953 through
1962. It was equal to nearly 80 percent of total fixed capital
formation and to 8 percent of GNP. Fixed capital formation was
a relatively constant 10 percent of GNP, and net foreign saving
(as measured by the current account deficit of the balance of
payments) averaged 9 percent of GNP for this decade (Table 36).

The next two years, 1963–1964, were an interim or transi-
tional period presaging the shift to export-led growth, increased
domestic saving, and reduced dependence on foreign assistance.
The evidence of this change is clearly recorded in the aid, trade,
and investment ratios for the post-transition high-growth decade,
that is, from 1965–1974. In the high-growth decade, fixed

capital formation averaged 23 percent of GNP, foreign saving held fairly constant at 9.5 percent, while aid-financed imports dropped to 4.4 percent of GNP. The aid imports were only 17 percent of total imports and 20 percent of fixed capital formation compared to the 70 to 80 percent ratio of the previous decade.

While these ratios of aid to imports, fixed capital formation, and GNP illustrate the magnitudes that were actually supplied, and in one sense can be described as measures of the contribution of aid to the Korean economy, they do not give a definitive indication of the contribution of aid to Korean development, which should be measured against what would have occurred if there had been no aid. Although the earlier development literature assumed that foreign assistance resulted in exactly matching increases in investment and imports, recently there has been greater recognition of the likelihood of some substitution of aid for domestic savings and for alternative means of financing imports.[26]

To the extent that external aid substitutes for domestic savings or exports, it basically adds to domestic consumption and contributes little to the growth of domestic production. It has been argued that the availability of aid encourages a pattern of economic policies that is conducive to such substitution,[27] and that this was specifically true in Korea.[28] But no one has yet come up with an adequate method for estimating the extent of substitution that has occurred in a particular historical experience. The best that can be done is a crude kind of sensitivity analysis of the potential effects on the rate of growth of varying assumptions about the degree of substitution of aid for domestic savings. Such an analysis is presented in Table 37.

The actual experience of Korea between 1953 and 1974 is shown on the left hand side of Table 37 with divisions into three periods: the first decade 1953–1962 characterized by low growth and high levels of foreign aid; then a brief transition period (1963–1964), followed by a decade of high growth and

TABLE 37 Per Capita GNP Growth Rates in Absence of Aid under Varying Assumptions about Substitution of Aid for Domestic Savings

	Actual Growth			Estimated Growth of Per Capita GNP with Assumed Substitution Rates of			
	GNP	Pop.	Per Capita GNP	0%	25%	50%	100%
1953–1962	4.2	2.7	1.5	-1.5	-0.7	0	1.5
1963–1964	8.7	2.7	6.0	1.6	2.7	3.8	6.0
1965–1974	10.7	2.1	8.5	6.5	7.0	7.5	8.5

Note: The estimated growth rate of per capita GNP ($\hat{g}$) is derived as follows:

$$\hat{g} = [1 - ((1-r)\,a)]\ g - n$$

where
r = assumed rate of substitution of savings for aid
a = aid financed imports as percent of fixed capital formation
g = the actual growth rate of GNP
n = the rate of population growth

much lower aid (1965–1974). The decline in the rate of population growth by 0.6 percent contributed only marginally to the rise in per capita GNP from 1.5 percent per annum in 1953–1962 to an average of 8.5 percent for the 1965–1974 decade.

The right hand side of Table 37 shows the estimated rates of growth of per capita GNP under the following assumptions:

1) No foreign aid.
2) Varying rates of substitution of domestic savings for foreign aid ranging from no substitution to 100 percent substitution.
3) A capital output ratio the same as it was in fact for the several periods.
4) No import constraint, that is, growth of output determined only by the availability of fixed capital.

The assumption of no substitution of domestic savings for foreign aid implies that investment would have been reduced by an amount equal to the lost foreign aid and, as shown in the column for 0 percent substitution, this would have resulted in an average growth rate of per capita GNP of –1.5 percent from 1953–1962 instead of the actual growth rate of +1.5 percent. For the latest period, 1965–1974, the loss of foreign aid would have been much less serious even with no substitution, in that the decline in per capita growth of GNP would have been only from 8.5 to 6.5 percent. At the other extreme, if there had been full substitution of domestic savings for foreign aid, there would have been no diminution of the growth rate.

Reality undoubtedly lies somewhere between these two extremes. Absence of aid would have resulted in some substitution of domestic savings, but this would have been more difficult to achieve in the immediate post-war period when per capita incomes were very low and many people were living at little better than a subsistence level. Table 37 suggests that anything less than 50 percent substitution of domestic savings for aid would have meant a decline in per capita income. Another interpretation is that a 50 percent reduction in aid with no substitution would have resulted in zero per capita growth for that period. Thus it seems reasonable to conclude that a flow of foreign aid in roughly the magnitude that occurred in the decade after the Korean War was necessary for achieving even the modest positive per capita growth rate of 1.5 percent. Thereafter the aid flow was much less significant as increased domestic saving, attributable in part to higher real incomes resulting from previous growth, and alternative sources of foreign saving made possible high rates of investment and growth even if there had been no foreign aid.

Also in the earlier period, when aid accounted for nearly 70 percent of total imports, it was the major factor in relieving the import constraint on domestic production. Between 1953 and 1960, the division of imports between consumer and intermediate goods changed from 75 percent consumer goods and 25 percent intermediate to one-third consumer goods and two-thirds intermediate goods[29] as Korean productive capacity was restored after the war. It is unlikely that Korea, even under the most favorable set of policies, could have achieved sufficient export levels at that time to finance a comparable flow of imported intermediate goods required to sustain the growing domestic production of consumer goods.

Later during the high growth decade when aid financed only 17 percent of total imports, its contribution to relieving the import constraint on domestic production was obviously marginal, and there were many alternative ways of achieving the needed flow of imports.

In addition to the change in the magnitude of foreign assistance since 1953, there have been substantial shifts in the source and the type of assistance. These are illustrated in Tables 38 through 40. During the post-Korean War decade, 95 percent of the foreign economic aid was supplied by the United States, the remaining five percent ($121 million) came through the United Nations Korea Reconstruction Agency, which received two-thirds of its contributions from the United States. Also, nearly all of the aid prior to 1964 was on a grant basis.

TABLE 38 Average Ratios of Grant and Loan Aid to
Total Imports

| | Aid as % of Total Imports | | | U.S. Aid as % of Total Imports | | |
	Grant	Loan	Total	Grant	Loan	Total
1953–1962	69	0	69	67	0	67
1963–1964	38	3	41	38	3	41
1965–1969	17	6	23	13	4	17
1970–1974	4	7	11	1	3	4

Source: See Table 43.

TABLE 39 Composition of U.S. Economic Assistance to Korea,
July 1953–December 1974

	Project	Program	Total
Supporting assistance grant	196	1,834	2,030
Development grant	325		325
PL 480 Title I		1,214	1,214
Title II & III		434	434
Development loan	280	142	422
Total	801	3,624	4,425

Source: AID Report: "AID Dollar Financial Expenditures for Korea Program,
through December 31, 1974," Washington, D.C.

Both these patterns changed in the 1965–1974 period. Loans
became the dominant form of assistance, and the U.S. share of
total assistance declined below 50 percent after 1970. (Table
38).

U.S. assistance to Korea has consisted of commodities and
technical assistance directed towards carrying out specific
projects (referred to as project aid) and financing specific
categories of imports (known as program aid). Program aid has
accounted for over 80 percent of the total, and nearly half of
the program aid has consisted of surplus agricultural commodities provided either under Public Law 480 or with $92
million of development loans that were used to purchase agricultural commodities in recent years. Other major components

TABLE 40 Distribution of U.S. Project Aid by Sectors, July 1953–December 1974
(million U.S. dollars)

	Grant Aid	Development Loans	Total Amount	Total %
Agriculture	36	0	36	4
Mining	14	9	23	3
Manufacturing	84	123	207	26
Electric power	66	87	153	19
Telecommunications	14	11	25	3
Transportation	186	40	226	28
Health and sanitation	25	7	32	4
Education	21	4	25	3
Social welfare	22		22	3
Other	53		53	7
	521	281	802	100

Source: Same as preceding table.
Note: Totals differ from preceding table due to rounding.

191

of program aid, especially through the mid-1960s, were fertilizer and petroleum products. Both these items were dropped out of the commodity aid program when Korean production and refinery capacity was built in the 1960s.

U.S. project aid was concentrated heavily in the areas of transportation, manufacturing, and electric power. Agriculture, education, health, and other social services received relatively minor allocations, generally amounting in each case to less than 5 percent of the total project assistance.

These statistics give a picture of the overall dimensions of aid to Korea, but give little indication of how that aid affected the pattern of development, or the influence it had on policies and politics. These matters are discussed in the following section.

AID PROGRAMS AND POLICIES IN THE HIGH-AID DECADE, 1953–1962

With the end of the Korean War, both the Korean and the U.S. governments shifted their attention to the problems of reconstruction and development of the Korean economy but, as already noted, there were some fundamental disagreements between the two governments over the appropriate approach. The Korean government of Syngman Rhee wanted to build a modern economy similar to, but independent of, the Japanese economy. Their desire was for new factories and heavy industry financed through foreign aid having little regard for the inflationary impact of the heavy investment programs or the longer-run issues of comparative advantage. The United States, on the other hand, was concerned about moving the South Korean economy towards self-sufficiency as rapidly as possible while holding down the aid requirement and minimizing instability and inflation in the process. Thus, there was clear disagreement over the issue of resource mobilization, with the Korean government wishing to rely mainly on external resources, or if necessary on inflation as a means of mobilizing domestic resources, and the American government urging greater Korean efforts at domestic resource mobilization through increased taxes and private saving. There was also disagreement as to the allocation of resources between heavy investment in factories and infrastructure, as desired by Korea, or less capital-intensive investment in the rehabilitation of light industry and infrastructure and fuller utilization of existing capacity as advocated by the Americans.

The Nathan report had suggested that South Korea could become self-sufficient in five years by a combination of rice, mineral, and textile exports to finance the imported intermediate and capital goods required by light, import-substituting industries. An aid input of $1.25 billion was proposed as necessary to achieve these objectives and bring the economy to both internal and external equilibrium. [30]

The Tasca report had recommended a bilateral aid structure that was supposed to give the United States effective bargaining power and improve the aid relationship. A new U.S. aid representative, C. Tyler Wood, was appointed in 1953 and charged with coordinating the various U.S. and U.N. assistance efforts. But his main problems were in trying to achieve coordination and agreement with the Korean government.

There are a number of accounts of the wrangling that went on between the U.S. and Korean governments over the aid program at this time. [31] Despite the disagreements on both objectives and approach, the aid continued to flow, its content largely dictated from the American side, while its ultimate uses and beneficiaries were strongly influenced by the framework of Korean economic policies. The United States undertook, in fiscal years 1954 and 1955, to support fifty-one new industrial projects which were mostly small-scale enterprises focused largely on import substitution. These projects moved very slowly, many taking five to six years to complete and some requiring protection or subsidy to survive. [32] Although the aid level more than doubled between 1954 and 1956, two-thirds of it was program or commodity aid which, from the Korean point of view, did little to promote long-term development.

The Korean government, through its budgetary actions and the allocation of bank credit and import licenses, determined the ultimate recipients of those aid resources. On the budgetary side, the counterpart funds derived from the sale of aid imports were a major source of budget revenue (as discussed in Chapter 9) which in the mid-1950s was going heavily into expansion of social services, especially education. The commodity imports were allocated by the import licensing system to various importers and producers. The overvalued exchange rate made import licenses a very valuable commodity and their distribution was a major concern of the government.

American efforts to force through a devaluation of the Korean currency were stoutly resisted by the Korean government. It was the American position that devaluation would restrain import demand, reduce the windfall profits and corruption associated with the import licensing system, encourage exports, generate more counterpart funds from a given volume of aid imports, and possibly permit some reduction in aid imports. The Korean government saw all these as disadvantages and particularly wished to keep the cost of imported capital and intermediate goods low as inducement to investment and production. The two devaluations that did occur in December 1953 and again in August 1955, as a result of great U.S. pressure, did not go far enough to compensate for the prior inflation and loss of purchasing power of the currency, so that excess demand for foreign exchange continued.[33]

Despite an inflow of foreign aid to Korea of over $1.25 billion from 1953 to 1957, which was the magnitude proposed by the Nathan report as necessary to achieve self-sufficiency, little progress was made in that direction. Aid imports in 1957 were still equal to 85 percent of total imports and nearly 100 percent of fixed investment. Inflation was averaging over 30 percent per annum, and the growth rate of GNP was less than 5 percent, which was relatively poor in comparison with North

Korea, or with other countries recovering from a war that had received similar levels of external assistance.

Largely as a result of this poor performance and growing American discontent with Syngman Rhee's intransigence, the U.S. government decided to start reducing its aid levels and to curtail new investment projects. Beginning in 1957, the United States forced the Korean government to agree to a series of annual stabilization programs as a condition for continued aid, so the Korean government had little choice but to go along. Starting with the setting of macroeconomic ceilings on fiscal deficits and monetary expansion, the stabilization programs over time became increasingly complex and detailed, thus providing the U.S. government with a mechanism for greater involvement in the allocative decisions.[34]

At the same time, the United States was cutting back on new aid projects and pressing for implementation of those initiated in prior years. Project aid disbursements dropped from an annual average rate of $88 million in 1954–1957 to only $38 million in 1958–1960. Program aid increased by nearly an equal amount so the total aid level did not change much, but there was a shift from investment projects to current inputs that was consistent with the U.S. stabilization objective while contrary to Korean desires for investment and growth.

The stabilization programs proved successful in slowing the inflation, but the positive repercussions on private investment and development that were predicted by U.S. officials never materialized. Fixed investment remained at slightly over 10 percent of GNP, while aid-financed imports dropped to 80 percent of fixed investment. The growth rate fell sharply and steadily from 1957 to 1960 for many reasons, and disillusionment with the stabilization policies increased. By the early 1960s U.S. officials had become extremely gloomy about the prospects of Korean development.[35]

A major impediment to development at this time was the growing inefficiency of the import-substitution strategy. First-stage import substitution had been largely accomplished, and many of the new producers were dependent on both cheap imported materials and on quotas or prohibition of competitive imports to maintain their profitability. New investment was directed more to obtaining a larger portion of the imported raw materials than to satisfying domestic demand which was not growing very rapidly. The level and composition of aid-financed imports of raw materials largely determined the level and structure of industrial production, and both U.S. and Korean officials were heavily and jointly involved in their allocation.

The interim government of 1960–1961 started dismantling this system by undertaking a major devaluation in early 1961. The Park Government continued the process after assuming power in May 1961. U.S. authorities were initially enthusiastic about the new spirit and policies of the Park Government. Their programs to reduce import restrictions, maintain a realistic exchange rate, and encourage exports were responsive to previously expressed U.S. concerns. Also, the new emphasis on planning and expansion of investment, and more open cooperation with the foreign aid officials, was viewed favorably. But this spirit of harmony soon deteriorated into one of discord and confrontation, as the military regime scrapped the stabilization program in 1961 and went on a binge of spending and lending that precipitated a return of inflation after mid-1962 and was aggravated by poor harvests in 1962 and 1963.

The years 1963–1964 witnessed some of the harshest bargaining over aid between the United States and Korean officials of the whole post-war period. Faced with severe food shortages, rising prices, and dwindling foreign-exchange reserves, the Koreans were in a very vulnerable position. The U.S. officials sought to take full advantage of this to press for major economic changes and also to see that the military leaders stuck to their commitment to restore an elected regime in 1963. The United States insisted upon resumption of the stabilization program in 1963, calling for curtailing the budget deficit and limiting growth of the money supply to 5 percent. The following year similar restrictions plus a 50 percent devaluation were imposed as conditions for continued aid.[36] While the Korean government acquiesced to these demands in order to assure an adequate grain supply for the coming months, they also began a realignment of policies and international relationships that would save them from ever being trapped in such a compromising position again.

RESTRUCTURING AND REDUCING THE AID RELATIONSHIP

By the end of 1965, Korea had reached a settlement with Japan that called for sizable financial flows from Japan over the next decade.[37] Korea also was negotiating a standby agreement with the International Monetary Fund (IMF) that could provide an alternative source of financing in times of need. Next, the Koreans prevailed upon the World Bank to organize an international consultative group of donor countries that would provide assistance to Korea. Finally, Korean access to the world capital markets in the latter half of the 1960s plus the explosive growth of Korean exports greatly reduced the dependence on foreign aid and provided multiple channels for financing Korean imports.

A turning point in U.S.-Korean aid relations occurred in 1965 in connection with a state visit by President Park to Washington.[38] Prior to this trip, there was a debate within the Korean government (reminiscent of the debates a decade before between the U.S. and Korean governments) as to whether to press for an indefinite continuation of supporting assistance grant aid or to accept a proposed U.S. commitment of $150 million in development loans. The supporting assistance financing of current imports was of interest primarily to the military leaders, who viewed it as an important source of counterpart funds to support their budget. Development loans, on the other hand, would be used mainly to import capital goods and carry out major development projects that were of primary concern to the Economic Planning Board. The decision of the Korean government to give up the budgetary support and take the development financing was made in large part because the Koreans interpreted the U.S. proposal as recognition of Korea's recent economic progress and development potential that had often been doubted in the past by both Koreans and Americans. It also reflected a shift from a mendicant mentality to greater self-reliance on the part of the Koreans.

U.S. economic assistance continued at a level of about $200 million a year throughout the period 1963–1975, though its composition changed markedly. As Table 41 indicates, non-project grants declined steadily and were discontinued in 1972. Project grants were at a low level throughout and amounted to less than $1 million in 1975. The principal sources of U.S. aid were development loans on concessional terms after 1965 and PL 480 sales and loans, again on concessional terms. In Korean calculations none of the loans, though concessional, were counted as aid.

Although U.S. aid totals were much smaller in the 1960s and 1970s than in the 1950s, their contribution to development per dollar of aid benefited from the more sensible economic policies followed by the Korean government. At least this might be said of the capital investments financed by development loans and project assistance. On the other hand, the easy availability of PL 480 grain supplies after the crisis of 1963–1964 had the effect of reducing farm incentives by holding down grain prices until the late 1960s when government policy was drastically changed (see Chapter 7). At the same time, low grain prices in the mid-1960s might well have been a stimulus to the production of non-grain crops, such as fruits, vegetables, and livestock, for which demand had been expanding rapidly with rising urban incomes.

The willingness to shift from grant to loan aid and, more important, to seek large amounts of foreign private commercial loans was strongly influenced by Korea's minimal foreign debt which, in turn, was due to the fact that previous foreign assistance had been almost totally in grant form. Prior to 1960,

TABLE 41 Total U.S. Aid Received by Source, 1963–1975 (millions of dollars)

	1963	1964	1965	1966	1967	1968	1969	1970	1971	1972	1973	1974	1975
Non-project supporting assistance	102.7	72.8	79.2	54.8	59.8	43.7	16.7	14.2	9.4	0.6	–	–	–
Project assistance (grants)	13.0	5.5	4.3	5.2	5.6	9.9	7.5	6.4	5.1	3.4	3.3	2.1	0.9
PL 480 sales	62.7	94.7	54.4	35.0	58.0	58.5	64.9	54.7	30.8	3.7	–	–	–
PL 480 Titles II and III	21.8	27.6	28.5	28.5	31.6	47.3	118.5	67.8	84.9	197.0	61.0	–	84.0
Development loans	20.0	4.5	2.6	49.7	74.8	38.0	31.9	38.8	55.7	36.8	27.7	44.1	192.2
	252.3	164.8	176.9	173.2	229.8	197.5	239.7	181.8	185.9	241.4	92.1	46.2	277.0

Source: USAID/Korea. Data provided by Aid Mission in Seoul.

Note: These data are on a calendar year basis. They differ from data presented in certain other tables because of differences in timing and valuations. The USAID payroll is included in this table.

the Korean government had undertaken no borrowing abroad, except for a small amount from the Development Loan Fund, and there had been no foreign direct investment in Korea. But, in January 1960, a Foreign Capital Inducement Law was enacted and amended in 1962 and 1966 to make it more attractive for investors and lenders. The first foreign direct-investment project approved by the Korean government was a joint U.S.-Korean venture producing nylon filament, established in 1962. From then until the end of 1976, the Economic Planning Board estimated a total of direct foreign investment of about $950 million. From 1962 to 1968, foreign investments were predominantly American, directed toward import-replacing activities. Since then, they have been predominantly Japanese, concerned mainly with production for export. Over the whole period, Japan and the United States accounted for 82 percent of total foreign direct investment. Of the 734 firms in which foreigners had an interest, as of the end of 1974, 684 (or 93 percent) were joint ventures. [39]

Modern industrial technology in South Korea is almost entirely a foreign import. It has been acquired in connection with foreign direct investment and also through technological licensing agreements entered into by Korean firms. By the end of 1975, some 580 agreements had been negotiated—397 with Japanese firms and 122 with American firms. [40] U.S. aid has made a considerable contribution to this transfer of technology through project financing, development loans, and the provision of large numbers of technical experts. Foreign direct investment grew slowly and reached substantial numbers only beginning in 1972. Borrowing from abroad was already sizable by 1965 and grew rapidly thereafter. It was a major source of investment financing as discussed in Chapter 9 (see Table 42).

U.S. technical assistance in the mid-1960s shifted away from massive involvement in the micro-allocative decisions of the Korean government to broader concerns for research, economic planning and policy, and assistance with the export program. Aid-generated local currency funds were used, beginning in 1964,

TABLE 42 Net Borrowing, Direct Investment, Debt Service,
And Export Earnings, 1965–1975
($ millions)

	Net Borrowing	Direct Investment	Total (1) + (2)	Debt Service	Exports	Debt Service Ratio	Capital Flows/ Exports
	(1)	(2)	(3)	(4)	(5)	(4)/(5)	(3)/(5)
1965	101.2	20.1	121.3	9.9	175.1	.057	.69
1966	218.2	2.2	220.4	15.6	250.3	.062	.88
1967	419.8	19.9	439.7	35.8	320.2	.112	1.37
1968	533.2	24.2	557.4	83.6	455.4	.184	1.22
1969	499.2	28.2	527.4	137.7	622.5	.221	.85
1970	420.0	61.4	481.4	261.9	835.2	.314	.58
1971	395.3	45.2	440.5	327.1	1067.6	.306	.41
1972	444.4	110.4	554.8	414.3	1624.1	.255	.34
1973	719.1	264.7	983.8	505.3	3225.0	.157	.31
1974	1170.6	139.9	1310.5	608.2	4460.4	.136	.29
1975	555.0	n.a.	n.a.	647.5	5081.0	.127	n.a.

Sources: Columns (1) and (4) from BOK, *Economic Statistics Yearbook* and Direct Investment from Wontack Hong, "Trade, Distortions, and Employment Growth," Table 4.15. Anne O. Krueger, *The Developmental Role of the Foreign Sector and Aid,* Table 41.

Note: Direct investment is recorded on a commitment basis. For the first ten months of 1975, direct investment approvals were $179 million. See Suk Tai Suh, "Statistical Report on Foreign Assistance and Loans to Korea," KDI Monograph 7602, (Mimeo, 1976), p. 71.

to support a series of economic and social studies of problem areas in the Korean economy, such as the financial system, grain marketing, and land tenure conditions. These studies were carried out by Korean academicians, many of whom had recently returned from foreign study and were interested in contributing to the analysis and solution of Korea's difficulties. While thousands of Koreans had gone abroad to study under both government and private auspices, especially after the Korean War, many had stayed overseas, and those who returned often felt that their training was underutilized. This aid-sponsored research gave many of them a first opportunity to do something other than writing articles critical of government policies in the local newspapers. It helped to open up a dialogue between the government and academics that was positive and mutually beneficial during the latter half of the 1960s.

Preparation of Korea's Second Five-Year Plan in 1965 and 1966 was supported by the USAID Mission and a number of American economists and technicians.[41] A second Nathan team and staff members from the AID Mission participated in joint working groups with Korean officials that formulated the basic guidelines for the plan as well as the detailed projects and policies. This undertaking represented a high point of mutual agreement on development strategy and the appropriate role of aid between the Korean and American governments. While the World Bank expressed some apprehension at overambitious plan targets, and the IMF worried about the inflationary potential, the U.S. government endorsed the basic dimensions of the plan that subsequently was substantially overachieved. In later meetings of the aid-donors group organized under World Bank auspices, there was general support for the plan and the development policies then being pursued by the Korean government.

Aid loans from the U.S. and Japan in the latter part of the 1960s helped to finance three new fertilizer plants and to expand power-generating and transportation facilities and other infrastructure. Commercial loans and suppliers' credits, mainly from the same two countries, contributed to the rapid expansion of the export manufacturing industries and soon became more significant than the aid funds.

The final innovative area for U.S. foreign assistance activity involved support for the creation of the Korea Institute of Science and Technology (KIST) in 1966, and the Korea Development Institute (KDI) in 1971. The former institution was intended to help Korean industry with the adoption and adaptation of modern technology. The latter was to assist the Korean government with research and analysis of critical economic policy and planning problems. Both institutions attracted many Korean scholars home from abroad and have achieved recognition, both within and outside Korea, for the quality of their work.

By the 1970s, foreign assistance was a relatively minor factor in Korea's external relations. Export earnings and foreign private capital were the major elements. U.S. assistance was increasingly concentrated in the surplus agricultural commodities. The World Bank and the Asian Development Bank became more active in financing infrastructure projects. But in the dynamic environment of 10 percent growth rates, the long delays generally experienced in approving and implementing foreign assistance projects often proved more of a drag than a help to Korea's development. The Korean government maintained cordial relationships with the international financial institutions but did not count on them for substantial financing even at the time of the oil crisis in 1973–1974, which they met initially mainly through private foreign borrowings and subsequently through exports of construction activity to the oil-exporting countries.

CONCLUSION

The massive inflow of foreign assistance before and during the Korean War was essential to the survival of South Korea as an independent country. Continuation of a high level of economic assistance for the decade after the war probably spelled the difference between some (1.5 percent per annum) and no growth in per capita income. Without this growth, the economic condition of the population would have remained desperate, political cohesion would have deteriorated, and the foundations for subsequent high growth would not have been forged. Thus, aid played a critical role for the two decades from the mid-1940s to the mid-1960s. Since then, it has added perhaps 1 percent to the already high growth rate and therefore can be characterized as relatively inconsequential. The fact that the earlier aid had been on a grant, rather than loan, basis made it possible to rely on large amounts of foreign commercial loans rather than aid in the latter half of the 1960s.

Attempts to use aid to bring about significant social and political change have not been very successful. Land reform was initiated by the U.S. Military Government, and although it did not involve a significant transfer into Korea of real resources from abroad, it was effectively supported through American technical assistance. Attempts at reform of the education system and of the banking system (described in Chapter 9) to make them more democratic and free of centralized control were tried, but largely failed. Notions prevalent in the mid-1960s, that rapid growth would be conducive to the maintenance of a more open democratic society, also proved unrealistic. As aid has become relatively less important to Korean development, the aid donors have lost their influence over political developments within Korea. There were substantial transfers of technology that have been put to good use, and a high proportion of the senior personnel in the government, business, and the academic spheres have been exposed to foreign training, mainly in the United States, under either the economic or military assistance programs. It is difficult to assess the impact this training has had on their performance and outlook.

Some specific types of aid-financed commodities had positive effects, such as the contribution of fertilizer to farm production and income and the stimulus to production and investment of the imports of industrial raw materials. Other types of aid were more questionable, for example, the adverse effects on farm incomes of high imports and low prices of grain and the inefficiency of the many small-scale import-substitute industrial projects financed by U.S. aid in the 1950s.

The high levels of aid and foreign capital inflow into Korea over the past three decades have, as will be discussed in Chapter 9, apparently acted as a depressant on the capability for mobilizing domestic savings and government revenues. It simply has not been necessary to push domestic savings rates to high levels to achieve high rates of growth; and Korea has managed in recent years to see that foreign savings were efficiently utilized. Attempts by the aid donors—principally the United States, in the 1950s and early 1960s—to force the Korean government to give greater emphasis to stability, either instead of growth, or as a necessary condition for growth, were ineffectual and probably misguided in that they diverted attention from the real impediments to growth, and delayed Korean assumption of responsibility for guidance of the economy.

TABLE 43 Aid-Financed Imports Relative to Total Imports
($ U.S. million and % of total imports)

		Aid-Financed Imports							
		Total				U.S. Share			
		Grant[a]		Loan[c]		Grant[b]		Loan	
	Total Imports	Amt.	%	Amt.	%	Amt.	%	Amt.	%
1953	345	201	58			171	50		
1954	243	149	61			132	54		
1955	341	233	68			215	63		
1956	386	320	83			304	79		
1957	442	374	85			369	83		
1958	378	311	82			314	83		
1959	304	211	69			220	72		
1960	343	232	68			245	71		
1961	316	197	62			199	63		
1962	422	219	52			232	55		
1963	560	233	42			216	39		
1964	404	143	35	25	6	149	37	25	6
1965	463	136	29	2	0	131	28	2	0
1966	716	148	21	50	7	103	14	47	7
1967	996	152	15	80	8	97	10	38	4
1968	1,463	168	12	90	6	106	7	70	5
1969	1,824	155	9	169	9	107	6	71	4
1970	1,984	187	9	101	5	82	4	51	3
1971	2,394	126	5	193	8	51	2	34	1
1972	2,522	66	3	342	14	5	0	194	8
1973	4,240	23	1	224	5	2	0	123	3
1974	6,851	30	0	186	3	1	0	20	0
1975	7,274	37		348	5				

Source: Suk Tai Suh, *Import Substitution and Economic Development in Korea,* (Korea Development Institute, December 1975), pp. 221–222. U.S. grant aid is from BOK, *Economic Statistics Yearbook.*

Notes: [a]Total grant aid includes Japanese grant funds from 1965 on.
[b]U.S. grant aid includes technical assistance costs in addition to commodity imports.
[c]Loan aid includes loans from international organizations and public bilateral loans.

TABLE 44 Relationships of Foreign Savings, Foreign Aid, Imports, and Fixed Capital Formation to GNP

	Fixed Capital Formation	Percent of GNP			Percent of Fixed Capital Formation	
		Imports	Foreign Saving[a]	Aid Imports[b]	Foreign Saving	Aid Imports
1953	7.2	9.7	7.7	5.7	107	79
1954	9.1	7.3	6.2	4.4	68	48
1955	10.1	9.8	8.2	6.7	82	66
1956	10.3	13.1	11.7	10.9	113	106
1957	10.6	12.0	10.5	10.2	99	96
1958	10.1	10.7	8.7	8.8	86	87
1959	10.9	10.1	7.5	7.0	69	64
1960	10.8	12.6	9.3	8.6	86	80
1961	11.6	14.8	9.5	9.0	82	78
1962	13.9	16.9	11.7	9.5	84	68
Average 1953–1962	10.5	11.7	9.1	8.1	88	77
1963	13.9	16.3	11.4	6.8	82	49
1964	11.6	13.8	7.8	6.2	67	53
1965	14.8	15.9	7.4	5.3	50	36
Average 1963–1965	13.4	15.3	8.9	6.1	66	46

207

TABLE 44 (continued)

	Percent of GNP				Percent of Fixed Capital Formation	
	Fixed Capital Formation	Imports	Foreign Saving[a]	Aid Imports[b]	Foreign Saving	Aid Imports
1966	20.2	20.1	9.8	6.6	49	33
1967	21.5	22.0	10.6	6.2	49	29
1968	25.8	26.1	13.0	5.4	50	21
1969	26.6	26.0	12.2	5.4	46	20
1970	25.1	24.8	10.1	3.8	40	15
1971	23.2	27.5	11.2	3.8	48	16
1972	20.2	26.3	5.2	4.5	26	22
1973	23.9	35.5	3.3	1.8	14	8
1974	26.0	43.2	12.6	1.3	48	5
1975	25.7	39.8	9.5	1.8	37	7
Average 1966–1975	23.8	29.1	9.8	4.1	41	18

Source: BOK, *Economic Statistics Yearbook,* and *National Income of Korea, 1975.* Aid imports are derived from Table 43.

Notes: [a]Foreign saving is the current account deficit of the balance of payments.
[b]Imports include goods and services measured at current prices.

SEVEN

Rural Development

As the previous chapter made clear, Korean development was led by industry and the export of industrial products. But until the 1970s, a majority of the Korean people lived in the countryside. Income distribution is dealt with in a later chapter, but clearly Korea's rapid growth could not have benefited large numbers of the Korean people unless it somehow managed to raise the productivity and income of farmers.

In many models of economic development, it is assumed that a revolution in agricultural productivity must precede entry into a period of industrial and overall economic development. In these models, agriculture is not simply the sector that sustains those left behind in the rush to modernization but is an essential source of food, capital, and labor for the modern sector. Because agriculture in a traditional economy is by far the largest sector, it is argued, it is not only a source of capital and labor for industry, it is the main source. Furthermore, farmers are the major source of demand for industry's output as well as the suppliers of industry's key inputs. In the current conventional wisdom of the 1970s, therefore, it is often assumed that economic development must begin with or at least encompass an all-out attack on the sources of rural poverty before there is much hope for progress elsewhere.

Korea's rural development experience provides little support for this new conventional wisdom. The Korean countryside is in the process of being transformed, and rural living standards have risen substantially, but this rural transformation has followed and been caused by industrial and urban developments rather than the reverse. In fact it would not be much of an exaggeration to say that a major lesson of Korea's rural development experience is that, if the growth rate of GNP is rapid enough over a ten-to-fifteen-year period, all sectors including agriculture will be dragged ahead whether or not a conscious government effort is made to promote rural development. When increases in average per capita national product are only one percent a year, it may take a long time before growth that is concentrated in a few urban centers spills over into the countryside. But at 7 or 8 percent per annum, the spillover occurs at a much earlier stage—at least in Korea's experience.

The one notable exception to this picture of rural progress following, rather than preceding, overall development is the land reform experience of the late 1940s and early 1950s. As will be pointed out later in this chapter and in subsequent chapters, successful land reform made it possible for Korean farmers to start from a basis of less inequality than that found in the rural sectors of many other developing nations. A lower level of rural inequality in turn had a substantial influence on much else that occurred in the Korean agricultural sector. The pace with which new techniques spread from one farm or region to another, to take only one important example, was undoubtedly accelerated by the absence of extreme inequality.

Data on growth rates in Korean agriculture and the sector's

share in GNP are presented in Tables 45 and 46. From these data
it is readily apparent that the agricultural growth rate, while
respectable in international comparative terms, was far below
the growth rate achieved by other sectors. The share of agriculture in GNP and the share of the farm population in the nation's
total, as a result, fell precipitously. By 1975 both shares were
well below what one would expect given the still relatively low
level of per capita GNP then prevailing in Korea ($374 in 1975
in 1970 prices).

TABLE 45 Agriculture's Share in GNP and Population,
            1955–1975

	Share of Agriculture and Forestry in GNP in Constant 1970 Prices (%)	Farm Population (millions)	Share of Farm Population in Total Population (%)
1955	45.5	13.30	61.9
1960	39.9	14.56	58.3
1965	37.6	15.81	55.8
1970	26.2	14.42	45.9
1975	19.2	13.24	38.2

Sources: BOK, *National Income in Korea, 1975*, pp. 144–147; and BOK, *Economic Statistics Yearbook, 1976.*

The limited contribution of agriculture to the overall growth
performance can be seen in other ways as well. Taxes on the rural
sector were very light, amounting to no more than 2 or 3 percent
of farm household income, and rural savings, for the most part,
stayed in the rural areas. In fact it was not until the 1970s that
there was any net cash flow out of rural areas. The main
contributions of agriculture to the urban sector, therefore, were
people and food. If the rural areas in 1975 had held on to the
same share of the population that they held in 1955, there would
have been 8 million fewer people in the cities.

The best evidence that agriculture not only lagged behind the
other sectors but was actually pulled along by those sectors is

TABLE 46 Growth Rates of GNP and of Agriculture
(%)

| | | Growth Rates Per Year | |
Period	GNP	Agricultural Production	Agricultural Value Added
1946–1952	–	0.83	0.70
1952–1954	–	10.87	10.48
1954–1965	6.2	3.99	3.80
1965–1973	11.0	2.79	1.51
1973–1975	8.0	5.60	5.33

Sources: Sung Hwan Ban, Pal Yong Moon, and Dwight H. Perkins, *Rural Development,* Studies in the Modernization of the Republic of Korea: 1945–1975 (Cambridge, Mass., 1980), p. 38.
Ministry of Agriculture and Fisheries, *Yearbook of Agriculture and Forestry Statistics 1976,* Seoul, pp. 392–393.

provided by data on the changing composition of farm output. In the two decades after 1955 total non-farm demand for food rose by 160 percent, accounting for roughly three-quarters of the total increase in demand for food in this period.[1] If Korean farmers had supplied the entire increase in demand, the composition of agricultural output would have been similar to what it was when most farm production was consumed by the farmers themselves. But Korean farmers were able to supply only a portion of this increase, with the remainder coming from abroad. As a result, Korean farmers were in a position to specialize on those crops on which they received the highest return.

Although surprising to some, there is no difficulty explaining how Korea, a major rice exporter in the 1930s, became a steadily increasing importer of grain in the 1960s and 1970s (see Table 47). As pointed out in Chapter 3, most of the rice exported to Japan in the pre-1945 period came from the surpluses of landlords, and those surpluses were wiped out by the land reform. With rising urban demand in the 1960s, farmers had a choice between attempting to accelerate the rise in the yields of grain crops or to shift more of their energies and other

TABLE 47 Imports and Exports of Grain
(1,000 metric tons)

	Exports	Imports
1915–1919	268	41
1925–1929	840	294
1930–1934	1,105	204
1956–1960	–	517
1961–1965	–	731
1966–1970	–	1,394
1971–1975	–	2,629

Sources: For 1915–1934 the data are from Wontack Hong, *Trade and Subsidy Policy and Employment Growth in Korea* (mimeographed, Korea Development Institute, 1976). The 1956–1975 data are from the statistical yearbooks of the BOK.

inputs to cash crops and livestock. Since the return on vegetables, fruit, and livestock was significantly higher than on grain, particularly in the 1950s and 1960s when PL 480 imports were used to hold down grain prices, most of the agricultural growth in this period was accounted for by non-grain crops.[2] Export demand for such commodities as silk further reinforced this trend away from grain. By the 1970s, cash crops and livestock had increased their share of an increased total value of agricultural product (in current prices) from 22.95 percent in the early 1960s to 40.08 percent (see Table 48). Even high grain prices and the introduction of new varieties of rice in the 1970s could not reverse this trend, although they probably did slow it down.

THE SOURCES OF AGRICULTURAL GROWTH

In a basic sense, therefore, it was rising urban and export demand that "caused" a large part of the increase in farm output. Initially this rising demand had its major impact on farmers living near major cities, but in the late 1960s and 1970s

Rural Development

TABLE 48 The Composition of Agricultural Product,
1955–1974

(%)

	1955–1957	1962–1964	1969–1971	1972–1974
Grain (including potatoes and pulses)	71.30	77.05	61.81	59.92
Cash crops	16.25	12.91	21.72	22.56
—vegetables	9.39	7.21	13.80	9.69
—fruit	1.84	1.83	2.98	3.32
Livestock	11.77	9.52	14.94	15.05
Cocoons	0.57	0.36	1.42	2.47
Total	100.00	100.00	100.00	100.00

Source: Ban, Moon, and Perkins, p. 50.

Note: The data in this table were derived from figures in current, not constant, prices.

Korea's road network was expanded dramatically (see Figures 1–4) bringing most of the nation's rural areas within economical reach of the cities.

If the rising demand was in a sense the ultimate reason for the rise in farm output, it was not the direct cause. Farmers respond to rising demand and higher prices, but plants respond to increases in land, water, and nutrients. Formal estimates of an aggregate agricultural production function from time-series data can take one part way toward the goal of identifying which of the various inputs accounted for the bulk of the increase in farm output but only part of the way. Among the various functions estimated in *Rural Development* by Ban, Moon, and Perkins, the one with the most plausible (or least implausible) results was the following:

$$\ln Y = 5.5790 + 0.7697 \ln LP + 0.1059 \ln NA + 0.1165 \ln WFC + 0.0260T - 0.0705D$$

S.E. 4.6724 0.1661   0.1119   0.1561   0.0085   0.0146

T 1.1940 4.6328**   0.9462   0.7465   3.040** 4.8399**

$R^2 = .9903$; $DW = 1.9239$

**Statistically significant at 99 percent level

214

where

> Y = Total agricultural production in 1,000 wŏn at 1970 prices;
>
> LP = Area of cultivated land in 1,000 hectares;
>
> NA = Labor used in agricultural production in 1,000-man equivalent units;
>
> WFC = Fixed capital services plus current inputs in 1,000-wŏn units at 1970 prices;
>
> T = Time trend;
>
> D = Dummy variable for weather (equals 0 in a good, and 1 in a poor, rice crop year).

These estimates were derived from data for the years 1955 through 1974. The high land coefficient presumably reflects the extreme scarcity of land in Korea, while the low and statistically insignificant labor coefficient reflects the opposite side of the same coin—low labor productivity resulting from labor having too little land (and capital) to work with. Other evidence to be presented below, however, indicates that this estimate of the share of labor's contribution in output may be too low. Attempts to separate out fixed and working capital also led to implausible results, notably a coefficient for working capital that was extraordinarily low, when there is ample evidence that working capital, particularly chemical fertilizer, was responsible for much of the increase in agricultural output. Finally, the time trend by itself accounts for much of the rise in output. This result could indicate that farm output benefited from large disembodied increases in the productivity of the various inputs, but a more likely explanation is that this time trend is picking up lagged responses of output to included inputs and the like. This theme will be pursued at greater length below.

Further attempts to formally estimate a production function for Korean agriculture are clearly called for. Estimation, however, must go beyond the aggregate time-series data that were the basis for these estimates and make use of the great

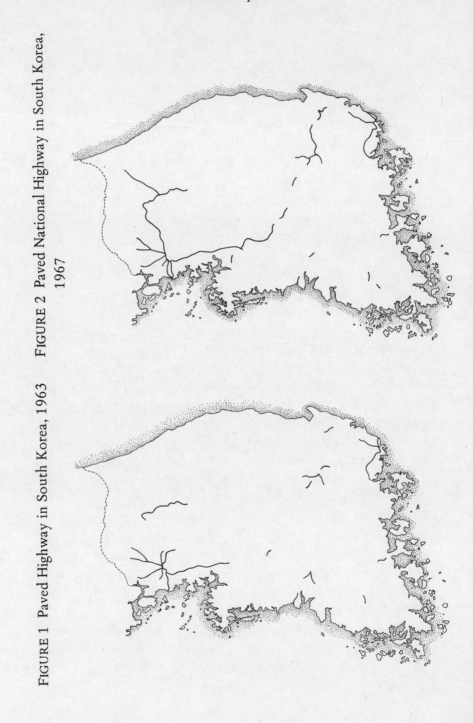

FIGURE 1 Paved Highway in South Korea, 1963　　FIGURE 2 Paved National Highway in South Korea, 1967

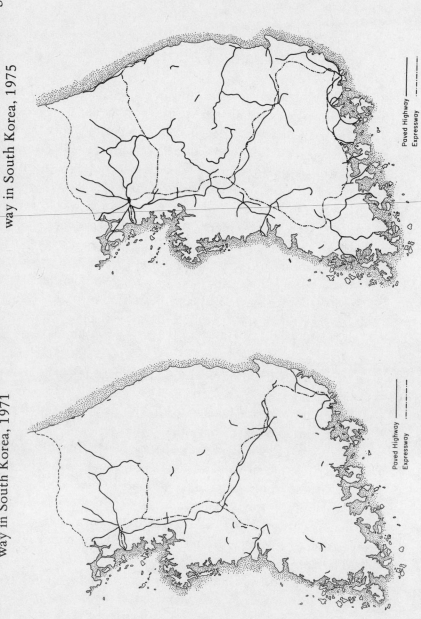

FIGURE 3 Expressways and Paved National High-way in South Korea, 1971

FIGURE 4 Expressways and Paved National High-way in South Korea, 1975

Paved Highway
Expressway

Paved Highway
Expressway

Source: Albert Keidel, "Regional Agricultural Production and Income," in Ban, Moon, and Perkins, pp. 150–153.

amounts of microdata available. Such an effort is beyond the scope of this study.

LAND DEVELOPMENT

Although the coefficient for land in the estimated production function is high, the increase in the area under cultivation in Korea over the past two decades and longer has been so small that increases in arable land account for only a small part of the rise in farm output. Data on the amount of land under cultivation in selected years are presented in Table 49. From these data, it is apparent that only in the early 1960s was there any substantial land development. After 1966, in fact, the amount of land planted to crops first stagnated and then began to fall as more and more land was alienated to industry and urban uses.

Most of the land development occuring in the early 1960s involved the conversion of upland pasture and forest areas into land suitable for crops. The cost of conversion of upland was substantial in terms of labor time, and the productivity of such land was usually well below that of existing arable land. In fact, productivity was usually low enough so that the land could not be rented out, because a prospective tenant could not earn enough on it to both take care of his own needs and pay a significant amount of rent to the owner.[3] Farmers who were already farming all the land they could exploit efficiently, therefore, had little incentive to develop additional land, and it was precisely these richer farmers who owned much of the upland with development potential. For these and other reasons, it is not surprising that much of the land that was developed was brought under cultivation only because of the payment of large subsidies through the use of PL 480 grain. When U.S. aid officials decided to stop subsidizing upland development because of the Korean government's lack of a comprehensive land use plan, upland development slowed almost to a halt.[4]

The major underlying reason why land development was slow,

TABLE 49 Land Under Cultivation

	Cultivated Acreage (1,000 hectares)			
Year	Total	Paddy	Completely Irrigated Paddy	Upland
1955	1,994.8	1,187.4	538.6[a]	807.5
1960	2,024.8	1,206.3	629.1	818.6
1966	2,293.1	1,287.1	730.7	1,006.0
1970	2,316.7	1,283.6	847.8	1,033.1
1975	2,239.7	1,276.6	892.7[b]	963.1

Source: Ban, Moon, and Perkins, p. 81.

Notes: [a]1956
[b]1974

however, was that there was not much land left that could be developed. One estimate in the early 1970s put the total upland area suitable for conversion into cultivated land at only 200,000 hectares.[5] The remaining 6.5 million hectares of "forest" land was on slopes too steep, in areas too remote from roads and people, or retained in forest for conservation purposes. In addition, another 600,000 hectares of tideland could be converted into 410,000 hectares of cropland but at a cost per hectare five times that involved in the conversion of upland. As these figures make clear, Korea is a land-short nation par excellence and, as will become apparent, this factor endowment has shaped fundamentally the kind of agricultural development strategies available to Korean planners and farmers.

It should also be clear from this discussion that land development is really a form of fixed capital formation, similar in key respects to fixed capital formation designed to enhance the quality of existing land. The most important form of fixed capital in this latter category is that connected with the expansion of irrigated land and the improvement of irrigation systems already in existence. Table 49 shows there has been a substantial expansion of completely irrigated areas over the past two decades. Increased irrigation, however, has not led to any dramatic conversion of dry land into paddy. Most of the fully irrigated land was previously either partially irrigated or rain-fed paddy.

LABOR

Given Korea's poor land endowment, it follows more or less automatically that labor productivity in Korean agriculture was extremely low prior to the introduction of modern capital inputs. It is unlikely that the marginal product of rural labor ever reached zero, since there is always more weeding or carrying of water to the fields that will have some positive effect on yields. A study, using 1959 data, demonstrates that there was no rural unemployment or underemployment during peak transplanting and harvest seasons (mainly June, July, and October), although there was substantial surplus time available in such months as January and February.[6] Increases in the farm labor force in the 1940s and 1950s, therefore, probably made some contribution to output.

Beginning in the early or mid-1960s, however, not only did the number of people living in rural areas begin to fall, but the number of labor hours spent per worker on the farm also declined. Not only were children spending a longer time in school and going off to the city to find work, but the adults who remained behind also began spending more of their time in off-farm activities. In 1975 as compared to 1963, for example, the average number of workers per farm household had fallen only 10 percent, but the number of labor hours per farm household had fallen by 36 percent.[7] And this fall occurred when the amount of land per household and per worker was rising by 20 percent.

This growing labor shortage began to be felt on both rural and urban labor markets by the mid-1960s. Wages of both factory and farm workers up to that point had shown no discernible upward trend, but in the late 1960s real wages for both groups began to rise markedly more or less in tandem. In effect, by the mid-1960s, Korea had ceased to be a "labor surplus" economy where wages were determined by "tradition" or "subsistence" rather than by the marginal product of work.

The declining rural work force also had a major impact on agricultural technique. Mechanization of some of the most onerous and labor-consuming tasks, notably the milling of grain, had begun in the 1930s and 1940s. But it was not until the 1960s that farmers began to mechanize such peak-season activities as threshing and the movement of water to the fields (see Table 50). Availability of government subsidies undoubtedly accelerated the introduction of machinery, but the growing labor shortage was the underlying driving force. In the 1970s,

TABLE 50 Farm Mechanization, 1951–1975
(number of units)

Year	Grain Processing Machinery	Power Pumps	Power Threshers	Power Tillers
1951	40,111	n.a.	93	0
1955	62,209	7,463[a]	850	0
1960	64,054	6,911	3,886	153
1965	89,516	26,029	18,909	1,111
1970	127,909	54,078	41,038	11,884
1975	109,166	65,993	127,105	87,722

Source: Ban, Moon, and Perkins, p. 75.

Note: [a]1956

farmers were also beginning to buy hand tractors (power tillers) in rapidly increasing numbers. By 1975, even peak-season activities were not fully mechanized, but Korean agriculture had moved a long way in the direction of substituting mechanical for human and animal power. Transplanting and harvesting of rice were the two major remaining labor-intensive activities.

FERTILIZER AND OTHER CURRENT INPUTS

Clearly neither increases in the labor force nor in the amount of land can account for much of the rise in farm output. The number of labor hours spent on the farm in 1975 was smaller than it had been twenty years earlier, and the amount of land under cultivation had risen only 12 percent over the same period, and most of that increase in land was in the form of relatively low yielding upland. Nor is it likely that increases in fixed capital (other than new land) accounted for a large share of the increase in agricultural production. Much of the farm machinery was used to substitute for the declining labor force. Improved and expanded irrigation had a positive impact, but the greatest influence of the new irrigation systems was in ironing out downward fluctuations in yield during periods of drought, not in raising yields in periods when rainfall was both timely and sufficient in quantity.[8] What then accounted for most of the rather considerable rise in farm output between 1955 and 1975?

An important part of the answer was chemical fertilizer. Korea's experience with chemical fertilizer was markedly different from that of other less-developed countries. Thanks to Japanese extension activities, Korean farmers were using over 20 kilograms of plant nutrient per hectare in the 1930s, mostly in the form of ammonium sulphate.[9] When American aid began subsidizing large-scale imports of chemical fertilizer in the late 1940s and 1950s, therefore, Korean farmers already had considerable experience with the proper use of this input. Except for the Korean War years, Korea, thanks to external assistance, was able to maintain sufficient imports to keep fertilizer use at around 100 kilograms of nutrient per hectare, a considerable figure (see Table 51).

Beginning in the 1960s, aid-financed imports began to decline and ended in 1969. The rising level of fertilizer use in this period was supplied partly from Korea's own foreign-exchange earnings but increasingly by the rapidly developing domestic

TABLE 51 Chemical Fertilizer Output and Consumption

Year	Consumption	Imports	Domestic Production	Consumption per Hectare
	(1,000 metric tons of nutrient)			(kg.)
1945	2.34	n.a.	0.75	1.1
1949	200.30	n.a.	–	97.6
1950	15.82	n.a.	–	8.1
1955	183.54	183.40	0.44	92.0
1960	279.42	262.20+	6.15	138.0
1965	393.10	425.00	75.27	174.2
1970	562.90	6.70	589.84	243.0
1975	886.21	240.90	859.72	395.7

Source: Various issues of MAF, *Yearbook of Agriculture and Forestry Statistics.*

chemical fertilizer industry. By 1975, Korea was using amounts of chemical fertilizer per hectare unmatched even in Japan (see Table 52).

TABLE 52 Fertilizer Consumption—International
Comparisons, 1972
(kg. per hectare of arable land)

	N	P	K
Japan	138	135	113
United States	40	24	21
Mexico	19	6	1
India	11	4	2
Korea (1972)	166	76	46
(1975)	215	106	75

Sources: These data were derived from data compiled by the FAO (except for the Korean data) and published in the 1975 and 1976 editions of the MAF *Yearbook of Agriculture and Forestry Statistics.*
Ban, Moon and Perkins, p. 106.

Chemical fertilizer, of course, cannot be applied in isolation from changes in other inputs. There must be plenty of water available, and the plant varieties used must be fertilizer-responsive. Korea had begun introducing high-yielding plant varieties under Japanese tutelage in the colonial period, and a number of new varieties of rice and other crops had also been introduced after 1945. The *t'ongil* and *yusin* rice varieties developed through the International Rice Research Institute in the Philippines and introduced into Korea in the 1970s, therefore, can be seen not so much as a new and sudden departure in technique as a continuation of a steady modernization of Korean agriculture that began long before. Further development of Korean agriculture will require new generations of high-yielding plant varieties beyond those already in existence.

PRODUCTIVITY AND THE "RESIDUAL"

As our formal estimate made clear, a large portion of Korea's increase in farm output cannot readily be accounted for by the increase in inputs. In part, however, this formal result is misleading. As suggested above, the increase in chemical fertilizer must have "accounted for" much of the rise in production, but there are a number of reasons why the formal estimation procedures used here would miss much of its impact. To obtain maximum impact, fertilizer had to be used with improved plant varieties. Thus a given increase in fertilizer use might have a modest effect until the farmer also began to use the new seeds. And when the new varieties were introduced, there was a probable lag of a year or more before farmers knew how to get the most out of these new varieties.

There were also improvements in the distribution of fertilizer. For the most part, chemical fertilizer in Korea has been distributed through a government supply network that in its early stages was riddled with corruption and inefficiency. Much of the supply ended up on the black market but, more important, fertilizer often did not reach the farmer at the time it was needed. By the 1970s the fertilizer distribution system was still far from perfect but, on the whole, farmers received as much fertilizer as they could use, and it came when it was most needed.

Another source of "productivity" increase was the previously mentioned shift from grain to higher-value-per-hectare cash crops. From the point of view of the individual farmer, the marginal return on inputs used on cash crops was higher than when those same inputs were used on grain, provided that the farmer could get those cash crops to market. Since the government built and paid for the roads that gave farmers this access, a major part of the cost of transport did not enter into the rate of return calculations of the individual farmer. Because the cost of improved transport also does not enter into the input side of our formally estimated production function, the impact of this improvement is picked up by the "time trend."

Finally, there are the many advances in farm management and technique that are no less real for being difficult or impossible to quantify. As subsequent discussion will make clear, there have been marked improvements in the government research and extension services following the virtual dismantling of these services in the aftermath of Liberation from Japanese rule. And the managerial qualities of the farmers receiving advice and information from the extension services have also improved. One important reason is that the Korean farmer of the 1970s is far better educated than his counterpart of the 1940s and 1950s. Even in the 1930s, there were very few farm households all of whose members were illiterate—only 9 percent of the total according to one survey.[10] By the 1970s, however, not only had three-quarters of the rural population received a primary school education, but most of the younger farmers had also gone through middle school and some (6 percent of the total rural population above preschool age) had graduated from high school.

FARM PRODUCTIVITY
IN INTERNATIONAL PERSPECTIVE

Another way to look at Korean agricultural productivity is in international comparative perspective. International comparisons of total factor productivity run into price and exchange rate conversion problems, discussion of which would take us too far afield from the main purposes of this study. But partial productivities can also be of interest.

Labor productivity in rural Korea is still low mainly because Korean farmers have fewer capital and land inputs per capita than do farmers in countries where labor productivity is much higher. Land productivity in Korea, in contrast, is very high by international standards in large part for the same reasons—that is, small amounts are used in combination with relatively large amounts of labor and capital. As the data in Table 53 indicate, Korea has one of the lowest arable land endowments of any nation in the world. In fact, if one excludes city states such as Singapore, Korea probably has the smallest amount of land per head of farm population of any nation in the world. Japan is worse off in terms of arable land per capita of total population (column #1) but a much higher percentage of the Japanese population lives in cities.

Given this land-short factor endowment, Korea either had to rely on food imports or achieve very high yields per hectare. As previous discussion has indicated, food imports have risen and can be expected to increase further, but Korean farmers have also achieved very high yields by international standards (see Table 54). Rice yields are nearly as high as those of the heavily subsidized rice farmers of Japan and are triple the yields achieved in South and Southeast Asia. In one sense, these high yields represent a major achievement. In another sense, however, they are a major problem. If Korea is to continue to achieve sustained increases in grain production, yields must continue to rise to what, in world terms, are unprecedented levels. New plant varieties not now in existence must be discovered and introduced,

Productivity in International Perspective

TABLE 53 Arable Land Per Capita—International Comparisons, 1968–1970

Country	(1) Arable Land (1,000 ha)	(2) Total Population (millions)	(3) Agricul- tural Population (millions)	(4) (1)/(2)	(5) (1)/(3)
Korea (Rep. of)	2,311	32.422	17.300	.071	.134
Japan	5,510	103.540	21.329	.053	.258
China (PRC)	105,000	800.000	640.000	.131	.164
India	164,610	550.376	372.605	.299	.442
Thailand	11,415	35.814	27.398	.319	.417
United States	176,440	205.395	8.216	.859	21.475

Sources: FAO, Production Yearbook 1971, except for the estimates for China, which were made by the author. Ban, Moon, and Perkins, p. 17.

TABLE 54 International Comparisons of Paddy Rice Yields

Country	Yield in kg/ha. of Sown Acreage			
	1952–1956	1961–1965	1970	1974
Korea (Republic of)	3,340	4,110	4,550	5,046
Japan	4,340	5,020	5,640	5,838
Taiwan	2,810	3,670	4,160	4,143[a]
India	1,280	1,480	1,700	1,640
Thailand	1,350	1,760	1,970	1,703
Philippines		1,257	1,780	1,614

Source: FAO, Production Yearbook, various years, except for 1975 figure for Taiwan.
Note: [a]1975

and this is an inherently more difficult process than introducing varieties and techniques that are already well known and require less major modification to adapt to a new environment. Furthermore, where other nations can raise grain output by expanding acreage as well as raising yields, Korea must rely almost entirely on yield increases alone. New land development will be sufficient only to offset land alienated to industrial and other urban uses, if that.

Korea, like most of the rest of East Asia, is now paying the price for centuries of population growth on limited amounts of arable land. Most of the rest of the world is more fortunately endowed, although current rates of population growth, if unchecked, will eliminate this advantage in the foreseeable future.

GOVERNMENT PLANNING
AND INVESTMENT

Government action is usually an important part of agricultural development. Farmers make up one of the few truly competitive industries which, by definition, implies that farmers as individuals are unable to control the prices they receive for their product. Because farmers are small operators, particularly in a country such as Korea, they also are unwilling or unable to finance research on new plant varieties or other modern techniques. Nor are farmers in a position to decide whether scarce foreign exchange should be allocated to import chemical fertilizer or machinery for urban factories. These actions and decisions, if they are to be done at all, must be carried out by the government.

Korean government action in the rural sector in the late 1940s and 1950s, except for land reform, was characterized either by neglect or a concern largely confined to recovery from wartime destruction. Furthermore, such positive efforts as were undertaken were more often the result of U.S. aid support than of any large-scale commitment of the Korean government to rural development. Koreans, in fact, had always reacted negatively to the often high-handed methods of the Japanese-built extension service of the colonial period and were perfectly content to allow the whole extension structure to disappear, which it basically did.

The largest commitment of government resources to agriculture in the 1950s was to the importation of large amounts of chemical fertilizer. Three-quarters of these imports were financed with U.S. aid funds, with the remaining quarter being provided out of Korea's foreign exchange earnings from exports.[11] By the latter half of the 1950s, also under U.S. aid impetus, the Korean government began to reconstruct a number of agricultural support institutions ranging from the Agricultural Bank to the Office of Agricultural Extension. There was even the formulation of a five-year production plan designed to run from 1958 through 1962, but this plan became inoperative in the economic confusion surrounding the student uprising of April 1960. Government investment in agriculture was low, amounting to about 2 percent of GNP in the late 1950s, and a high if unknown portion of this figure was financed by the United States.

The changes that occurred in government agricultural policy in the 1960s were not dramatic. As data in Tables 55 and 56 indicate, the level of government investment in agriculture actually declined slightly relative to GNP in the early 1960s, although the government made up for lost ground and more in the late 1960s. In the middle and late 1960s, the burden of chemical fertilizer imports fell increasingly on Korea's own foreign exchange receipts from exports, although U.S. aid played a new and major role in initiating Korea's domestic chemical fertilizer industry in the early 1960s. Another important aid initiative was the backing given to the creation of the Office of Rural Development, a largely independent agency that, in effect, removed control over research and extension from the Ministry of Agriculture and Forestry (MAF). The Seoul-centered MAF, with its urban elitist bureaucratic character, had not only been ineffective but had consistently diverted U.S. aid funds to "informal" purposes. Since its formation, the Office of Rural Development has expanded its activities greatly and is now opening up offices at the sub-county level, but the organization has been plagued throughout by the inability to hold onto well-trained effective workers.[12]

By the early 1970s, two further changes of a fundamental sort had occurred in government policy towards agriculture. On the one hand, the role of U.S. aid in rural development was phased

TABLE 55 Government Expenditures on Agriculture
(Real Index)

Year	GNP (constant 1970 prices) (1963 = 100)	Government Expenditures on Agriculture, Forestry, and Fisheries (constant prices) (1963 = 100)
1957–1959	80.0	96.2
1963	100.0	100.0
1964	108.6	62.4
1965	115.2	94.7
1966	129.4	137.8
1967	139.5	105.0
1968	157.1	199.3
1969	180.7	219.2
1970	194.9	204.6
1971	212.8	179.0
1972	227.6	193.4
1973	265.2	213.3
1974	288.0	324.1
1975	309.2	(budget) 335.3

Source: Data are taken or derived from various statistical handbooks of the BOK and MAF.

Notes: These expenditure data, unlike those in Table 56, exclude government loans. The current price data were converted into constant prices using the price index derived from prices paid by farmers. This index is far from ideal, but an index for agricultural investment goods and the like was not available and prices paid by farmers were the closest approximation.

out. On the other hand, the Korean government, in part spurred by evidence of a decline in rural political support in the 1971 election, began to make a major rural effort on its own. The center of this effort was the New Community Movement (Saemaul Undong) begun in the winter of 1971–1972. At its core this movement is a local self-help effort led, sometimes with excessive zeal, by local officials of the Ministry of Home Affairs. Even in its initial years, there is no doubt that the

TABLE 56 Government Investment and Loans to Agriculture,
1962–1975
(million current wŏn)

Category	Period		
	1962–1966	*1967–1971*	*1972–1975*
Total investment + loans	170,347	769,803	1,462,908
—In Agriculture, forestry, and fisheries	45,185	198,768	340,128
of which			
Improvement of production	14,600	46,003	120,055
Irrigation	10,035	36,976	
Agricultural experiment and extension	1,970	7,402	6,943
Sericulture	1,404	6,160	3,505
Agricultural mechanization	765	8,815	15,026
Forestry	4,633	16,364	34,470
Fisheries	6,555	29,803	18,284

Source: Ministry of Finance, *Summary of Financial Implementation* for FY 1962–1975 as reported in Ban, Moon, and Perkins, Chapter 5.

movement led to the local construction of many new roads, bridges, wells, washing facilities, and toilets. By 1974, however, the government not only raised its own financial commitment to the program (see Table 55), but also put greater emphasis on voluntarism on the part of the rural villagers themselves. There was also a shift in emphasis from improvements in the quality of rural life (for example, the elimination of thatched roofs) to renewed efforts to raise agricultural production.

RURAL CREDIT

Two agricultural support efforts of the government require special comment—the creation of a modern system for providing rural credit and the government's grain purchase policy. Land reform in many ways left rural Korea of the 1950s starved for credit, both short- and long-term.[13] Not only were most landlords, the main source of credit, wiped out by the reform, but even those who had money were unwilling to lend because of the lack of adequate collateral. Farmers could not mortgage their land because tenancy, except in a few severely circumscribed cases, was not allowed.

Finding an adequate substitute for the ubiquitous landlord-moneylender has proved to be a difficult task in all poor countries and Korea was no exception. The government formed an Agricultural Bank in 1956 to replace the wholly inadequate Financial Associations then in existence, and a "new" Agricultural Bank was formed in 1958 to replace the old one. But as data in Table 57 make clear, the funds available through these banks (and all other banks) were woefully inadequate. In U.S. dollar terms, loans provided amounted to well under $100 million per year.

The new Agricultural Cooperatives Law of July 29, 1961 merged the functions of the Agricultural Bank into the National Agricultural Cooperative Federation (NACF) which was cooperative in name only. The NACF is, in fact, an arm of the government. The new law called for loans to be made on such criteria as trust in the recipient rather than on good collateral. At the same time, the government introduced an "anti-usury campaign" but lack of adequate funding, the problem that plagued so many agricultural programs in this period, ensured that this campaign did not succeed. Loans of 23 billion wŏn (U.S. $90 million) in 1964, for example, were not sufficient to provide even the working capital requirements of what was then a 300-billion-wŏn industry (larger if agricultural gross value rather than value added were used).

By the 1970s, funds available to the NACF, only a small portion of which came from farmers' own deposits,[14] had managed to rise considerably faster than had agricultural output (in current prices), so that by 1974 252 billion wŏn (over U.S. $600 million) was lent out to farmers. Still, with interest rates on NACF loans of from 8 to 15 percent, as compared to

TABLE 57 Lending Trends, 1955–1974
(million wŏn)

| | Source of NACF Funds | | | As % of Agricultural Value Added |
	Government Sector (BOK, etc.)	Credit Sector	Total	
1955	—	—	1,639	
1956	—	—	3,577	2.3
1957	—	—	7,286	8.2
1958	—	—	7,871	9.2
1959	—	—	8,216	10.7
1960	—	—	11,536	12.7
1961	8,554	8,134	16,688	14.0
1962	11,193	7,418	18,611	14.6
1963	12,195	7,509	17,704	8.6
1964	12,257	10,882	23,139	7.2
1965	11,899	11,360	23,259	7.5
1966	12,913	14,195	27,108	7.4
1967	16,112	18,265	34,377	8.6
1968	18,840	33,974	52,814	11.6
1969	31,053	53,360	84,413	14.1
1970	34,372	70,988	105,360	14.5
1971	35,420	87,648	123,068	13.5
1972	45,262	102,984	148,245	13.5
1973	47,506	116,894	164,400	12.8
1974	60,867	191,282	252,149	14.7

Source: National Agricultural Cooperative Federation as reported in Ban, Moon, and Perkins, Chapter 6.

50 to 60 percent on loans from private sources, demand for credit greatly exceeded supply. Among the several problems created by this excess demand was the tendency for loans to be made to richer farmers who were better risks and, not incidentally, had more local political clout. A law on guaranteeing credit-worthiness and designed to channel more funds to poorer farmers passed in 1971, but has not yet fundamentally altered this bias in loan allocations.

GRAIN PRICE POLICY

The Korean government has attempted to influence or determine the prices paid to and received by Korean farmers since the 1940s. Sales of chemical fertilizer and many kinds of farm machinery, for example, have been subsidized in various ways in order to stimulate their greater use. Grain prices, notably those for rice and barley, however, have been by far the most important under government control.

During the Korean War, the government was mainly concerned with acquiring enough grain to meet such basic needs as feeding the armed forces. After 1955, the government had available to it large imports of virtually free PL 480 grain from the United States and heavy pressure from the donor to use grain imports to fight the inflation then rampant in the country.[15] For the next decade grain prices were held down, although the margin between the market price and the government purchase price of rice did narrow somewhat in the 1960s (see Table 58).

The poor harvest of 1968, however, led to a marked change in government grain price policy. Not only did the government raise rice and barley purchase prices substantially during the next several years, it did so without a comparable rise in the price at which rice and barley were sold on urban markets (Table 59). The result was a substantial deficit on the grain account that had to be made up out of overdrafts on the central bank, thus contributing substantially to the annual rise in the money supply. Whereas throughout much of the 1960s the government sacrificed a stimulus to agricultural production in order to curb inflation, in the 1970s grain prices were used to improve agriculture's terms of trade (Table 60) in order to raise farm incomes and stimulate production even at the cost of some increase in inflationary pressure. To prevent the urban population from bearing the brunt of the increased cost of grain, the government channeled the inflationary pressure more generally throughout the economy.

TABLE 58 Market Prices and Government Purchase Prices for Rice, 1949–1974

(wŏn per 80 kg. bag)

Year	(1) Government Purchase Price	(2) Market Price	(3) Ratio (1/2)
1949	2.67	13.21	.202
1955	390.56	962.00	.401
1960	1,059.00	1,687.00	.628
1965	3,150.00	3,419.00	.921
1970	7,000.00	7,153.00	.979
1974	15,760.00	17,821.00	.884

Source: Ban, Moon, and Perkins, Table 105, p. 240.

TABLE 59 Government Purchase and Selling Prices for Rice, 1956–1975

(wŏn per 80 kg. bag)

Year	Purchase Price	Selling Price	Price Differences	Handling Costs
1956	1,059	1,216	157	157
1960	1,059	1,216	157	157
1965	3,150	3,350	200	394
1968	4,200	5,200	1,000	496
1970	7,000	6,500	−500	662
1973	11,372	11,264	−108	905
1975	19,500	16,800	−2,700	1,560

Source: Ban, Moon, and Perkins, Table 109, p. 247.

TABLE 60 Terms of Trade for Agricultural Products, 1959–1975

| Year | Index of Prices Received by Farmers | | Index of Prices Paid by Farmers (C) | A/C | B/C |
	All products (A)	Rice (B)			
1959	17.4	18.0	24.8	70.2	72.6
1960	20.9	21.8	26.6	78.6	82.0
1961	24.6	27.1	28.7	85.7	94.4
1962	27.1	28.7	31.8	85.2	90.3
1963	40.1	45.8	35.3	113.6	129.8
1964	50.2	57.0	44.8	112.1	127.2
1965	52.2	55.3	51.8	100.8	106.8
1966	55.4	56.5	58.1	95.4	97.3
1967	63.5	62.2	65.8	96.5	94.5
1968	74.3	73.2	78.8	94.3	92.9
1969	84.8	90.8	86.8	97.7	104.6
1970	100.0	100.0	100.0	100.0	100.0
1971	121.4	125.6	114.4	106.1	109.8
1972	147.9	159.5	130.5	113.3	122.2
1973	164.2	167.7	143.1	114.7	117.2
1974	215.6	242.8	192.5	112.0	126.1
1975	267.6	305.7	237.9	112.5	128.5

Sources: Computed from an NACF 1975 Rural Price Survey.
Ban, Moon, and Perkins, p. 244.

LAND REFORM

Even if the improvement in agriculture's terms of trade in the 1970s had not contributed to a rise in farm output, it would have led to an improvement in rural living standards. Put differently, the rise in agricultural production per farm family has been one source of an improved rural standard of living, but it has not been the only source. Of almost equal importance have been deliberate efforts to redistribute income to farmers.

Land-reform legislation can be found on the books in dozens of countries around the globe, but in only a few has that legislation led to a major redistribution of land. Korea is one of the exceptions. As pointed out in Chapter 3, over 60 percent of the arable land in what is now South Korea was owned by landlords in the 1930s. Some of these landlords were Japanese, and these lost their land more or less automatically with the restoration of Korean independence. Korean landlords, however, also carried the taint of collaboration with the Japanese, at least in the eyes of most of their countrymen, and these landlords, as a result, were not in a politically strong position. The North Korean invasion further weakened this already weak position.[16]

If the political context was favorable to thoroughgoing reform, such questions as how much compensation to pay to landlords for loss of their land remained. The legislation of the U.S. Military Government set payment at 3 times the average annual product of the land, but the new Korean government in 1949 changed the ratio to 1.5 times payable over five years. The landlords were to receive bonds from the government, and the government was to take on the task of collecting the payments from the former tenants. In actual practice, landlord bonds with a face value of 30 sŏk (equals 5.12 U.S. bushels) of rice sold on the market for the equivalent of only 3.5 sŏk, in effect virtually wiping out landlord assets.[17] An average former tenant, on the other hand, might be paying 6 sŏk a year to the government, 30 percent of his harvest. Under such circumstances, both landlords and tenants had a powerful incentive to make a private deal outside of the land-reform legislation. In fact roughly half of the total amount of land transferred from owners to tenants appears to have been handled through private channels.[18]

Whatever the channel, land reform led to a major redistribution of both land and income from landlords to the new owner cultivators. Land redistribution is in the very nature of the reform process, but income redistribution resulted not so much from land reform per se as from the fact that landlord assets were confiscated with only minimal compensation. Along with the redistribution of land and income went a real if unmeasurable increase in farmer independence. Where in 1947, 83.5 percent of the farm population (see Table 61) was dependent on a landlord's decision for access to all or part of his main source of livelihood, in 1964 only 30.5 percent of all farmers were in that position, and all but 7 percent had at least some land of their own.

TABLE 61 Owner-Tenant Distribution of Farm Households (%)

	1947 (end)	1964
Full owner	16.5	71.6
Owner-tenant	38.3	14.8
Tenant-owner		8.4
Tenant	42.1	5.2
Farm laborer and burnt field farmer	3.1	–
TOTAL	100.0	100.0

Source: Ki Hyuk Pak et al., *A Study of Land Tenure System in Korea* (Seoul, 1966), pp. 87, 89, 131.
Ban, Moon, and Perkins, p. 286.

Land reform's impact on farm output was mixed in part because increased incentives to invest in the land by farmers were offset by the already mentioned disruption of rural capital markets. Korean landlords had also played a number of other positive roles in the promotion of agricultural improvements. If the net impact of land reform on productivity is unclear, however, no such uncertainty surrounds the impact of land reform on rural incomes.

It is not possible to come up with completely comparable estimates of per household farm income for both the 1930s and the 1960s, because the earlier period household surveys appear to have an upward bias. From the data presented in Table 62, however, it is clear that the impact on average per household income was large. If farm household income (gross of rent) was roughly the same in 1962 as it was in 1938, then income net of rent would have risen by nearly 40 percent. Put differently, in 1975 farm income per household net of rent was roughly 80 percent higher than in the 1930s. About half this increase in income was due to increases in agricultural production per family, but the other half was caused by land reform. Confiscation and redistribution of the land and income of a relatively small number of landlords thus can be seen to have had a large impact on a great many people.

TABLE 62 Farm Household Income Net of Rent Payments, 1933–1975

(constant 1934 yen)

	(1) Farm Income Per Household	(2) Rent per Household	(3) (1) – (2)
1933	299.12 (370.55)	68.04 (84.29)	231.08
1938	327.89 (406.19)	94.80 (117.44)	233.09
1962	327.89	3.83	324.06
1965	327.74	6.00	321.74
1970	382.44	9.69	372.75
1975	436.82	9.29	427.53

Sources and Methodology: The 1962–1975 data are from MAF, *Report on the Results of Farm Household Economic Surveys,* various years, and the original 1933 and 1938 income and rent data were derived from material in the Chōsen Sōtokufu, Nōrin-Ryoru, *Nōka keizai gaikyō chōsa.* The original estimates for 1933 and 1938 are given in the parentheses but, because the original survey was believed to contain a substantial upward bias, the 1938 figure was reduced to make it equal to 1962 and all other figures were deflated accordingly. There is evidence from other sources to suggest that household income in the early 1960s was roughly equal to that in the 1930s.

If in deflating farm household income, the index of prices paid by farmers had been used instead of the index of prices paid to farmers, farm household income in 1975 would be another 10 percent higher than the figure presented in Table 62. Deflating by prices paid by farmers is in fact a better measure of changes in the standard of living of farmers, since it is those prices that determine how much a farmer can consume out of a given money income.

The purpose of these calculations is to illustrate one major point. Deliberate attempts by various Korean governments to redistribute income towards farmers accounted for as much or more of the very considerable transformation of rural standards of living as did efforts, private and public alike, to increase agricultural output. This impact of land reform on rural incomes will be discussed further in Chapter 11.

THE QUALITY OF RURAL LIFE

Income alone, however, is not a complete guide to changes in the quality of rural life. Income, for example, does not really capture the greatly expanded opportunities open to rural Koreans, particularly the young. The already-mentioned rapid expansion of rural education has combined with the great increase in non-farm jobs to give rural youth a real choice of occupations and lifestyles. This represents a major change from a world where the only real option was to become a farmer or a farm laborer.

Other changes in rural life that have an impact that is inadequately captured by measures of income include the spread of paved roads and rural electrification. Most rural people in Korea today are within quick and inexpensive reach of Seoul or other major cities. Electricity by 1975 reached most rural villages (but not all) and, while most electricity is used for productive purposes, electricity-based consumption activities (television, and so on) are not likely to lag far behind.

Health is one area, on the other hand, where the degree of transformation in the quality of rural life has been less impressive. One measure of the relative neglect of rural health is the inadequacy of government statistics dealing with the subject. The worst killer communicable diseases, to be sure, have been largely eliminated in Korea, although there were still 600 to 800 cases of typhoid fever in 1973 and 1974. But such major scourges as tuberculosis and parasite infections remain widespread, and there is little readily available data with which to judge whether the incidence of these diseases is rising or falling. Perhaps the best available measure of the trend over time in rural health is a series on infant mortality compiled from various sources by researchers at Seoul National University. These data, presented in Table 63, indicate that infant mortality in the 1960s was about half that in the 1940s, but was still high. In Japan and the United States in 1970, for example, the comparable rates were 13.1 and 19.8 per thousand respectively.

CONCLUSION

One theme of this discussion of rural development in Korea has been that specific interventions by various Korean governments, notably land reform in the late 1940s and early 1950s and subsidized rice prices in the 1970s have had a major impact on rural life. But another theme has been that, except for these few major interventions, prior to the 1970s the government's attitude toward farmers could be described as basically one of neglect. Successive United States aid missions made an effort to overcome some of this neglect through support for fertilizer imports, for the creation of effective extension services, and the like. But American aid was also used to hold down prices paid to farmers as part of a general attack on inflation. Furthermore, no likely amount of foreign aid was an adequate substitute for a commitment by Koreans themselves to do something about the rural areas.

TABLE 63 Rural Infant Mortality, 1944–1970

Year	Rural Infant Mortality (per 1,000 live births)	Size of Sample
1944	160.9	230
1945	258.7	201
1946	143.7	327
1947	125.0	280
1948	168.9	302
1949	85.8	338
1950	87.6	331
1951	119.3	285
1952	92.5	346
1953	105.5	256
1954	–	–
1955	–	–
1956	59.2	359
1957	63.8	470
1958	59.3	337
1959	67.1	432
1960	68.5	394
1961	66.7	1,289
1962	61.2	1,372
1963	55.7, 67.6	1,508, 1,375
1964	60.7	1,317
1965	59.6	6,645
1966	26.5	226
1967	63.3	5,952
1968	49.3	223
1969	–	–
1970	42.2	2,083

Sources: Various sample survey results by D. J. Yun (Tŏk-chin Yun), S. J. Lee (Sang-jae Yi), and others were compiled by Ok Ryun Moon (Ong-nyun Mun) and Jae Woong Hong (Chae-ung Hong), "Health Services Outcome Data: A Survey of Data and Research Findings of the Provision of Health Services in Korea" (Seoul, unpublished paper, December 1975), pp. 18–20. Ban, Moon, and Perkins, p. 303.

And yet, for all this comparative official neglect, there were major changes for the better in both agricultural production and the rural standard of living. The real "lesson" of Korean rural development, therefore, is that, if growth in the rest of the economy is rapid and sustained, the rural areas will receive substantial benefits. If, in addition, overall growth has been preceded by a successful land reform, the great majority of the rural population, not just a privileged few, will enjoy these increased benefits.

EIGHT

Government and Business

Since the early 1960s, Korea has been governed by a highly centralized and authoritarian government which has espoused economic growth as its principal objective. The course of development has been shaped in large part by government direction via increasingly effective planning mechanisms and policy formulation in the hands of relatively few decision-makers. Policy decisions have been effectively implemented by a competent bureaucracy backed by firm political authority. At the same time, government decision-making has been essentially pragmatic and non-ideological. Political authority has not hesitated to use the instrument of public ownership when this has seemed useful, with the result that the public sector has accounted for a larger share of value added than is true of a number of developing economies ostensibly pursuing a "socialist" pattern of development. On the other hand, the main source of the rapid growth of industrial output has been the private sector led by a rapidly expanding group of vigorous entrepreneurs.

After a consideration of the colonial period and a short reference to the Rhee regime, we go on to examine the governmental decision-making process, the implementation of policy and the instruments of control, public enterprise and the economic activities in the public sector, large-scale enterprise and the development of entrepreneurship, and economic concentration and the emergence of the *chaebŏl*.

THE COLONIAL HERITAGE

Japanese penetration and colonial rule in Korea brought both exploitation and modernization in a mixture that is difficult to disentangle. There can be no doubt concerning the character and intensity of the exploitation, as Chapter 3 has indicated. From 1910 on, Korea was operated as a Japanese fief with agricultural and industrial activities directed towards satisfying Japanese requirements. It was, however, impossible to accomplish this objective without at the same time introducing Koreans to the technical and managerial practices of a modernizing economy. In no area was this more significant than in the industrial sector.

It is a commonly held view in Korea, for understandable reasons, that the course of industrial development since 1963 owed little to the period before 1945. The reasons customarily cited to support this belief are: 1) that under the Yi dynasty there were no industrial enterprises in an economy that, apart from an overwhelmingly dominant agricultural sector, was populated by small-scale cottage industry and weak merchantile establishments; 2) that, during the colonial period, modern activity was not only thoroughly dominated by the Japanese but possessed an enclave character that minimized spread effects; and 3) that such limited indigenous industry as survived the Japanese period and the years of U.S. Military Government was wiped out before and during the Korean War. It follows from this argument that Korean industrial development must be seen as a phoenix born from, and rapidly becoming full-feathered in, a purely indigenous environment. While it is true that there was little industrialization during the Yi dynasty, the Japanese left behind a substantial growth potential in impressive stocks of physical and human capital and an experience of the characteristics of modern management and technology that were by no means completely dissipated in the immediate post-war years.

During the first two decades of the Japanese colonial period, Korea was regarded by Japan as principally a supplier of foodstuffs and raw materials. From 1910 to 1920, manufacturing activity was actively discouraged and new corporations were formed only with government approval. An abandonment of restrictions in 1920 led to the establishment of a large number of small factories, but it was not until the late 1920s that the rate of growth of factory output exceeded that of household industry. The beginning of Japanese war preparations in the 1930s resulted in a substantial expansion of heavy industry which grew from 23 percent of manufacturing net commodity-product in 1930 to 30 percent in 1940. The output of producer goods was funneled to Japan with the result that the share of exports in total manufacturing increased from about a third in the 1930s to two-thirds in 1940. There is no doubt that the "colonial enclave" character of Korean industrial development seriously lessened the spread effects of rapid economic growth. The impact was further reduced by the dominant role of Japanese ownership, management, and technical competence.

Although the dominance of Japanese management and the enclave character particularly of heavy industry certainly diminished learning opportunities and industrial experience for the Korean population, the influence of these decades of rapid growth and export expansion was far from negligible. Korean employment in manufacturing increased from 23,000 household heads in 1910 to 440,000 in 1940. By 1944, there were nearly 1,900 Korean engineers and technicians employed in manufacturing, another 1,300 in mining, and 2,000 in service industries. Table 64 below indicates there were more than 7,000 Korean managers and 28,000 professional and technical workers. As early as 1937, there were 2,000 Korean-owned factories and 100 of these employed more than 50 workers.

TABLE 64 Occupations of Active Male Population, 1944
(1,000s)

	Japanese	Koreans
Managerial	3.4	7.2
Professional and technical	14.5	27.9
Clerks and other white collar	53.4	172.4
Civil servants and small businessmen	38.2	122.1
Laborers	74.6	6,292.3
TOTAL	184.1	6,622.3

Sources: George M. McCune, *Korea Today* (Cambridge, Mass., 1950), pp. 330–331. Leroy Jones and Il SaKong, *Government, Business, and Entrepreneurship in Economic Development: The Korean Case,* Studies in the Modernization of the Republic of Korea: 1945–1975 (Cambridge, Mass., 1980), p. 26.

Japanese, of course, occupied the higher managerial and technical positions and Koreans the lower, still the Koreans' experience in industry and government was impressive. The importation from Japan of technology and forms of organization were also important. Two further modern reflections of the colonial heritage deserve to be mentioned—the nature of government-business relations and export orientation. The growth-oriented, interventionist, and export-led characteristics of the 1960s and 1970s were somewhat similar to the pattern of the colonial period. To be sure, neither the government's role nor the export orientation were passed directly to the Park regime, but the reintroduction of these characteristics in the 1960s may well have been substantially eased by familiarity with a similar pattern two decades earlier.

A few of the largest enterprises inherited from the Japanese were turned over to be managed by nascent government departments (for example, electricity, railways, communications, tobacco, and coal mining). We shall consider later what happened to these enterprises. The bulk of the manufacturing enterprises, however, were entrusted to the American Office of the Property Custodian which delegated operating responsibility to selected Korean managers. In January 1948, toward the end of the period of American military-control, not more than 20 percent of these enterprises were in full or partial operation. Although economic circumstances were highly unfavorable to an effective transfer, the unpreparedness of the American forces beset, moreover, with continual policy changes, and the political and social chaos in South Korea were even more important deterrents. As an American official reported, "The property custodians were subject to all sorts of pressures from high-ranking military officers, representatives of national agencies, their civil officer colleagues, and Korean friends."[1] Efforts at reliberating from American control what had already been liberated from the Japanese took every form from outright theft, to padded payrolls, to byzantine legal efforts to prove prior title. Success in such efforts provided a stake for not a few budding entrepreneurs who were later to be heard from in Korean industrial development.

Under these circumstances, it is not surprising that the new government was unable to utilize effectively the vested properties. The land reform of 1949 provided an opportunity for the transfer of a number of these properties into private hands. Landowners were paid in part with land bonds which, in accordance with the Law on the Disposition of Vested Properties, were redeemable through purchase of former Japanese enterprises. A large number of properties, usually in a serious state of deterioration, were acquired in this fashion only to experience the devastating consequences of the Korean War. It is estimated that, during the war, some 45 percent of industrial units nationwide suffered "substantial" damage. In Seoul, "over 80 percent of industry, public utilities and transport, three-quarters of the office and more than half the dwellings were in ruins."[2]

As a result of these economic, political, and military vicissitudes, the physical capital inherited from the colonial regime was badly dissipated. The same, however, cannot be said of the inheritance in trained manpower and the cultural changes in a population that had lived thirty-five years in a highly dynamic economy in which effective management and modern technology had been clearly visible. The Japanese managed in their repressive and exploitative regime to give Korea an introduction to industrial development, the effects of which were still visible in the renewed period of rapid development in the 1960s and 1970s.

GOVERNMENT AND BUSINESS DURING THE RHEE REGIME

The close cooperation between government and business that developed in the 1960s and 1970s and was a large contributor to economic growth was quite different from the government-business relations that characterized the period from the Korean War to Syngman Rhee's disappearance from the scene in 1960. The development strategy of the 1950s, while neither well articulated or planned, was, as described in Chapter 5, based upon import substitution, over-valued exchange rates, and heavy reliance on foreign assistance. Access to controlled supplies of foreign exchange and domestic credit were the chief ingredients of business success, and for those who could obtain such access, frequently through contact with corrupt officials, high protection of domestic output and quantitative restrictions on imports assured the possibility of highly profitable operations. The foundations for a number of entrepreneurial fortunes of later members of the *chaebŏl* were laid during this period. A by-product of this system was a fairly rapid growth of manufactures, concentrating mainly on import-replacing consumer goods, and the development of considerable entrepreneurial talents.

The industrial development that took place during the period of the Rhee Government was directed mainly to nondurable consumer goods. For the years, 1960–1961, food, beverage, tobacco, textiles, clothing, and footwear accounted for nearly 70 percent of total manufacturing output. The most rapidly growing areas of manufacture, however, were chemicals (mainly fertilizers) and metal products, including machinery and transport equipment. As noted in previous chapters, "By the early 1960's Korea had almost exhausted the possibility of 'easy' import substitution in non-durable consumer goods and their inputs."[3] Despite the relatively rapid growth of manufactured output after 1953, Korea, on international comparison, had a manufacturing sector smaller than the average for countries of similar per capita income and a volume of exports very much smaller.[4] The period of export-led rapid industrial growth was not yet visible on the horizon.

This is not to deny that, in some respects, the developments of the 1950s laid the foundations for later industrial growth. A group of able entrepreneurs emerged and, if their success was due as much to expert manipulation of government policies and officials as to the production of goods, still the base of a sizable number of firms able to survive under a different regime had been laid. A base had been laid, but the effective exploitation of this base depended on a different political regime, a different set of economic policies, and a different relationship between government and business.

GOVERNMENT ECONOMIC DECISION-MAKING

The government that emerged in 1961 and put an end to the Student Revolution of 1960 lost no time in indicating that it favored economic development directed by a strong governmental hand. To General Park and his associates, this required effective planning machinery and a bureaucracy capable of implementing central government decisions. Even before the military takeover, Park Chung Hee had unofficially directed one of his ten associates to draft a five-year economic plan. As soon as the Park Military Government assumed power in May 1961, it wasted no time in announcing its intention to launch a five-year plan beginning in 1962. At the same time, the Park Military Government introduced various institutional changes necessary for effective decision-making.

The primary goal of the Park Military Government, carried over into the civilian regime elected in 1963, was an acceleration of economic growth. Park Chung Hee proclaimed in 1962, "In human life, economics precedes politics or culture."[5] As he explained later,

> In order to ensure efforts to improve the living conditions of the people in Asia, even undemocratic emergency measures may be necessary . . . It is also an undeniable fact that the people of Asia today fear starvation and poverty more than the oppressive duties thrust upon them by totalitarianism . . . In other words, the Asian peoples want to obtain economic equality first and build a more equitable political machinery afterwards . . . The gem without luster called democracy is meaningless to people suffering from starvation and despair.[6]

No one can deny that President Park was a man of his word in the economic as well as the political sphere. Irma Adelman and Cynthia Morris observe, on the basis of a cross-country study of the development process:

> The extent to which economic change can take place is significantly conditioned—by a single political characteristic, the extent of leadership commitment to economic development . . . It is—the absence of national mobilization for development which in general constitutes the prime political obstacle to development.[7]

In the South Korean case, there can be no doubt concerning the political commitment of the Park Government.

A major step towards assembling the necessary government machinery took place in 1961 with the organization of the Economic Planning Board (EPB) centrally located in the government. The board took over planning responsibility from the recently established Ministry of Reconstruction and absorbed the Bureau of Budget from the Ministry of Finance and the Bureau of Statistics from the Ministry of Home Affairs. Since it was the Bureau of Budget rather than the Ministry of Finance that monitored public expenditures, including development expenditures, the EPB was at the center not only of medium-term planning but also short-term planning and policy-making. The head of the Economic Planning Board was given the title of Deputy Prime Minister (DPM). This elevated position signified the seriousness of the regime's planning intentions, and the EPB was expected to play a prominent role in adjudicating and controlling conflicts among the various economic ministries. The Park Military Government also established a Central Economic Committee, consisting of the Prime Minister as chairman, the DPM as vice-chairman, all the ministers concerned with economic affairs, and a few outside experts.

This emphasis on planning does not signify either that South Korea had previously lacked plans (indeed there were many) or that the Economic Planning Board immediately assumed the direction of economic policy. There was, however, a marked difference between the planning efforts of the Rhee Government and what came later.

As early as 1948, an Office of Planning was established under the Prime Minister's office with responsibility for budgeting, economic planning, resource mobilization, pricing policy, and research activities. This office prepared a five-year plan during the Korean War and issued it in revised form in 1953. It was essentially a collection of recommended projects most of which were never carried through. The office dealt primarily with short-term stabilization policies until it was merged into the Ministry of Reconstruction in 1955. In 1952 the United Nations Korea Reconstruction Agency (UNKRA), as we noted in Chapter 6, hired Robert Nathan Associates to prepare a post-war reconstruction program. The resulting "Nathan Plan" submitted in 1953 never got off the ground, in part because the commitment to employ Nathan had been made without consulting President Rhee but mainly because of its unrealistic terms of reference.

The establishment of the Ministry of Reconstruction in 1955 evidenced a certain interest in improving the planning machinery, and the minister, who was made chairman of the Reconstruction Committee of Economic Ministers, was charged with the responsibility for overseeing and coordinating overall planning regarding the rehabilitation of the industrial economy. In 1958, an Economic Development Council was established within the ministry and was able to attract a capable young staff, many of whom had been trained abroad. Within a year of its appointment, the council prepared a three-year development plan for the period 1960–1962. This plan, however, was postponed by the Rhee cabinet for a year and came into effect only a few days before the Rhee regime fell victim to the April Student Revolution of 1960. When the democratic government of Chang Myon came to power, the Economic Development Council was directed to prepare a five-year economic plan and invited a Rand Corporation expert to advise in its formulation. This plan shared the fate of the other initiatives of the Chang Myon regime when the military coup brought that regime to an end.

There was, then, no dearth of plans and planning activity before 1961. The reason this activity had so little effect on policy was, essentially, that President Rhee was more interested in other things than in economic development. As in so many of the new states, the leader who fought for independence proved not to be a man capable of effective administration. Like others with similar careers—Sukarno, Nkrumah, Sheik Mujib —Rhee was more adept at bringing a new nation into being than directing its development. He seemed to be unable to understand the relation of economic growth to the attainment of his own goals. Thus his anti-Japanese measures retarded the resumption of trade with a natural and traditional partner, and his yearning for reunification was carried to the extreme that "there was an unwillingness to build up the South as an independent and integrated economy. The possibility that unification would again give access to the electric power and heavier industries of the North was given as a reason for holding up the growth of such facilities in the South."[8]

The Park regime changed all that. Not only did economic growth become the primary objective, but it was understood that the attainment of this objective required superior government management. As Hahn Been Lee observes, "The most general contribution of the military to the development of administration in Korea was its introduction and vigorous application of a 'managerial approach.'"[9] Rhee was a politician; Park was a military man who knew how to use a staff. Rhee manipulated political parties, youth groups, and cronies; Park relied on a reorganized and strengthened bureaucracy.

The rapid economic growth that began in South Korea in the early 1960s and has accelerated since then has been a government-directed development in which the principal engine has been private enterprise. The relationship between a government committed to a central direction of economic development and a highly dynamic private sector that confronts the planning machinery with a continually changing structure of economic activities presents a set of interconnections difficult to penetrate and describe. Planning in South Korea, if it is interpreted to include not only policy formulation but also the techniques of policy implementation, is substantially more than "indicative." The hand of government reaches down rather far into the activities of individual firms with its manipulation of incentives and disincentives. At the same time, the situation can in no sense be described in terms of a command economy. If we conceive of economic activity as resulting from a continuum of decisions ranging from the broadest enunciation of policies down to the decision to put zippers rather than buttons on pants, we proceed from an area in which government is the primary decision-maker (although influenced by business), through an area of policy implementation in which government and business cooperate (though government, at least in Korea, is the senior partner), to an area in which the decision belongs to the firm or the household. The process of implementation is a sort of dividing area between government-dominated and private decision-making. We shall discuss this area in the next section. Here the emphasis is on planning and policy-making in the Park regime.

Since 1962, South Korea has seen the preparation of four five-year plans and has experienced the completion of three plan periods. Inevitably there has occurred substantial change in planning techniques and procedures. The major changes can be described as follows: a persistent broadening of participation in plan formulation; a shift from a somewhat mechanistic attempt to achieve consistency between available resources and target requirements to a greater concentration on central policy issues; a substantial increase in the quantity and quality of the available data; and a declining dependence on foreign advice. The First Five-Year Plan (1962–1966) was relatively hastily prepared under broad directives from the Supreme Council by the relatively inexperienced staff of EPB with mutual consultation with concerned ministries. Relevant data were lacking, and the consistency of the plan was in doubt. The plan had a bad start due to a poor harvest and the fiasco of monetary reform in 1962. It was revised in 1964, but even the new version was largely ignored. In the event, the rate of growth substantially exceeded plan targets even though these had been considered by U.S. advisers and Korean experts to be too optimistic.

The Second Five-Year Plan (1967–1971) was much more carefully prepared and involved the participation of concerned ministries, members of the Economic and Scientific Council, representatives of economic research institutes, business associations, and foreign aid missions.[10] Because the First Five-Year Plan formulation had suffered from lack of reliable statistics, the Second Five-Year Plan stressed data collection and processing. It utilized a dynamic input-output model in testing the consistency of the overall plan and in estimating sectoral investment and import requirements. As a result, the Second Five-Year Plan document, as a technical achievement, was widely admired both in Korea and abroad. It also had a significant influence on current policy decisions to delay construction of Korea's first steel mill to release resources for more investment in the export-oriented industrial sectors. The Second Five-Year Plan was, nonetheless, rapidly outstripped by events, as investment and growth exceeded plan estimates. To help the government keep abreast of changing conditions and policy problems the practice was introduced, in 1967, of preparing annual Overall Resource Budgets (ORBs). These provided a framework for consistent short-run policy-making. They reviewed past performance, set short-term targets and allocations, and formulated appropriate implementation policies. The annual preparation of ORBs brought the staff of the Economic Planning Board into much closer touch with relevant policy-making, and this became evident during the formulation of the Third Five-Year Plan (1972–1976). There was a shift from modeling and an emphasis on macro consistency towards "policy planning." The focus was on how "to formulate policies which will lead to the desired allocation of resources within the framework of private decision-making in response to price incentives. Analytical work focuses on the system of incentives and the government's role as an economic catalyst."[11] Ministerial influence was also in part responsible for this shift, as the various economic ministries outside of EPB gained greater confidence in their planning capabilities and experience in the choice of policies needed to implement their investment proposals.

The Fourth Five-Year Plan (1977–1981) was prepared in much the same manner as the Third Five-Year Plan but with a somewhat greater emphasis on decentralized procedures. There were twenty-two working groups, each headed by a high government official from a concerned ministry. Each group consisted of government officials from the relevant ministries, and experts from research institutes, banks, business associations, and ministries. EPB officials acted as secretaries to each team. Much of the economic analysis was undertaken by the Korea Development Institute (KDI), established in 1971. These groups developed detailed plans for their area following guidelines prepared by EPB and subjected to the scrutiny of the Economic Plan Deliberation Committee chaired by the Prime Minister. This time around, although there were many foreign experts involved in data collection and analysis, they played a minor role in comparison with the participation of foreign experts in the preparation of the second and third plans.

Economic planning is taken seriously in South Korea. Yet, as Table 65 indicates, planned magnitudes have departed rather far from actuals. This is, of course, characteristic of medium-term plans, the main difference being, in the Korean case (as in Japan), that realizations have tended to exceed targets. We conclude that medium-term planning has not been as important in charting a particular course for the economy as it has been in providing a forum for the consideration of alternative strategies, in stimulating a dialogue among divergent interests, in training government officials, and in announcing the government commitment to a particular set of policies.

The fact that actual growth has consistently exceeded planned targets is presumably to be attributed, at least in part, to the existence of a highly dynamic private sector and to a government-business relationship that has stimulated, released, and guided the energies of private enterprise. We postpone consideration of the characteristics of Korean entrepreneurship and enterprise to direct attention here to the nature of policy formulation under the Park regime. It can be described as executive-dominated and highly centralized with all significant decisions not only made in Seoul but involving relatively few people; speedy and flexible in the sense that wrong decisions were quickly corrected; pragmatic and particularistic; and, despite the fact that political discussion was strongly repressed, discussion of economic policy was relatively open.

The emasculation of the legislature in all significant matters of policy is well known to the most casual observer of the Korean

TABLE 65 Plan Targets and Actual Performance
(%)

	First Five-Year Plan (1962–1966)		Second Five-Year Plan (1967–1971)		Third Five-Year Plan (1972–1976)	
	Planned	*Actual*	*Planned*	*Actual*	*Planned*	*Actual*
GNP Growth Rate (annual average)	7.1	8.3	7.0	11.4	8.6	11.2
Agriculture, forestry and fisheries	5.7	5.5	5.0	2.0	4.5	5.8
Mining and manufacturing	15.1	14.8	10.7	20.9	13.0	20.1
Social overhead capital and other services	5.4	8.9	6.6	13.2	8.5	8.5
Industrial structure (terminal year)						
Agriculture, forestry and fisheries	34.8	37.9	34.0	24.2	22.4	20.3
Mining and manufacturing	20.6	19.8	26.8	29.9	27.9	36.0
Social overhead capital and other services	44.5	42.3	39.2	45.9	49.7	33.7
Investment as share of GNP (annual average)	22.6	16.9	19.0	30.6	24.9	27.0
Domestic savings as share of GNP	9.3	6.7	11.6	15.5	19.5	17.0
Foreign savings as share of GNP	13.3	10.2	7.4	15.1	5.4	11.8
Allocation of resources by industrial sector [a]						
Agriculture, forestry and fisheries	17.4	15.4	16.3	9.5	11.8	11.5
Mining and manufacturing	33.2	26.2	30.7	23.8	25.8	25.8
Social overhead capital and other services	49.4	58.4	53.0	66.7	62.4	62.7

TABLE 65 (continued)

Sources: Jones and SaKong, pp. 54-55. Kyŏngje Kihoegwŏn (Economic Planning Board), *Kyŏngje paeksŏ* (Economic white paper), 1972, 1976, 1977. Kyŏngje Kihoegwŏn (Economic Planning Board), *Che samch'a yondo ch'ongjawŏn yesan, 1977* (Overall resources budget for 1977). Bank of Korea, *Monthly Economic Statistics*, January 1977.

Note: [a]Input-output tables 1965, 1970, 1978. ROK inventory changes are included in the plan estimates, but the "actual" national income accounts data do not provide this on a sectoral basis. These data were therefore estimated from IO tables to provide consistent sectoral allocations inclusive of inventory adjustments.

scene. Within the executive branch the ultimate power is, of course, the President, and major decisions and disputes are ultimately decided by him. Given Park's preoccupation with growth, this is no rubber stamp formality. His office is equipped with a strong secretariat and, between the secretariat and the Korean CIA, the President is remarkably well informed. The formal mechanism for conflict resolution is the Economic Ministers' Meeting. The meeting is chaired by the Deputy Prime Minister and consists of all economic ministers and the Minister of Foreign Affairs. The meeting is currently held twice a week. More formal interaction takes place every Saturday morning at the "Economic Ministers' Round-Table." Economic policy proposals agreed to at the formal meeting are sent to the cabinet meeting, which is largely a rubber stamp. The former is the forum within which decisions are made. Of course there is consultation with concerned interests, in some cases a great deal of consultation. The introduction, for example, in 1975 of the proposal for a value-added tax was followed by prolonged and active discussion in business and academic circles and the media.

Personal contacts with government officials are a traditional means of influence in East Asia, and Korea is no exception. Important Korean businessmen have regular opportunities to discuss economic policy with the government officials. An important forum is the Monthly Export Promotion Meeting and it, and the more select luncheon that follows, were both attended regularly by President Park. The President or, in default, the Prime Minister, also attends quarterly meetings with academics, giving them an opportunity to question proposed economic policy. And, as we mentioned above, there is a surprising amount of discussion and debate on economic issues in the press. Interests outside the government certainly have influence on economic policy, but in most cases this influence appears to be in the presentation of facts that need to be taken into account, but perhaps would not have been, in the absence of public discussion. The Park Government showed no hesitation in overriding these interests in a manner impossible in a more democratic government, when it seemed important on developmental grounds to do so. There has been in recent years a good deal of criticism, both within and outside government circles, of the narrowness of this decision-making process. It may well be that, as the economy becomes more complex, a wider net will have to be cast.

The highly centralized decision-making process obviously facilitates speed and flexibility in policy formulation with some advantages and some disadvantages. One example of how the process works is provided by the Korean reaction to the oil crisis of October 1973. It required perhaps a month for the full implications of the situation to sink in but, in December, the President's secretariat began an intensive effort to produce a policy response. After consultation with a minimum number of experts, a sophisticated document was produced that led to a Presidential Emergency Decree issued on January 14, 1974, some three weeks after the study began. This became the centerpiece of Korea's energy policy. The contrast with the efforts of the United States to achieve an energy policy is illuminating.

Speedy decision-making also has its costs. Major adverse effects or better alternatives are often found after a new policy has been announced. But the government has shown itself quick to reverse a policy decision under these circumstances. To date, the government obviously considers that benefits of speed and flexibility outweigh the cost.

Government policy is also highly pragmatic in the sense that it shows no hesitation in devising means most appropriate to the end in view without significant ideological bias. The result is a balance between market forces and direct government intervention and between government ownership and reliance on private entrepreneurship. Where the market works, fine; where it does not, the government is quick to intervene. Policy is not only pragmatic but particularistic in the sense that the activities of a single firm may form the object of government intervention. Witness the example of the Export Room in the Ministry of Commerce and Industry where officials monitor the performance of firms in foreign markets and take action when results fall below targets. Particularism gives great scope for official discretion (with possible corruption) and is examined in the next section.

The close relationship between government and business and their mutual interest in economic growth raises the question whether it is appropriate to refer to a "Korea, Inc." as is alleged to be in the case of Japan. If it is, the operations of "Korea, Inc." are very different from those of "Japan, Inc." A recent study of government-business relations in Japan concluded that "big business (is) predominant and unrivaled as an influence in Japanese politics. Its wishes are tantamount to commands, and the government does not dare to take them lightly."[12] Whether this accurately describes the situation in Japan, it certainly is not accurate for Korea, partly because there is little political activity that big business might influence. The pattern of government-business relationships under Park was set in the first few months of the regime. One of the first acts of the new government was the implementation of a Special Law for Dealing with Illicit Wealth Accumulation. Under its provisions many of the country's leading businessmen were arrested and threatened with confiscation of their assets. Soon thereafter, ten of the leaders were summoned to a meeting with Park, then Vice-Chairman of the Revolutionary Council.[13] A deal was struck whereby:

1) The government would exempt most businessmen from criminal prosecution.
2) With the notable exception of commercial bank shares, existing assets would not be confiscated.
3) Businessmen would instead pay off their assessed obligations by establishing new basic industrial firms and donating a share to the government.

In the event, few new firms were established, and most of the delinquents paid fines in cash. But Park was interested in more than punishment; he was eager to enlist business support for the growth policies for the new government. It was largely on the basis of business recommendations that the industrial port at Ulsan was established and an association that evolved into the Federation of Korean Industries was created. Since these early years, government-business relations have mellowed and, as we noted above, personal relations between business and government officials can be close, and the advice of business associations listened to. Still, in these relationships, the government clearly has the whip hand. If there can be said to be a "Korea, Inc.," it is the government that is the Chairman of the Board, with business holding a few of the directorships.

IMPLEMENTATION OF ECONOMIC POLICY

In most LDCs the weakest link in the efforts by government to direct or influence economic resource use lies in the implementation of plans and policies. Nehru's judgment on India—"The real question is not planning but implementing the Plan . . . I fear we are not quite so expert at implementation as at planning"— is reflected in a growing emphasis in planning literature on the importance of implementation and its general inadequacy. It is our view that South Korea is a notable exception. It does not follow, however, that Korean procedures and experience are easily transferable to other countries. Implementation mechanisms are deeply imbedded in the social and political fabric and are inherently difficult to transfer. In Korea, they are a part of a particular set of government-business relations and are heavily influenced by the political structure of the Park regime.

Intervention mechanisms may be classified in two ways: first, in terms of the instruments of intervention (taxes, exchange rates, rationing, subsidies, and so on), and second, in terms of the kinds of pressure brought upon an individual's or enterprise's behavior in order to insure compliance. There is a good deal of discussion in other chapters of various instruments of intervention; here we are primarily concerned with behavioral compliance mechanisms.

Behavior may be modified by the use of incentives and disincentives or by command. The former expands an individual's opportunity set, leaving him free to alter his behavior or not, while the latter constricts it. Subsidies and tax differentials are examples of the manipulation of incentives; uniform tax obligations and rationing involve command procedures. Both incentive manipulation and command may be discretionary or non-discretionary, depending on the degree to which administrators are free to alter their applicability. Government action can, obviously, also affect business behavior through the provision of information and the lessening of uncertainties. It has come to be a tenet of economic liberalism that the use of non-discretionary incentives is to be preferred both on grounds of efficiency and equity. A change in the incentive structure permits an individual or a firm to adjust his activities to his own best advantage while complying with government policy. And a limitation or denial of administrative discretion favors an impersonal rule of law rather than a personal rule of men. Gunnar Myrdal describes the heavy reliance of LDCs on discretionary controls and classes the users as "illiberal states." He argues forcibly for liberalization on the ground that

> the scarcity in South Asia of administrative personnel with both competence and integrity should make discretionary policies all the more difficult to execute with reasonable effectivness and reliance on them more hazardous even morally. With this consideration in mind . . . it would be desirable, if non-discretionary controls were used to a maximum extent possible. [14]

In fact, the Korean government makes extensive use of discretion, both in the manipulation of incentives and in its command procedures, with apparently good effect. In an economy in which government attempts a detailed direction of resource use and, on occasion, reaches far down into the decision-making processes of individual firms, there is much to be said for a considerable discretionary scope in choosing the firms and the processes to be manipulated, provided the administrator knows what he is doing and is not amenable to counterproductive pressures. On the whole, Korean bureaucrats, at least at upper levels, know what they are doing, and although it is too much to say that government officials are not amenable to corruption, their intervention rarely leads to a slowing down of production or a failure to meet prescribed targets. There is too much pressure from a well-informed and growth-oriented government to permit serious dislocation.

There is one other aspect of the Korean implementation procedure that deserves emphasis—the interrelationships among incentive and command devices to secure compliance. A firm that does not respond as expected to particular incentives may find that its tax returns are subject to careful examination, or that its application for bank credit is studiously ignored, or that its outstanding bank loans are not renewed. If incentive procedures do not work, government agencies show no hesitation in resorting to command backed by compulsion. In general, it does not take a Korean firm long to learn that it will "get along" best by "going along." Obviously, such a system of implementation requires not only cooperation among the various government agencies that administer compliance procedures but continuous consultation between firms and public officials. Such a system could well be subject to corruption, and there is some evidence that payments are, in fact, made and received for services rendered, but again it must be emphasized that there is very little evidence that such corruption as exists interferes in any serious way with production processes.

In theory, non-discretionary manipulation of incentives is the preferred form of intervention, since it achieves a desired deviation from pure market behavior while taking maximum advantage of the motivational and informational advantages of the invisible hand. In Korean practice, non-discretionary manipulation is not so pervasive as one would gather from the writings of some economists, but it nevertheless plays an important role. The single most important realm of application has been in the market for foreign exchange. The basic change in exchange-rate regimes between the Rhee and Park periods is generally characterized as a move from a disequilibrium system. Under Rhee, the wŏn was heavily overvalued, with the demand price, on the average, about one-third the official rate. Following the 1964 exchange-rate reform, the demand price was only some 15 percent below the official rate, and this declined steadily to about 7 percent in 1975.

During the whole of the period since 1953, however, foreign exchange has been available to importers and exporters at rates significantly influenced by tax, tariff, and financial incentives and disincentives, and by other promotional schemes. Wontack Hong has listed some 38 major promotional schemes that have been in operation at one time or another since 1953 and which have affected the terms on which foreign exchange was available to domestic purchasers. Many of these took the form of non-discretionary incentives. The net result of this foreign exchange regime was, during the Rhee period, that, while these incentive schemes only partly offset the disadvantages of an overvalued wŏn for exporters, the effective exchange rate for importers remained very low.[15] The result was that, if an importer obtained foreign exchange at the official rate, and many did, he could earn a profit of from 100 to 175 percent if he bought a tariff-exempt commodity. Access to imports during the Rhee regime was allocated by quantitative restrictions, a command mechanism, which was subject to a high degree of discretion. The implementation procedures during the Park regime have been mainly non-discretionary manipulation of tariff and financial incentives.

The surge in exports beginning in the late 1950s and early 1960s is usually attributed to a more favorable effective exchange rate for exporters. But, if the calculations of Charles R. Frank, Kwang Suk Kim, and Larry Westphal are accepted, the effective exchange rate on exports, inclusive of subsidies, has remained remarkably stable from 1958 through 1970. We suggest that one of the main reasons for the shift from an import-substituting to an export-oriented economy was the disappearance of the rich opportunities for profit from import substitution provided by the foreign exchange regimes under Rhee. Entrepreneurs in Korea found it necessary to turn their efforts elsewhere after 1964 to the benefit of exports. The critically important influence was not the absolute level of incentives to exports, but the level relative to other opportunities for entrepreneurial gain. The rise in exports came less from an increase in the level of export incentives than from a reduction in returns to alternative uses of funds.

The close relation between government and business permitted other stimulants to exports. Assured political stability tended to lengthen time horizons and made manufacturing a much more feasible alternative to commerce as a field of entrepreneurial activity. In the export field itself, the Monthly Export Promotion Meeting chaired by the President not only permitted an exchange of information but was a potent indicator of the government's interest in this area. In 1962, the Ministry of Commerce and Industry began setting annual export targets classified by commodity, region, and country of destination and monitored the performance of firms in approaching these targets. As we have noted elsewhere, the government established or expanded a variety of special-purpose entrepreneurial support institutions. The best known of these is the Korean Trade Promotion Corporation (KOTRA). Other support institutions include a variety of special purpose banks and other financial intermediaries.

Although the relations of government and business were probably closer in export promotion than in other areas, the government's hand has been felt in all activities of large-scale enterprise. The most potent instruments for implementing economic policy have undoubtedly been control of bank credit and access to foreign borrowers. These instruments involve the manipulation of incentives on a presumably non-discretionary basis but, in fact, involve a considerable element of administrative discretion. Credit is the lifeblood of business enterprise everywhere, but it is particularly critical in Korea where the debt-equity ratios in manufacturing have been in the range of three or four to one in the first half of the 1970s. Over the entire period of 1963 to 1974, only 14 percent of cash flows of manufacturing corporations came from new equity. Another 20 percent was generated internally, but two-thirds came from borrowing. Of the borrowing, 53 percent came from domestic banks and financial institutions, 29 percent from foreign sources, and 19 percent from miscellaneous sources, including the curb market.[16] Since the commercial banks and other financial institutions that undertake corporate financing are owned by the government, the heavy borrowing of Korean corporations gives the government substantial influence over the direction of corporate expansion.

Since corporate borrowing from abroad can only be undertaken with government authorization and a government guarantee, this constitutes a substantial augmentation of government influence. There are currently three mechanisms of foreign credit allocation. Public loans (that is, those to the government from international agencies or other governments) have since 1974 been covered by the Public Loan Inducement and Management Law that specifies the process for government guarantee. The second category is private long-term loans (over three years maturity). These are covered by the Foreign Capital Inducement Law that allows guarantee by the government, the Korea Exchange Bank, or the commercial banks. The third category is private short-term credit, which comes under the Foreign Exchange Management Laws. In contrast to the first two forms, transactions under this law are relatively automatic so long as the terms conform to international banking practice. This exception does not weaken the government's control over all foreign borrowing for capital investment.

Bank interest rates are controlled by government in Korea as in most less-developed countries. The general bank rate has usually been well below the curb rate and, in real terms, it has often been negative. The result has been excess demand, creating the need for credit rationing. This has introduced a command feature into what would be, if interest rates governed access to credit, an incentive system. During the Rhee regime, there can be no question that the rationing of credit was highly discretionary and frequently politically motivated. Under the Park Government, there has been a serious attempt to specify desirable end uses and the differential rates to be allowed, and to target industry allocations. The priority system, however, would have to be impossibly specific (and undesirably rigid) to permit the exclusion of administrative discretion; in fact, it has not been that specific.

Although implementation procedures in Korea have leaned toward incentive structures and administrative discretion in the application of both incentives and commands, there has been no hesitation to use non-discretionary commands and to enforce these commands with compulsion where necessary. Taxation and the field of sumptuary legislation are two areas in which non-discretionary command implementation procedures are widely used. Indirect taxes are, of course, predominantly administered in non-discretionary fashion in all countries. With few exceptions, unit quantity and value are easily ascertainable and a per-unit or percent-of-value tax readily calculable. This clarity of assessments facilitates non-discretionary command procedures in all countries, including Korea. Where the Korea case differs from most LDCs at similar income levels is in the assessment and collection of direct taxes on personal and corporate incomes and on inheritances.

The Office of National Tax Administration was established in 1966 to increase tax revenue and to make tax administration as non-discretionary as possible by eliminating corruption, tax evasion, and arbitrary tax assessment procedures. Since then, tax collections as a percent of GNP have grown rapidly from an average of about 8 percent in 1964 and 1965 to an average of about 17 percent in 1975 and 1976. Enforcement is reflected not only in the level of collections but in its composition. Korea as compared with other LDCs at similar income levels has a substantially larger than average reliance on direct taxes.

(The Korean tax structure is discussed further in Chapter 9).

Enforcement of direct taxation is generally via the selective application of police action. An example was the announcement in July 1976 of a tax investigation of 27 corporations based on the Law for Punishment of Tax Criminals. If tax evasion is discovered, the corporations not only have to pay the taxes due plus a penalty of twice the additional tax, but the management is also subject to criminal prosecution. The latter is a serious matter in Korea, and corporations consequently dread a tax investigation. We should not be understood as implying that tax evasion is unknown in Korea. In a dynamic society where the information gap is large and personal connections are traditionally strong, tax "irregularities" are probably widespread. But Korea has done considerably better than most LDCs in applying non-discretionary command procedures in the field of taxation.

These procedures are also applied in the area of consumption. Under both the Rhee and Park regimes, the government has endeavored to control luxury imports, the difference being that, under Park, control has tended to be non-discretionary and prohibitions have been enforced. An example is the case of cigarettes. The Cigarette Monopoly Law of 1972 provides explicit and severe penalties for buying, selling, and using foreign cigarettes. The result has been that, although one sees foreign cigarettes, usually available from a handy PX, in private homes, they are rarely seen in public. Other luxury imports were banned under the 1961 Law Prohibiting Sales of Special Foreign Products. Offenders are severely punished with sentences of up to ten years' imprisonment and/or a fine of five to twenty times the price of the commodity. In sum, non-discretionary command procedures are widely used in Korea. Such use is not unique among LDCs but the fact of enforcement may well be.

Price controls under the Park regime have usually employed discretionary command procedures, and there has been no hesitation in bringing various forms of government "persuasion" to bear when commands showed signs of being ignored. Controls have generally been selective and short-term, with specific goals in view. An exception was the 1972–1973 period when a broad-based non-discretionary effort to control prices was attempted. As might have been expected, success was limited. Producers resorted to under-the-table payments, product mix realignments, and other devices usually encountered in such circumstances. The government rather quickly abandoned the attempt at across-the-board controls in 1974.

The first instance of short-term price controls under Park occurred in May 1961 when the new Military Government announced a temporary freeze on prices at their pre-revolutionary levels. Two months later, the freeze was replaced by the Temporary Law on Price Control that placed price ceilings on "critical" commodities such as rice, barley, coal, and fertilizer. A few more items were added later but, apart from grain prices, controlled during most of the 1960s to subsidize the cost of living in the cities, explicit price controls were largely abandoned in favor of aggregate-demand management in 1963. During most of the 1960s, there existed what might be called informal price supervision. There were no formal control procedures, but the government exercised "persuasion" on various producer associations. Persuasion was fortified by various disincentives, implicit threats of credit restraint, tax investigation, stricter regulation of sanitary standards, and so on. As Soon Chough puts it, "There is no legal basis for the working of this system, but the government influence goes beyond what laws or regulations stipulate."[17]

The interventions of the 1960s and early 1970s were principally justified by the existence of temporary disequilibria and the desire to alleviate the price consequences therefrom. A new chapter was added in December 1975 with the Law on Price Stability and Fair Trade that sought to control oligopoly and monopoly markets. This has reflected the government's increased concern with problems of industrial concentration. It seems probable that discretionary command will be the favored method of implementation, supplemented by the various incentives and disincentives available in a system of close government-business interaction.

A further example of this close interaction and its effect on implementation procedures is provided by government efforts to induce and enforce closely held Korean corporations to "go public." We shall have occasion to refer to these efforts later in discussing private economic power in the Korean economy.

PUBLIC ENTERPRISE

As we have emphasized previously, government policy in Korea is essentially pragmatic in the sense that the choice of means is determined by the ends to be achieved without significant ideological predilection. One indication is the degree of dependence on public enterprise in an economy that proclaims the virtues of private initiative and the free market. The public-private boundary is a continuum in several dimensions, and it is only the ownership dimension that permits a statistical estimate of the size of the public enterprise sector. We here define a public enterprise as a productive entity which is owned or controlled, via ownership, by a public authority and which produces a marketable product. Ownership is defined as a public-equity holding of more than 10 percent. An output is "marketed" if sales cover more than half of current costs. According to this definition, the public-enterprise sector, in 1972, consisted of slightly over one hundred enterprises producing 9 percent of GNP or 13 percent of non-agricultural GNP. This is a rather high level, being similar to that of India (on the basis of non-agricultural GDP) and probably larger than that of Italy or the United Kingdom (in the late 1960s) despite substantial socialist advocacy in all three countries.

Knowledgeable Koreans are prone to explain this large public-enterprise sector as a part of the Japanese colonial heritage. At best this is a partial truth. Of the thirty-six enterprises in the sector as of December 31, 1960, over three-quarters were directly traceable to activities run by the Japanese Colonial Government or confiscated from private Japanese firms. By the end of 1972, however, the number of public-sector enterprises had more than tripled. Value-added estimates of the size of the sector are available only from 1963, but from 1963 to 1972 the average annual growth rate of value added in the public sector was 14.5 percent as against 9.5 percent for the economy as a whole and 12.2 percent for the non-agricultural economy. It is thus misleading to view the current size of the sector as a passive residual of the colonial era.

Certain characteristics of the Korean public-enterprise sector are worth noting. The sector as a whole shows extremely high forward linkages but modest backward linkages relative to the entire non-agricultural economy. But, since public-enterprise goods and services are usually priced to cover costs and yield a profit, the private enterprises purchasing these goods and services are not indirectly subsidized, as frequently happens in other economies with a large public sector. The public-enterprise sector is more than three times as capital-intensive as the Korean economy and more than double Korean manufacturing. This means that the sector tends to absorb a large fraction of total investment and a small fraction of total employment. In the late 1960s and early 1970s, the sector accounted for about 30 percent of total investment but, between 1962 and 1973, only 5 or 6 percent of the increase in employment.

Public-sector enterprises are, in general, large firms located in monopolistic or oligopolistic markets. At most, 10 percent of the value added by these firms was sold in competitive markets. Given this high correlation between public enterprise and imperfect competition, what is the direction of causation? One possibility is that government uses its powers to protect its enterprises from competitive pressures. This is clearly the case with the Office of Monopoly dealing with the sale of cigarettes, ginseng, and a few other luxury products, where the goal is straightforward profit maximization. In most other cases, however, public enterprises have been established because markets were imperfect.

Finally, public-sector enterprises are generally import-substituting or they deal in non-tradeables. In sum, enterprises operating in the public sector are characterized by high forward linkages, high capital-intensity, large size, market concentration, and the production of non-tradeables or import substitutes rather than exports.

Although it is a matter of common belief that public enterprise must inevitably be inefficient, we are prepared to argue that, at least in comparison with public enterprise in other less-developed countries, Korean public enterprises are relatively efficient. At the crudest level, this follows from the fact that, when an economy is growing at a real rate of 10 percent annually, a sector that absorbs 30 percent of investment cannot be using its resources too inefficiently. Furthermore, it is simply not possible to find in Korea examples of the sort of conspicuous inefficiency it is rather easy to discover in other countries. Industrial studies of iron and steel and fertilizers suggest that, at least in some cases, Korean public-enterprise engineering is extraordinarily high by LDC standards and not markedly deficient when compared with similar operations in industrial nations. It is commonly believed in Korea that public enterprises are less cost-efficient than their private counterparts, and this may well be so. In our judgment, however, the public-private gap tends to be much smaller than in most LDCs.

The reasons for this do not seem to lie in any particular Korean organizational or managerial practice. Public-enterprise salaries in Korea are generally below those in their private counterparts, with no particular added incentives to stimulate production. The heads of public enterprise are not generally professional managers. In 1972, two-thirds of the presidents of public enterprises, and half the vice presidents, were formerly either military officers or civil servants. Further, 60 percent of the presidents had spent less than three years with the company and 95 percent had spent less than five years. Nor do Korean public-enterprise managements enjoy a scope of action denied to managements in other countries. At least on paper, Korean public enterprises are responsible to a variety of ministries and agencies for a multitude of mundane details, and managers spend much of their time worrying about these bureaucratic relationships.

We suggest that, in Korea, the public-enterprise sector functions relatively well for the same reasons that other forms of government intervention are effective. Public enterprise is one form of discretionary command, and the potential for abuse of this form of intervention is minimized by leadership commitment to growth, with power in the hands of a competent bureaucracy. Throughout the world, public enterprises tend to be "unlimited liability companies" in that they are never allowed to die and are seldom divested. In Korea, there have been numerous cases of divestiture, most notably in the 1967–1969 period. And if a Korean public enterprise considered important for development shows signs of becoming moribund, it is likely to be vigorously kicked back into life by drastic changes in management and operating procedures.

PRIVATE ENTERPRISE

While the role of public enterprise has been impressive, the bulk of Korean growth has come in the private sector. From 1961 to 1976, real private non-agricultural GDP grew at a compound rate of over 13 percent per annum. Despite the pervasive activity of the government's visible hand, most of the decisions leading to output expansion were taken in the private sector.

Since government-business relationships and entrepreneurship had attracted little scholarly attention in Korea, Jones and SaKong were induced to undertake a series of case studies of selected small enterprises, large conglomerates, and particular industries and to supplement the information so gathered by an intensive questionnaire survey of entrepreneurship and management. The results of these enquiries, summarized here, are reported in detail in *Government, Business, and Entrepreneurship in Economic Development: The Korean Case.* [18] (The universe covered by the survey was defined as 311 manufacturing enterprises listed in the Directory of Korean Business as employing more than 50 workers as of June 20, 1975. This resulted in a population of 1,867 firms. Application of a 1-in-6 equal probability of selection procedure resulted in a sample size of all enterprises. The characteristics of this sample in terms of location, asset size, and industry represented, are given in Jones and SaKong.)

All Korean firms regardless of size and legal form are individual or family enterprises, usually dominated by a single head. Since the growth of the private sector has been recent and rapid, a large percentage of these enterprises are still in the hands of the original founders, as Table 66 indicates. The government has, in recent years, made a serious attempt to induce, and later to compel, a public distribution of equity shares, with results to be reported in the next section. But even the largest of combinations and conglomerates are still dominated by families, usually founding families. If one accepts J. A. Schumpeter's distinction between entrepreneurship and management, the leadership of most Korean medium and large firms is distinctly entrepreneurial in character. According to Schumpeter, the formation of "new combinations," which constitutes entrepreneurship, includes the introduction of new goods or goods of different quality, the introduction of new methods of production, the opening of new markets, a conquest of a new source of supply, and the carrying out of new forms of organization. [19]

If "new" refers to newness within the Korean context, more than two-thirds of the companies in the sample represented "new combinations." Furthermore, over half of the companies' expansion projects involved entrepreneurship by the same standard. Clearly Korean industry has not been routinely managed with executives following beaten paths. (See Table 67.)

TABLE 66 Relationships Between Chief Executives and Founders
(%)

Current chief executive is:	
Founder	61.4
Direct descendant of founder	7.8
Other relative of founder	12.0
Unrelated	18.8
	100.0
Where current chief executive is not the founder, the founder is:	
Deceased	8.0
Retired	16.0
Active in related company	24.0
Active in other company	16.0
Other	36.0
	100.0

Source: Jones and SaKong, p. 179.

TABLE 67 Type of Innovation Among Sample Firms
(%)

	At Establishment	At Expansion
Product new to Korea	31.3	20.7
Production new to Korea	20.9	11.0
Production process new to Korea	13.4	23.2
Product new to firm (but not to Korea)	34.3	14.6
Production process new to firm (but not to Korea)		18.3
Existing product and process (within firm)	—	12.1
TOTAL	99.9	99.9

Source: Jones and SaKong, p. 178.

At the bottom level of the Korean enterprise pyramid, life tends to be brutish and short, as in most less-developed countries and, indeed, in developed ones as well, with a large number of entrants and an almost equally large number of exits. In-depth interviews of some dozen or so small-scale businessmen by Vincent Brandt, published in the Jones-SaKong study, gives the flavor of this entrepreneurial experience. And, of course, most manufacturing enterprises are small. In the 22,632 manufacturing establishments listed by the Economic Planning Board in 1974, over 20,000 employed less than 50 workers. Even among the firms included in the Entrepreneurship Survey, the failure rate of the younger and smaller firms tended to be high. Roughly a third of the sample firms failed within five years of their founding. Of the new entrants that survive, a sizable percentage are the offspring of already existing firms. Jones and SaKong estimate that, over the entire period of rapid growth (1963–1973), the net flow of new entrepreneurs (mainly small) has been of the order of 400 per year, with a much smaller number per year since 1965.

The tremendous expansion of manufactured output during this period has come from the growth of existing enterprises and not from the entrance of new ones. From 1962–1974 the number of establishments increased by less than 40 percent, while average size tripled in terms of employment and rose ninefold in terms of value added. Ninety-seven percent of the increase in value added thus comes from an increase in average size and only 3 percent from a net increase in numbers. Once a firm is securely established, it tends to grow rapidly. Some evidence on this question is provided by the corporate histories of the firms in the Entrepreneurship Survey. Their average employment at establishment was 97 workers, and they averaged nearly 2 expansion projects with a mean increase in employment per project of 114 workers. At the top of the heap were some 46 *chaebŏl* who, in 1975, controlled 382 subsidiaries, and there were many smaller corporate groups as well.

The fact that most of the expansion of manufactured output

during the period of rapid growth came from existing enterprises rather than from new entrants argues that Korean entrepreneurs moved quickly along the learning curve and, presumably, that they were assisted in doing so by an increasing availability of managerial and technical expertise. The development of the Korean fertilizer industry provides a relevant example. There was a dramatic difference between progress of the first two plants, started in the late 1950s, and the next three, built in the mid-1960s. The first two were highly inefficient by contemporary Korean standards, though quite typical of LDC projects in general, and reflected the entrepreneurial barriers encountered in the early stages of development. Gestation periods for the first two plants were 67 and 54 months respectively; the next three, though larger and more complex, took only 17, 18, and 21 months, respectively. Nor is such experience limited to the fertilizer industry. As shown in Table 68, the average time from conceptualization to operation of projects declined steadily over time among sample firms in the Entrepreneurship Survey.

TABLE 68 Average Lead Time from Conceptualization to Operation of New Plants

	Months	Number
1962 and prior	16.5	12
1963–1968	14.1	14
1969–1975	10.2	36

Source: Jones and SaKong, p. 183. Only new establishment projects are included, as we recorded only seven expansion projects prior to 1969.

These results are not conclusive, since the sample is small with a high variance. Nevertheless, allowing for the greater size and complexity of later projects, we believe that this is a fair reflection of a fundamental trend in entrepreneurial and managerial ability.

The ownership of Korean firms is typically in the hands of individuals or family groups with, as we have seen, the founder of the firm, more often than not, as chief executive. As enterprises have increased in size, however, their effective administration has required the assistance of a growing number of managerial and technical collaborators both inside and outside the firm. Even in medium-size firms there is a good deal of differentiation in. the managerial function, with the chief executive particularly dependent on collaborators in obtaining financing, introducing new technology, and providing technical training. Although much of this is supplied from within the firm's own rapidly expanding stock of trained technicians, outside sources, including foreign firms, government agencies, and banking, research, and other service institutions, have been important.

The medium-size and large Korean firm resembles Japanese enterprises at an earlier stage of Japanese development before decentralized professional management became the rule. The firm normally provides housing, hospital, and recreation facilities for its workers, and there are the company-organized social and training groups, company songs, and other paternalistic efforts to bind the employee to the firm, practices long familiar in Japan. It is not usual, however, for the Korean enterprise to guarantee lifetime employment to its managerial employees and workers, and there is a good deal more employee mobility among firms than was customary in Japan. The manufacturing work force is industrious, highly disciplined, and works long hours, unimpeded by significant trade union intervention. Managerial employees and chief executives work even harder. Replies from chief executives to the entrepreneurial questionnaire report that their ordinary employees average 52 hours weekly, their senior staff 53 and they themselves 54. To judge from the expressed opinions of foreign visitors, these estimates are, if anything, conservative. The long hours of chief executives and management not only distinguish successful from unsuccessful entrepreneurs, but are characteristic of the entire economic system. As one example, the regular working hours of the fastest growing large-scale enterprise in Korea, Daewoo, are from 8:00 A.M. to 7:00 P.M. To staff its thirty-six foreign branches, language training is provided from 6:00 to 8:00 A.M. daily, with any absences "affecting promotion."

The emergence of a thriving entrepreneurial class in South Korea is intriguing, since supposedly it runs counter to the traditional value system. Confucianism places commerce and industry at the bottom of the *sa, nong, kong, sang* (scholar-official, farmer, artisan, merchant) status hierarchy. It is evident, however, that this value system has hardly proved an insuperable obstacle. This does not mean, however, that the difficulties to be overcome were not serious.

Studies of many LDCs find that business leaders come from narrowly defined sub-strata of the population, frequently religious or ethnic, rather than being randomly distributed. Korea has had over two thousand years of unified history in roughly its present border with no significant influxes of foreign elements. The result is one of the world's most homogeneous populations and, in consequence, there are no ethnic, caste, or tribal minorities from which entrepreneurship might have sprung. The Entrepreneurship Survey investigates provincial origin, religion, work history, parental occupation, and education as possible differentiating factors. The last two variables must also serve as proxies for class, since it is impossible to distinguish traditional status classes in modern Korea.

Geographically, the survey considers the place of birth of various Korean elites (private entrepreneurs, private managers, public-enterprise managers, public officials, and politicians). The results indicate that, with respect to entrepreneurial and business managers, the northern population that emigrated south is by far the most highly represented, with roughly four times the representation for the country as a whole. This may be attributed mainly to a process of (un)natural selection. Those who choose to flee a Communist regime will be disproportionately educated, wealthy, and from industrial and commercial backgrounds. A comparison of the backgrounds of northern- and southern-born entrepreneurs indicates that the two groups are similar in the level of their own and their father's educations, the place raised (city versus country), and job experience. Major differences occur only for father's jobs and religion. Northerners were more heavily influenced by Christianity (30 percent versus 18 percent) and correspondingly less influenced by Buddhism and Confucianism (37 percent versus 54 percent). More than one-third of the northerners' fathers had been engaged in some form of trade as opposed to only one-seventh of the southerners. Southerners were more likely to have come from landowning backgrounds (23 percent versus 15 percent) and industry (15 percent versus 9 percent). Although these differences are real, the important fact is that, both for northerners and southerners, the business leaders have come from elite backgrounds.

The major religious minorities in Korea are the Protestants and Catholics. Heavily persecuted under the Yi dynasty, they have since prospered and have played a prominent role in national affairs. In politics they were particularly visible during the Rhee regime (Rhee himself was a Christian), and Christians have been in the forefront of the protest movements from the colonial period down to current civil rights efforts; in education, three of the five finest universities are Christian-sponsored. The question here is whether or not the Christian minority has played a similarly disproportionate role in industry.

Confusing estimates of the Christian share of the population, which vary from 3.5 percent to over 13 percent, make it difficult to give a quantitive answer. This is due, in part, to the religious inhibitions of Koreans. When a Westerner is asked his religion, it is difficult to say "none"; for Koreans, it takes a conscious dedication to say anything other than "none." The result is that many individuals with a strong religious upbringing nevertheless express no religious preference. Most of the respondents in the Entrepreneurship Survey maintained that religion was irrelevant to their business success. In sum, neither the available data nor a priori theorizing allow us to form definite judgments on the degree of over- or under-representation of Christians in the business elite. In comparison with other societies, religion appears to play a minor role in differentiating the business elite from the population as a whole.

Of considerably more interest is the opportunity for movement from low- to high-status occupation. Between generations in South Korea this appears to be negligible. Entrepreneurs' fathers were large-to-medium landowners (47 percent), merchants (19 percent), factory owners (16 percent), civil servants (6 percent), teachers (4 percent), or professionals (7 percent). Ninety-eight percent of the fathers thus came from occupations representing perhaps 15 percent of the male Korean cohort. The industrial elite were recruited from the pre-industrial elite rather than from society as a whole. The younger entrepreneurs (under 40) come from different backgrounds than their elders, with nearly two-thirds having parents in trade and manufacturing (compared with just over a quarter for the older group). There is still no evidence here of recruitment from the poorer segments of society.

Closely related to the narrow recruitment of the Korean business elite is the critical role of education in a Confucian society. Popular opinion in Korea holds that entrepreneurs are not particularly well educated. In fact, business leaders are extraordinarily well educated, in both an absolute and relative sense. Nearly 70 percent of the survey sample had some college education, a level attained by less than 10 percent of the male cohort. Compared to the Korean norm, entrepreneurs constitute part of the minority of educated elite. Since the traditional occupational choice of the educated is government, it is interesting to note there is no significant difference between the level of education of business leaders and higher civil servants of similar age. There remains the question whether business leaders attained their positions because of superior education or whether they received this type of education because they came from ranks in society from which business leaders are normally chosen. Doubtless there is much in the latter view, though it can be claimed that superior education is a requirement for successful management of at least the larger export-oriented firms. In the Confucian tradition, it is difficult for an uneducated man to manage educated men; in the close government-business relations of Korea, it would be difficult for an uneducated business executive to deal effectively with highly educated civil servants; and education probably contributes to sophistication valuable in dealing with foreign firms.

The work history of the sample is not particularly noteworthy. Business leaders had an average work period of some 22 years. Over that period they spent an average of 8.5 years in each of the 2.5 jobs. While this is a stable occupational pattern by Western standards, it is much more mobile than in Japan, where executives typically stay with a single company for life and average 1.8 jobs in a career.

In sum, the Korean experience does not conform in any respect with those theories holding that entrepreneurs tend to come from subordinated groups frustrated by the culture from attaining traditional positions of prestige. While northerners are heavily overrepresented in the entrepreneurial population and Christians, perhaps, to some extent, this is not the result of subordination but of correlation with other variables. Other groups with similar occupational and educational backgrounds are similarly represented. The dominant fact is that South Korea's business leaders come from privileged families representing not more than 15 percent of the population. The present day industrial elite has descended from the pre-industrial elite.

Jones and SaKong also undertake an examination of the backgrounds of the more successful entrepreneurs as compared with those who are less successful. Not surprisingly, they conclude there are no significant differences. The explanation of unusual success presumably lies in personal characteristics that elude the grasp of statistical averages.

There remains the perplexing question why the Confucian culture, which assigns so low a value to business activity, has accommodated itself to the rise of so many successful entrepreneurs. This heritage is, of course, not limited to Korea. The dramatic achievements of entrepreneurship in Japan, Taiwan, Hong Kong, and Singapore also beg for explanation. One possibility is that the modernization process is subtly, or not so subtly, changing the rank order of Confucian values. In South Korea, indeed, there is substantial evidence that business careers, once denigrated, are now regarded as acceptable rivals to those in government officialdom.

PRIVATE ECONOMIC POWER

A consideration of business concentration and sources of private economic power in South Korea leads directly to an examination of the *chaebŏl*. The Chinese characters for *chaebŏl* are the same as for the Japanese zaibatsu, and there are common characteristics. There are also some significant differences.

Zaibatsu has been defined as "a system of highly centralized family control through holding companies."[20] Hirschmeier and Yui identify three stages in their evolution. During the first, from the Meiji Restoration to the Sino-Japanese War (1868–1895), the "old" zaibatsu emerged under driving individual leadership and with no particular pattern of corporate control.[21] Early in the second stage (1895–1946), the "old" zaibatsu faced increasing problems of coordination and control over their expanding empires and turned to a holding-company model with heavy reliance on non-family managers selected on a basis of merit. In the post-war stage three, the zaibatsu were initially broken up but reemerged as one set of nuclei for modern *keiretsu*—"independent enterprises, clustering around one or several core city banks, with some coordination of policies, some joint action even, and personal regular meetings of the presidents."[22]

Contemporary Korean *chaebŏl* correspond most closely in structure to the stage-one zaibatsu of the Meiji era. At the center of each group is the *hoejang,* a "chairman" who is the dynamic

and cohesive force of the group. Typically he is an entre-
preneur in the true sense, founding one enterprise and then
leaving its management to a relative (or, more recently, to a
trusted associate) as he moves on to a new venture. Majority
shares in the various enterprises are held by the *hoejang* and his
immediate relatives. There is an important difference between
large-scale business organization in Korea and Japan which we
have emphasized earlier. Pre-war zaibatsu included, and post-war
keiretsu are centered on, their own banks and other financial
institutions. *Chaebŏl*, on the other hand, must rely on
government-controlled credit institutions. This is a central fact
in government-business relations in Korea and has an important
bearing on the extent of private economic power.

Jones and SaKong, with the assistance of the Federation of
Korean Industries, have prepared a list of 46 *chaebŏl* ranging
from Samsung, the largest (in terms of value added), with 18
companies and 353 billion wŏn in sales, to the smallest, Han
Yang, with only 2 companies and 387 million wŏn in sales.
Together these large firms account for a sizable share of Korean
business as indicated in Table 69.

TABLE 69 *Chaebŏl* in the Korean Economy, 1975

Number of Chaebŏl	Chaebŏl Value Added as Cumulative Percentage of		
	GDP	Non-Agricultural GDP	Manufacturing GDP
5	5.1	7.1	14.5
10	7.7	10.7	21.8
20	10.6	14.7	30.2
46	13.4	18.6	36.7

Source: Jones and SaKong, p. 266.

The *chaebŏl* sector is significantly larger than either the
public-enterprise or government sector, in terms of value added,
but is only one-third the size of other private non-agricultural

enterprise. How do these magnitudes compare with other Asian nations? Business concentration appears to be substantially higher in Japan though current Japanese estimates are unavailable. At the end of World War II, the four largest zaibatsu controlled one-fourth of all paid-in capital of Japanese incorporated business.[23]

Korean business in 1975 was substantially less concentrated than business in Pakistan in 1958 (when large-scale business was privately owned) or than in India in 1948, 1958, and 1968. Although data for comparison are somewhat less than adequate, the four largest Korean groups accounted for 13 percent of manufacturing in 1975 versus 23 percent for India in 1968; the 16 largest Korean groups accounted for 26 percent as against 34 percent in Pakistan in 1958.

The relatively low level of business concentration in Korea runs counter to popular perception, but it is not too surprising, given the fact that everyone started from a near-zero base in 1951. On the other hand, the share of *chaebŏl* value added in non-agricultural GDP has grown rapidly in recent years as shown in Table 70.

TABLE 70 Trends in *Chaebŏl* Concentration, 1973–1975
(cumulative percent of non-agricultural GDP)

Number of Chaebŏl	1973	1974	1975
5	5.2	5.6	7.1
10	7.9	8.5	10.7
20	10.9	11.8	14.7
46	15.0	15.3	18.6

Source: Jones and SaKong, p. 268.

This is a rapid rate of increase and, if it continues, it forecasts a high level of business concentration in Korea in the near future.

The *chaebŏl* do not enjoy a good press in South Korea, though perhaps it is no worse than large-scale enterprise suffers from in most countries. Kyong-Dong Kim expresses a typical view in referring to *chaebŏl* leaders as "political capitalists" who:

> accumulated capital mainly through such "non-rational" processes as speculation, price-fixing, tax evasion, and taking advantage of cumulative inflation. More crucial to this process, however, was that they played on political connections to gain economic favors in exchange for political contributions.[24]

While there is some element of truth in this as applied to modern business leaders, its application to the Rhee period is much more exact. Then the description of business leaders as "political capitalists" was no less than the truth. As one student of the period comments:

> It is well known that Japanese properties and aid dollars were distributed at ridiculously low prices. Even these acquisitions were made with cheap bank loans under the existing situation of hyper-inflation. And cheap bank loans were mostly concentrated in a few *chaebŏl*. Hyper-inflation, shortage of supply, high import tariffs, import restrictions, protected *chaebŏl* monopoly prices and the domestic tax structure were all favorable for *chaebŏl*.[25]

The major sources of *chaebŏl* accumulation during the Rhee period were considered to be noncompetitive allocation of import quotas and import licenses, bargain-price acquisition of former Japanese properties, the selective allocation of aid funds and materials, privileged access to cheap bank loans, non-competitive awards of government, and U.S. military contracts. A particular source of discrimination in AID allocation was the favoritism said to have been shown to members of Rhee's Liberal Party.

Some of these accounts may be exaggerated, but there is no doubt that the foundations of a number of *chaebŏl* fortunes were based on political influence during the Rhee regime. Nevertheless, there also occurred, as we have seen, a fairly rapid growth of industrial output and employment. An exaggerated price in business profits was paid for this growth, but there was still growth.

Under Park the most egregious sources of privileged access to profit-making opportunities have been eliminated, though there remains privileged access to domestic credit and, to a certain extent, foreign exchange. Ready access to credit and foreign exchange, when taken in conjunction with the highly leveraged structure of Korean corporations, can lead to a rapid growth of profits and that the profits of *chaebŏl* have, indeed, grown rapidly is an established fact; but so have the output and exports of manufactures. To obtain preferred access to credit and foreign exchange, it is sufficient that a convincing argument be made to the bureaucracy that the privileges thus conferred will be used productively. To make such an argument effectively, it is also necessary that one be well connected with the bureaucracy. This condition clearly provides an advantage for those who are already wealthy and for those with backgrounds paralleling the backgrounds of top bureaucrats. It may well be that the dynamics of discretionary allocations of industrial credit result in economic rents beyond the minimum necessary to induce the existing level of entrepreneurial effort, but how much beyond we are unprepared to estimate.

Our view is, then, that under Rhee much of *chaebŏl* accumulation took place as a result of government-controlled transfers which produced unnecessarily few compensatory benefits for the society as a whole. Under Park such transfers remained, but they are decidedly ancillary to accumulation resulting from socially beneficial growth of productive activity. This change is not to be attributed to any consciousness-raising on the part of entrepreneurs but rather to a shutting off of certain unproductive channels of moneymaking and the opening of others that are productive.

Business concentration in South Korea, though not as impressive as in certain other Asian countries, is still large and seems, in recent years, to have been increasing rapidly. Furthermore, it is a concentration that has clearly been favored by government policy. Nevertheless, it has not led to the kind of exercise of private economic power that might have been expected from the growth of the *chaebŏl*. The government has mixed its encouragement to growth with concern for the use of accumulated wealth and, beginning in the 1970s, had introduced a series of measures designed to modify capital structures, to limit certain forms of investment, and to increase public participation in equity holdings. And at no stage has there been any doubt that government is in charge.

This was made clear early in the Park regime in the enforcement of the Special Law For Dealing With Illicit Wealth Accumulation which we have already discussed. Although criminal sanctions were withdrawn in favor of fines that totalled $16 million, the *chaebŏl* were convinced that what the government could give, it could also take away. While, during the 1960s, there was encouragement of *chaebŏl* wealth accumulation, it is important to note there have been real restraints on its utilization. As we have argued throughout this chapter, wealth has not been translated into significant political influences. Second, a high proportion of profits has been reinvested and remarkably little diverted to conspicuous consumption. Third, there have been limitations on the utilization of wealth to acquire certain forms of economic power—most effectively in precluding *chaebŏl* control of banks, and more recently, in a period of restraints on *chaebŏl* asset use.

The limitation of conspicuous consumption is partly a result of public policy and partly of self-imposed standards of austerity. Income and property taxes are progressive, and the inheritance tax is somewhat higher than in most LDCs. Furthermore, as we shall see in Chapter 9, these taxes are collected. Public policy clearly discourages luxury consumption. Taxes on luxury vehicles (over 4 cylinders) in 1975 were numerous: a tariff of 250 percent, a commodity tax of 40–60 percent, a lump sum automobile tax, and a purchase tax of 15 percent. The houses of the rich may be opulently furnished and constructed, but they are not of gargantuan size.

By Asian practice, the standards of living of the Korean rich are relatively austere. Korean wealth is largely first-generation, and this austerity may well not be accepted by a more profligate second generation. Of course standards vary widely among rich Korean families. Casual empiricism, however, suggests that Korean excesses pale by comparison with the Southeast Asian practices among the rich of hiring jetliners to host birthday parties in Europe. While the Korean rich live supremely well by Korean standards, their houses, cars, and entertainments appear to us to be decidedly frugal in comparison to their counterparts elsewhere in Asia.

Beginning in the 1970s, there has been a marked upsurge in government attention to the *chaebŏl*, stimulated, no doubt, by the rapid growth of large-scale enterprises. The new government concern has manifested itself in a series of measures aimed at opening the *chaebŏl* to public ownership, lowering their debt-equity ratios, and prohibiting real estate speculation. These efforts began in 1972 with a law designed to induce business firms to open themselves to public participation by selling their shares on the stock market. The rather feeble response to this measure has led to successively more stringent measures. Over time the result of the various laws and directives aimed at the *chaebŏl* may significantly reduce their rate of wealth accumulation since:

1) The reduction in the debt-equity ratio reduces the earnings from leverage.
2) It becomes more difficult to use low-interest industrial credit to finance profitable land speculation.
3) The public offerings are made at well below recognized market value, giving an immediate transfer to buyers. Insofar as the market undervalues current offerings there will be a further transfer as economic rent from earlier entrepreneurial acts accrues to new equity holders.

Particularly since the Presidential Special Directives of May 29, 1974, it may well be that a turning point has been reached in the government's attitude toward the *chaebŏl*. At this writing,

the ramifications are not entirely clear, but this seems to be a
distinct possibility.

CONCLUSION

Although Korea, before the incursion from Japan, had accomplished little in the area of industrialization and, indeed, was
extraordinarily remote from the winds of industrial change that
were sweeping the developed world, its population proved to be
highly adaptable to industrialization—first under the leadership
of Japan and, later, under its own leadership. Japanese penetration began in 1876 and, by the time Korean independence was
lost in 1910, nearly 80,000 Japanese resident in Korea had
thoroughly permeated the economy. By the end of World War
II, there were nearly 800,000. Although Japanese exploitation
could hardly have been more systematic, it was impossible to
develop industry this rapidly and efficiently without affecting
Korean experience and know-how. While it is true that Japanese
occupied the top positions in business, there had emerged by the
end of Japanese rule many thousands of capable Korean
technicians and managers. The expansion of educational facilities
assisted the growth of the supply of trained labor, and the
experience of modern technology and forms of business organization had lasting effects.

This Japanese heritage was, in part, but only in part, dissipated
for South Korea by the division of the peninsula, the elimination
of the Japanese management and the Japanese market, the dis-
organization of the period of U.S. Military Government, and the
destruction of the Korean War. The loss in physical facilities was
great, but most of the human capital remained, augmented by
the return of Korean nationals from Japan and Manchuria and
the influx from North Korea. Furthermore, the experience of
how modern industrial establishments operate was there to stay.

The regime of President Syngman Rhee, which took the place
of the U.S. Military Government in 1948 and lasted until 1960,

was a highly personal government manipulated by a skilled politician who showed little interest in, or capacity for, the formulation of sensible development policy. Nonetheless, industrial investment, financed largely by U.S. aid, grew at a respectable rate, although it was accompanied by a degree of corruption sufficient to keep Rhee's party in power and to lay the basis for a number of private fortunes. The expansion of manufactured output met increased domestic demand and substituted for imports; the export of manufactured products was negligible. Still many of the entrepreneurs and business organizations that emerged during this period managed to survive and flourish in the 1960s and 1970s.

The Park Military Government that succeeded the short-lived democratic regime of Chang Myon adopted economic growth as its top priority and announced its ambition of becoming independent of foreign assistance and influence. The highly centralized decision-making process that emerged was speedy, flexible, and thoroughly pragmatic. Although private enterprise was the principle agent of growth, it was enterprise operating under firm government direction. The government developed effective planning procedures that increasingly concentrated on an examination of policy alternatives.

It was, however, in the implementation of policy that the Park regime particularly distinguished itself from governments in most less-developed countries. It exhibited a discriminatory use of incentives and disincentives and command procedures that left an unusual degree of discretion in the hands of the administrative bureaucracy. Policy implementation required close cooperation between government agencies and business enterprise, but there was never any question as to who held the whip hand. Although many devices were used to persuade, cajole, and command business compliance with government objectives, the most powerful instruments were undoubtedly the taxing power, control of credit from the government-owned banks, and control of access to foreign loans.

The pragmatic character of public policy in South Korea is

well illustrated by the ready resort to public ownership in an essentially private enterprise economy. The relative size of the public industrial sector is comparable to that in countries subject to large socialist influence. The attitude of the Korean government has been—if the market works, fine; if not, there are other ways of accomplishing the public purposes.

But, while the role of public enterprise has been impressive, the major part of Korean growth has come in the private sector. A remarkably effective group of entrepreneurs have headed these private enterprises, exhibiting an ability to introduce new products and processes and, with considerable government assistance, to find their way into new markets. In general this business elite has sprung from the old preindustrial elite. Immigrants from the north and the Christian element in the population have accounted for more than their share of entrepreneurial talent, but it is rather striking that, despite the diminution of class barriers since the war, there has not been more upward mobility into positions of business leadership.

A substantial number of these firms have grown into large conglomerates popularly known as *chaebŏl* which resemble in some respects the zaibatsu of pre-war Japan. But there are also notable differences; in particular the absence of control of commercial banks which, in Korea, are all in government hands. Although the *chaebŏl* are fairly numerous and large, economic concentration in South Korea is not as pronounced as in India, Pakistan, and a number of other less-developed countries. This, however, may be in the process of change, since the recent growth of *chaebŏl* has been extremely rapid. Government has been concerned with this growth and has recently adopted a number of policies to check it. How successful this will be is, as yet, unclear. But, in any case, it seems unlikely that large-scale enterprise in Korea will achieve anything like the political influence exerted by the pre-war zaibatsu in Japan. In "Korea, Inc." the government is definitely the senior partner.

NINE

Korean Fiscal and Financial Development

The taxing and spending powers of the fisc and the borrowing and lending powers of financial institutions are potentially powerful instruments for mobilizing and allocating the resources of a society. The Western tradition has conceived of these two as quite separate with the fisc in the public sector and finance primarily a responsibility of the private sector that has only been brought under public regulation within this century. In East Asia the two institutions have not been so sharply separated. Farming out tax collections to private individuals is a long-standing practice. Payment of tribute to a powerful sovereign for protection and the right to trade within his territory is another tradition, as is the lending of grain and cloth by governmental bodies and the abuse of that power to the benefit of the officials and the detriment of the peasantry. Governmental mingling of fiscal and financial functions and the use of both to support favored groups, or punish the recalcitrant, has been part of the fabric of Chinese, Japanese, and Korean society for centuries.

The Japanese began the introduction of modern financial institutions in Korea in 1876. They subsequently developed both the fiscal and financial systems in Korea to relatively high levels of sophistication during their colonial reign. These systems were very much in the Japanese style, based on close association and cooperation between government and business. The main objective of the Japanese was to mobilize financial resources in Japan and Korea, initially for the expansion of Japanese enterprises in Korea, but eventually to support the Japanese war effort. The collapse of the Japanese regime in Korea in 1945 removed the experienced managers and engulfed the fiscal and financial institutions of Korea in a tidal wave of inflation.

The U.S. Military Government sought to overcome the continuing inflation with a large inflow of foreign aid. Subsequently, as the inflation subsided, the Americans attempted to introduce reforms that would have cast both the fiscal and financial systems more in the Western democratic mold. The Korean War intervened and brought with it a resumption of inflation, reliance on external aid as the primary source of finance, and reinforcement of governmental control over the allocation of finance. For the next decade, there was a continuing struggle between the American and Korean governments over the basic directions of the fiscal and financial systems. American aid, and the resulting generation of counterpart funds, provided a major share of total savings, budget revenues, and loanable funds for the financial institutions. The Americans sought to reduce this role and the Koreans to expand it. At the same time, the Americans were urging the Korean government to reduce its control over financial institutions, to make the tax system more effective and uniform in its enforcement, to improve budgetary and planning practices, and to stabilize prices.

Finally, in the mid-1960s, faced with declining aid levels, the Korean government turned its attention to exploiting the potential for resource mobilization of both the tax and banking mechanisms. The approaches adopted, which embodied the East Asian traditions of strong governmental guidance and discretion as to tax assessments and loan allocations, have been remarkably successful. They have been a major factor in more than doubling the ratio of investment to GNP and channeling resources into manufacturing and economic infrastructure rather than social services and consumption. In this chapter we shall review some of the historical antecedents and show how they were transformed into the efficient, controlled and controlling set of instruments and institutions that exist today.

THE COLONIAL LEGACY

The Kanghwa Treaty of 1876 authorized the opening of trade relations between Japan and Korea and the establishment of Japanese-owned businesses within Korea. The first branch of a Japanese bank commenced operations in Pusan that same year and was soon followed by others that extended their activities to the other major port cities. Japanese currency circulated freely in Korea by the turn of the century,[1] and in 1905 the note issue of the Daiichi Ginkō (Bank) became the official legal tender in Korea.

With the annexation of Korea by Japan, which occurred in stages between 1905 and 1910, several new banking institutions were established in Korea under Japanese governmental sponsorship to carry out specialized financial functions. These included: the Bank of Chosen, which functioned as a central bank, the Agricultural and Industrial Bank, and the Oriental Development Company, both destined to become important sources of financing for Japanese industrial investment, and the Local Financial Associations, that were designed to mobilize rural savings and provide financing to agriculture. From 1910 to 1945 the financial institutions in Korea were predominantly owned by Japanese, controlled by the Japanese Government

General, linked closely to parent or sister institutions in Japan, and operated to serve Japanese interests. While several Korean-owned banks were established during this period, they were clearly junior partners, and they followed the lead of their masters.

The growth of the financial and fiscal system in relation to the current value of output (as measured by commodity-product) is depicted in Table 71. During the first decade of colonial rule, while output and prices were rising significantly, both the fiscal and the financial systems were relatively small, and revenues actually declined towards the end of the decade. Over the next decade there was rapid expansion of both systems while the price level and the growth rate were declining. Government revenues nearly doubled as a proportion of output between 1920 and 1930, and broad money (currency plus demand deposits and time deposits) expanded from 17 percent to 40 percent of commodity-product. Between 1930 and 1940, fiscal and financial growth continued after a brief hiatus due to world recession. High output growth and mild inflation also characterized this period of colonial expansion into Manchuria and China. By the end of the decade, however, as Japanese military preparations accelerated, the potential inflationary impact of large increases in money supply was offset by price controls, and suppressed inflation distorted the financial ratios. Thus, while the war-directed expansion of the late 1930s brought the revenue and monetary ratios up to levels that have not been matched in recent Korean experience, these ratios contain an upward bias, and those for the mid-1930s are more indicative of normal conditions. A comparison of the revenue and money ratios for 1935, 1940, and 1975 is shown in Table 72. It is based upon a conversion of the commodity-output estimates for 1935 and 1940 into estimates of GNP in order to derive the ratios of revenues and money to estimated GNP for those years.[2] This shows that the ratios of 1975 moderately exceeded those of 1935, but were less than the distorted ratios of 1940.

These figures suggest that fiscal and financial development

TABLE 71 Comparisons of Government Revenue and Money Supply to Commodity Output, 1911–1940

	Net Value of Commodity Output (million yen at 1936 prices)	Deflator	Net Value in Current Prices	Growth Rate	% Ratios to Net Output[d]		
					Revenues[a]	M_1[b]	M_2[c]
1910–1912	682	58.3	398		12 (1911)	11	12
1919–1921	929	145.7	1,354	3.5	10 (1920)	13	17
1929–1931	1,256	93.7	1,177	3.1	17 (1929)	20	40
1939–1941	1,658	177.0	2,935	3.1	36 (1939)	42	76

Sources: Commodity output and growth rate data are from Kim and Roemer, Chapter 2, which in turn are based on Sang Chul Suh Growth and Structural Changes, pp. 169–170. The revenue ratios are derived from Chong Kee Park, Development and Modernization of Korea's Tax System (Seoul, Korea Development Institute, 1977) p. 11. The money ratios are from David C. Cole and Yung Chul Park, Financial Development in Korea, 1945–1978 (Seoul, Korea Development Institute, 1979), p. 22.

Notes: [a]Revenues are those of the Central Government in Korea and include public bonds, borrowing and subsidies from the Japanese government, in addition to regular revenues from taxes and government-owned enterprises and property.
[b]M_1 or narrow money consists of currency in circulation plus demand deposits of banks.
[c]M_2 or broad money is M_1 plus time and savings deposits of banking institutions. Postal savings deposits are not included.
[d]The M_1 and M_2 ratios are for 1911, 1920, 1930, and 1940 rather than three-year averages. The revenue ratios are for the years indicated in parentheses.

TABLE 72 Fiscal and Financial Ratios to GNP
(%)

	1935	1940	1975
Government revenues	13	21	16
M_1	13	24	13
M_2	29	44	34

under the Japanese was considerable even prior to the period of suppressed inflation, and that the ratios to GNP were not very different from those of recent years. Such high levels of development in the late 1930s accentuate the collapse of the fiscal and financial sectors over the two decades 1945–1965, that will be described in the next sections, and also suggest that the subsequent expansion of these sectors after 1965 was more of a restoration than a new creation.

THE WAR AND INTER–WAR YEARS

Fiscal and financial conditions in Korea during World War II were dominated by credit creation and price controls that burst forth in an inflationary surge when the Japanese were defeated in 1945. Within several months, prices had risen 24-fold, the banks practically ceased to function, and government revenues were negligible in real terms. The U.S. Military Government, attempting to fill the breach in South Korea, initially retained the existing Japanese tax regulations, but found that they produced very little revenue because of the inflation and the breakdown in the administrative machinery. Monopoly profits were the main source of revenue at this time, eventually supplemented by funds derived from the sale of aid supplies from the United States.

In 1947 the U.S. Military Government introduced some reforms in the income and property taxes in an effort to make them more equitable. Both a progressive rate structure and self-assessment were incorporated in the income tax, following the U.S. pattern. The following year after the new Korean government was established, a Korean Tax System Reform Committee recommended reduced reliance on income taxes, heavier taxes on luxury consumption, and simplification of the tax system.[3] This was the first of a series of interactions over the structure of the tax system in which the American side generally espoused greater reliance on self-assessed, progressively structured income and property taxes, and the Korean officials indicated their preference for selective commodity taxes and administratively assessed business and income taxes. The Koreans generally believed that self-assessment would not work and that discretionary tax enforcement was preferable for a number of reasons, only one of which was to obtain adequate revenues.

The financial system deteriorated drastically after 1945. The volume of banking activity declined, and the Bank of Chosen was mainly engaged in financing government deficits. The various specialized banks, which were first taken over by the U.S. Military Government and then transferred to the Korean government in 1948, shifted over to doing general banking business in order to survive. The system described in 1950 was a far cry from the highly developed modern institutions of the 1930s.

> There are no money or capital markets in the accepted sense of the terms and no really adequate facilities for mobilizing such savings as are currently made and for channeling them into productive investments. The government has relied exclusively on borrowing on overdraft from the central bank for financing its deficits, and only recently has it announced its first pending issue of bonds, which are to be sold to the public and banking institutions on a more or less compulsory basis. The use of the check is highly undeveloped and the bulk of the country's monetary transactions is consummated in currency. A large fraction of the aggregate turnover of goods and services does not, in fact, even involve the use of money at all, but takes the form of payments in kind and barter transactions.[14]

In an effort to revive the financial sector, two experts from the U.S. Federal Reserve System, Arthur Bloomfield and John Jensen, worked out a program in collaboration with Korean officials that called for:

1) Transforming the Bank of Chosen into a strong, autonomous central bank to be renamed the Bank of Korea;
2) Strengthening controls over the commercial banks and transferring them as rapidly as possible to private ownership;
3) Implementing forceful anti-inflation policies to encourage financial growth.

The first two points of the program symbolized the American policy of democratizing the banking system, and the economy in general, by creating separate and equal monetary and fiscal authorities and private ownership of the banks, so that economic power could not be concentrated in the hands of either strong government or powerful businessmen.[5] While the new banking regulations were only partially implemented in the spring of 1950 and then largely nullified by the advent of the Korean War, the Bloomfield and Jensen proposals provided the basis for a struggle between the Bank of Korea and the Ministry of Finance, and more broadly between the advocates of concentration and dispersion of economic and political power that lasted into the 1960s.

The Korean War dealt a second devastating blow to the fiscal and financial institutions. The price index, which had declined in the spring of 1950 for the first time in five years, went up by 100 percent during the third quarter of the year. The newly created Bank of Korea set up operations in its Pusan branch and began financing the government's war effort on a massive basis as internal revenue sources disappeared. The influx of U.N. forces also required financial resources that were provided simply by expansion of central bank credit, because no suitable agreement was reached for over a year in regard to the terms of payment for local currency advances by the Bank of Korea to the United Nations Command.[6] The inflationary potential of these factors was counterbalanced in part by the quick military recovery of most of South Korea, the arrival of food and relief supplies from the United States, and the basic commitment of support by the United States and some other U.N. members to the government and people of South Korea.

During the three years of the war, from mid-1950 to mid-1953, the money supply increased at an average rate of 28 percent per quarter, and prices rose at slightly over 30 percent per quarter. Money supply statistics only present part of the picture, because U.S. currency and Military Payment Certificates entered the country in substantial but unknown quantities and served as a more stable store of value and medium of exchange than the steadily depreciating local currency. Throughout this period, money dealers and other unorganized money market institutions assumed increasing importance as borrowers and lenders as well as currency dealers. Such unorganized financial institutions have had a long tradition in Korea.[7] They have tended to take on more active roles when the regular banking institutions are not functioning effectively and vice versa. During the war years they were very active.

The broad lines of the fiscal problem from 1949 through 1953 are shown in Table 73. Starting from a large deficit in 1949, the increase in defense expenditures in 1950 resulted in a deficit equal to three-fourths of total expenditures. Thereafter, the deficit diminished but was still equal to half of total spending in 1953. Monopoly profits, mainly from the manufacture of cigarettes, accounted for half of total revenue in 1949, but dropped to only about 20 percent over the next four years. This was due in part to the destruction of production facilities, but probably more important were the large quantities of foreign cigarettes supplied through military channels.

The main source of revenues during the war years was an agricultural land tax collected in grain, which was adopted in 1951, and was a major factor in the tenfold increase in revenues over 1950. The significance of the land tax is understated in the statistics, because the grain was valued at well below prevailing market prices. Chong Kee Park has estimated that at market

TABLE 73 Government Revenues and Expenditures, 1949–1953 (million wŏn)

	Government Revenues	Government Expenditures			Deficit	% of total expenditures
		Non-Defense	Defense	Total		
1949	33	64	24	88	55	62.5
1950	59	112	132	244	185	75.8
1951	505	442	330	772	267	34.6
1952	1,332	1,389	946	2,335	1,003	43.0
1953	2,655	2,420	2,260	5,680	3,035	53.4

Sources: Revenues are from Chong Kee Park, p. 30. Expenditures are from Chuk Kyo Kim, "The Growth Pattern of Central Government Expenditures," in Chuk Kyo Kim, ed., *Planning Model and Macroeconomic Policy Issues* (Seoul, Korea Development Institute, 1977), p. 284.

prices it would have amounted to 50 percent of total revenues.[8] Haskell Wald reports that the government collected 11 percent of the total rice crop in 1952 through this mechanism.[9] The tax in kind, reminiscent of the land tax in the imperial period, was also critical for meeting government wages that were partly paid in kind to offset the inflation.

Thus a number of expedients, such as the land tax and wage payments in kind, use of foreign currency, and the unorganized money markets were relied upon during the war years to cope with the continuing inflation and to carry on the war. With the ending of hostilities in the summer of 1953, attention was turned to the reconstruction of the country and its institutions.

POST-WAR DEVELOPMENTS: AN OVERVIEW

During the early post-war years much greater attention was devoted, in the fiscal and financial spheres, to the mechanics of spending and lending than to the means of mobilizing revenues or voluntary savings. Given the depressed state of the economy and the impoverished condition of the people, it was not unreasonable to conclude that the potential for mobilizing financial resources from within Korea was limited, and the prospects of substantial foreign aid seemed to make such efforts unnecessary. The problem was, as discussed in Chapter 6, that the principal aid donor, the United States, and the Korean government never achieved real agreement as to the appropriate level or role of foreign assistance, and both sides tried to manipulate the instruments at their command to support their position on the aid level. The Korean side sought to expand government expenditures and bank credit to finance the reconstruction program. It did little to increase domestic resource mobilization and insisted upon a flow of aid sufficient to fill the gap between investment plus government current expenditures on the one hand and domestic savings plus government revenues on the other. The Americans for their part sought to impose ceilings on government spending and bank lending, and a floor on government revenues, and to make their aid conditional upon achieving agreement on these matters.[10]

For the first three years (1954–1956) the Korean government had its way. Expenditures and loans grew rapidly, revenues grew slowly, and deposits declined as shares of GNP. Despite a rapid increase in aid (from 4.4 to 10.9 percent of GNP between 1954 and 1956) inflation was still rampant. Over the next four years (1957–1960) the American side was dominant. The revenue and money ratios rose sharply, credit and government spending were somewhat curtailed, the aid level declined as did the inflation rate, but so too did the growth rate. This was followed by two years of expansion (1961–1962) by the Park Government and two more years of American-imposed contraction (1963–1964). In general, the Koreans were overly ambitious and gave little consideration either to the inflationary consequences or to the need to mobilize domestic resources. Conversely, the Americans were overly restrictive, believing that greater stability would lead to more growth. Despite the oscillations of policy from expansion to restraint, the ratio of fixed investment to GNP remained remarkably steady between 10 and 11 percent until 1961–1963, when it moved up to an 11–14 percent range. Finally the Koreans came to appreciate the harmful consequences of this seesaw pattern and recognized both the limitations and costs of obtaining foreign aid under such circumstances. They then turned their efforts to mobilizing domestic resources and non-aid foreign financing. This turn-about in the mid-1960s ushered in the period of high fiscal, financial, and output growth that has been noted many times already in this study. By the 1970s the Korean economy had been transformed into an open, high-growth pattern. As shown in Chapter 5, the fiscal, financial, savings, investment, and trade ratios had been elevated to new levels, and the problems of stabilization emanated more from outside than inside the economy.

The consequences of these broad shifts in policy are illustrated by the changes in the fiscal and financial ratios shown on a quinquennial basis in Table 74. All the ratios rose sharply between 1955 and 1960; most of them declined over the next five years and then recovered and rose to new highs after 1965.

With this brief overview, it is possible to turn to a more detailed examination of the fiscal and financial sectors during the post-war decades.

GOVERNMENT EXPENDITURES

In the post-war period, government expenditures have fluctuated widely as a share of GNP over a range of 12 to 24 percent. There were two expansionary phases from 1956 through 1962 and 1965 through 1972, each followed by a short, severe contractionary phase. There have also been sizable shifts in the composition of government expenditures involving reductions in the shares of defense and social services, and expansion of infrastructure investment and economic services that have supported the accelerated growth efforts of the government.

The cyclical movements of government expenditures and their effects on the fiscal deficit are readily discernable from

TABLE 74 Fiscal and Financial Ratios, 1955–1975 (as % of GNP)

| | Flow Variables | | | | | | Stock Variables | | | | |
| | Government Revenues | | | Government Expenditures | | | Money | | Credit | | |
	Regular	Counterpart	Total	Non-Defense	Defense	Total	M_1	M_2	Bank Loans	Foreign Loan Guarantees	Total
1955	6.2	4.0	10.2	7.4	4.5	11.9	8.1	8.1	6.0	0	6.0
1960	12.0	4.9	16.9	12.2	6.0	18.2	9.2	12.5	16.3	0.2	16.5
1965	8.6	3.5	12.1	9.0	3.7	12.7	8.1	12.1	13.5	9.3	22.8
1970	15.4	0.6	16.0	15.1	3.9	19.0	11.9	34.6	32.9	28.9	61.8
1975	16.2	0	16.2	14.4	4.3	18.7	13.1	34.4	38.5	32.8	71.3

Sources: Revenues are from Chong Kee Park, Development and Modernization of Korea's Tax System, p. 39. Expenditures are from Chuk Kyo Kim, "The Growth Pattern of Central Government Expenditure," p. 284. Money and Credit data are from David C. Cole and Yung Chul Park, Financial Development of Korea, 1945–1978, pp. 22 and 26.

FIGURE 5 Central Government Expenditure and Deficit
as Percent of GNP
(at current prices)

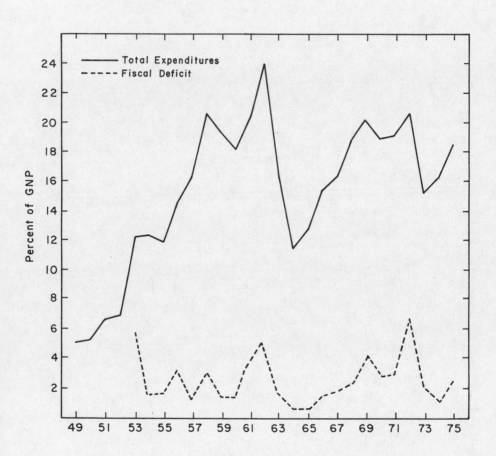

Source: Chuk Kyo Kim, p. 271.

Figure 5. Government expenditures expanded during the Korean War and then leveled off in the immediate post-war period. They were again expansionary from 1956–1958 but were contracted as part of the stabilization effort from 1958 to 1960. The rise in government spending and the fiscal deficit in 1961–1962 contributed to the subsequent inflation; and the drastic cutback in spending, from 24 percent to 11.5 percent of GNP between 1962 and 1964, was the main element of the government's stabilization program. Recovery of government spending over the next five years was more gradual (and consistent with revenue growth) than in previous periods and thus avoided serious inflationary consequences. From 1968–1972, expenditures were fairly constant in the range of 18–20 percent of GNP, but the deficit grew as revenues stagnated and then declined in 1972.

The decline in the government-expenditure share in 1973–1974 was largely in response to the decline in the revenue-to-GNP-ratio in 1972 resulting from a mild recession. The government's intention was to hold down the budget deficit and thereby limit inflationary pressure. But an export boom in 1973, plus the oil price increases in late 1973, injected both demand-pull and cost-push pressures into the picture that overwhelmed any contractionary effect of the restraint on government spending. These external factors became the predominant causes of instability in the 1970s and, as a consequence, internal fiscal and monetary policy instruments were much less effective than the management of external debt in dealing with instability of prices and the balance of payments. Massive external borrowing in 1974 made it possible to ride out the rise in oil prices and the softness in export markets due to worldwide recession with only a mild decline in Korea's GNP growth rate to 7 percent in 1974–1975.

While variations in the rate of government spending were an important factor in both generating and curing instability in the 1950s and 1960s, they become less significant in the 1970s for two reasons. The amplitude of the swings in the expenditure ratio diminished, and the rise in both the export ratio and the fluctuations around the trend of that ratio became the dominant influence on instability of aggregate demand. Fluctuations of government expenditures were still important, but more in terms of whether they offset or exacerbated the cyclical movements of exports than as a destabilizing force in their own right.

The composition of government spending has undergone some significant shifts since the Korean War. Defense expenditures moved very narrowly in a range around a mean of 5.75 percent of GNP for the decade 1953–1962 and then dropped to a mean of 4 percent of GNP—again with minimal variation thereafter (see Table 75). This negative displacement of nearly 2 percent of GNP that occurred after 1962 coincided with the shift from an expansionary to a stability-oriented budget policy, a sharp decline in counterpart revenues (part of which had been earmarked for the defense budget), and a political transition from an openly military regime to an elected regime dominated by ex-military officers who sought to play down their military origins. All three of these factors contributed to the decline in the relative share of defense spending, but it undoubtedly helped to have an ex-general as President who could both restrain the fiscal demands of the military and assure them that they were not being neglected. The absence of serious threats from North Korea during the mid-1960s helped to make the decline in defense resources palatable. Later in the decade, the increase in U.S. military assistance and equipment, associated with South Korea's involvement in the Vietnam War, and a constant 4 percent share of a rapidly growing GNP gave the military an adequate, if not an abundant, flow of real resources.[11]

Non-defense spending by government had risen steadily and steeply throughout the post-Korean War decade, that is, from 5 percent of GNP in 1953 to 18.2 percent in 1962. It was cut back to 8 percent by 1964 and then recovered to a 14.5 percent average, around which it has fluctuated since 1968. The negative displacement of government non-defense spending between 1962 and 1964 was achieved through a cutback on all types of

TABLE 75 Government Revenues and Expenditures as
Percent of GNP, 1953–1975

Year	Government Revenues			Government Expenditures		
	Regular	Counterpart	Total	Non-defense	Defense	Total
1953	5.5	0.3	5.8	5.0	6.8	11.8
1954	6.5	4.2	10.7	7.7	4.6	12.3
1955	6.2	4.0	10.2	7.4	4.5	11.9
1956	7.1	5.0	12.1	9.2	6.1	15.3
1957	7.5	7.7	15.2	10.8	5.7	16.5
1958	8.7	9.0	17.7	14.5	6.2	20.7
1959	12.0	6.1	18.1	13.1	6.3	19.4
1960	12.0	4.9	16.9	12.2	6.0	18.2
1961	9.6	7.4	17.0	14.6	5.6	20.2
1962	10.8	8.1	18.9	18.2	5.9	24.1
1963	8.9	5.5	14.4	12.1	4.2	16.3
1964	7.2	3.6	10.8	7.9	3.6	11.5
1965	8.6	3.5	12.1	9.0	3.7	12.7
1966	10.8	3.1	13.9	11.6	3.9	15.5
1967	12.1	2.2	14.3	12.4	4.0	16.4
1968	14.4	1.6	16.0	14.8	4.1	18.9
1969	15.1	0.9	16.0	16.3	4.0	20.3
1970	15.4	0.6	16.0	15.1	3.9	19.0
1971	15.6	0.3	15.9	14.7	4.4	19.1
1972	13.5	0.0	13.5	16.2	4.5	20.7
1973	13.2		13.2	11.7	3.6	15.3
1974	15.1		15.1	11.6	4.7	16.3
1975	16.2		16.2	14.4	4.3	18.7

Source: Roy W. Bahl and Chuk Kyo Kim, "Modernization and the Long Term Growth
of Korean Government Expenditures," mimeographed (Syracuse, N.Y., 1976).

expenditures but, as Bahl and Kim show, social services were
relatively the hardest hit.[12] Government support of health and
welfare programs has never been significant, as much of the
health care is provided by the private sector, and welfare or
social security has been considered a family responsibility.[13]

But in the early 1960s, the government cut back its support for education and pushed much of the burden of education costs over onto direct private payments. (see Chapter 11).

The changing composition of government spending is shown from a somewhat different perspective in Tables 76 and 77. The

TABLE 76 Functional Distribution of General Government
Expenditures, Selected Years
(in constant prices)

	Percent of Total Expenditure					
	1953	1958	1965	1971	1974	1975
General services	19.8	9.5	15.0	11.2	9.7	9.0
Defense	56.0	37.4	32.3	21.6	24.9	24.6
Social services	5.5	17.2	23.5	24.6	21.3	22.4
Economic services	18.0	29.1	24.9	31.0	34.1	37.3
Unallocable	0.9	6.8	4.3	11.6	10.1	6.8

	Percent of GNP					
	1953	1958	1965	1971	1974	1975
General services	2.4	1.9	2.0	2.2	2.1	1.6
Defense	6.9	7.4	4.4	4.2	5.5	4.5
Social services	0.7	3.4	3.2	4.8	4.7	4.1
Economic services	2.2	5.8	3.4	6.1	7.6	6.8
Unallocable	0.1	1.3	0.6	2.3	2.2	1.2
Total	12.5	19.8	13.6	19.6	22.1	18.2

Source: Bahl and Kim, "Modernization and the Long Term Growth."

decline in general services and defense, both as a share of total government spending and as percent of GNP, is apparent. Social and economic services rose sharply in the 1950s, dipped in the mid-1960s, and increased thereafter to account together for more than half of total government expenditures and over 10 percent of GNP. Economic services have been consistently greater than social services, and the disparity has widened since the mid-1960s.

TABLE 77 Composition of Economic and Social Service Expenditures, Selected Years

	Percentage Distribution						
	1953	*1958*	*1965*	*1971*	*1974*	*1975*
Economic Services	100.0	100.0	100.0	100.0	100.0	100.0
Agricultural and non-mineral resources	38.6	37.6	32.1	27.1	12.8	15.3
Fuel and power	5.1	2.1	4.4	9.2	9.2	6.3
Mining, manufacturing, and construction	47.0	27.0	18.7	15.7	19.4	14.8
Transport, storage, and communications	9.3	32.0	37.3	41.1	32.0	40.2
Other	—	1.4	7.4	6.9	26.7	23.3
Social Services	100.0	100.0	100.0	100.0	100.0	100.0
Education	40.2	61.0	63.1	66.1	56.2	64.7
Health	10.8	8.4	5.4	5.4	4.0	2.5
Social security and welfare	42.4	17.5	24.3	20.0	22.6	15.4
Community services	3.7	7.9	5.5	4.9	14.5	8.0
Other	2.8	5.1	4.0	3.6	2.6	2.1

Source: Bahl and Kim, "Modernization and the Long Term Growth."

There has also been a shift within the economic services away from expenditures on manufacturing and mining towards investment in transportation, storage, and communications. The apparent decline in expenditures on agriculture is somewhat misleading because the large increase in "other economic services" in 1975 is mainly due to grain price supports that benefit primarily the agriculture sector. The composition of social services, in Table 77, shows the preponderance of education and the very limited allocations for health. Other social services have been a relatively constant share of the total since the end of the Korean War.

The other significant shift that occurred in the transition years of the mid-1960s was that the government moved from a position of net dissaver to that of net saver as a result of the severe curtailment of government consumption expenditures and the subsequent increase in government revenues. Fixed investment by general government and government enterprises moved from 3 percent of GNP in 1964–1965 to 7 percent of GNP in 1968–1970, while government consumption moved up from 9 percent to only 11 percent (see Table 78). In the 1970s, government saving and investment diminished as shares of GNP, but during the latter half of the 1960s they contributed significantly to moving the economy to a high growth path.

THE EVOLUTION OF GOVERNMENT REVENUE POLICIES

While the ratio of total government revenues to GNP has changed markedly over the post-war years, the composition of total revenues has not changed very much (see Table 79). National government revenues have accounted for 90 percent of the total and local government for the remaining 10 percent in most years, except the early 1960s when national revenues declined sharply and several taxes previously collected by the national government were shifted to the local level.

TABLE 78 Government Consumption, Saving, and Fixed
Investment as Percent of GNP, 1953–1975

Year	Consumption	Saving	Fixed Investment
1953	7.8	–2.4	0.8
1954	10.1	–2.7	1.7
1955	8.7	–2.3	2.0
1956	9.1	–2.9	2.1
1957	10.8	–3.0	4.0
1958	12.6	–3.1	3.5
1959	14.0	–2.7	3.7
1960	14.4	–2.0	3.4
1961	13.5	–1.8	3.7
1962	14.2	–1.4	4.4
1963	11.2	–0.3	3.8
1964	8.9	0.5	2.5
1965	9.4	1.7	3.2
1966	10.2	2.8	4.4
1967	10.4	4.1	4.7
1968	11.0	6.3	6.4
1969	10.7	6.2	7.9
1970	10.9	7.0	6.3
1971	11.3	6.0	6.2
1972	11.3	3.9	5.6
1973	9.7	4.6	4.5
1974	10.9	3.0	4.6
1975	12.1	5.3	5.0

Source: BOK, National Income In Korea, 1975 (Seoul, 1975).

Direct taxes increased as a share of total revenues, especially
during the latter half of the 1960s, but have declined in
importance since then. Indirect taxes followed a reverse pattern,
while custom duties and monopoly profits declined fairly
steadily from the early 1960s. Collections of the personal
income tax have been the most volatile, ranging from 8.5 percent
of total revenues in one high tax period (1959–1960) to nearly

TABLE 79 Composition of Total Government Revenues

	1954– 1955	*1959– 1960*	*1963– 1964*	*1969– 1970*	*1974– 1975*
Total Gov't Revenues as % of GNP	6.4	12.0	8.1	15.3	15.6
Composition of Total Revenues					
National	89.6	92.2	82.9	91.6	89.3
Local	10.4	7.8	17.1	8.4	10.7
Composition of National Revenues					
Direct Taxes	25.9	27.3[a]	30.0	38.3	31.7
Personal income	13.0	8.5	18.5	23.8	16.6
Corp. income	3.5	3.2	9.1	11.6	11.1
Other	9.4	15.6[a]	2.4	2.9	4.0
Indirect Taxes	44.0	47.0[a]	39.1	38.5	46.2
Business	9.5	4.1	7.4	8.3	12.9
Liquor	8.3	4.2	7.4	5.8	6.0
Petroleum	0	0	5.5	5.5	9.8
Commodity	18.2	14.7	9.7	9.7	8.9
Other	8.0	24.0[a]	9.1	9.2	8.6
Customs Duties	17.9	16.8	18.7	14.8	13.9
Monopoly Profits	12.2	8.9	12.2	8.4	8.2

Source: Chong Kee Park, *Development and Modernization of Korea's Tax System,* pp. 30, 40.

Note: [a]An adjustment is made to Park's data by shifting the foreign exchange tax from other direct taxes "to other indirect taxes." Gilbert T. Brown, *Korean Pricing Policies and Economic Development in the 1960s* (Baltimore, 1973), p. 61, records that the foreign exchange tax was 18.2% of national taxes in 1960.

24 percent in another (1969–1970). The corporate income tax, since it achieved some importance in the early 1960s, has been a much more stable source of revenue.

A special tax on foreign exchange imposed in 1958 in lieu of a devaluation was a major factor in raising the overall revenue ratio and causing the temporary increase in other indirect taxes. The foreign exchange tax rate was reduced after the devaluations of 1960–1961 and was discontinued in 1963. The agricultural land tax, collected in kind, contributed to the high percentage of other direct taxes in the 1950s, but it was replaced in 1961 by a tax payable in money and became a revenue of the local governments.

The business tax on gross receipts of most types of business activity, except farming, has been a steadily increasing source of revenue since the 1960s. Tax rates have been raised over the years from a range of 0.15–2.5 percent in 1960 to 0.5–3.5 percent in 1975, but the average tax rate has increased only moderately from 0.46 to 0.59 percent for the same years. The income elasticity of the tax has been 1.33 as the tax base has grown very rapidly relative to GNP (see Table 80). As a multistage, gross-receipt tax, its base is a multiple of GNP even though it omits agriculture.[14]

The selective commodity tax on manufactured and imported goods has also had a rapidly expanding base and an average effective tax rate that rose from 15 percent in 1958 to 21 percent in 1975. Petroleum and textile products have accounted for over half the total revenues from the commodity tax, but their relative importance has shifted (see Table 81). Much of the recent increase in the tax on petroleum has been due to the rise in the price of imported oil. The government has sought to discourage private ownership of cars and consumption of gasoline by maintaining very high taxes on both. Thus, gasoline was only 6 percent of the petroleum tax base in 1975, with bunker C oil (for power plants) and diesel oil accounting for 51 and 27 percent of the base respectively.[15]

While the indirect taxes, customs duties, and monopoly profits have produced 60 to 75 percent of total national revenues over the years, the direct taxes and especially the personal income tax have received most of the attention from both tax officials and foreign advisors, partly because the continuing inflation required frequent adjustments of the exemptions and bracket tax rates and partly because the Korean tax was a schedular one with differing rates for different types of income, thus presenting

TABLE 80 Tax Base, Yield, and Rate Change for Main
Indirect Taxes

	1960	*1964*	*1970*	*1975*
Business Tax				
Tax base (bil. wŏn)	217.3	774.7	6,215	33,613
Tax yield (bil. wŏn)	1.0	3.2	31	198
Effective tax rate (%)	0.46	0.42	0.5	0.59
Tax base/GNP (%)	88.2	110.6	240	370
Tax yield/GNP (%)	0.41	0.46	1.2	2.18
Income elasticity		1.33		

Commodity Tax[a]	*1958*	*1966*	*1975*
Tax base (bil. wŏn)	9.7	85.5	1,331.8
Tax yield (bil. wŏn)	1.5	12.4	279.0
Effective tax rate (%)	15.0	14.5	20.9
Tax base/GNP (%)	4.6	8.3	14.7
Tax yield/GNP (%)	0.7	1.2	3.1
Income Elasticity		1.35	

Source: Chong Kee Park, pp. 105, 126.

Note: [a]Includes petroleum taxes, which are shown separately in Table 81.

TABLE 81 Shares of the Commodity Tax for Selected Years

	1958	*1966*	*1975*
Petroleum products	19.1	26.2	43.2
Textiles	34.6	27.3	9.2
Sugar	20.0	14.7	7.2
Other	26.3	31.2	40.4
	100.0	100.0	100.0

Source: Chong Kee Park, p. 103.

some obvious inequities that begged for correction. Finally, because the personal income tax symbolizes modern taxation, tax specialists generally focus first on it and treat other taxes as secondary.[16]

The Korean income tax has gone through many changes of rates and coverage. In 1969 a global overlay was superimposed on the schedular system, and in 1974 the tax was shifted completely to a global system. Despite the many changes in the law, the major factor contributing to the observed income elasticity of the tax of 1.24 has, according to Park, been "the result primarily of the expansion in the tax base rather than the graduated statutory rates."[17] He shows (see Table 82) that the tax base as a percent of non-agricultural personal income rose by 50 percent in the period of fiscal restraint (1957–1960), held steady through 1965, soared through 1970, and fell off in 1973–1974. These changes go far beyond statutory changes in the tax base or changes in the composition of taxable income. They reflect mainly changes in tax administration.

TAX ADMINISTRATION

Fluctuations in the ratio of tax revenues to GNP over the past two decades have resulted much more from variations in the effectiveness of administration than in legislative changes. One exception to this generalization was the spurt in revenues in the late 1950s due to the foreign exchange tax, collections of which were automatically linked to payment for imports. But the decline in tax revenues in the early 1960s and the spectacular rise in the latter half of the 1960s was mainly due to changes in the commitment of the government to collect taxes. In the early years of the Park Government, the main concerns were with expenditure and economic expansion. When this led quickly to inflation and real decline in fiscal resources, the government, with strong encouragement from the United States, the International Monetary Fund (IMF), and the International Bank for

TABLE 82 Tax Base of Personal Income Tax in Relation to
Non-Agricultural Personal Income, 1957–1974

Year	Non-Agricultural Personal Income (billion wŏn)	Tax Base (billion wŏn)	Tax Base as % of Income
1957	102.9	18.7	18
1958	113.3	23.5	21
1959	130.5	33.5	26
1960	138.6	35.6	26
1961	159.9	40.4	25
1962	193.9	50.1	26
1963	250.2	66.0	26
1964	351.9	87.5	25
1965	448.1	118.3	26
1966	594.9	181.2	31
1967	766.4	263.6	34
1968	963.2	376.2	39
1969	1,276.5	560.5	44
1970	1,566.2	815.6	52
1971	1,896.8	998.1	53
1972	2,312.8	1,220.4	53
1973	3,058.9	1,440.8	47
1974	4,248.0	1,947.2	46

Source: BOK, *National Income in Korea, 1975* (Seoul, December 1975), pp. 152–153,
182–183. Tax base data from Chong Kee Park, Table 20, p. 85.

Reconstruction and Development (IBRD), shifted priorities and initiated an all-out campaign to expand tax revenues and other financial resources. This led to a doubling of the tax ratio from 7.2 percent to 14.4 percent in the four years between 1964 and 1968 with only minor changes in the tax laws.

A key element in the improvement of tax administration, as discussed by Gilbert Brown,[18] was the insulation of the tax collectors from political interference. This was symbolized by the creation of the Office of National Tax Administration in early 1966 and appointment as director of that office of Nak-sŏn Yi, a close associate of the President, who was given a clear mandate to expand revenues. Upon assuming office, Yi announced that his objective for the first year was to collect 40 percent more revenues than prescribed in the budget through more efficient enforcement.

In addition to the normal techniques for strengthening tax enforcement, such as more thorough tax audits, tighter supervision of tax officials, and publicity campaigns on the importance of paying taxes, the tax office used a system of tax targets, or quotas, broken down by geographic area and type of tax, and applied a system of awards and penalties to the tax officials for exceeding or falling short of the targets. These measures had their main impact on the income taxes, under which evasion had been most extreme. This was manifested in the rise of the income tax *base* from 25 percent of non-agricultural personal income in 1964 to 53 percent in 1971 (see Table 82). Similarly the taxable *income* under the corporate income tax went from 2.26 percent of GNP in 1965 to 3.51 percent in 1970.[19] Richard Musgrave, after reviewing the Korean revenue scene in 1965, concluded that the "Korean tax structure . . . comprises an extensive and sophisticated set of tax statutes . . . the main task is to narrow the gap between tax law and practice."[20] By 1970, there had been considerable progress towards this objective.

In the ensuing years, tax revenues declined as a percent of GNP for a number of reasons. The economy experienced a recession in 1971 and 1972, and many of the larger businesses were caught in a serious financial squeeze between rising debt-service costs on foreign loans (because of devaluation) and slower growth of exports. Also, the increasing importance of tax incentive measures for new investment and "public" corporations (as opposed to closely held family corporations) reduced both the tax base and the effective tax rates. As Chong Kee Park shows,[21] taxable income of corporations dropped from an average of 3.54 percent of GNP in 1970–1971 to 3.08 percent in 1972–1973, and the effective corporate tax rate declined from 45.6 percent (1967–1971) to 38.7 percent

(1972–1975). There is no evidence of any diminution in the effectiveness of tax enforcement in recent years, but rather the normal responses to changing economic conditions and the effects of new incentive measures on potential tax yields.

One of the consequences of the strengthened machinery for tax administration has been that the government also has had a more powerful instrument for monitoring business performance and applying pressure to businessmen who were not operating in ways consistent with national policy objectives. The highly organized export promotion efforts have already been discussed (see Chapter 5), whereby the government followed closely the export performance of all significant exporting firms. The credit system, as discussed below, and the tax system provided mechanisms for rewarding good performance and punishing bad performance. While the influence of political favoritism was largely eliminated from the tax system, economic penalties have remained a part of tax enforcement, and both rewards and penalties are important aspects of the credit system.

DISTRIBUTIONAL CONSEQUENCES OF THE FISCAL SYSTEM

While recognizing the difficulties inherent in the process, Roy Bahl has undertaken an analysis of fiscal incidence for Korea that gives some interesting indications of the distributional changes over time.[22]

He attempts to estimate the incidence of both revenues and expenditures for both urban and rural areas. The many assumptions and allocation decisions are spelled out in his study and need not be repeated here, except for one that has a significant impact on the results. Bahl's estimate of property income, which is underreported in household survey data, is derived from the national income accounts, allocated between farm and non-farm households in proportion to their shares of total household income, and then imputed to the top income bracket in each category.[23] This increases the inequality of income distribution in comparison with that derived directly from the household surveys.

The main conclusions of his incidence study, before taking account of the fiscal effects, are presented in Table 83. They show that the gap between farm and non-farm household income not only was very low, but narrowed even further between 1965 and 1974. The degree of inequality diminished in the non-farm areas, whereas it increased in the farm areas. While there was greater inequality in the non-farm households than in farm households in 1965, this difference was greatly reduced by 1974.

TABLE 83 Distribution Patterns from Incidence Study

	1965	1974
Ratio of farm to non-farm income per household	0.82	0.88
Gini coefficients for non-farm families	0.526	0.485
farm families	0.347	0.413
Percent of total income going to top decile		
Non-farm families	44.9	45.6
Farm families	29.8	37.1

Source: Roy W. Bahl, "The Distributional Effects of the Korean Budget During the Modernization Process," (Mimeo, Syracuse, NY, October 1977), pp. 27, 30.

The fiscal effects on these distributional patterns are shown in Tables 84 and 85 covering the non-farm and farm households respectively. For the non-farm households, the tax incidence was substantially regressive in both years and, while the expenditure incidence was progressive, the net effect on incomes of all but the lowest two income brackets was negative in 1965, and it was negative for all brackets in 1974. This was due to the fact that the non-farm households bear a much heavier share of the tax burden and receive less of the expenditure benefits than the farm households. As shown in Table 86, the disparity has narrowed over time, but the farm households still are the main beneficiaries of budgetary incidence because of their very low taxes.

TABLE 84 Tax, Expenditure, and Net-Budget Incidence for
Non-Farm Households, 1965, 1974

	Cumulative percent of			
Decile	Income	Taxes	Expenditures	Change in Income
1965				
1	2.4	1.7	5.1	11.6
2	5.9	5.8	11.7	0.8
3	7.3	10.5	18.5	−0.7
4	11.5	16.0	26.0	−1.7
5	16.7	22.5	34.4	−2.8
6	22.3	29.8	43.4	−3.7
7	29.0	38.8	53.5	−5.4
8	37.0	49.7	65.0	−6.2
9	55.1	68.1	80.0	−8.5
10	100.0	100.0	100.0	−6.5
Gini Coefficient	0.521	0.415	0.225	
1974				
1	2.7	3.9	6.0	−2.5
2	6.1	8.8	12.9	−4.4
3	10.3	13.6	20.3	−1.7
4	14.9	18.8	27.9	−2.8
5	20.1	24.7	36.0	−4.7
6	26.1	31.3	45.3	−4.1
7	32.5	38.4	55.3	−3.8
8	40.2	46.7	66.6	−4.6
9	54.4	60.9	80.4	−10.4
10	100.0	100.0	100.0	−15.4
Gini Coefficient	0.485	0.406	0.199	

Source: Bahl, "Distributional Effects," pp. 46, 58, 65.

TABLE 85 Tax, Expenditures, and Net-Budget Incidence for
Farm Households, 1965, 1974

| Decile | Cumulative percent of | | | Change in Income |
	Income	Taxes	Expenditures	
1965				
1	4.5	5.0	6.6	12.3
2	9.0	9.9	13.2	12.3
3	13.4	14.9	19.8	12.3
4	19.7	21.0	27.7	10.5
5	27.3	28.1	36.7	9.7
6	34.9	35.2	45.7	9.7
7	43.4	43.0	55.4	9.3
8	54.0	52.7	66.8	8.5
9	70.2	68.4	81.0	6.2
10	100.0	100.0	100.0	3.0
Gini Coefficient	0.347	0.344	0.195	
1974				
1	2.5	3.1	5.1	22.7
2	6.5	7.1	11.4	17.4
3	11.5	11.7	18.6	15.5
4	16.6	16.3	25.7	15.5
5	23.5	22.0	34.3	13.6
6	30.9	27.9	43.3	13.3
7	39.6	34.6	53.3	12.5
8	49.7	42.0	64.5	11.9
9	62.9	51.2	78.0	11.1
10	100.0	100.0	100.0	−2.0
Gini Coefficient	0.413	0.468	0.232	

Source: Bahl, "Distributional Effects," pp. 46, 58, 65.

TABLE 86 Division of Population Income, Tax Burden, and Expenditure Benefit Between Sectors

	Rural as a Percent of Urban	
	1965	1974
Population	113.9	62.0
Income	93.4	54.9
Tax burden	23.3	21.4
Expenditure benefits	101.1	58.1

Source: Bahl, "Distributional Effects," pp. 27 and 50.

In sum, the Korean fiscal system has imposed taxes most heavily on urban consumption and has used the proceeds to invest in the infrastructure of economic development while maintaining adequate defense forces (with the help of military assistance) and minimal public expenditure on social services. In comparison with other countries at comparable stages of development, government revenues are close to the norm (based on Chenery-Syrquin predictions),[24] but government consumption is below the norm. This is the case despite relatively large defense expenditures, which further emphasizes the very low level of other current government expenditures. Government investment spending, on the other hand, has been high, especially over the past decade.

THE FINANCIAL SYSTEM

At the end of the Korean War, the financial system was in disarray. The new central bank, the Bank of Korea, had spent its first three years printing money to finance the war and was left with an accumulation of uncollectable claims on the government, continuing inflationary pressures, and very low levels of money and credit relative to GNP. The commercial banks, starved for deposits and loanable funds, and subject to pervasive controls, were barely operating. The effective part of the financial system was based upon U.S. dollars and Military Payment Certificates (MPCs) and was managed by the unorganized currency dealers and loan brokers, because the organized financial institutions could not deal in such illegal currencies.

In the decade after the war, there was a continuing struggle between those who wished to create an independent, competitive, democratic financial system based on the American model, as prescribed by Arthur Bloomfield, and those who wished to use the financial system to finance their favored activities regardless of the longer-run consequences for the development of the financial system itself. This tug of war resulted in frequent changes in direction and considerable instability.

Finally in the mid-1960s the government, under various external pressures, turned its attention to building up the financial system, concentrating on the mobilization of financial savings. This led to a phenomenal expansion of both internal and external financial resources that played a major role in financing the investment boom of the latter half of the 1960s. The government retained total control of the organized financial system, thus rejecting the "democratic" model espoused by some American advisers, and also precluding the emergence of a zaibatsu model in which the financial institutions are controlled by powerful business interests. Instead, the Korean government used the financial system to guide the allocation of investment, to reward good economic performance, and to retain some leverage over the independent-mindedness of the businessmen. While there have been moves in recent years to create new short- and long-term securities markets that may diversify potential sources of financing and even in time dilute direct government control, the present system has been remarkably effective in achieving the dual objectives of mobilizing finance and preserving the government's power over the private sector.

INFLATION AND REPRESSION, 1953–1960

The struggle over the basic directions of the financial system during the 1950s led to the pattern of financial repression so aptly described by Edward Shaw.[25] The Bank of Korea, attempting to carry out its mandate as the guardian of price stability, sought to restrict the growth of credit, but since it could not resist the demands of the government to cover the fiscal deficit, it ended up restricting credit through the commercial banks to the private sector. Deficit financing amounting on average to 2 percent of GNP through 1956 (see Figure 5) led to high rates of inflation which, together with interest rate ceilings on both loans and deposits, caused excess demand for loans and minimal demand for deposits. Counterpart funds, derived from the sale of foreign-aid goods, were used to cover part of the fiscal deficit. They also became the main source of funds for newly created lending institutions, such as the Korea Reconstruction Bank, that were designed to provide long-term loans to key enterprises and thus get around the restrictions on commercial bank lending. These new institutions were largely outside the control of the Bank of Korea, being responsible to the Minister of Finance. The commercial banks, viewed as relatively unimportant by the government, were sold off to private owners in 1957, as Bloomfield had recommended, and their share of total bank lending dropped from 45 percent to 29 percent between 1955 and 1958. The domain over which the Bank of Korea exercised authority shrank accordingly.

Beginning in 1957, annual financial stabilization programs were drawn up and were intended to coordinate the internal fiscal and financial demands with the inflow of foreign aid and the resulting counterpart funds (see Chapter 6). These programs, involving quarterly ceilings on credit expansion and budgetary expenditure, proved successful in bringing down the rate of inflation (to a negative 6 percent in 1958) and reducing the flow of aid. They also contributed to an increase in the real size of the financial system in the late 1950s, mainly due to the lower rate of inflation. Domestic bank credit rose from 10.2 percent of GNP in 1957 to 15.3 percent in 1960, but this greater availability of credit was not sufficient to offset the many other factors discouraging investment and growth.

FINANCIAL EXPANSION AND CRISES, 1961–1964

It was not surprising that the Park Military Government that came to power in 1961, dedicated to getting the economy moving again, immediately set aside the financial stabilization programs, took back the ownership of the private commercial banks, and initiated a number of institutional reforms centered around the financial system. But most of the military leaders had little appreciation of the functioning of a financial system, other than as a means for providing funding for the programs they wished to carry out, and they soon got into difficulty.

During their first months in office, the Park Government created a new bank to serve small industry and commerce. They reorganized the agricultural credit institution, canceled much of the outstanding indebtedness of low-income farmers, and initiated an expanded agricultural credit program. All these measures were designed to redress the favored treatment the new government felt had been granted to Syngman Rhee's cronies, and to help the lower-income groups expand their production and income. By the middle of 1962, bank credit and the money supply had expanded greatly, and the government became concerned about potential inflation—although prices had remained remarkably stable. They also feared that the rich businessmen and moneylenders were holding large cash balances that they would exchange for goods at the first sign of rising prices. Thus, the government decided to carry out a monetary reform that both changed the denomination of the currency and froze all bank deposits.[26] The immediate effect of the reform was to bring business to a standstill so that within days the government had to remove the restrictions on deposits. The longer-run effect was to undermine confidence in the government and the financial system and to trigger the shift from holding financial assets to the holding of real assets that the government was trying to prevent. Poor crops accentuated the problem and brought on two years of accelerated inflation.

The instability also led to a resumption of the annual stabilization programs jointly agreed upon by the Korean and American governments. These programs in 1963 and 1964 imposed very restrictive credit and money supply ceilings that led to a severe liquidity squeeze and imaginative searches for sources of financing that were not covered by the ceilings.

The major innovation that emerged at this time was the system of foreign loan guarantees. Korean businesses would work out loan agreements with foreign lenders, often in the form of suppliers' credits. After approval by the Economic Planning Board and the National Assembly, these loans were guaranteed by the Korea Reconstruction Bank (later the Korea Development Bank) and the Bank of Korea. (In later years the other special and commercial banks were authorized to issue the guarantees and the Korea Exchange Bank took over the responsibility from the Bank of Korea for guaranteeing the foreign exchange convertibility of the loan repayments.) By thus eliminating most of the risk for foreign lenders, the Korean financial authorities opened the door to massive foreign borrowing. As shown in Tables 87 and 88, the increase in foreign loans nearly offset the real decline in domestic bank loans during 1963 and 1964 and reached approximate parity with the domestic loans by 1966. These foreign loans also served as a substitute for foreign aid which was declining during this period. The fact that Korea had received almost all of its foreign aid on a grant basis and had incurred negligible foreign debt prior to the 1960s meant that its foreign borrowing capacity was considerable, especially with the shift to export led growth described in Chapter 5.

While the foreign loan guarantee scheme relieved some of the

TABLE 87 Financial Indicators, 1953–1964

Year	M_2/GNP	Credit/GNP Comm. Banks	Credit/GNP Spec. Banks	Guarantees of Foreign Loans/GNP	Real GNP Growth Rate (% per year)	Change in Wholesale Price Index (% per year)	Highest Bank Interest Rate on Deposits (% per year)	Real Deposit Interest Rate (% per year)
1953	6.8	3.1	1.5			+25.0	5.0	−16.0
1954	9.4	2.8	1.0		5.5	+28.4	12.0	−12.8
1955	9.7	2.7	1.6		5.4	+81.1	12.0	−38.1
1956	9.1	3.6	4.7		0.4	+31.4	12.0	−14.8
1957	8.2	3.0	7.2		7.7	+16.3	12.0	− 3.7
1958	10.5	3.7	9.0		5.2	− 6.5	12.0	+19.8
1959	13.3	4.2	10.5		3.9	+ 2.6	11.0	+ 8.2
1960	12.5	4.7	11.6		1.9	+10.7	10.0	− 0.6
1961	13.9	4.3	13.3		4.8	+13.2	12.5	− 0.6
1962	14.8	6.0	13.4		3.1	+ 9.4	15.0	5.1
1963	11.3	4.7	11.0	3.7	8.8	+20.6	15.0	− 4.6
1964	9.1	3.3	8.8	5.5	8.6	+34.6	15.0	−14.6

Source: Cole and Park, *Financial Development*, p. 204.

TABLE 88 Financial Indicators, 1965–1975

Year	$\frac{M_2}{GNP}$	Credit/GNP Domestic	Credit/GNP Foreign	Real GNP Growth	Change in Wholesale Price Index	Highest Bank Rate on Time Deposits	Real Deposit Interest Rate
1965	12.1	13.5	9.3	6.1	10.0	30.0	+18.2
1966	15.2	14.4	14.0	12.4	8.9	30.0	19.4
1967	20.0	18.1	15.4	7.8	6.4	30.0	22.2
1968	27.3	24.9	19.0	12.6	8.1	26.0	16.5
1969	33.8	31.6	25.4	15.0	6.8	24.0	16.1
1970	34.6	32.9	28.9	7.9	9.2	22.8	12.5
1971	34.4	34.2	34.4	9.2	8.6	22.0	12.3
1972	37.6	37.2	27.0	7.0	14.9	15.0	0.1
1973	38.8	38.7	28.0	16.5	7.0	12.6	5.2
1974	35.8	42.1	31.2	8.7	42.2	15.0	-19.1
1975	34.4	38.5	32.8	7.4	26.5	15.0	-9.1

Source: Cole and Park, p. 209.

Note: Real interest rate = $\frac{1+r_t}{1+w_t}$ where r_t is the current year's nominal interest rate and w_t is the current year's change in wholesale prices. Domestic credit includes the loans of both commercial and special banks which are presented separately in Table 87.

pressure of the tight money policies in 1963–1964, it provided little relief for the short-run operational demands for local currency. To satisfy this demand, the unorganized money markets were again drawn into a very active role of reallocating the scarce supply of domestic credit. Businesses or households with any temporary cash surpluses would loan them on a call basis at 3–5 percent monthly interest rates to private money-lenders or brokers who would relend them at 4–7 percent also on a call basis to businesses in urgent need of cash. This system provided a relatively efficient mechanism for economizing the available liquidity, but it also entailed some risk and frequently encountered difficulty at year-end when, by tradition, out-standing debts are supposed to be settled.

Because the unorganized money markets in Korea are unregulated and in many instances engaged in activities that are proscribed by law, but tolerated in practice, information on their operations is very imprecise. Still, estimates have been made of the volume of their lending[27] which suggest that they reached a peak in 1964–1965 when their loans were equal to about 40 percent of total bank loans.[28] It was partly out of recognition of the effectiveness of the unorganized money markets in mobilizing and allocating savings that the Korean financial authorities turned their attention to financial reforms that would make the banking system somewhat more competi-tive with the unorganized money markets.

FINANCIAL REFORM AND EXPANSION

After more than a decade of focusing on the supply of liquidity as the principal instrument of monetary policy, with only occasional success and some notable failures, the Korean government finally in 1965 shifted the emphasis to measures that would influence the demand for liquidity.[29] The principal feature of the financial reform of September 30, 1965, was an increase in the interest rate on time deposits from 15 percent to

30 percent per annum. Interest rates on some types of loans were also raised to a range of 26–30 percent, and the controls over bank lending were relaxed somewhat, but these were less significant and lasting elements of the reform.

In the three months following the interest rate changes, the level of time and savings deposits increased by 50 percent and grew at a compound annual rate of nearly 100 percent over the next four years. The ratio of such deposits to GNP rose from 3.8 percent at the end of 1965 to 21.7 percent by the end of 1969. As shown in Table 88, broad money (M_2) grew from 15.6 percent of GNP in 1965 to 36.1 percent in 1970. Such rapid increases in the size of a financial system are unparalleled in recent world experience.[30]

Much has been claimed for the interest rate reform: that it was largely responsible for the rise in the private saving rate from an average of 5 percent of GNP in 1962–1965 to 10 percent in 1966–1970,[31] and that it contributed to higher levels and more efficient allocation of investment. On the other hand, there have been objections to these claims, and suggestions that the effects of the reform were overrated: that the banks largely drew funds away from the unorganized money markets; that the rise in savings was mainly due to rising income, or statistical error, and that the investment boom was demand- rather than supply-induced.[32]

The basic obstacle to rigorous analysis of these issues is that several other major developments were occurring simultaneously in the Korean economy: the massive inflow of foreign capital as a result of the foreign loan guarantee system and the treaty with Japan, the fiscal reform raising the tax ratio and increasing public savings and investment, the export boom, and involvement in the Vietnam War. These factors added either to the available savings or to incomes from which additional savings might derive.

It is clear that both the average and the marginal propensity to save of the private sector increased significantly after the interest rate reform, that households and corporations shifted their asset holdings to include a greater portion of financial assets, and that time and savings deposits assumed increasing importance within the financial assets. It is also clear that the ratio of private investment to GNP jumped from 11 percent in 1964–1965 to 18 percent in 1966–1970, and that bank loans financed a significant share (roughly 40 percent) of corporate investment, which in turn accounted for about three-fourths of total private investment. The other major source of financing was the guaranteed foreign loans, which were roughly equal in amount to the domestic bank loans and thus made an equivalent contribution to the financing of investment.[33]

The investment boom of 1966–1970 undoubtedly would not have been so large if there had not been both the demand for new capacity arising from the export boom and the available financing from both domestic bank loans and guaranteed foreign loans. The interest rate reform made possible the growth of domestic bank loans by stimulating the demand for time deposits and, to that extent, contributed to high growth of investment and output. Without either the export drive or the foreign loans, the results would have been less spectacular.[34]

It is also important to recognize that the government used the financial system to provide incentives to exporters and generally controlled the allocation of both foreign and domestic credit to support those investments considered most conducive to development. Exporters received automatic financing of raw material and production costs at low interest rates (generally 6 percent per annum). This financing, which often exceeded current needs, could be reloaned in part in the unorganized money markets at 24–30 percent per annum, thus giving a healthy subsidy that has been estimated equal to 4.5 percent of the value of exports in 1968.[35] Similarly, the foreign loans, the term loans of the special banks, and even many of the loans of the commercial banks carried interest rates that were low in nominal terms and often negative in real terms. This pattern of loan interest rates was criticized on the grounds that it created constant excess demand for loans and encouraged unnecessary borrowing.[36] It was also claimed that the system invited bribery and misallocation of resources. Finally, some have considered it a pure subsidy and have estimated the distribution of the subsidy among different sectors of the economy.[37]

There is obviously some inconsistency between the notions that the difference between the nominal and some "realistic" interest rate was a pure subsidy and that it was a major source of bribery. If bribes had to be paid, then the subsidy element was reduced accordingly as was the incentive for excessive reliance on loan financing. In this connection, the loans for financing export production were distinctive in that they were granted automatically upon receipt of an export order or letter of credit. For the other loans, the subsidy element was quite variable, depending in part on the institution from which it was being obtained, the government agencies involved in the approval process, the degree of competition for particular types of credit, the interest of the government in promoting a particular type of investment, the political influence of the borrower, and, finally, the political climate or financial exigencies of the government's political party. All these factors were subject to change over time, and therefore the amount of credit subsidy was quite erratic.

The Korean government has viewed control over the allocation of credit, both domestic and foreign, as an important element of economic and political policy. It has resisted repeated advice (mainly foreign) to let interest rates and competition among independent financial institutions determine the allocation of credit. (Few Korean businessmen have ever advocated such a policy.) Instead, the government has kept loan interest rates below equilibrium levels and has intervened pervasively—although generally unofficially—in allocation decisions. The reasons for this appear to have been both economic and political: the credit instruments could be used to mobilize businessmen for major economic programs such as export promotion or development of the machinery and petrochemical industries, while on the political side they served to maintain control over, and cooperation from, the business community. All Korean businessmen, including the most powerful, have been aware of the need to stay on good terms with the government to assure continuing access to credit and to avoid harassment from the tax officials. Rapid growth of domestic and foreign loans in the latter half of the 1960s added to their importance as instruments of government policy.

INSTABILITY AND INSTITUTIONAL CHANGE

Despite the remarkable progress of the Korean economy and financial system from 1965 through 1970, there were some fundamental distortions that eventually created problems when the driving force of export growth slowed down in 1971. The most serious distortion was the increasing overvaluation of the currency, as the government used expanded export subsidies rather than depreciation to bridge the gap between external and internal price movements. This avoided serious balance-of-payments disequilibrium, but it unfortunately led to unrealistic expectations as to the stability of the exchange rate that encouraged greater borrowing abroad. A constant exchange rate meant that foreign loans could be repaid at lower real cost than if the wŏn was depreciated, so that businessmen, including exporters, who were heavy borrowers abroad were opposed to depreciation so long as export incentives were sufficient to maintain the profitability of their exports.

Finally, in 1971, in the face of a growing current account deficit and the first significant decline in foreign exchange reserves since 1963, the wŏn was devalued by 18 percent, followed by another 7 percent in 1972. This raised the cost of repaying foreign loans by comparable amounts and imposed a severe financial strain on those favored businesses that had borrowed heavily under the foreign loan guarantee scheme. Despite a large reduction in bank reserve requirements in 1971 (from 32 to 18 percent on demand deposits and from 18 to 12 percent on time deposits), the banks were unable to finance the increased foreign loan repayments. Many businesses were forced to borrow from the unorganized money markets to avoid defaulting on their foreign loans or forcing the domestic banks to make good on their guarantees.

Obviously such short-term high-cost financing was only a temporary solution that would soon lead to more serious financial difficulties. After considering a number of alternatives, the government came forth in the summer of 1972 with the August 3rd Emergency Measures that provided relief to the large business interests at the expense of the unorganized money markets and those who had invested in them.[38] All unorganized money market loans were required to be registered and were then transformed into five-year loans after a three-year grace period with a maximum interest rate of 18 percent. Although many loans probably were never registered because either the borrower or lender did not want to be exposed, a total of 346 billion wŏn of loans was recorded, equal to 25 percent of the total bank loans outstanding at that time.[39]

The decapitalization of the curb market in August 1972 attested to the increased ingenuity and sophistication of the government's financial policies in the decade since the disastrous currency reform of 1962. Where the earlier reform had brought business to a standstill and had to be largely repudiated within weeks, the 1972 measures were implemented quickly and thoroughly. They had their desired effects of relieving the debt burden of the larger businesses and practically wiping out the assets of the unorganized money market. While some thought this would be a lethal blow, such has not proven to be the case. Before long the unorganized money market dealers were back in operation, although on a reduced scale.

The government also endeavored to develop other financial institutions that would become alternatives to the unregulated private moneylenders. The most important of these are the securities markets and the finance companies. Since the early 1960s, there have been efforts to develop the stock market. In

1963 there was a débâcle, as manipulators, with government support, generated a speculative boom that soon collapsed and left the market a shambles. Then in 1968, tax incentives were provided to encourage closely held companies to make public stock offerings (see Chapter 7). The corporate tax rate was set one-third lower for publicly held corporations. Even this incentive had very little effect as most corporations preferred to keep their financial operations out of the public domain and to rely primarily on loan financing. Finally, in 1973, the government initiated a more aggressive approach by requiring each year those companies to "go public" that the Ministry of Finance deemed suitable. The ministry has also set the prices on the new equity issues and has seen to it that they were attractive. Thus, each new issue has been heavily oversubscribed and has immediately risen in value after being put on the market. As shown in the previous chapter, the corporate sector has not raised much new capital through these initial public offerings, but at least a market has been established and, in time as prices become based more on prospective earnings than current book values, new equity issues may become a more important source of funding.

The finance companies deal mainly in short-term bills, either of their own issue or issued by corporations. These companies, which are subject to government supervision, have grown rapidly since their inception in 1972, attesting to the fact that they serve a real need and probably are competitive with the unorganized money lenders.

CONCLUSION

Modern fiscal and financial institutions in Korea were first created by the Japanese and were well established by the 1930s. They were nearly decimated by the immediate post-World War II inflation and again by the Korean War. The fiscal and financial systems stagnated in the decade following the Korean War, because they were caught up in the struggle over the aid level.

When that issue was finally set aside and attention given to promoting fiscal and financial growth, the results from 1965 to 1970 were remarkable. Following the upward surge in the fiscal and financial ratios during the latter half of the 1960s, the ratios have stopped rising in the 1970s and are currently at levels typical of countries with similar per capita incomes. At the same time, there has been continued, heavy reliance on external resources to augment domestic savings. These two streams of finance—external and internal—made possible an extremely high level of investment and growth. Since 1970, however, the marginal savings and tax rates out of rapidly rising incomes have been unimpressive, but higher rates were not needed, given the abundance of external resources.

Over the past three decades, the fisc and the financial system have been used more to allocate and control than to mobilize resources. Government has seen them as instruments for guiding the economy and rewarding good performance. Attempts to democratize institutions and reduce the degree of centralized control over them, and through them, have been rejected for various reasons, not least of which is the fact that in their present form they have contributed to such rapid and efficient growth of the economy.

Some changes are occurring around the edges of the systems that may in time transform their character. Local banks and finance companies are regulated, but not closely controlled, by government. Publicly owned corporations and the related securities market may before long open up significant new channels of financing and help to move the tax system to a more open, legal process. Whether these new institutional arrangements will prove efficient remains to be seen. The unregulated financial institutions that played a critical role at certain stages in the past seem to be receding in the face of periodic governmental attack and increasing competition.

The fiscal system has done much to build up the economic infrastructure while neglecting the social areas, in line with basic governmental policy. Little attention has been given to the most suitable techniques of financing health, education, or social services, and the attempt to disguise a major tax increase in the form of a social security program was repudiated in 1975, even by the government-controlled National Assembly. With rising incomes and rapid urbanization, the growing demands for social services, on top of continuing needs for defense and economic infrastructure, are likely to require substantial growth and improvement of the fiscal apparatus.

TEN

Education[1]

This chapter focuses on the contribution of human resources to the development of the Republic of Korea. Poor in land and minerals, Korea is rich in culture and education, and some see in the high levels of educational attainment among the Korean population and the almost insatiable demand for further learning the explanation of the nation's rapid economic development. Typical of this widespread enthusiasm as a major factor in the modernization of Korea is this statement by a UNESCO mission:

> The remarkable and rapid economic growth that has occurred in Korea over the last decade has been based to a large degree on human resources, and education has assisted in the production of a literate and industrious people.

The arguments to support these conclusions are as follows:

1) Korea has (compared to other countries at a similar level of GNP) a highly developed education system, which reaches all its population.
2) This educational system was developed after 1945.
3) There is a close positive relationship between the expansion of education and the growth of the economy.
4) The content of Korean education fits the economic requirements of the country and is a "modernizing" influence.

This chapter examines the propositions and summarizes the arguments and evidence to support various views of how education may have contributed to the development of Korea. Three major questions are asked. How was it possible for Korea to achieve rapid expansion of its educational system, beginning from a low level of GNP per capita? How much and in what ways has education contributed to Korea's rapid economic growth since 1945? What can the Korean experience tell us about the potential contribution of education to the development of the poor countries?

THE DEVELOPMENT OF EDUCATION

Traditional education in Korea was based on the Confucian Classics, the detailed understanding of which was tested by examinations that screened candidates for positions in the court bureaucracy. Memorization of the Classics was done in the home under the guidance of tutors and was limited mainly to children of the aristocratic, *yangban* class. Modern education was introduced into Korea under the Japanese, who established the full panoply of educational institutions in Korea for their own children, but limited the Koreans mainly to the primary grades. Education was used by the Colonial Government to Japanize the Koreans, who were required to adopt Japanese names, speak only Japanese in the schools, wear uniforms, declare their allegiance to the Emperor, and accept strict discipline. Nevertheless, primary education for males had become widespread by the end of the colonial period.

The schools were well supplied with Japanese teachers and texts and, particularly in the rural areas, were reported to have provided instruction that was relevant to the needs of the farm population. Thus, the Japanese schools had both political and economic purposes: to convert the Korean youth into loyal subjects and to ˙train them for subordinate roles in both agriculture and industry. Some Koreans were able to go beyond these limits within Korea, and somewhat more readily in Japan, but they were not numerous. At the end of World War II, only 2 percent of the Korean population over 14 years of age had completed secondary school. Of all students enrolled in the school system at that time, 93 percent were in the primary grades.

Schools under the U.S. Military Government (1945–1948) also had clearly defined political and economic purposes: to convert Korean youth and adults to the American conception of democracy and to provide basic skill training. American educators in Korea had more freedom in applying concepts of progressive education than they had experienced in conservative communities in the United States, and they went at their task with enthusiasm. All schools became coeducational. Control was shifted from national and provincial governments to the township or county level. Local school boards were created to select and supervise teachers and to allocate locally collected funds, the principal source of financial support for schools. The revision of curriculum was total, with an abandonment of Confucian Classics and the development of textbooks in Han'gŭl that taught democratic principles and the scientific method. Emphasis was placed on problem-solving and learning-by-doing. Teachers were trained to encourage students to challenge their authority in the classroom. Academic secondary schools received little attention, in favor of the creation of the comprehensive high school, only then being adopted widely in the United

States, and secondary-level vocational-technical schools. Not much attention was given to higher education at this time.

Educational efforts went beyond formal schooling. Under American direction, a national Boy Scout movement was started that at one point enrolled approximately one in every two male youths in South Korea. The movement put strong emphasis on anti-communism and community development. Another large program of the U.S. Military Government was civic schools, designed to provide education to out-of-school youths and adults. In addition to literacy training in Han'gŭl, these schools sought to develop support for the new Korea and basic democratic values. By 1947, there were 15,400 civic schools.

Increasing political instability, following the establishment of the Republic in 1948, was a major factor in the suppression of many of the American-imposed changes. Control of schools (but not financing) was taken back by the national and provincial governments. Teachers were carefully screened for loyalty to the government. Traditional authoritarian practices returned to the classroom, and schools and students were used regularly to organize demonstrations of support for the government.

The Korean War destroyed much of the investment made in education during the first five years after Liberation. Not only did the Republic lose much of its physical capital, but many teachers either were killed or disappeared during the conflict.

Following the war, American aid again played an important role in shaping Korean education, but this time giving more attention to higher education. American military and civilian groups made important contributions to the rebuilding of schools and in training primary school teachers. But perhaps the most significant, and successful, involvement of American aid in education came with the strengthening of undergraduate faculties and the development of graduate level programs in public administration, agriculture, and medicine.

The present structure of the Korean school system is described in Figure 6. Under the Japanese, formal schooling had consisted of six years of primary school, five years of secondary, and four years of higher education. After several changes the present 6-3-3-4 pattern, like that found in most countries of the world, was adopted.

The American contribution to school construction, plus local sacrifices, had a significant impact on primary school enrollments, as displayed in Table 89 showing enrollments from 1945. Despite lack of government support for higher education, enrollments grew very rapidly (from a small base), especially when for a short period college attendance exempted students from military service.

Under the U.S. Military Government, enrollments in academic high schools grew slowly (2.4 percent per year), while those in vocational high schools (which included the American-type comprehensive high school) grew rapidly. After 1952 this pattern of growth was reversed. During the first years of the Park Government (1961 on), vocational high school education again grew more rapidly than academic high schools, but this pattern was reversed in 1971–1975, despite government policy to enroll about two-thirds of the high school population in vocational high schools.

Higher education includes not only four-year colleges and universities but also two-year junior colleges, two-year teacher training colleges, technological institutes, and other post-secondary institutions. As Tables 89 and 90 show, enrollments in these schools grew most rapidly immediately after Liberation from the Japanese and have declined in rate of growth since that time. (It should be noted that high rates of growth in the late 1940s reflect the small base, rather than a large absolute growth.) Of the approximately 300,000 students in formal higher education institutions in 1975, about 209,000 were in four-year colleges, 9,000 in junior teachers' colleges, 4,000 in junior colleges, and 59,000 in junior technical colleges.

Not all the expansion of enrollments has been made possible by governmental action. As Table 91 shows, the private sector

FIGURE 6 The School System

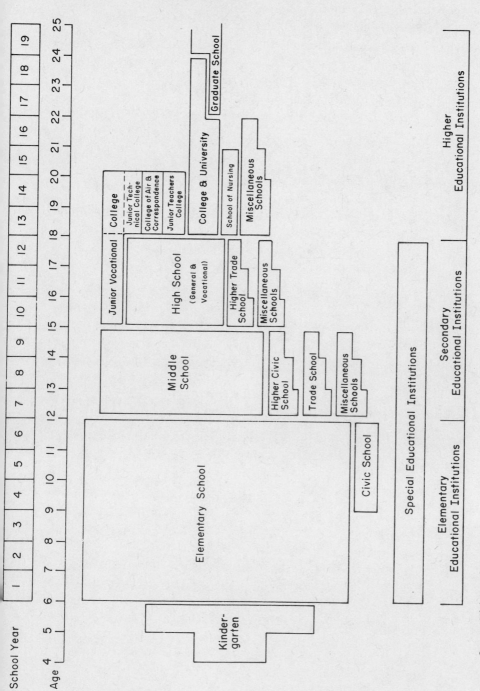

Source: Ministry of Education

347

TABLE 89 Increase in School Enrollments, 1945–1975

Type of School	1945	1952	1955	1960	1965	1970	1975
Elementary Schools	1,366,024 (100)	2,369,861 (173)	2,947,436 (216)	3,622,685 (265)	4,941,345 (362)	5,749,301 (421)	5,599,074 (410)
Middle Schools		291,648 (100)	475,342 (163)	528,614 (181)	751,341 (258)	1,318,808 (452)	2,066,823 (709)
Academic High Schools	50,343 (100)	59,421 (118)	141,702 (281)	164,492 (327)	254,095 (505)	315,367 (626)	648,149 (1,287)
Vocational High Schools	33,171 (100)	74,463 (224)	118,911 (358)	99,071 (299)	172,436 (520)	275,015 (829)	474,868 (1,432)
Higher Ed. Institutions	7,819 (100)	34,089 (436)	80,391 (1,028)	101,045 (1,292)	141,626 (1,811)	193,591 (2,476)	296,640 (3,794)

Sources: Ministry of Education, *Statistical Yearbooks of Education.* McGinn et al., *Education and Development in Korea*, p. 5.

Note: Indexes of increase are in parentheses, 1945 = 100.

TABLE 90 Rate of Growth in School Enrollments, 1945–1975

Type of School	1945–1952	1952–1960	1960–1970	1970–1975
Elementary	8.2	5.4	4.7	–0.5
Middle	–	7.7	9.6	9.0
High School	7.0	8.8	8.4	13.7
Academic	2.4	13.6	6.7	15.5
Vocational	12.2	3.6	10.7	11.5
College	23.4	14.5	6.7	8.9

Source: McGinn et al., p. 6.

TABLE 91 Public School Share of Enrollments
at Various Levels

	Percentage of Students in Public Schools		
	1965	1970	1975
Elementary	99.5	98.9	98.8
Middle School	55.6	51.4	59.4
Academic High	42.5	40.0	39.6
Vocational High	61.2	51.9	47.6
Junior College	3.2	0	0
Junior Technical	55.0	50.0	32.0
Junior Teaching	100.0	100.0	100.0
College and University	27.4	24.6	27.2
Graduate School	42.9	39.1	30.5

Sources: Ministry of Education, *Statistical Yearbooks of Education 1965, 1970, 1975.*
McGinn et al., p. 8.

has a large and increasing share of education in Korea. Only at the primary and middle levels, where there has been a public commitment to universal education, has the government acted to increase its share of enrollments in schools. The expansion of private education indicates a high unsatisfied demand for education, a theme to which we shall return.

Entrance to four-year colleges and universities has been determined by an entrance examination since 1968. Students are assigned to the institution of their choice according to their score on the examination. Because of the belief that graduates from several of the universities (Seoul National, Yonsei, Korea) have a better chance of obtaining employment in government or leading businesses upon graduation, places in those universities are in high demand, while provincial universities may have assigned to them students who are low scorers on the examination. Since 1971 the government has attempted, with limited success, to control the expansion of higher education enrollments.

Korea has the usual collection of publicly and privately supported programs in non-formal education. These include the Korean Junior College of Air and Correspondence, which enrolled 19,000 students in 1974, and a variety of non-accredited secondary and college-level schools or academies, mostly privately funded, that enrolled 62,000 students in 1975. Adult education also is provided by voluntary organizations such as the YMCA, the Korean Mothers Association, and the Korean Association of Women College Graduates. There is a government-run agricultural extension service, the Office of Labor Affairs, that runs training programs for industrial workers, and there are libraries and museums. These programs in Korea are no different from those of other countries in either their nature or level of activity.

Korea's more interesting ventures in non-traditional education cannot be claimed to have produced an economic takeoff beginning in the early 1960s, as they were not begun until the latter half of that decade. These include the Korean Mothers Association, or the mothers' clubs, that are said to have had a significant impact on the birth rate during the past ten years, and the Saemaul Undong, or New Community Movement, which provides a wide range of educational and technical assistance services to small rural communities.

The impressive aspect of Korean education that could be considered as contributing to development is the tremendous expansion of enrollments at all levels since 1945. Table 92 shows the extent to which education has been extended to members of the appropriate age cohort. Primary schooling has become universal (percentages greater than 100 reflect the presence of students older than the corresponding age group) and the government expects to have all eligible children enrolled in middle school by the early 1980s. This increase in educational opportunity has resulted in a dramatic rise in literacy, as measured by ability to read and write simple phrases in Han'gŭl. In 1945, it was estimated that 78 percent of the adult population was illiterate; by 1970 that figure had been reduced to less than 12 percent, and the average adult had completed almost six years of schooling.

THE REASONS BEHIND EXPANSION

The rates of expansion of school enrollments that Korea has experienced are high, although not unprecedented among low-income countries. Yet, enrollment growth in Korea has not been accompanied by the fiscal strains experienced elsewhere. How was such a poor country able to afford such an impressive expansion of its educational effort? Important aspects of an answer are: the efficiency of the Korean educational system, the pattern of educational finance, and the role of foreign assistance.

EFFICIENCY OF THE SYSTEM

Korean education is efficient in several senses. One of these is its low per-pupil cost. Student-teacher ratios have been unusually high, particularly in elementary school—although this ratio has been reduced gradually through time (Table 93). In the early years, there was considerable double- and triple-shift use of school buildings. This, too, has been reduced as more classrooms have been built (Figure 7). Another factor holding down per-pupil cost is the fact that motivated, well-trained

TABLE 92 School Enrollments as Percentages of
Corresponding Age Group, 1945–1975

Type of School	1945	1953	1955	1960	1965	1970	1975
Elementary (ages 6–11)	—	59.6	77.4	86.2	91.6	102.8	107.6
Middle (ages 12–14)	—	21.1	30.9	33.3	39.4	53.3	74.0
High School (ages 15–17)	—	12.4	17.8	19.9	27.0	29.3	40.5
College (ages 18–21)	—	3.1	5.0	6.4	6.9	9.3	8.6
% of total to the total population	5.7	13.3	17.2	18.5	22.0	25.3	28.8

Sources: For the statistics of the 1950s, see UNESCO, *Republic of Korea: Educational Services in a Rapidly Growing Economy*, 2 vols. (Paris, 1974), p. 9. For the 1960s, see Taehan Sanggong Hoeŭiso, *Kyŏngje kaebal kwa kyoyuk t'uja* (Seoul, 1973), Chapter 2. For the 1970s, see Han'guk Kyoyuk Kaebal Yŏn'guwŏn, *Kyoyuk kyehoek e kwanhan kich'o t'onggye charyo* (Seoul, 1975), p. 41. McGinn et al., p. 47.

TABLE 93 Students per Teacher, 1945–1975

Type of School	1945	1952	1956	1960	1965	1970	1975
Elementary	69.3	66.5	61.2	58.6	62.4	56.9	51.8
Middle		37.4	44.8	40.7	39.3	42.3	43.2
High	25.9	27.3	38.1	27.2	30.2	29.8	31.4
College	5.2	26.7	32.5	25.7	20.8	19.4	19.5

Source: McGinn et al., p. 51.

teachers have been available at modest salaries; this fact may be attributable to the traditionally high social status of the scholar-teacher and the opportunities to earn additional income from tutoring outside regular teaching hours.

Korean education is also internally efficient, in the sense used by educational planners. Most educators agree that schools should carry students to some meaningful level of achievement and, therefore, that early leaving or desertion or dropouts reflect

FIGURE 7 The Gap Between Classes and Classrooms
in Elementary Schools, 1945–1974

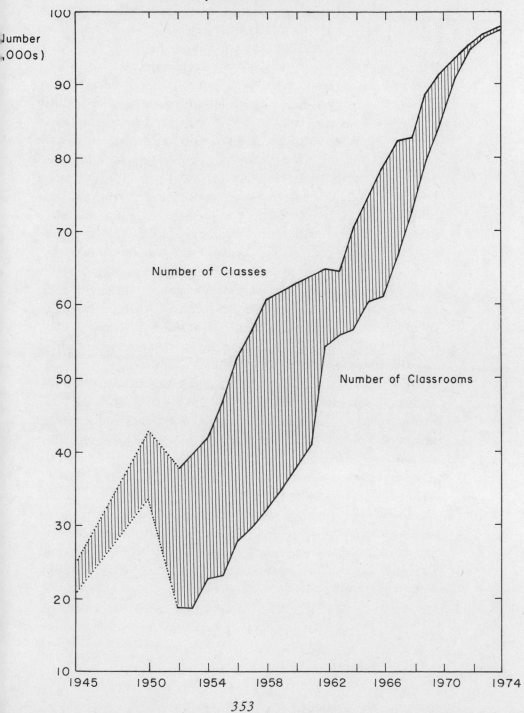

negatively on the educational system. A common assumption is that the cycles in the educational process are integral, so that leaving school before completing 6th grade, for example, is regarded as desertion. Desertion rates are high in nearly all developing countries, but not in Korea. As Table 94 shows, transition rates within the Korean system have been stable over time and, within particular levels of schooling, have been very high. At all levels, almost all children beginning school finish within the specified time period. There are few dropouts and very few repeaters because of a policy of automatic promotion from grade to grade. The transitions from grade 6 to 7 and from 9 to 10 have improved over time. This, too, probably is largely a matter of policy, however, rather than of the quality of applicants or the teaching-learning process. By 1980, the government hopes to admit all children to middle school, so that the transition rate will approach 1.000. Unlike most developing countries, Korea has maintained a policy of automatic promotion within each level. All children are expected to pass to the next highest grade; teachers are not supposed to screen out the least capable or to fail those at the lower end of an ability distribution. The high internal efficiency of the system is one determinant of the contribution of schooling to income distribution.

A final efficiency concept is external efficiency, that is, how well the outputs of the educational system articulate with national needs. The government has not systematically applied manpower planning or other techniques for relating education to job market needs, and considerable unemployment of secondary and tertiary school graduates occurred in the late 1950s and early 1960s. Since 1965 the results have been mixed. Graduates of vocational schools and colleges, who experienced the highest rates of unemployment in the earlier period, have generally found it much easier to find suitable jobs. This is more likely a result of rapid expansion of the skilled labor market than a consequence of planning.

TABLE 94 Flow Rates of School Enrollments

Grades	1956–1957	1959–1960	1964–1965	1969–1970	1974–1975
1–2	.999	.950	.950	.967	.978
2–3	.996	.972	.975	.986	.989
3–4	.957	.964	.970	.992	.992
4–5	.977	.962	.992	.989	.992
5–6	.968	.954	.957	.987	.989
6–7[a]	.448	.397	.454	.621	.747
7–8	.938	1.000	1.000	.962	.978
8–9	.924	.937	.947	.995	.970
9–10[b]	.646	.733	.751	.698	.711
10–11	.949	.954	.966	.932	.939
11–12	.906	.956	.963	.989	.945

Sources: Shin-Bok Kim, "A Systematic Sub-Optimization Model for Educational Planning with Application to Korea," unpublished PhD dissertation, University of Pittsburgh, 1973. McGinn et al., p. 54.

Notes: [a]Proportion of elementary school graduates going on to middle school.
[b]Proportion of middle school graduates going on to high school.

FAMILY CONTRIBUTIONS TO PUBLIC EDUCATION
The second factor holding down the cost of education to the government was the unusually large share of the financial burden shifted to private households. The central government, which provides most of the public sector financing for education, has increased its outlays many fold in real terms since 1948, as Table 95 shows. But as a percentage either of the total government budget or of GNP, these expenditures have been kept well below levels prevailing in other countries that have undergone comparable enrollment expansions. This has been made possible by virtue of the fact that private households have paid approximately two-thirds of the direct costs of education (see Table 96), as opposed to perhaps one-third in a more typical developing country.

Private educational expenditures take several forms. In the elementary schools, it has long been customary to supplement

TABLE 95 Central Government Expenditures on Education, 1948–1975

	Central Government Expenditures on Education (million *wŏn*)		Ratio of Central Government Expenditures on Education (%)	
	Current price	1970 price[a]	to Government Budget	to GNP
1948	2	n.a.	8.0	n.a.
1951	15	n.a.	2.5	n.a.
1954	575	7,668	4.0	0.9
1957	3,217	16,495	9.2	1.6
1960	6,237	28,611	14.9	2.5
1963	10,523	28,596	13.8	2.2
1966	24,346	40,510	17.2	2.4
1969	57,301	66,091	15.5	2.8
1972	116,577	91,289	16.4	3.0
1975	199,776	90,642	15.5	2.2

Sources: Yung Bong Kim, "Education and Economic Growth," Working Paper 7605, Korea Development Institute, October 1976, p. 29. McGinn et al., p. 16.

Note: [a]Deflated by GNP deflators.

TABLE 96 Educational Expenditures Paid by Students
(million wŏn)

	1966	1967	1968	1969	1970
A) In-School Expenditures	19,208	22,681	29,332	39,242	74,619
Rents and Fees	10,587	13,597	18,380	22,402	29,638
Others[a]	8,621	9,084	10,952	16,840	34,981
B) Out-of-School Expenditures	45,142	53,708	63,493	76,580	95,149
C) Expenditures Paid by Students (A+B)	64,350	76,389	92,825	115,822	169,768
D) Total Educational Expenditures	90,789	112,661	137,490	184,288	251,288
E) C/D (%)	70.9	67.8	67.5	62.8	67.8

	1971	1972	1973	1974	1975
A) In-School Expenditures	82,876	102,611	112,398	142,208	174,833
Rents and Fees	42,349	57,497	63,326	79,084	100,191
Others[a]	40,527	45,114	49,072	63,124	74,642
B) Out-of-School Expenditures	113,653	138,063	160,832	216,368	283,472
C) Expenditures Paid by Students (A+B)	196,529	240,674	273,230	358,576	458,305
D) Total Education Expenditures	309,962	372,692	418,816	537,532	692,992
E) C/D (%)	63.4	64.6	65.2	66.7	66.1

Sources: Yung Bong Kim, "Education and Economic Growth," p. 36. McGinn et al., p. 28.

Note: [a]Includes school-support fund, experimentation and practical training expenses, and student self-governing expenses.

budgetary allocations with "voluntary" parental contributions made through the Parent-Teacher Associations (called Yuksŏnghoe since 1970). Out-of-school expenditures include the usual cost of books (even most elementary school students must buy their own), school supplies, transportation, extra-curricular activities, and (for some) room and board. In addition, large sums are frequently spent on after-school tutoring to prepare students for the crucial national examinations. Finally, three-fourths of government expenditures in education have gone for compulsory (elementary) education. Expansion of the higher levels of schooling has been largely a private matter. As we saw in Table 91, above, increasing shares of secondary and higher education enrollments have been in private institutions.

ROLE OF FOREIGN AID

A third, but much less important, factor in explaining Korea's ability to expand its educational system so rapidly is the role of foreign aid. The initial attempts to satisfy pent-up demand for education were made by the U.S. Military Government in 1945–1948. Although local communities were generally expected to provide facilities, the U.S. Military Government apparently covered about two-thirds of operating costs at the primary level. A second significant foreign input came in the rebuilding process that followed the widespread destruction of the Korean War. Between 1952 and 1956, foreign aid to Korea for education totaled about $100 million. This sum was spent on classroom construction, secondary and vocational education, higher education, and teacher training. Foreign aid at least made a significant contribution to the process of closing the classroom gap depicted in Figure 7, above. In the longer view, however, the amount of aid provided was not large, and ways in which it was spent were not necessarily those which would provide maximum benefit to Korea.

In conclusion, Korea was able to expand its educational system rapidly while the country was still very poor primarily because of its ability to design an efficient, low-cost system and through the extraordinary willingness of Korean families to shoulder heavy financial burdens on behalf of their children's education. Foreign aid also helped, but it was a significant factor only in the period immediately following the Korean War.

CHARACTERISTICS OF KOREAN EDUCATION

The previous section fails to bring out some important qualities of Korean education. Some of its attributes should, in terms of conventional wisdom, contribute to low educational quality. For example, class sizes in Korean schools are very large; on the average, teachers face about twice as many students as developed-country educational specialists claim is desirable. Classes are large not only in primary schools but also in secondary and technical-vocational schools. Second, although many educators favor automatic promotion as a device for reducing inequalities introduced by "streaming" and "screening" in education, it runs counter to recommendations for ability grouping and special training of the more talented students. Automatic promotion is complete in Korea at all levels of the system. Third, educational specialists argue that the most effective education is one that teaches students *how*, not *what*, to think. Emphasis on rote memorization, learning of facts rather than principles, encyclopedic curricula—all these are seen as counterproductive and are often cited as typical of education in backward areas. Yet these features also characterize education in Korea.

There have been four major influences on the nature and content of Korean education:

1) Confucian traditions
2) political pressures for national survival, anti-communism
3) democratization, Deweyism
4) desire for modernization, interpreted to mean increased familiarity with, and competence in, science and technology

There has been much conflict among the proponents of these four perspectives. In the early years of independence, advocates of democratization dueled with traditionalists. Although one prominent Korean educator decried the influence of Deweyism to us, it would seem that today the democratizers have lost out. The character of Korean schools owes more to historical factors predating the U.S. Military Government than to the post-war period during which American advisors and some American-trained Koreans tried to implant a different educational philosophy.

On the other hand, there are other features of Korean education that would be looked on positively by most education specialists. Most striking is the extent of private spending on schooling. Strong "social demand" for education appears in most underdeveloped societies (and, for that matter, high-income societies) in the world today. In nearly every developing country, there is steady growth in the demand for school places, placing tremendous pressure on governments to expand enrollment capacity, first at the primary level and then at progressively higher levels as ever-larger cohorts of the schooled move up into the proper age ranges. This demand is present in Korea, too, but what distinguishes Korea from most other countries is the pattern of educational finance. In all countries, higher levels of education are associated with higher incomes and higher social status. In most countries, then, education is a highly attractive opportunity for economic and social mobility, because it is available at little cost to students and their families (although even this cost is sufficient to weigh heavily on the poorest families); most of the cost is borne by the public. Not so in Korea. We have seen that Korean families have had to carry most of the financial load, paying fees even in public schools and relying heavily on private schooling when the government was slow to expand the capacity of the public schools. It is the willingness of large numbers of Korean families to pay substantial sums, especially large relative to their modest incomes, that is perhaps the most impressive feature in Korea.

One can ask *why* social demand has been so strong in the Korean case. Part of the answer is no doubt cultural—that is, the importance accorded to study and the role of the scholar in Confucian tradition. Perhaps even more important, however, is that Korean society is unusually homogeneous in terms of language, religion, and culture; moreover, its traditional system of social class was all but destroyed in the upheavals created by foreign military occupation, war, and national partition. As documented in *Education and Development in Korea,* these events weakened many of the influences that strongly condition social mobility in other countries and left education as a uniquely important means of individual advancement. This explains the observed fierce competition for places in the higher levels of a school system, which may do little to make people more productive but has practically everything to say about whether they will be successful in gaining access to higher-income jobs and enviable social or powerful bureaucratic positions.

Associated with this importance of education is the privileged social position of the teacher, a cultural heritage from the Chinese, reinforced under the Japanese. In Korea the teacher's social status is so great that it has been possible to attract large numbers of educated *men* to teach in primary grades. In relatively few other countries does one find a majority of teachers who are both male and highly educated.

This attribute goes hand-in-hand with the ability of Korean teachers to command absolute respect from their students. While teachers in many other parts of the world may spend much of their class hour on problems of discipline rather than instruction, the Korean teacher can expect that students will discipline themselves.

This last feature of Korean education must provoke mixed feelings in American educators. Bowing to the teacher, uniforms, mass calisthenics, and reciting in unison are educational practices long ago abandoned in favor of statements promoting student freedom to develop his or her capacities to the fullest and consequent restriction of teacher control over student behavior. Behavior conformity is, for Americans, anti-modern. On the other hand, it is clear that schools cannot teach, let alone socialize, if teachers cannot control students.

The examination system is a dominant facet of Korean education that casts its shadow widely. Prior to 1969, the most significant examinations were given for admission to middle schools, and the results largely determined the individual's future role in society. This was true because the exams were not universal but given separately by each school, and there was a well recognized rank ordering of schools. Kyŏnggi was the "best," Seoul second best, and so on. The graduates of Kyŏnggi were destined for the highest positions after passing through Seoul National University—the prestige institution at the university level. Students could only sit for one examination at one of the first-ranked middle schools and, if they failed in the intense competition, they either had to wait a year or drop down to a second-ranked school.

Preparation for these examinations began early in a child's life and became more intense as the examination time approached. Students worked long hours outside school with tutors to memorize the subjects likely to be covered. For many of them, this was a physical and psychological ordeal that marred them for life, especially if they failed. For the families, it was a risky gamble to decide in which contest to enter their child; if he failed, the family fortunes would suffer while, on the other hand, if he succeeded in a lesser institution, the long-term benefits would be less than if he had gotten into a top school. The odds were assessed with great care.

This system was changed in 1969, because of many complaints about adverse effects on the children, inequity, and its unreliability as a screening process. In its place was substituted a uniform national examination for admission to high school under which those who passed were assigned to specific schools on a random basis. This had the effect of removing the middle and high schools from the role of final arbiters of status and shifted the focus to the universities, which continued to use examinations for screening candidates for admission to individual institutions. At the university level, Seoul National is regarded as the top institution, but below that the ranking is somewhat blurred, so that a top student at any of the major national universities can be expected to begin his career with substantial advantages. Attendance at a provincial university is much less helpful.

Another feature of the use of examination as the sole determiner of which students can pass on to higher levels of education is that it undercuts the importance of grades and performance in school. As a consequence, all students are automatically promoted, and schools concentrate on teaching the material that will be covered in the examinations. This is consistent with the large classes and absence of individual attention in the schools supplemented by the use of private tutors outside the schools.

EDUCATION AND DEVELOPMENT

The oldest argument for a causal link between education and development states that schooling is critical for the development in individuals of those skills and attitudes required for economic growth and political stability. According to this theory, education makes people more entrepreneurial, more productive, more efficient, more mobile. This happens, it is asserted, because of a process in which individuals are transformed through education.

The specific contributions of education—its "value added"—are assumed to be recognized by the market, and therefore one can look to the economic value of education as evidence for its contribution to development. This value is recognized in various ways. The more highly educated people are paid more than those with less education. People want education because they know it contributes to individual advancement.

The statistical relationships on which these assumptions are based hold for Korea as much as in other countries. Those with higher levels of education do (in most cases) receive higher salaries than those with lower levels of education. Figures 8 and 9 demonstrate this relationship with respect to one limited segment of the work force.[2] There are data that suggest a positive relationship between education and economic growth. But, we shall argue, there are other and more convincing explanations of these relationships than the assumptions stated above. First, we shall review the evidence for positive relationships, as provided by rate of return and residual analysis. Then we shall examine whether there were changes in the content, kind, and quality of education that could have contributed to modernization.

RATE OF RETURN AND RESIDUAL ANALYSES

The "rate of return to investment in education" is often calculated as a means of getting at the private and social benefits of education. Rate-of-return calculations for Korean education have been made by Kwang Suk Kim (1968) for USAID, John Chang (1971) for the Florida State University educational planning team, and Chang Young Jeong (1977) for the Korea Development Institute. The results of these calculations are shown in Table 97. We believe that all the rates given in this table are marginal social rates. That is, they are marginal in the sense that they reflect the additional income earned by graduates of a particular level of education over those who have completed the preceding, lower level, as well as the cost of obtaining that marginal level of education. They are social in that they reflect the part of educational costs borne by society as a whole through the government, as well as the costs met by the individuals being educated and their families. These calculations entail a number of arbitrary assumptions and technical difficulties but, for what they are worth, the studies (particularly those by Kwang Suk Kim and Chang Young Jeong) indicate rather low rates of return to investment in education, relative both to the roughly 20 percent rate of return on industrial and commercial investment thought to exist in Korea in the late 1960s and to rates of return on investment in human capital

FIGURE 8 Average Monthly Earning in Industry by
Age and Education, Males, 1972

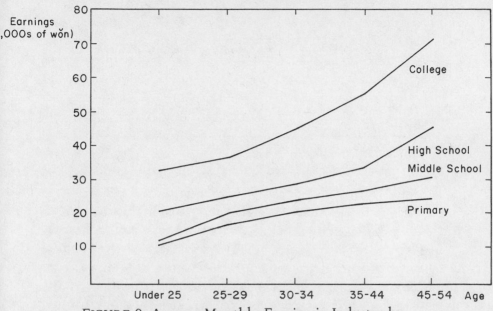

FIGURE 9 Average Monthly Earning in Industry by
Age and Education, Females, 1972

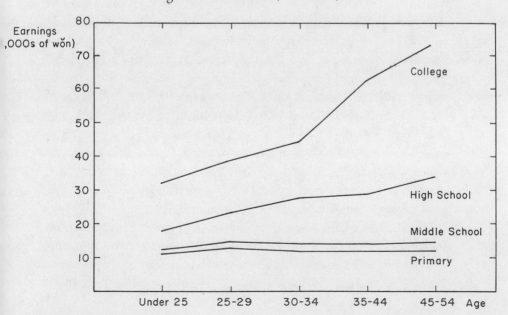

Source: Based on Office of Labor Affairs, *Wage and Employment Survey* (Seoul, 1972).

TABLE 97 Estimated Rates of Return
To Investment in Education

| | Kwang Suk Kim (1968) | John Chang (for 1967) | | Chang Young Jeong (for 1971) |
		Adjusted for Unemployment	Unadjusted	
Middle school	12.0	20.0	26.5	8.2
High school	9.0	11.0	13.5	14.6
College	5.0	9.5	9.5	9.3

Source: McGinn et al., p. 178.

calculated for other countries.[3] These results could be read to indicate that Korean education is over-expanded and should be cut back in favor of other investments. An alternative interpretation is that Korea has had (for a variety of reasons) a tight earnings structure, and that this causes low rates of return to be measured. The latter interpretation is consistent with a view of education as a major social selection device, attractive to those who seek high-status positions in the society and economy, despite the comparatively modest financial returns.

Another analytical approach to establishing a connection between education and economic growth is that of Edward Denison, in which improvement in labor quality as a result of additional education is treated as a factor of production. Calculations employing this methodology suggest that education accounted for less than 10 percent of the total growth of output between 1960 and 1974, and that its contribution was less than 5 percent in the period of high growth since 1966 (see Table 98). Many questions can also be raised about this methodology, but the fact remains that it, like the rate-of-return approach, suggests that education's contribution to economic growth was smaller than many have supposed.

There is no doubt that the social demand for education is high in Korea. Its role in prompting expansion of secondary and higher education well in advance of government intentions has already been noted. What is less certain, however, is that these

TABLE 98 Growth Rates of Factor Inputs and Their
Contributions to Economic Growth

	1960–1974	*1960–1966*	*1966–1970*	*1970–1974*
Growth of inputs and output (annual percentages)				
GNP	9.07	7.25	10.78	10.14
Capital	7.19	3.75	10.43	9.27
Labor	3.55	2.11	6.26	3.06
Education	1.18	1.72	0.82	0.73
Percentage contribution of factor inputs to output growth rate				
Capital	2.88	1.50	4.17	3.71
Labor	2.13	1.27	3.76	1.84
Education	0.71	1.03	0.49	0.44
Others	3.35	3.45	2.36	4.15
Contribution of factor inputs to output growth rate (GNP growth=100)				
Capital	31.8	20.7	38.7	36.6
Labor	23.5	17.5	34.9	18.1
Education	7.8	14.2	4.5	4.3
Others	36.9	47.6	21.9	40.9

Sources: Computed from BOK, *National Income in Korea, 1975*, pp. 268–269;
Tables 33 and 34; and Wontack Hong, "Statistical Data on Korea's Trade
and Growth," Appendix to *Exports and Employment in Korea* (Seoul, 1975),
Table A-27. McGinn et al., p. 123.

findings of a positive relationship between education and economic growth confirm the assumptions with which they are
associated. If education is rewarded because the skills taught
meet the needs of the economy, there should be little educated
unemployment, and a good fit between manpower requirements
and the output of schools. If there is a value-added process in
education, it should be possible to associate differences in
educational quality that people experience with differences in
the economic rewards they receive. The returns to education
might be expected to increase the more education one has.

CONTENT AND QUALITY OF EDUCATION

If education changed to be congruent with the Korean economy over time, we would expect to find that the content of schooling evolved from a traditional to a modern emphasis. If education contributed to development through provision of specific, work-related skills, we should find an evolution from an academic to a vocational-technical curriculum. We should find an expansion of non-formal or out-of-school training programs important in the development of the labor force. Over time the quality of education should have improved; improvements in quality would be reflected in increased unit costs, or smaller class sizes and higher teacher salaries.

The evidence we have reviewed at best only partially fulfills these expectations. Education expanded much more rapidly than could the economy prior to 1960, to such an extent that educated unemployment was regarded as a serious problem. For several years, the number of graduates, especially in certain technical fields, exceeded the manpower requirements of the economy. Some analysts feel that the situation has never been fully rectified, that there is still *too much* investment in human capital.

An alternative formulation has been to suggest that it was the *pool of available talent*—that is, the prior development of education—that made possible the economic takeoff of Korea. To support this argument it would be necessary to distinguish the effects of prior education from those arising simply from the existence of a large unemployed and underemployed labor force that could be put to work with minimal training at low wages in the new labor-intensive export industries.

Research from a number of countries fails to demonstrate a powerful relationship between differences in conventional measures of educational quality received by students, and either the amount of learning they have acquired, or rewards handed out by society. That is, it seems to make little difference whether a student has a well-trained teacher or not, is in a large or small classroom, has access to textbooks, or uses a modern curriculum;

how long one is in school is important, but apparently not what happens to him there.[4]

There are no research results of this kind for Korea. But if they were similar to those from all other countries in which studies have been done, they would read as follows: graduates from Seoul National University command higher salaries than those from a provincial university, irrespective of their grades or position in the class. A graduate from a university commands a higher salary than one from high school, no matter what his level of intelligence or knowledge. More important, when one introduces social class measures into the predictive equation, school differences (of the order Seoul National versus a provincial university) become small, and social class (education and income levels of parents) account for most of the variance in earnings of graduates.

These comments should not be interpreted as disparagement of the Korean educational system. It has many praiseworthy features. Even though the rote learning tradition and heavy reliance on national examinations seem unlikely to foster creativity and productivity, the system is relatively open to students from varying social backgrounds (much more so than in many other developing countries), and there is no doubt that Korean students are bright. We believe that students learn in schools all around the world, and that much is learned in Korean schools. The argument, however, is over whether *differences* in the amount and kind of that learning are a result of differences in the quality and amount of school inputs, or a function of antecedent factors associated with social class.

We have seen that in Korea, as elsewhere, there is a positive rate of return to education. But the rates of return in Korea are lower than rates of return to physical capital, a finding unlike that of other countries. Second, the rate of return to higher education is lower than that of returns to secondary education. (Hence the assertion that there is too much education). Finally, it is possible for individuals to have high rates of return to their investment in education without any equivalent increase in gross national product, as can be seen in a number of countries with very low growth rates and high returns to education. What most influences the rate-of-return calculation are income differentials between persons with different levels of educational attainment. It can be argued that these differentials are more a function of structural factors in the economy and polity—specifically access to power by those with more education—than they are a result of differences in contribution to national productivity.

If the development of education in Korea *after* 1945 was a contributor to modernization and growth, then one would expect an evolution of the changes in the system from that time forward. There were changes. Some were lasting; others were not. The system expanded and new curricula were tried out. But many of the more "modern" innovations were abandoned (coeducation is an exception), and new curricula have elements that seem contrary to the modernization hypothesis. The evidence suggests that, although objectives were set for the introduction of a vocational-technical emphasis in schools, in fact not much progress was made toward that goal until well after the economic takeoff had occurred. Although there was emphasis on individualism and productivity in the curriculum in the 1950s, that was replaced in the 1960s with more emphasis on collectivity and conformity. What distinguishes the curriculum of Korean schools from that of countries whose attempts at development have not resulted in both rapid growth and relative equity is *not* its emphasis on science and technology. The major difference seems to be that Korean education places a heavy stress on moral education and discipline. It is hard to fit this characteristic into the human resources development explanation of education's contribution.

Nor does the explanation seem to lie in the creation of a large non-formal education system that provides relevant skill training. As reviewed earlier, these programs do exist. A significant effort has been made in family planning education, and the Saemaul Undong is making a contribution in rural development. But these programs began in the past decade, and would not seem to have had a major impact on the economy until the last five years. Korea seems to have invested relatively small amounts in skill training, either in out-of-plant training programs, apprenticeship training, or supervised work-study programs. There is an increasing interest in programs of that kind today, but they were not common in earlier years. There has, no doubt, been much skill acquisition through job experience, but it seems unreasonable to presume that workers were better disposed to skill acquisition through an education that emphasized rote learning and moral education.

The absence (during the 1960s) of large investments in skill training is not, after all, surprising, given the path towards industrial development that Korea chose. Unlike other countries in which worker training has been an important part of the development plan, Korea avoided large-scale heavy industrial production in favor of labor-intensive, low-technology enterprises of fairly modest scale. The skills required of workers were easily learned, especially given basic literacy and the manual dexterity which might be associated with people fresh from rural areas, accustomed to working with their hands.

Ironically, perhaps the most important type of out-of-school education in the Korean experience has been one that directly supports students' performance in the formal school system. We refer to the extensive use of after-hours tutoring in academic subjects noted above.

As we have pointed out, it strains credulity to suggest that the formalistic education imparted by Korean schools, from the 1st grade through the university, was directly functional for the kind of industrial employment associated with the Korean economic miracle. Korean schools teach a good deal, but not what workers need to know in agricultural and low-technology industrial employment or what managers need to know to run modern businesses. We expect that what Korean students learn in school, even those graduating from the middle school, far exceeds what they need to know for gainful employment.

INDIVIDUAL MODERNIZATION AND
INSTITUTIONAL EFFECTS OF EDUCATION

An alternative rationale for the human-resources-development-leads-to-national-development theory argues that it is not really skills that are so important but rather attitudes and values that dispose individuals to modernization. There are at least two variants of this approach. One would argue that modern attitudes and values lead *individuals* to act as entrepreneurs, to act to increase their personal productivity, and that it is the aggregate effect of these modernized individuals that results in economic growth. Another version would argue that development occurs through planned and organized efforts for which compliance and conformity by individual citizens are important: modernity is defined in terms of identification with a nation-state and active participation as a consumer as well as producer in the national economy. There are also positions that combine these two emphases.

In both cases education is seen as a critical factor for the development of modernity in individuals. In the simplest approach, the presumption is that this transformation of persons is a function of the content of the educational process, that is, of the school curriculum. We have presented evidence that suggests both that the content of Korean education is not, on face value, modernizing, and that changes in curricula over time seem to be moving away from what we could consider "modern" values, or at least those consistent with individual entrepreneurship. Especially at the higher levels of education, curriculum and examination content would seem to discourage creativity and innovation.

On the other hand, there are data for Korea which show that educated persons tend to be more "modern" in their perspective than those with lower levels of education. The explanation offered to account for this paradox is that what transforms individuals, at least in terms of these attitudes and values, is not so much the content of the educational process as the structure of the schooling process. In schools students learn rules, the importance of time, the use of non-personal evaluation, the importance of quantity, and a variety of other social facts which constitute the syndrome of "modernity." These attitudes are not so much taught as built into the experiences of schooling.

In studies conducted in other countries, persons with more years of education tended to have those attitudes that most people would agree were consistent with life in a "modern" society, especially one in which strong emphasis was placed on acquisition of material goods and social participation. What data are available for Korea are consistent with the findings from other countries. The data for Korea also indicate, however, that persons with higher levels of education are increasingly critical of government policies; university students particularly react against the attempt to associate development with a verticalist society in which collective conformity replaces individual freedom as a value.

Education has collective as well as individual effects. In Korea these effects may have been more important in the modernization process than the value-added effect on individuals. One of the more important collective effects is the definition of who is competent to fill various social and economic roles. In "modern" societies, education is a principal criterion for the assignment of persons to these roles. Government officials must be university graduates. Only engineers (that is, those who have a degree in engineering) are allowed to direct certain kinds of industrial and construction projects. Only lawyers can practice in courts— a lawyer is a person certified on the basis of his education.[5]

Persons in positions assigned to those with certain levels or kinds of education take on the attitudes and values that go with those positions. High school graduates are expected to think and act in ways which are different from primary school graduates. The university graduate in turn has a different set of role expectations. Because these expectations are widely shared in a modernized society, a person with a degree finds that others are willing to accord him certain privileges with no need to demonstrate his abilities. At the same time, these expectations push the degree-holder into a certain pattern of behavior.

Those who have not gone to school also have a role definition —the person who is "intelligent," although he has not gone to school, is so rare that his appearance merits public comment. Even though there is ample evidence that there is tremendous overlap in terms of intellectual ability between those who have finished university and those who have not, people automatically assign to the graduate respect denied the dropout. Korean students who fail examinations tend to accept their lower incomes and status with no questioning of the system. With those lower incomes and status are also accepted certain definitions of self-worth. The acceptance of lower levels of income is critical in a strategy of economic development that calls for low levels of consumption and high levels of productivity.

By the end of the period of Japanese colonial rule, about half the primary-school-age population of Korea was involved in the educational system. The only route to participation in the Japanese colony was through education. Teacher training and military training were the principal routes for a number of Koreans who later became leaders in the Republic of Korea (including President Park, who attended normal school in Japan and a Japanese military school in Manchuria).

Occupation by the Americans reemphasized the role of education as a means to identify those areas of knowledge that were of importance, and therefore the persons who wield special competency. In addition to a rapid expansion of primary education, the Americans invested heavily in expansion of higher education, in Korea, and through scholarships for Koreans to study abroad. Economics, law, public administration, medicine, agriculture, and engineering, programs that previously had received less attention, were now the best financed, and became the most promising route to a prestigious job in the government.[6] Public-sector employment in Korea was always more sought-after than private-sector employment, given the Confucian legacy and the impositions of the Japanese Colonial Government. When the Republic of Korea created new educational programs and categories, it was to be expected that graduates of these programs (especially those from the prestige universities) would soon occupy critical positions in the government. Management of the nation's affairs thus passed from the hands of those trained in traditional bureaucracy and public administration to a new generation of technocrats. In addition to the new roles created by the universities, specialized competence also came from an expansion of the military with a heavy emphasis on formal training in modern management concepts and techniques. It was this new category of competent leaders that was to take power in 1961.[7] These new leaders were certified by the educational system as possessing elite status, because they were trained in the best schools and in the "new knowledge." The preparation of students in "modern" knowledge and status imparted only by the school demands the employment of these persons in important positions, and justifies assigning them salaries equivalent to, or higher than, those received by persons with more traditional training. Even if no learning took place in the middle and high schools and universities of Korea, one could argue that the expansion of these kinds of institutions, and the repeated insistence of public figures on their importance for society, would result in employment of their graduates.

The effect would also be to persuade parents that their "educated" sons (and, in a few instances, daughters) could accept employment in an industrial occupation, could take positions previously occupied by persons with low levels of education, or could encourage entrepreneurial activity, even if *traditional* Confucian values frowned on that kind of activity. Education—meaning in this case the possession of a certificate—would replace scholarship as the defining characteristic of a respectable person, and in time would replace occupation as the source of prestige. Because in Korea respect was based less on material wealth of an individual than on his standing (as demonstrated by successful performance on examinations), it was possible for the expansion of a new source of respect (the university degree) to occur without serious distortions to a reasonably equitable distribution of national income. That is, the expansion of education in Korea did not lead to widening income gaps as educational expansion has in the great majority of developing countries, not because educated persons in Korea were less productive than those in other countries, but because the social value of·education was not in the salary it could command but the social position of the graduate.

Another function of education is to strengthen the foundation of a nation-state by providing a common language, a common set of heroes and myths, the basis for a common civic order, and common perspective on reality. Given the homogeneity of the Korean population, the high level of education already present in the society, and the existence of, and allegiance to, local and national political structure, it is doubtful that this particular function of education was important in Korea. As we have described earlier, considerable attention was given, however, to defining a set of values that would legitimate the current regime. Both during the period of Syngman Rhee and under the present government, education has been designed to reinforce the authority of the government. Ross H. Cole writes:

> The fervor with which anti-communist education was stressed as the Park government solidified power had other implications. The original position of the military junta . . . was to destroy the communists and reunify the fatherland. That stance was particularly beneficial to the government at a time when the junta leader-turned-president was striving to unify the people of South Korea . . . Exploiting the presence of the hungry aggressors to the North who were lurking in wait to crush South Korea, added emotional tenor and near religious fanaticism to the sense of urgency and utter necessity of preparing and building Korea immediately . . . Anti-communism became the basic rationale for economic development. [8]

Through direct socialization of students in schools (where even today anti-Communist posters are common), the organization of university students into paramilitary units with the mandate to seek out subversives, the repeated pronouncement and analysis of the National Charter of Education, the use of school students in demonstrations in favor of the government and other activities, the educational institution reinforces a national culture in which the president is defined as a benign authority pursuing the interests of all Koreans. Until 1975 this policy had not been successful, but in recent years the government has made additional efforts to command university student support.

Education not only specifies what knowledge and values are important for participation in the nation-state, it also certifies that individuals are competent as citizens and, therefore, entitled to the rights and responsible for the duties of citizenship. With the expansion of education comes the expansion of citizen participation in the political process. This has occurred in Korea as in other countries, although, as we have noted, in recent years the government has tended to thwart movements for increased participation. The movement away from an open parliamentary democracy to a more paternalistic and corporate form of government has necessarily required a reduction in the rights of citizens to free expression and redress of grievances, or so the government sees it. We would predict that, with continued expansion of education, the Korean government must also continue to be repressive, or permit a fundamental change in political structure.

What we have learned in this analysis of the educational system of the Republic of Korea can be summarized as follows: Both the expansion of education, and the growth of the economy of Korea are unique events in the history of development. There is a relationship between the two phenomena, but it is not a simple cause-and-effect or facilitation linkage. The evidence is not consistent with a conclusion that education generated growth through some transformation of individuals from traditional to modern men or through the formation of "human capital." It does seem likely that changes occurring in other sectors of the Korean society occurred also in education, and that consistency was helpful in the development process.

Education in Korea does not appear to have expanded as a response to technological improvements in the economy requiring higher levels of ability among workers. Nor is there evidence that increases in the number of educated people anticipated (in some causal way) the economic boom of the 1960s. The latter statement does not deny, of course, the possibility that the availability of large numbers of literate and modestly educated workers facilitated the organization of the economy under the Park Military Government in the early 1960s. What is clear is the role assigned to education in the socialization of the population, both as students and adults, into the basic attitudes of compliance with a strong central government. Although the government promotes education as contributing to economic development, major trends have not been towards skill acquisition and developmental values (as Westerners may see them) so much as towards identification of students with the future of Korea as a corporate state. The expansion of education obeyed, therefore, not only social demand for increased educational opportunity (because educational attainment is a key determinant of occupation) but also the desire to legitimize the new economic and political system. We believe that education did play a critical role in the modernization of Korea—primarily by assisting a strong government with "modernizing" policies to impose its will upon the nation.

ELEVEN

Population, Urbanization, and Health

As the previous chapters have shown, Korea has experienced two eras of rapid growth, the first as a colony and the second as an independent country. The consequences of these two divergent developmental experiences for the distribution of benefits and impact on the structure of the society have been immense. This chapter will explore the effects on the population in terms of its growth, location, and health. The following chapter will take up the more direct measures of income distribution.

One of the more fascinating aspects of recent Korean development has been the pattern and determinants of its demographic transition. While there has been general recognition that economic growth and rising incomes have implications for both birth and death rates, there has been less agreement on the impact of income distribution, access to health services, fertility control programs, and other government policies on those rates. Korean experience sheds some light on their relative effectiveness.

Migration has been another major factor in Korean life in this century that is in marked contrast with its previous history. During the colonial era, part of the population explosion was absorbed by emigration to Japan, Manchuria, and China. Repatriation at the end of World War II added roughly 10 percent to total population. The subsequent division of the country and civil war led to further sizable migration from North to South Korea. Since the war there has been a massive influx from the countryside to the cities. Such mobility has had positive effects on productivity and income distribution and has enhanced the degree of homogeneity of the population.

Rapid urbanization and industrialization have generated strong demands for housing, transportation, and other urban services such as sanitation, health, and education. These services have been met to an unusual degree by the private sector which generally operates under considerable governmental guidance. It is interesting to assess this private-public model in terms of the extent to which it has satisfied the demand for services, the efficiency with which it has operated, the degree of equity or inequity in the distribution of benefits, and, finally, the extent to which these services have contributed to the development process.

AN OVERVIEW

Before proceeding into the forest, it is useful to have an overall impression of the major changes that have occurred in Korean population, its location, and health since the beginning of the colonial period. This is provided in Table 99. It is clear that a population explosion began during the colonial era. From a fairly stable and manageable differential of 5 per thousand between the crude birth and death rates, the 1920s saw a widening of the gap to 20 per thousand as the birth rate rose and the death rate declined, both by roughly 20 percent. The gap between the birth and death rates stayed roughly the same

TABLE 99 Demographic Transitions in Korea, 1910–1975

Year	(1) Crude Birth Rate (per 1,000)	(2) Crude Death Rate (per 1,000)	(3) Urban Population (%)	(4) Agricultural Labor as % of Total Employment
1910	35–40	32–37		87.5 (11)
1915	38	34	3.1	
1920	40	33	3.3	91.5
1925	42	30	3.5	89.3
1930	45	26	4.5	87.9
1935	44	24	7.4	85.8
1940	44	23	11.6	
1945	42	23	14.5	78.2 (47)
1950	42	23	18.4	79.4 (49)
1955	40	33	24.4	79.5
1960	44.7	16	28.3	65.6
1965	41.7	15	33.9	58.6
1970	32.0	13	43.1	50.5
1975	30.5	9	50.9	45.9

Sources: Columns (1) and (2), Tae Hwan Kwon, Hae Young Lee, Yunshik Chang and Eui-Young Yu, *The Population of Korea* (Seoul, Seoul National Univ., 1975), p. 12. Column (3), Mills and Song, Table 1, p. 8 and Table A-3-1, p. 201–203. Column (4), Mills and Song, Table A-2-1, p. 185 through 1950, Kwon for 1955 and 1960 and EPB for 1970 and 1975.

Notes: Columns (1) and (2), crude birth and death rates, are 5-year averages for the preceding 5 years. Figures in parentheses show years for which figures are reported when they differ from the year indicated. Urban population refers to number of persons living in municipalities with populations of 50,000 or more.

Figures through 1945 cover all Korea, thereafter only South Korea.

level for two decades until 1950. Then the Korean War brought on a sudden rise in the death rate followed by a precipitous decline that has brought it down to 9 per thousand by 1970–1975, a level generally found in much more affluent countries.

In the 1960s the birth rate also plummeted in what has been described as "one of the fastest [fertility declines] recorded in any nation in history."[1] These two remarkable events—the decline in the birth rate by 17 per thousand between 1960 and 1975, and the decline in the death rate by roughly the same amount (setting aside the unusually high rate resulting from the war) in twenty-five years—raise many questions. Why didn't something similar happen during the earlier high economic growth period? What was the constellation of factors in the 1960s that was so different from the earlier period? Was it the direct effects of health services or indirect effects of changing economic conditions and social services?

Some indication of parallel movements of similar scale in other key variables is also given in Table 99. According to Mills and Song, "The pace of Korean urbanization during much of the middle half of the 20th Century may have been as rapid as any ever observed during a substantial historical period in a country larger than a city-state."[2] Opposite movements in the share of agricultural, forestry, and fisheries workers in the total employed labor force show that Korea was predominantly a rural agricultural country through 1955 but, over the next twenty years, the urban, industrial, and service workers and inhabitants achieved parity with their rural, agricultural counterparts.

The spurt in educational expansion, discussed in the preceding chapter, preceded the recent demographic changes. In the fifteen-year period immediately after World War II, primary school enrollment rates doubled, females moved close to equality with males at that level of schooling, and literacy rates more than tripled.

The most significant indicator of improvement in health conditions is the decline in the crude death rate. The extremely low figure of 9 per thousand in 1975 is open to some question and, if accurate, is probably not sustainable in the future as it reflects, in part, an abnormal age structure of the population. Even so, a somewhat higher figure would still be a considerable achievement considering the relatively low expenditures on health care and sanitation facilities. The basic question about health conditions in Korea is—Why are the death and infant mortality rates so low, when the health services are so limited and maldistributed? So far there is not enough information to answer this question adequately, but some preliminary hypotheses will be suggested.

THE DEMOGRAPHIC TRANSITION

At the turn of the century, the population of Korea was about 17 million and growing very slowly according to the best available estimates.[3] Economic and cultural pressures for farm hands and male heirs encouraged early marriage and moderately high birth rates, estimated at 35–40 per thousand. Poor health and sanitation, low incomes, and neglect of unwanted female babies kept the crude death rate in a range slightly below the birth rate.

This relatively stable pattern of gradual population growth was transformed into one of high growth in the 1920s as a result of both a rise in the birth rate and a decline in the death rate. As Tai Hwan Kwon has shown, the rising birth rate reflected two opposing movements: initially there was a substantial rise in the fertility rate of married women which continued for the next forty years (until 1960), but this was offset, at least after 1925, by a steady rise in the age of women at first marriage from 16.6 in 1925 to 17.8 in 1940. These countervailing forces led to a decline in the age-specific fertility rates in the 15–24 year age bracket and a rise for the higher age levels. During the first two decades of the colonial period, higher fecundity dominated and the crude birth rate rose (see Table 99); thereafter it declined slightly.

The main reason given by Kwon for the rise in fecundity is improved health conditions.[4] The Japanese introduced mass inoculations against smallpox in 1915 and other measures to prevent the spread of infectious disease. Also some hospitals and schools for training medical personnel were established.

While these health measures undoubtedly had some effect in increasing fertility, their main impact was on mortality as evidenced by the drop in the crude death rate from 34 to 24 per thousand between 1910–1915 and 1930–1935. Such changes in the mortality rate have often been associated with periods of rapid economic development, and this was clearly taking place in Korea at that time. As shown in Chapter 3, real output per capita grew at roughly 4 percent per annum from 1910 through 1940, with higher rates in the first and third decades. But to what extent did this affect the Korean population?

There is considerable evidence (see Chapter 3) that consumption levels of Koreans did not improve during the colonial period. Rice consumption per capita is reported to have declined from 112 kilograms per year in 1912 to 80 in 1944,[5] since Koreans were forced to substitute inferior grains to release rice for export to Japan. Those who experienced the rising incomes and consumption levels were primarily the Japanese, who were expanding their landholdings and industrial and commercial ventures in Korea.

The combination of rapidly increasing population, originating mainly in the rural areas of Korea, and limited opportunities for increasing agricultural incomes and employment as the Japanese consolidated and expanded their landholdings, forced many Koreans to look to the cities or abroad for some means of livelihood. Between 1910 and 1940, the total population in Korea went from 17.4 to 23.5 million. During the same period the urban population rose from about 500,000 to 2.7 million, while the net migration from Korea to Manchuria and to Japan was 1.4 million and 1.2 million respectively.[6] The net increase in the rural population over the three decades was about 4 million or less than half what it would have been without the urbanization and emigration.

The contrast between the colonial and post-World War II demographic changes for all of Korea and South Korea is illustrated in Tables 100 and 101, where account is taken of the emigration during the earlier period and the return flow to South Korea from Japan, Manchuria, and North Korea in the 1945–1955 decade. In the 1910–1940 period, the rural areas

TABLE 100 Demographic Changes in All Korea, 1910–1940 (in millions)

	Total Population in Korea	Urban	Rural	Net Migrants	Approximate Total Korean Population Incl. Emigrants
1910	17.4	0.5	16.9		17.4
1940	23.5	2.7	20.8	-2.6	26.1
Change 1910–1940	6.1 35.1%	2.2 440%	3.9 23.1%	-2.6	8.7 51.1%

Sources: Tai Hwon Kwon et al. and Dae Young Kim "Migration and Korean Development" in Robert Repetto (1977) for migrant estimates. Urban population based on Mills and Song criterion for urban areas as those with 50,000 or more inhabitants.

TABLE 101 Demographic Changes in South Korea, 1945–1975

	Total Population in South Korea	Urban	Rural	Net Migrants	Total Population Incl. Emigrants
1945	16.1	2.3	13.8	+2.5	18.6[a]
1955	21.5	5.2	16.3		21.5
1975	34.7	17.7	17.0		34.7
Change 1945–1955	5.4 33.5%	2.9 126.1%	2.5 18.1%		2.9 15.6%
1955–1975	13.2 61.4%	12.5 240.4%	0.7 4.3%		13.2 61.4%
1945–1975	18.6 115.5%	15.4 669.5%	3.2 23.1%		16.1 86.5%

Source: Dae Young Kim in Repetto.

Note: [a]This figure includes the 0.5 million who subsequently imigrated to South Korea.

absorbed nearly half the total population expansion; emigration accounted for 30 percent and urbanization the remainder. After 1945, there was a large return flow of migrants from Japan and Manchuria, mainly to South Korea (whence most had originated) and an influx of refugees from North Korea. This inflow accounted for nearly half South Korea's population increase between 1945 and 1955. Also, over half of the population increment occurred in the urban areas, but this was only a precursor of the shift that was to occur thereafter. Between 1955 and 1975 practically the total increase in population was in the urban areas. The rural population hardly increased at all. Thus where the colonial period saw the beginnings of urbanization, large-scale emigration, and increasing rural population pressure, the three post-colonial decades have been marked by explosive urbanization absorbing both the return flow of émigrés and subsequent migrants from the rural areas where population pressure has scarcely changed.

With urbanization came rising industrial and service employment and many other modernizing influences. Primary education achieved complete coverage of both sexes and in both rural and urban areas by 1970. Access to higher education was greatly broadened. Health services were expanded, particularly in the urban areas, while preventive health services became generally available throughout the countryside.

After the disruption, destruction, and death of the Korean War, these modernizing influences began to have a marked impact on the death rate that declined from 33 per thousand during 1950–1955, and a pre-war rate of 23 per thousand, to 16 per thousand in 1955–1960. A concurrent rise in the birth rate reflecting a post-war baby-boom caused a rapid expansion of nearly 3 percent per annum in the total population which began to cause some real concern in official Korean circles.[7] Because Syngman Rhee was opposed to institutionalized family planning programs, his removal in 1960 opened the way to more forthright discussion of population policies and family planning programs. Family planning was one of the seven key programs for promoting economic development adopted by the Park Government in 1961, and the First Five-Year Economic Development Plan, approved in early 1962, mentions that "population control measures will be required" to bring about a gradual reduction in the population growth rate. [8]

This was the beginning of an extensive well-funded, public-private effort to introduce family planning in Korea. [9] The program concentrated on educating women in contraceptive techniques, and was accompanied by free distribution of contraceptive devices. The spread of contraceptive practices was rapid (see Table 102) and pervasive, reaching women in the rural areas as well as urban, and women of all educational levels. As expected, the usage rate of contraception increased with both the age of the women and with parity, that is, the number of children already born. It has been estimated that from 1962 through 1975, contraception resulted in averting over 1.5 million births.

In addition to these impressive achievements of contraception through the family planning program, abortion has been an important supplement to contraception (or recourse when contraception failed) in reducing the fertility rate. As reported by Tai Hwan Kwon, there has been a decline in the total fertility rate for all Korean women from 6.3 in 1955–1960 to 3.9 in 1973. [10] Over roughly the same time period, there has been a rise in the total abortion rate from 0.7 to 2.1 (see Table 103). While abortion rates and fertility rates are not directly comparable because some women have more than one abortion per year, the rising abortion rate accounted for a significant portion of the drop in the fertility rate. By 1973, the rate of abortions among rural women was nearly as high as that of urban women, but the fertility rate in rural areas was still well above the urban rate (see Table 104).

The desired number of children dropped from 3.9 in 1965 to 3.1 by 1973, and the desire for more children depended heavily

TABLE 102 Percent of Married Women Currently Using
Contraception by Selected Characteristics
and Years

Characteristic	Year					
	1964	*1965*	*1967*	*1971*	*1973*	*1976*
Total Using	9.0	16.4	20.2	24.6	34.5	43.9
Age: 20–24	4.4	5.7	4.0	6.9	12.9	15.9
25–29	9.8	12.7	14.2	15.5	27.4	31.7
30–34	13.2	23.6	26.9	27.4	36.4	55.5
35–39	13.9	24.1	33.1	38.0	49.8	61.2
40–44	5.8	10.4	16.3	26.8	33.7	44.8
45–49	1.9	n.a.	n.a.	n.a.	n.a.	n.a.
Parity:						
0	n.a.	(5.5)	(0.9)[a]	(3.0)	3.4	4.6
1	n.a.	4.3	2.4	5.9	14.6	17.9
2	n.a.	12.2	11.9	20.2	33.2	43.9
3	n.a.	14.9	22.2	28.7	49.1	56.2
4	n.a.	20.3	29.9	31.9	44.2	59.0
5 or more	n.a.	23.2	30.6	31.6	41.8	48.8
Residence:						
Urban	n.a.	21.4	26.0	27.4	36.5	47.6
Rural	n.a.	14.0	17.3	22.7	32.7	39.8
Education:						
None	4.6[b]	9.8	15.7	20.9	27.5	37.2
Literate	n.a.	15.9	15.4	24.6	33.8	45.5
Primary school	13.8	16.8	21.7	24.5	35.2	42.4
Middle school	35.5	30.8	25.7	32.4	42.9	44.2
High school or more		33.5	36.4	39.5	47.8	50.6

Source: Published and unpublished tabulations from fertility and family planning
surveys conducted by the Korean Institute for Family Planning.
From Donaldson in Repetto.
Notes: [a]Figures in parenthesis are based on too few cases to be reliable.
[b]Data refer to "ever use" which includes both past and current users.

TABLE 103 Total Abortion and Fertility Rates

Year	Abortion Rate	Year	Total Fertility Rate
		1955–1960	6.3
1961	0.7	1960–1965	6.0
1963	0.7	1965–1970	4.6
1966	1.4		
1971	2.0		
1973	2.1	1970–1975	3.9

Sources: Abortion rates are from Repetto, p. IV-32.
Fertility rates are from Tae Hwan Kwon et al., p. II–26.

TABLE 104 Rural and Urban Fertility and Abortion Rates, 1973

Urban		Rural		National	
Abortion	Fertility	Abortion	Fertility	Abortion	Fertility
2.2	3.3	2.0	4.7	2.1	3.9

Source: Repetto, pp. 28–29, 49, based on Kun Yong Song and Seung Hyon Han *National Family Planning and Fertility Survey: A Comprehensive Survey* (Seoul, Korean Institute for Family Planning, 1974).

on the number of sons already in the family. Education and urbanization of parents also have been correlated with declining fertility.

Robert Repetto has suggested that the relatively egalitarian pattern of Korea's recent development has had a significant effect on fertility decline.[11] He has demonstrated statistically that fertility is negatively associated with family income, and that the effect is stronger for lower, than for higher, income groups. Thus, he suggests that a more equal distribution of income has contributed to lower aggregate fertility in Korea. Also, parental aspirations for the education of their children have tended to limit fertility. A third major factor affecting fertility has been the greatly increased urban employment opportunities for women which have caused them to delay getting married and to limit the number of children once they are married. These are the main considerations that have created the demand for contraception and abortion and reduced the birth rate so rapidly since 1960.

Two other aspects of the fertility transition should be noted. First, the government gave full support to the ostensibly privately run contraception program and approached it much like a military campaign, as it did with the export and the tax programs. National and local targets were set for adoption of various types of contraceptives, and performance was carefully monitored at the national level to see that targets were met. This undoubtedly led to some abuses and misreporting, which have recently been mentioned by the World Bank,[12] but it was typical of the government's approach to mass programs. The growing demand for contraceptive services removed much of the need for coercion.

A second feature was the government's lack of concern for legal technicalities, such as the law prohibiting abortion which was not abolished until 1973 despite the widespread practice of abortion. The government obviously did not oppose abortion and in fact encouraged it, but did not see the need to make the law consistent with its programs.

In sum, Korea started the demographic transition in the 1920s under a colonial regime that introduced a limited range of public health measures which caused a rise in the birth rate and a decline in the death rate. Growing population pressure in the rural areas was exacerbated by increasing Japanese landlordism, but relieved in part by urban and external migration. Limited job opportunities and education, especially for women, kept the mass of the Korean population illiterate, poor, rural, and fecund, while the Japanese reaped most of the benefits of the substantial output growth that occurred.

After Liberation in 1945, the return flow of migrants, plus refugees from the north, initiated the burgeoning urbanization that has characterized South Korea for thirty years, despite the devastation of most cities in the Korean War. High death rates during the war, and birth rates after the war, temporarily distorted the population trends, but by about 1960 the second phase of the demographic transition began. Since then, both birth and death rates have declined sharply, but the drop in the birth rate has been greater, so the overall population growth rate has diminished from nearly 3 percent in 1960 to 2 percent or less since 1970.

This very significant decline in fertility seems to derive from the egalitarian development pattern, greatly expanded employment opportunities for females, easy access to contraceptives and abortion, and changing social attitudes resulting from urbanization and modernization.

URBANIZATION[13]

Rapid urbanization has been a recent phenomenon in Korea. Although the process started during the colonial period, it accelerated greatly after Independence. In 1950, the portion of South Korea's population living in urban areas was similar to that of other developing countries. By 1975, it was nearly double that of the other developing countries and roughly equal to that of the developed countries in 1950 (see Table 105).

Korea's cities are characterized by high population densities and a high degree of concentration of population in the central district of the major cities. But Mills and Song suggest that these patterns are to be expected in a densely populated country that has been experiencing rapid urbanization. They show that the three largest cities—Seoul, Pusan, and Taegu—have been undergoing a process of decentralization since the middle 1960s and expect that other cities will follow the same path in time.

The rate of urbanization has been linked to the rate of economic growth, particularly of the urban-oriented manufacturing and service sectors which in Korea have both grown rapidly and been relatively labor-intensive. Rapid urbanization has also had a strong impact on the demand for land in the urban areas.

TABLE 105 Urban Population Percentage in Developing and
Developed Countries, 1950 and 1975

Area	Year	
	1950	*1975*
All Developing Countries	16.5	28.3
All Developed Countries	51.6	66.9
World Average	28.2	38.9
Korea	18.4	50.9

Sources: Korean data for 1950 refer to 1949 and are obtained from Pyŏng-nak Song,
"Han'guk sudokwŏn ŭi konggan kyŏngje punsŏk," Korea Development
Institute, Research Report No. 75-16 (December 1975), p. 72. Data for
other countries are obtained from The World Bank, "The Task Ahead for
the Cities of the Developing Countries," Staff Working Paper No. 209
(July 1975), p. 3.

It has been estimated that the average real rate of appreciation
of urban land values was 14 percent per annum between 1963
and 1974, and that in 1975 urban land, which was only 4
percent of the total land area, accounted for 45 percent of the
total land value in the country, and, finally, that the total land
value was 1.85 times annual GNP. This is more than double the
ratio in the United States (0.7 times) but less than Japan (3.3
times). It reflects the relative scarcity of land in Korea and
Japan, and continuing expectations of high rates of growth and
urbanization.

Rapidly rising land values are said to have attracted savings
away from more productive froms of investment and to have
reduced the rate of recorded private savings.[14] Rising land values
have also exerted strong pressure for efficient use of space and
have induced a sizable shift from single- to multiple-family units
and from owner-occupancy to tenancy. The extreme scarcity of
organized financing for purchase of dwellings has made it very
difficult for families to purchase their own homes. Urban
landlordism has become widespread, but rents appear not to
have risen as rapidly as land values (which capitalize both current income and expected appreciation).

The stock of housing was severely damaged during the Korean

War, particularly in the urban areas, and in the post-war years investment in housing accounted for about 18 percent of total fixed investment or 2 percent of GNP. In recent years, housing investment has increased to over 3 percent of GNP, but this has done little to improve the availability of housing on a per capita basis, probably because of the higher cost of urban housing.

The government has granted no tax incentives for investment in housing and has provided minimal financing of mortgages. Housing development has been mainly a responsibility of private enterprise which relies on its own financial resources. Bank financing is estimated to have amounted to less than 5 percent of the value of homes purchased in all cities in 1974.[15] Furthermore, the government has regulated development of new areas on the urban fringe, and the slowness in approving new sites has contributed to the shortage and high price of housing sites. When the government approves new developments, it lays claim to part of the land, some of which is used for building infrastructure, and the rest of which is sold to recoup the costs of the infrastructure. This system of self-financing has further served to limit the government's financial contribution to housing development.[16]

One of the most successful aspects of urban development in Korea has been the heavy reliance on privately owned buses for public transportation systems which move large numbers of people at low cost with minimal traffic congestion.[17] As shown in Table 106 a traffic count in the city of Seoul in 1974 indicated that one-third of the trips were made on foot, and of the remaining two-thirds over 85 percent were by bus. Taxis and private autos each accounted for about 5 percent of the vehicular travel. A new subway started operation in 1974 and is changing the pattern somewhat, but not drastically.

Since the Korean War, the government has restricted the importation of cars and imposed heavy use taxes on privately owned vehicles. Buses have been imported in large numbers by privately owned bus companies which compete over the same routes both within and between cities. Government has regulated

TABLE 106 Purpose of Trips by Transportation Modes, Seoul, 1973
(%)

Purposes	Commercial Bus	Commercial Taxi	Private Autos	Train	Walk	Other	Total
School	49.2	0.2	0.8	0.3	48.2	1.3	100.0
Work	64.3	4.9	4.7	0.5	19.3	6.4	100.0
Shopping	55.4	4.6	1.1	0.3	34.9	3.6	100.0
Business	52.5	14.9	11.2	0.5	15.7	5.2	100.0
Recreation	69.1	8.4	3.3	0.4	18.4	0.5	100.0
Home	57.4	2.3	2.2	0.4	34.7	3.0	100.0
Travel	53.2	18.9	3.5	12.6	11.9	0.0	100.0
Other	60.0	9.5	4.2	0.5	23.2	2.5	100.0
Average	56.8	3.0	2.8	0.4	33.7	3.3	100.0

Sources: Han'guk Kwahak Kisul Yŏn'guso, *Sŏul [Seoul] T'ŭkpyŏlsi t'onghaeng silt'ae chosa*, 1974. Mills and Song, p. 146.

the bus operations but has not been overly restrictive in granting operating permits. Fares are low and service is almost continuous on the main routes. Domestically produced taxis are relatively abundant and provide an effective supplement to the bus service.

Thus, urban transport is an example of reliance on the private sector operating under government surveillance which has resulted in an efficient system that economizes on capital and direct government-financed support. Where this approach has broken down is in connection with those public services that cannot be provided by the private sector and that require heavy capital investment. Examples are sewage, water supply, and, to a lesser degree, electricity. They have been characterized by underinvestment and continuing shortages, lack of service to outlying areas, and considerable inefficiency. Large amounts of raw sewage and human excrement are dumped directly into the Han River near Seoul, and several major sources of the city's water supply are downstream from the sewage discharge points. Water supply from these latter sources is said to be of low quality and a potential source of waterborne disease and parasites.[18] Large investments will be required to bring these facilities up to acceptable levels.

Air pollution is a growing problem in Korea's cities, with coal-burning home heating units and industrial emissions accounting for much of it. Motor vehicles and power generation have been relatively minor sources because of the preponderance of diesel buses and oil-fired generators, both of which have relatively low emissions of pollutants. Antipollution laws have existed since 1963, but little has been done to enforce them. The oil crisis and high prices of imported oil since 1973 have encouraged continued use of coal for home heating, and thereby frustrated one of the government's main programs for controlling air pollution. In the meantime, according to Mills and Song, "Large Korean cities are now reaching air pollution levels at which some health damage is almost inevitable."[19]

Over the past thirty years, Korea's cities have absorbed massive numbers of new inhabitants who have found jobs in the burgeoning industrial and service sectors. Transportation has been good, housing fair, and most other public services poor. The private sector has outperformed the public sector in meeting urban needs. Decentralization, which is now underway in the larger cities, if accompanied by sufficient public investment, could provide an opportunity to remedy some of the deficiencies.

HEALTH[20]

The health picture in Korea provides a number of intriguing contrasts. The mortality rate has fallen to a very low level, and correspondingly life expectancy has achieved a high level. On the other hand, infant mortality is still relatively high and activity-restricting morbidity is a substantial problem. Government has given very low priority over the years to provision of health services, effective implementation of mass inoculation programs, improvement of water supply, and sanitation. Demand for health services has been growing, however, and has been met mainly by private expenditures for private services. Sellers of traditional medicines and prescribing druggists are major purveyors of health services, especially in the rural areas where trained health professionals are very scarce. Despite a relatively favorable ratio of doctors to population, it has been estimated that approximately 90 percent of the births in Korea are unattended by either a physician or a qualified midwife, and that in one rural area less than a quarter of the instruments used to cut the umbilical cord were sterilized, resulting in high incidence of neonatal tetanus.[21]

The Korean people have a reputation for being hardy and hard working. Those who survive the hazards of childbirth and early childhood diseases seem to have sufficient food to overcome the effects of ubiquitous parasites and poor sanitation. Respiratory ailments are a serious problem, especially in the winter months, while the effects of air pollution and tension arising from urbanization and modernization are becoming more significant. Given the uneven and uncoordinated nature of the health system and services bearing on health, health conditions are better than would be expected.

HEALTH STATUS

Health status has improved considerably in Korea in recent years and now compares favorably with that of other developing countries. As shown in Table 107, life expectancy has risen by about one-fourth, or twelve years, for both men and women between 1955 and 1970. Infant mortality declined by nearly 40 percent and was a major factor in the similar decline in the crude death rate. The recent infant mortality rate in the urban areas is in the range of 30–35 per thousand live births, while that in the rural areas is 40–60 per thousand.

When compared with other Asian countries, the crude death rate is lower than that of any country except Japan. The infant mortality rate, however, is still well above that of Taiwan, Thailand, and Malaysia as well as Japan, but it is far below the Philippines, Indonesia, and India. Life expectancy in Korea is near that of Japan and above that of the other countries (see Table 108).

The major causes of death as well as morbidity in Korea have been respiratory diseases. Although the incidence declined appreciably from the late 1950s to the mid-1960s, pneumonia, bronchitis, and tuberculosis were still the main killing diseases. Gastrointestinal illnesses were the second most common cause of morbidity, but the fatality rate from them has diminished over time. They remain major causes of incapacity, loss of working hours, and reduced productivity as well as serious discomfort.

DETERMINANTS OF HEALTH STATUS

The major determinants of morbidity and mortality include nutrition, sanitation, and other environmental conditions of the population, the availability and utilization of health services, and the level of knowledge and practice of health care throughout the population. In Korea the pattern has been mixed.

TABLE 107 Health Status Indicators, Korea, 1955–1970

	1955	*1960*	*1965*	*1970*
Life expectancy:				
Men	51	54	54	63
Women	54	58	60	67
Infant mortality:				
(per 1,000 births)	78	69	52	49
Crude death rate:				
(per 1,000 population)	14.3	13.0	11.9	8.5

Sources: Hakchung Choo and James Jeffers, "Health and Economic and Social Development," unpublished paper prepared for the Korean Modernization Study, (KDI, Seoul, 1976), p. 13.

Life expectancy figures were taken from Hakchung Choo (5 p. 2) with the exception of 1955 and 1970 figures which were reported by the Economic Planning Board, "Abridged Life Table of Korea," *Data on Population Statistics,* No. 23 (1965 and 1974).

Infant mortality statistics were also taken from Choo (5 p. 2), except 1955 figures which were provided by the Ministry of Health and Social Affairs.

Crude death estimates for 1955 are E. H. Choe's (unpublished). Crude death rate estimates for 1960 and 1970 are from the Economic Planning Board, *Korea Statistical Yearbook,* 1970. The crude death rate in 1965 was estimated by I. S. Kim et al, "Recent Mortality Trends in Korea," *The Korean Journal of Preventive Medicine,* 2.1:61–76 (1969).

Nutrition

Average nutritional levels appear to have risen substantially in recent decades and to have reached satisfactory levels of most nutrients. According to one estimate, per capita food expenditures have risen by over 50 percent in real terms between 1960 and 1973.[22] This undoubtedly reflects some shift from lower- to higher-priced foods, but that shift is likely to contribute to the nutritional value of the expenditures through greater consumption of meats and vegetables. An analysis of the calorie and protein content of the average Korean diet in 1975 is displayed in Table 110. Overall calorie and protein intakes appear to be relatively favorable, but the fact that they come so largely

TABLE 108 Health Indicators in Selected Countries, 1973

Country	Crude Death Rate (per 1,000 population)	Life Expectancy	Infant Mortality (per 1,000 births)
Korea	8.5	65	49
Japan	6.6	73	12
Taiwan	10.2	62	18
Thailand	10.4	59	23
Malaysia	9.8	59	38
Philippines	10.5	58	62
India	16.3	49	139
Indonesia	18.9	45	125

Sources: Korea, Table 107.
Japan, Chong Kee Park, *Financing Health Care Services in Korea* (KDI, 1977).
Other countries: World Bank, *Health Sector Policy Paper* (Washington, D.C., March 1975), pp. 72–75.

TABLE 109 Major Cause Specific Death Rates in Korea (per 100,000)

Cause of Death	1958–1959	1966–1967
Vascular lesions affecting central nervous system	19.6 (5)	26.1 (3)
Tuberculosis	39.5 (2)	35.8 (2)
Pneumonia and bronchitis	73.8 (1)	43.8 (1)
Heart diseases	8.5 (6)	11.7 (7)
Gastroenteritis	31.0 (3)	14.2 (5)
Accidents	8.2 (7)	12.8 (6)
Malignant neoplasm	25.8 (4)	25.8 (4)

Source: Hakchung Choo and James Jeffers, "Health and Economic and Social Development," mimeo (Seoul, Korea Development Institute, 1977).

TABLE 110 Calorie and Protein Nutrients in Average
Korean Diet, 1975

	Consumption (kg. per year)	Calories (per day)	Protein (per day)
Food-grains	215.5	2,123	46
Fruit and vegetables	144.9	150	6
Meat and fish	33.4	131	15
Milk and eggs	14.8	35	2
TOTAL	422.6	2,448	70

Source: The World Bank, *Growth and Prospects of the Korean Economy* (February 1977), p. 45.

from food-grains suggests that there are deficiencies of some vitamins and minerals. Also, it should be remembered that these are national averages, and they cover up the deficiencies at the lower end of the consumption scale. A survey of 4,000 school children in 1967–1968 found that they had serious deficiencies of calcium, Vitamin A, riboflavin, and ascorbic acid. Another survey of 6th grade children over the years 1968–1972 found that rural children were significantly shorter and lighter than urban children, suggesting a less favorable pattern of consumption for the rural population.

A recent assessment by The World Bank states:[23]

> The consistent conclusion of both budget studies and nutritional surveys is that Koreans suffer little gross undernutrition, but that specific nutrient deficits are prevalent. The pattern of undernutrition appears to be primarily due to dietary customs and, to a lesser extent, to be attributable to the unavailability outside of cities of fresh fruits and vegetables in the off-season. Malnutrition does not appear to contribute significantly to disease.

Sanitation

Just the opposite is true in the domain of sanitation. Inadequate sewage, waste disposal, and water supplies are the source of very high incidence of parasites and other intestinal ailments. The

Korean tradition of using human waste (night soil) for fertilizer meant that cities developed without any sewage system for removal of such waste, and it has been very expensive to build the systems into the existing cities. Only in recent decades has the pattern of direct collection of human waste given way to central sewage systems, and most of these, as noted in the discussion of urban problems, discharge untreated waste directly into the major rivers from which downstream water supplies are drawn.

In the countryside, much untreated human waste is still used as fertilizer, especially for vegetable gardens, although this has been illegal since 1968.[24] A study in a typical rural area in 1974 found that nearly half of the vegetable farms were infested with parasitic eggs, and more than half of the vegetable samples were contaminated.[25]

Since vegetables are mainly fermented rather than cooked before being eaten, the parasites are not likely to be destroyed. A 1973 study in one rural district found three-fourths of the population with enteric parasites.[26] Thus, while food intake for the average Korean is generally adequate, its nutritive value is shared with the ubiquitous parasites, and the consequences are reflected in lower average height and weight and in the high incidence of diseases of the digestive system.

About 90 percent of the inhabitants of the city of Seoul are now served by central sewage and water supply facilities,[27] but only 39 percent of the total population of the country had piped water supply in 1973,[28] and there is no assurance that such water supplies are free of contamination. Improved water supply and treatment of human waste are major objectives of the Saemaul Undong (see Chapter 9) and much progress has been made under this program, but because the facilities were so grossly inadequate before, it will take a long time to eliminate the health hazards of poor sanitation.

Health Services

While the numbers of trained health personnel and health facilities have grown appreciably in the post-war period, they have tended to concentrate in the major urban centers, and many of the more highly trained are practicing or training abroad. Thus the quantity and quality of health services available to the rural population and also the urban poor has been limited.

The trends in health personnel and facilities between 1955 and 1975 are shown in Table 111.

TABLE 111 Health Personnel and Facilities, 1955–1975

Health Personnel	1955	1965	1975
Physicians	6,141	10,854	16,800
Dentists	967	1,762	2,595
Nurses	2,487	8,898	23,632
Pharmacists	1,985	10,028	19,750
Herb doctors	2,078	2,849	2,788
Midwives	2,369	5,714	3,773
Total	16,027	40,105	69,338
Health Facilities			
Hospitals	90	200	168
Clinics	2,800	5,002	6,087
Health centers	16	189	198
Herb clinics	1,284	2,247	2,367

Source: Ministry of Health and Social Affairs, Republic of Korea as quoted by Choo and Jeffers.

The total number of licensed health personnel has quadrupled over the two decades, with the most rapid increases in the numbers of nurses and pharmacists, both of which have risen approximately tenfold. Physicians and dentists have roughly tripled, while the numbers of herb doctors and midwives have increased much more slowly. Health facilities have roughly doubled except for the health centers, scattered throughout the country, that were established in significant numbers between 1955 and 1965. Among the hospitals and clinics, privately owned facilities accounted for 99 percent of the 6,200 institutions and 73 percent of the 41,000 beds in 1975.[29]

The numbers of licensed health personnel appear to overstate the numbers actually engaged in practice by about one-half. According to one estimate, there were over 15,000 Korean health professionals working abroad in 1975, including 4,500 physicians and 11,000 nurses. These estimates for the physicians and nurses would largely account for the discrepency between the numbers licensed, as recorded in Table 111, and the numbers submitting annual registrations in 1975, reported in Table 112. Because nearly half the licensed nurses are overseas, the pharmacists are the largest group of health professionals actively engaged within Korea, accounting for over one-third of the total.

The concentration of health personnel in the major cities is also clearly visible in Table 112. Nearly half the total active health professionals are located in Seoul and another 10 percent in Pusan, although these two cities account for only 20 and 7 percent of the population respectively. Midwives are the only professional group of which a majority is located outside the two main cities, and the fact that 40 percent of the midwives are in Seoul and Pusan attests to the fact that they have a continuing role even in the urban areas. (There may well be a considerable number of unregistered midwives and herb doctors operating in the rural areas.)

Another indicator of the importance of pharmacists is found in the rates of medical care utilization in 1973 reported in Table 113. Three out of five visits to some kind of health facility consist of visits to pharmacies. Another 30 percent are to private clinics, and less than 10 percent to hospitals. The limited use of hospitals is not due to a lack of facilities, but more likely to their inaccessability or high cost. The bed utilization rate in hospitals has increased somewhat in recent years, but it is still only 64.5 percent.[30]

TABLE 112 Distribution of Active Medical Personnel
in Korea, 1975

	Seoul	Pusan	Two Main Cities	Rest of Country	Total
Physicians	5,094	1,141	6,235 (55.4)	5,023 (44.6)	11,258
Dentists	1,097	158	1,255 (61.2)	796 (38.8)	2,051
Nurses	5,039	1,054	6,093 (55.4)	4,905 (44.6)	10,998
Pharmacists	7,568	1,368	8,936 (58.1)	6,443 (41.9)	15,379
Herb doctors	1,180	243	1,423 (59.7)	959 (40.3)	2,382
Midwives	453	185	638 (39.3)	987 (60.7)	1,625
TOTAL	20,431	4,149	24,580 (56.3)	19,113 (43.7)	43,693

Population estimates (in millions) for 1975 are:

Seoul	6.9	19.8%
Pusan	2.4	7.1%
Two Main Cities	9.3	26.9%
Rest of Country	25.0	73.1%
TOTAL	34.7	100.0%

Source: Ministry of Health and Social Affairs, *Yearbook of Public Health and Social Statistics* (Seoul, 1976).

Note: Figures are based on annual registration, not licenses granted.

TABLE 113 Medical Care Utilization by Type of Health
Facility, 1973
(per 1,000 population per month)

	Amount	Percent
Private clinics	68.4	29.4
Hospitals	17.6	7.6
Health centers	1.1	0.5
Pharmacy	136.0	58.5
Dental visits	0.9	0.4
Herb doctors	8.3	3.6

Source: Adapted from Table 3-1. Ok Ryun Moon and Jae Woong Hong, "Health Services Outcome Data: A Survey of Data and Research Findings on the Provision of Health Services in Korea," *Journal of Family Planning Studies,* Korea Institute of Family Planning, Vol. III, April 1976, p. 181.

The share of private consumption expenditures devoted to health care has increased over the years, as is to be expected with rising per capita incomes. Between 1960 and 1974, it has risen from 2.3 percent to 3.6 percent. The ratios are reportedly much the same for both rural and urban populations, but the rural population, again as expected, devotes a greater portion to pharmacists and herb doctors and less to physicians and hospitals than the urban inhabitants. Private hospitals and clinics have even lower utilization rates in the rural than the urban areas, reportedly because of poor quality and lack of effective demand. [31]

The government's share of gross national health expenditures has been low and declining in recent years. In per capita terms, government health expenditures are low even by Asian standards (see Table 114). This limited governmental effort in the field of

TABLE 114 Government Health Expenditures Per Capita in U.S. Dollars for Selected Asian Countries, 1973

Korea	1.33
Philippines	1.06
Thailand	2.45
Malaysia	7.18
Japan	5.45

Source: Choo and Jeffers, p. 47.

health services and in sanitation, is symptomatic of the government's approach to social services in general. They have been left largely to the private sector with resulting unevenness and inequity in the distribution of services, especially for those services that have the inherent properties of public or social goods.

The rural population especially has had limited access to modern health services and facilities, so they have relied on pharmacists for modern medicines and diagnosis to treat the illnesses arising from their environment. The urban population has fared somewhat better, especially those in the upper income groups who have been able to afford the relatively abundant, private, modern health services. The absence of health insurance programs, either public or private, has served to concentrate further the access to such services. Rising incomes and improved nutrition have probably contributed more than modern health services to the betterment of health status.

Rapid urbanization and environmental pollution has increased the potential health hazards for the urban population but, at the same time, a greater part of the populace has been brought within the domain of modern facilities and services. If the economic access to these services can be facilitated and, some relatively simple preventive health measures adopted more widely, the health status of the total population could be improved appreciably.

CONCLUSION

Korea started its demographic transition, urbanization, and modernization of health and other social services during the colonial era, but the Japanese occupied the top of the pyramid in Korea and reaped most of the benefits of those services. Faced with limited opportunities and growing population pressure at home, many Koreans migrated to the cities of Japan and Manchuria, whence they returned in large numbers after World War II. After Independence, education underwent rapid expansion followed by accelerated urbanization and then a precipitous decline in the fertility rate, signaling the second phase of the demographic transition. The health of the population has improved considerably, despite poor sanitation and unevenly distributed health services, mainly due to better nutrition and access to modern drugs dispensed mainly through private channels.

All social services have been supplied to a considerable extent by the private sector, generally operating under government regulation and supervision. Examples of regulated private activities include secondary and higher education, urban transportation, urban land development, and the family planning program. Purely governmental services, such as sanitation, water supply, and public housing, have been underfunded and inadequate. Others, such as primary education, have been able to elicit some private financial support and have fared better. Purely private services in the health area, such as private clinics, pharmacies, and herbal practitioners, which attract little government attention, have tended to concentrate in the urban areas, leaving the rural population seriously underserved.

TWELVE

Income Distribution

One of the most striking features of Korean economic development since 1945 is that development has been achieved without requiring or causing a highly unequal distribution of income. In World Bank publications and in other international forums, Korea has been hailed as a prime example of how growth can be achieved with equity. According to the data presented in these forums, Korea is among only a handful of less-developed nations that have achieved a level of equality comparable to that of the advanced world economies.

As this chapter will indicate, there is no reason to challenge the conclusion that the degree of income inequality in Korea is substantially less than that existing in many other less-developed countries. The data most often used to support this conclusion, however, are flawed in the extreme. The real basis for the belief that Korea at least entered into its period of rapid economic growth with a low degree of inequality rests not so much on these data but on an understanding of the nature of land reform and the Korean War.

A central theme of this chapter is that income distribution can only be understood at other than a superficial level if that distribution is disaggregated into its component parts. Disaggregation not only brings out the nature of the shortcomings of the data, it is also an essential step in any attempt to analyze how growth has influenced distribution or how distribution has affected growth. For those interested in the growth-equity relationship, the key division is the tripartite one between farm households, urban households, and businesses. The major determinants of incomes in each of these three sectors are so different in any less-developed country that it is virtually impossible to analyze the sectors together. A second level of disaggregation is to break the three sectors down along regional or geographic lines. Regional differences in income in less-developed countries are often large and play a major role in the overall national level of inequality. With the exception of regional differences in business income, all the other components of the disaggregated distribution of income will be discussed in the sections that follow.

KOREAN INCOME DISTRIBUTION DATA

There are a variety of statistical measures that can be used to present income distribution data in a form that makes possible comparisons over time and between countries. The three that will be used here are the percentage income shares of various proportions of the population (top 20 percent, bottom 40 percent, and so on), the Gini coefficient, and the Theil or entropy measure.[1] The first measure is useful, because one is often most interested for economic, social, and political reasons in what is happening to the poorest part of the population, or the middle or richest parts. The Gini coefficient has the advantage of being frequently calculated and easily understood, so that there are many international figures available for comparative purposes. The major advantage of the Theil statistic is that, unlike the Gini coefficient, it is easy to disaggregate into its component parts. Thus the Theil statistic allows one to identify changes in inequality as coming from either within a given sector or from changes in the position of a given sector in comparison to that of another.

The most widely quoted figures on Korean income distribution in international comparison are those of a World Bank study, and there are a number of other studies that have attempted to look explicitly and in greater depth at the Korean data.[2] With the exception of one or two special surveys, most of the figures used to estimate the Korean income distribution come from farm and urban household surveys, from wage and salary surveys, and from income tax reports.

Estimates of income inequality from the farm and urban household surveys tell much the same story. From the beginning of these surveys in the early 1960s to 1975, within-sector inequality has been low, and there is no discernible trend (see Table 115). Both surveys, however, exclude all or most business income and neither includes the richest families. The farm households do not include many rich families, because few such families live in rural areas, but the urban surveys simply did not investigate families whose income was above roughly U.S. $5,000 a year.[3] The problem, thus, is how to come up with an estimate of business income and of the income of urban upper-income groups in general. The most common answer to this question has been to resort to the national income tax reports.

Income tax data for the 1960s and 1970s are readily available but difficult to interpret. To begin with, until the concept of "global income" for very high income groups was introduced in the 1970s, business income and wage and salary income were reported separately (and still are for those with lower incomes) even though an individual might earn income from both sources. In this chapter, as in most other studies of Korea's income

TABLE 115 Within-Sector Income Inequality

Year	Rural Income Inequality		Urban Income Inequality		Business Income Inequality	
	Gini	Theil	Gini	Theil	Gini	Theil
1963	n.a.	n.a.	.337	.180	.541[b]	.779[b]
1967	.357	.200	.315	.172	.570	.908
1970	.296	.143	.273[a]	.148[a]	.636	1.132
1974	.322	.172	.259	.113	.733	1.326
1975	n.a.	n.a.	.313	.161	n.a.	n.a.

Sources and methodology: The rural data were taken from various farm household surveys and the urban data from various urban household surveys of wage and salary worker households. The business income data are from various issues of Office of National Tax Administration, *Statistical Yearbook of National Tax.* Business income as used here includes both income taxed as "business income" together with "global income," a term used to cover very high income taxpayers. Although most of the income of this latter group is business income, some portion also includes salaries of senior managers and the like. Rural income data include inventory appreciation, since there was no way of separating out such appreciation from the data classified by income class.

In calculating the Theil statistic, each sector's sample was normalized to 1,000 households. In the case of the urban and rural surveys this step involved only minor adjustments, since each was based on samples of nearly 1,000 households anyway. The business income data, however, were normalized to 1,000 households from tax data on all households paying the tax. The purpose of normalization was to eliminate differences in the Theil statistic due solely to differences in the size of the population (or sample) whose inequality was being measured.

Because these measures are all derived from grouped data, it is likely that these measures of inequality understate the "true" degree of inequality. Some of the trend in inequality, particularly the increase in business income inequality, may simply reflect the greater disaggregation of the data for 1970 and 1974 (7 and 9 categories of income respectively) when compared with those of 1964 and 1967 (4 and 6 categories of income respectively).

Notes: [a]1971
[b]1964

The Gini coefficient can vary between 0 (perfect equality) and 1.0 (perfect inequality). The Theil statistic can vary between 0 (perfect equality) and the natural log of the size of the sample or population (perfect inequality). Since all the calculations in this chapter are based on samples of 1,000, the maximum figure for the Theil statistic is 6.9. Any figure over 1.0, however, can be considered to be a high level of inequality.

distribution, it is necessary to act as if business income was received only by households with no other source of income. The probable effect of this assumption is to make the distribution appear less unequal than it is in reality, since combining business and wage and salary income for those households with both would probably swell the ranks of the well-to-do more than other groups.

An even more serious problem with the business income data is their incomplete coverage. Because of definitional differences, tax avoidance, and outright evasion, there is an enormous gap between business income as reported in the national accounts and what shows up in the tax records (see Table 116). There seems little reason to doubt that the national accounts give a truer estimate of the magnitude of business income than do the tax records. To use the tax data at all, therefore, one must assume that they accurately reflect the relative (to each other) shares of the various business income groups even if they greatly understate the total income of those groups. To say the least, this is a strong assumption.

How one deals with business income has a very large impact on the overall estimate of income inequality for the Korean nation as a whole. The nature of this impact can be seen from the calculations in Table 117 based on a disaggregated version of the Theil entropy statistic. If one follows the procedure used by some others, of assuming that the tax records accurately reflect the level as well as the distribution of business income, then the higher level of inequality within the business sector has little impact on the nationwide overall figure. The reason is simple—farm and urban household income swamps the small amount of taxed business income. But when the share of business income in the total is taken from the national accounts, the overall Theil statistic doubles. The much heavier weight given to business income by this method roughly doubles the Theil statistic by increasing both within-sector and between-sector inequality.

The rising *trend* in inequality is also more pronounced when business income is given a greater weight. Part of this increase in inequality reflects a rising weight given to business income because of the rising share of business income in total national income. Another part of the rise, however, may only reflect a statistical artifact. Over the decade from the mid-1960s to the mid-1970s, the taxable business income data were disaggregated

TABLE 116 Tax and National Account Data
on Business Income

	Business plus Global Income (from the tax tables) (million current wŏn)	Unincorporated Business Income— Excluding Agriculture (from the national accounts) (million current wŏn)
1964	18,060	91,880
1967	56,459	180,030
1970	143,593	348,470
1971	190,445	437,110
1973	269,064	873,380
1974	371,799	1,276,500

Sources: Office of National Tax Administration, *Statistical Yearbook of National Tax* (various years) and EPB, Bureau of Statistics, *Korea Statistical Yearbook, 1976*, pp. 374–375.

into a greater number of income groups with much of this disaggregation occurring among the upper income tail of the distribution. This greater number of income groups would account for some of the rise in the Theil statistic for business income.[4]

If this analysis suggesting that Korea's income distribution is somewhat more unequal than indicated by some previous calculations is correct, one must be careful not to jump to the conclusion that Korea has had a greater degree of inequality than that of other less-developed nations. Figures for other less-developed nations, with which Korea is often compared, are subject to the same kinds of biases, often in a more extreme form.

Data limitations are not the only reason for staying away from comparisons of Korea with other nations. As is well known but frequently ignored in studies of income distribution, the degree of inequality is heavily influenced by the age distribution of a nation's population and by the way in which people are organized into families.[5] Such life cycle effects as the fact that retired people generally have low incomes whereas people in

TABLE 117 Between- and Within-Sector Inequality (Theil [Entropy] Statistic)

Year	Between-Sector Inequality		Within-Sector Inequality		Overall Inequality	
	Assumption A	Assumption B	Assumption A	Assumption B	Assumption A	Assumption B
1963	.086	.010[a]	.329	.202	.415	.212
1967	.096	.010	.364	.231	.460	.241
1970	.072	.001	.365	.251	.437	.252
1974	.183	.002	.440	.257	.623	.259
1975	.138	n.a.	.403	n.a.	.541	n.a.

Source: For the data used in making these calculations, see Table 133.

Notes: [a]1964 data.
Assumption A: The income share of the business sector was assumed to be equal to the share of unincorporated non-agricultural income plus dividend income in the national accounts.
Assumption B: The income of the business sector was assumed to be equal to the amount of business plus global income reported in the *Statistical Yearbook of National Tax*, and total income was obtained by adding this income to agricultural and wage salary income in the national accounts.

their 40's and 50's are at their peak earning power have a marked influence on national income distribution statistics. Like most less-developed countries, Korea's population is quite young (see Table 121) and those few who are retired often live with their children in an extended family household. Furthermore, large numbers of adult Americans live alone, whereas relatively few Koreans live in single person households. In rural Korea, for example, where the transformation of family structure has proceeded least far, only 1.9 percent of the "families" were single person households in 1970 and only 16.3 percent lived in households with 3 or fewer persons.[6] For "households" of the United States in 1970, the comparable figures are 18.5 and 45.1 percent respectively. Although proof is lacking, it is likely that restructuring Korea's age and family composition along American lines would increase Korean measures of income inequality. Such a statistical transformation, of course, would be of little significance, since it is an income distribution based on large numbers of people living alone or in small families, when in fact they live together in large families and share to some degree in the income of all family members. The point is simply that less-developed versus advanced-country comparisons of income distribution are very difficult to interpret.

Family size and life cycle effects not only make it difficult or impossible to make meaningful international comparisons, they also have an important influence on how one interprets the relationship between economic growth and income distribution over time within Korea. The rapid pace of both urbanization and the demographic transition in Korea are bound to have a major impact on Korean family structure if they have not had such an impact already. We know, for example, that the average size of both urban and rural households has been dropping steadily since the mid-1960s. Data, such as those from the agricultural censuses of 1960 and 1970, indicate only modest changes in the prevalence of large family units (see Table 118), but more recent data are unavailable and one would expect family structure to change more slowly than say the pace of urbanization in any case.

TABLE 118 Farm Households by Size of Family
(by % share of all farm households)

No. of Persons per Household	1960 census	1970 census
1 – 2	5.5	7.7
3 – 4	21.2	20.5
5 – 6	31.8	33.9
7 – 8	25.8	26.9
9 – 10	11.1	9.0
11 and up	4.5	3.9

Sources: MAF, *Agricultural Census, 1960* (Seoul, 1964), pp. 80–81
MAF, *Agricultural Census, 1970* (Seoul, 1974), pp. 68–69.

Even crude attempts to eliminate family size and life cycle effects from the Korean data make it clear that interpretations that ignore these effects are likely to be misleading. Figures in Table 119 and 120 were obtained by recalculating urban and rural household income on a per capita basis. Estimates of household per capita expenditure were also made on the belief that consumption expenditures are likely to reflect better a family's permanent income than do income estimates which are more likely to include transitory elements. Whereas urban household income of the highest income group is eleven times the income per household of the lowest income group, on a per capita basis the ratio is only nine to one and the expenditure ratio per capita is only four to one. Similar differences occur in the rural figures. In short, much of the inequality observed among urban and rural households has little to do with the kind of inequality that implies that one group is better off than another.

Where taking proper account of shortcomings in methods of estimating business income tends to widen the difference between income groups in Korean society, recalculating the figures to account for household structure and life cycle effects has the opposite impact. Again, however, one must caution the reader not to attempt to relocate Korea within an

TABLE 119 Family Size and Life Cycle Effects on Urban Household Income, 1976

Category	Average	Income Group							
		I	III	V	VII	IX	XI	XIII	XV
(1) Household monthly income (1,000 wŏn)	88.3	21.1	44.3	64.2	85.1	104.6	125.4	145.2	235.4
(2) Household monthly expenditures (1,000 wŏn)	75.5	34.3	42.2	57.8	72.6	87.4	106.1	122.8	174.4
(3) Family size (persons)	5.05	4.58	4.57	4.94	5.04	5.18	5.42	5.48	5.51
(4) (1) / (3)	17.5	4.60	9.69	13.00	16.89	20.20	23.14	26.49	47.72
(5) (2) / (3)	15.0	7.48	9.23	11.70	14.40	16.87	19.58	22.40	31.65
(6) Group household income relative to average	100.0	.24	.50	.72	.96	1.18	1.42	1.64	2.67
(7) Group income per capita relative to average	100.0	.26	.55	.74	.97	1.15	1.32	1.51	2.44
(8) Group expenditure per capita relative to income	100.0	.50	.62	.78	.96	1.12	1.31	1.49	2.11

Source: EPB, Annual Report on the Family Income and Expenditure Survey, 1976, Seoul, pp. 82–83. The data are for salary and wage earners' households.

TABLE 120 Family Size and Life Cycle Effects on Farm Household Income, 1973

Category	Average	Farm Size				
		Under 0.5 chŏngbo	0.5	1.0–1.5	1.5–2.0	over 2.0
(1) Size of farm household	5.72	4.83	5.45	6.30	6.50	6.98
(2) Farm household income (1,000 wŏn)	480.7	284.0	400.4	542.6	685.9	971.6
(3) Living expenses per household (1,000 wŏn)	337.4	235.8	309.2	381.2	434.4	523.3
(4) (2) / (1) (1,000 wŏn)	84.0	58.8	73.5	86.1	105.5	139.2
(5) (3) / (1) (1,000 wŏn)	59.0	48.8	56.7	60.5	66.8	75.0
(6) Group household income relative to the average	1.000	.591	.833	1.129	1.427	2.021
(7) Group income per capita relative to the average	1.000	.700	.874	1.025	1.256	1.656
(8) Group living expenses per capita relative to the average	1.000	.828	.962	1.026	1.139	1.271

Source: MAF, *Report on the Results of the Farm Household Economic Survey, 1974,* Seoul.

TABLE 121 Age Distribution of Population in Korea and
the United States, 1970

Korea		United States	
Age	Share in Population (%)	Age	Share in Population (%)
0–19	51.9	0–20	39.5
20–34	22.0	21–34	18.6
35–64	22.7	35–64	31.9
65+	3.3	65+	9.9

Source: Department of Commerce, *Statistical Abstract of the United States, 1971*
U.S. Government Printing Office (Washington, D.C., 1971) and EPB, Bureau
of Statistics, *Korea Statistical Yearbook, 1976.*

international framework on the basis of these calculations until
enough similar work has been done on other nations.

The real case for the equitable nature of Korea's income distribution is based not so much on these national measures as on
an analysis in greater depth of what has occurred within specific
sectors.

RURAL INCOME DISTRIBUTION

Central to the existence of a comparatively high degree of
equity in Korea is the fact that the country underwent in the
late 1940s and early 1950s a thoroughgoing land reform. Under
Japanese colonial rule, landlordism, already high at the beginning,
rose until, at the time of regaining independence in 1945, only
13.8 percent of all Korean farmers owned all the land that they
cultivated, and a full 51.6 percent of all farm households owned
no land whatsoever (see Table 122).

Beginning in November 1945, the U.S. Military Government
established the New Korea Company, Ltd. to administer and
distribute to cultivators land formerly owned by the Japanese.
With the establishment of the Republic of Korea on August 15,

TABLE 122 Owner-Tenant Distribution of Farm Households
(%)

	1945	1947	1960	1964	1970
Full owner	13.8	16.5	73.6	71.6	64.6
Owner-tenant	34.6	38.3	19.6	23.2	31.9
Tenant	48.9	42.1	6.8	5.2	0.6
Farm laborer and burnt field farmer	2.7	3.1	—[a]	—[a]	2.9
TOTAL	100.0	100.0	100.0	100.0	100.0

Sources: The 1945, 1947 and 1964 data are from Ki Hyuk Pak et al., *A Study of Land Tenure System in Korea* (Seoul, Korea Land Economics Research Center, 1966), pp. 87, 89, and 131. The 1960 and 1970 data are from Ministry of Agriculture and Forestry, *Agricultural Census 1960,* and *1970,* Seoul. Ban, Moon, and Perkins, p. 286.

Note: [a]Data on the number of farm laborers were not given for these years.

1948, and the passage of land reform legislation on June 21, 1949 and March 10, 1950, the government began redistributing the land of the more numerous Korean landlords as well. Together the U.S. Military Government and the Korean government redistributed some 577,000 hectares from landlord to tiller, or 39 percent of all land farmed under conditions of tenancy.[7] One of the interesting features of Korea's land reform is that approximately another 573,000 hectares were sold directly by landlords to their tenants.[8] The incentive behind these arrangements was straightforward. Landlords were paid by the government with bonds that rapidly deteriorated to only about 10 percent of their face value. The former tenants, however, had to pay the government off at the face value rate which was equivalent to 30 percent of the annual harvest each year over a period of five years. That left a considerable range within which the landlord and tenant could strike a deal of benefit to them both at the expense of the government.

Prior to land reform, about 4 percent of the rural population (the landlords) had received roughly half the main crop or about one-quarter of all farm income. After land reform, Japanese landlords had lost everything, and Korean landlords on the average had received compensation equivalent to perhaps one-sixth to one-fourth of their former land assets. Like most successful land reforms, Korea's had involved a substantial amount of what in effect was confiscation of landlord property without compensation.

The ultimate beneficiaries of this transfer of income were the former tenants, although initially the government took a large cut as already explained. A tenant farmer with no land of his own, who had previously paid half his main crop or one-quarter of his net income to a landlord, now received that income himself, a per capita rise of 33 percent. Tenants who also owned part of the land they cultivated on average received an increase in income ranging from just above zero to nearly 33 percent depending on the ratio of owned to rented land. [9]

Since the completion of the land reform, there has been little in the way of a trend in the distribution of income within the rural sector. The shares of the various income groups in total income have remained virtually unchanged (Table 123), and there has been only a very modest tendency for land ownership to become more concentrated (Table 124). Laws preventing most forms of landlordism, although sometimes evaded, together with a 3-chŏngbo (approximately 3-hectare) limit on farm size have probably helped prevent the return of some sources of inequality. A booming investment climate in the cities and the lack of any comparable boom in agriculture may also have inhibited the flow of money from the urban rich to the countryside, such money being a major source of demand for tenant-farmed land in Asia including Korea. Finally, the rural population, at least that part young enough to move, has had the option of taking up jobs in the cities if conditions in the countryside appeared unattractive. Whether most migrants came disproportionately from the poor or from any other income group is unknown, but we do know that the rural sector has not had to absorb the rapid rise in Korea's population. If this increase in population had been absorbed by Korea's agricultural sector

TABLE 123 Distribution of Farm Households by Income
          per Household
                      (%)

	1963	1967	1970	1974
Top 10%	31	24	—	25
Top 20%	44	40	39	41
Next 40%	36	40	40	40
Next 30%	17	17	18	16
Bottom 10%	3	3.5	3	3

Source: Ban, Moon, and Perkins, p. 307.

Note: This table was derived from the same farm household data used to calculate
the Gini coefficients in Table 115. However, because assumptions had to be made to
obtain estimates for the groupings used here, one cannot directly use the figures here
to derive the Gini coefficients in Table 115.

TABLE 124 Total Per Capita Rural Output by Selected Regions
           (South Korea average = 100.0)

	1938	1947	1960	1966	1970	1975
Kyŏnggi province	158.4	105.7	113.6	108.3	125.2	123.0
Kangwŏn province	42.6	79.9	72.3	77.9	79.1	85.0
North Ch'ungch'ŏng province	99.1	88.5	81.5	103.2	103.5	110.4
South Chŏlla province	97.9	95.3	83.1	87.4	88.3	89.2
South Kyŏngsang province	97.6	88.2	81.5	106.1	104.7	91.8
South Korea	100.0	100.0	100.0	100.0	100.0	100.0

Source: Derived from Albert Keidel, "Regional Agricultural Production and Income,"
     in Ban, Moon, and Perkins, *Rural Development,* Table 56, p. 137.

Note: For reasons of clarity and economy, this table presents data for only 5 of
South Korea's 9 provinces.

with its essentially fixed land base, the result might have been smaller and more fragmented farms, increasing numbers of land-less laborers, and the like. The within-sector Gini coefficient might or might not have changed for the worse, but the average level of per capita income in agriculture would almost certainly have been lower than it is today.

A major source of rural income inequality that is relatively impervious to redistribution efforts such as land reform or even collectivization is the inequality that exists between different regions of the country.[10] In many countries great geographic size and cultural diversity make for very large differences in income among regions. In Korea, cultural homogeneity and the relatively small size of the peninsula limit the degree of regional inequality, although some still remains. As indicated by the data in Table 124 the average per capita output of the richest province (Kyŏnggi) was only 45 percent above that of one of the poorest (Kangwŏn).

As Albert Keidel has shown, two major developments in rural areas in the 1960s and 1970s have had a considerable impact on the regional distribution of rural income. Urbanization and the development of an extensive road network have led to the rapid growth of vegetable production and other cash crops destined for urban markets. The major beneficiaries of this trend have been those provinces with large quantities of upland located near enough to roads and cities to have access to these urban markets. North Ch'ungch'ŏng, Kangwŏn, and Kyŏnggi provinces have thus benefited from this development, while such tradi-tional rice bowls as South Chŏlla province have not.[11] Some-what offsetting to the impact of cash crops, however, has been the government's policy since 1969 of raising rice and barley prices paid to farmers while maintaining lower prices for urban residents. These high grain prices, needless to say, have had a greater impact on the traditional grain-producing areas.

In summary, therefore, the relatively high degree of equality within rural Korea can be largely explained by land reform and the homogeneity of the peninsula in cultural and geographic terms. The differences that remain are largely the result of differences in size of farms, particularly landholdings, and degree of access to major urban markets.[12] Isolated areas, Keidel has demonstrated, are generally the poorest.[13]

URBAN WAGE AND SALARY INCOME DISTRIBUTION

Even if one accepts the view that urban household income as reported in the surveys excludes most business income, the low level and lack of trend in urban household income inequality are more difficult to explain. One reason for this difficulty is that so little work has been done on what determines the structure of wages and salaries in less-developed countries. Work by David Lindauer suggests that worker attributes (skills, sex composition) and firm attributes (size of firm, regional location, capital-labor ratios) together explain over 70 percent of the differences in interindustry wages and salaries in Korea.[14] Wages and salaries, of course, represent the income of individuals, not of households. Trends in the number of wage and salary earners per household, therefore, could either offset or reinforce trends in the distribution of wage and salary income. Still, the trends in wages and salaries are of interest in themselves and probably have a significant influence on urban household inequality.

Regional differences in wages are clearly on the decline as Figure 10 from Lindauer's study indicates. Korean workers, and the Korean people in general, are highly mobile and, although regional loyalties and prejudices exist in a mild form, they do not appear to have much influence on the ability of workers in one province to find employment in another. The growth in the urban labor market has itself presumably been a major reason for the steady decline in the degree of labor market fragmentation along regional lines, as rapidly growing labor requirements have led employers to draw workers from whereever they can find them.

In contrast to the regional distribution, the size distribution of wage and salary income on a national basis has become more, not less, unequal (Tables 125 and 126).[15] The major explanation appears to be an increasing gap between white and blue collar workers[16] caused perhaps by the rising salaries and increasing size of the urban executive class, a group poorly represented in the urban household surveys. Exclusion of these higher salary households may be an important part of the reason why the urban household Gini estimates do not show a trend toward greater inequality. Distribution within the blue and white collar categories did not change significantly between 1958 and 1972 (Table 126). If Korea follows the Japanese pattern in this area, as it has in many others, these wage differentials will eventually narrow,[17] but clearly such a narrowing has not yet occurred.

URBAN-RURAL INCOME DIFFERENTIALS

In Korea as in most countries, there has been a substantial and persistent gap between urban and rural incomes even if, as is usually the case, most business income is not included in the income of urban households. As indicated by the data in Table 127, this gap can at times reach substantial proportions. In fact, surveys taken in the 1950s suggest that the narrow gap between urban and rural incomes in the 1963–1965 period was an aberration. More typical of the pre-1963 period were kinds of differences that existed in the late 1960s when rural income was only half that in the urban areas on a per capita basis.[18]

Two comments on the quality of these data, however, are in order. First, they are not adjusted for differences in prices between rural and urban areas. Such an adjustment would narrow the gap by a substantial, but otherwise unknown, degree. Second, the concept of farm household income used in Table 127 differs from that most commonly appearing in public print and which has been used to argue that farm incomes are now actually above those in the urban areas. The income concept

FIGURE 10 Regional Wage Distributions

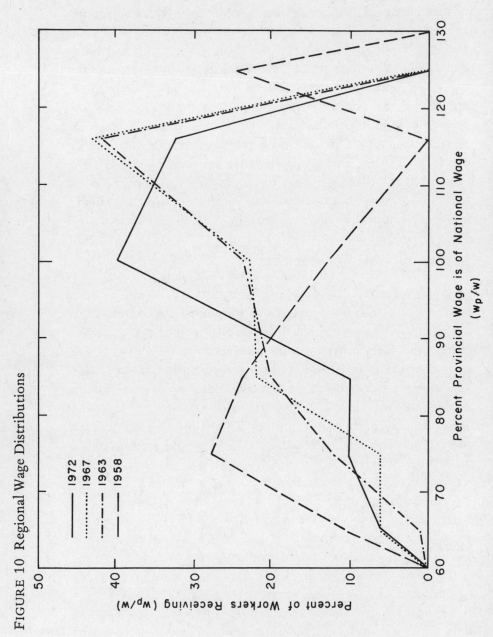

1972
1967
1963
1958

Percent of Workers Receiving (w_p/w)

Percent Provincial Wage is of National Wage (w_p/w)

Source: David Lindauer, "Labor Market Behavior in Developing Countries," unpublished PhD dissertation, Harvard University, forthcoming.

TABLE 125 Distribution of Earned Income in Korean
Manufacturing

Percent of Workers	Percent of Income	
	Year	
	1958	1972
Bottom 10%	4.5	4.2
10 – 20	6.4	5.8
20 – 30	7.3	6.4
30 – 40	8.0	7.2
40 – 50	8.2	7.8
50 – 60	8.5	8.3
60 – 70	11.4	9.0
70 – 80	11.7	11.2
80 – 90	13.5	15.1
Top 10%	20.5	25.0

Source: Lindauer, "Labor Market Behavior."

TABLE 126 Distribution of Earned Income of Blue and
White Collar Workers, Separately

Percent of Population	Blue Collar Workers Percent of Income		White Collar Workers Percent of Income	
	Year		Year	
	1958	1972	1958	1972
Bottom 10%	5.0	4.8	4.5	5.1
10 – 20	7.0	6.9	7.6	6.8
20 – 30	7.7	7.5	8.3	7.4
30 – 40	8.6	8.2	8.5	8.2
40 – 50	8.9	9.2	9.1	8.6
50 – 60	9.6	9.5	10.0	9.4
60 – 70	10.9	10.2	10.7	10.6
70 – 80	11.9	10.8	11.5	11.7
80 – 90	13.2	13.1	12.5	12.8
Top 10%	17.2	19.8	17.3	19.4

Source: Lindauer, "Labor Market Behavior."

TABLE 127 Urban and Rural Household Income
(1,000 wŏn in current prices)

| | Urban Household Income | | | Rural Household Income | | | Ratios | |
	(1) Per Household	(2) Per Capita		(3) Per Household	(4) Per Capita		(5) (3)/(1) × 100	(6) (4)/(2) × 100
1963	80.16	14.42		82.80	12.96		103.3	89.9
1965	112.56	20.32		109.84	17.46		97.6	85.9
1967	248.64	45.54		138.72	22.67		55.8	49.8
1969	333.60	61.55		186.85	31.19		56.0	50.7
1971	451.92	85.59		317.24	54.42		70.2	63.6
1973	550.20	104.80		426.76	74.61		77.6	71.2
1975	859.32	166.86		722.72	128.37		84.1	76.9

Sources: The urban data are from EPB, Bureau of Statistics, *Annual Report on the Family Income and Expenditure Survey, 1975. The* rural data are from various issues of Ministry of Agriculture and Fisheries, *Report on the Results of Farm Household Economic Survey.* Household income in the farm surveys has been adjusted to eliminate asset appreciation using a methodology explained in Ban, Moon, and Perkins, p. 310.

used here as elsewhere in this book excludes the appreciation in value of farm household assets. These assets are, for the most part, the household's stores of grain for its own use and later sale. During periods of inflation these assets rapidly increase in value, but only rarely does this increase involve any real improvement in the farm household's standard of living.

The most significant change in the urban-rural income relationship is the substantial narrowing of the gap that has occurred since 1969. To a significant degree this gain in the relative position of farm households reflects the improvement in agriculture's terms of trade due to changes in government grain price policies together with market forces. In the absence of these price changes, the ratio of rural to urban income in 1975 would be around 67 percent rather than 77 percent.[19] The remainder of the gain in farm income was a result of the acceleration in the rate of growth of farm output per household after 1970 which was itself at least in part the result of the improvement in the terms of trade.

By itself, the closing gap between urban and rural incomes should lead to a decline in national aggregate measures of income inequality. Such was the case in the Theil statistic estimated in Table 117 above, but the impact of this change was more than overcome by the opposite influence of the gap between rural and urban incomes on the one hand and business incomes on the other. This latter gap was widening.

BUSINESS INCOMES

As indicated earlier in this chapter, there are no really good data on business income and its distribution in Korea or on the incomes of the upper tail of the income distribution in general. There are indications, however, that this income has been rising more rapidly for a number of years than has income in the other sectors.

Perhaps the best data we have on this subject come from the

national accounts. Income from unincorporated enterprises and other business-related income is not only several times the level of business income taxed (see Table 116); the share of this income in total national income has been rising since the early 1960s. This rising share is confirmed both by the national accounts data themselves (Table 128), but also by the fact that GNP has been growing more rapidly than combined agricultural income and employee compensation (Table 129).

What is far less clear is the question of who has received this increasing share of national income, or what the underlying causes of the rise have been. It is conceivable, for example, that the rapid growth in unincorporated business income reflects an equally rapid expansion in the number of small family shops and the like. It is possible, but not very likely. A more likely explanation is that this growing share reflects the rising profits of Korea's modern sector enterprises.

Anyone who has been in Korea during the past decade is aware of the rise of large conglomerates (*chaebŏl*) which often developed from extremely modest beginnings to annual sales of hundreds of millions of U.S. dollars worth of products. Complicated tax laws, benefits that appear as costs in corporate records, and other such considerations obscure what this rising enterprise income means for the size distribution of individual income. Automobile ownership gives some indication of what is happening. Because of a deliberate government effort to discourage private automobile ownership, through high taxes on automobile sales, monthly taxes on owners of cars, and very high gasoline prices, the annual cost of automobile ownership comes to several thousand dollars a year. No family earning $5,000 a year (the upper cutoff in the urban household surveys) could seriously consider the purchase and maintenance of a private automobile. As the data in Table 130 indicate, however, the number of private automobiles in Korea has been rising very rapidly from under 2,000 in 1961 to 50,000 in 1975. Although some of these automobiles are no doubt shared by several families or executives within a corporation, much of the rise in

TABLE 128 The Source of Korean National Income

	1956	1960	1963	1965	1970	1973	1975
Employee compensation + agricultural income	71.1	71.3	71.1	65.7	64.6	60.8	62.9
–Employee compensation	28.2	37.1	31.2	30.9	39.0	37.2	38.8
–Agricultural income	42.9	34.2	39.9	34.8	25.6	23.6	24.1
Other sources[a]	28.9	28.7	28.9	34.3	35.4	39.2	37.1
Unincorporated enterprises (non-ag.)	17.7	14.2	14.1	17.6	16.0	21.5	19.4

Source: BOK, *Economic Statistics Yearbook, 1976*, pp. 272–273.

Note: [a]These other sources include rent, interest, dividends, corporate transfer payments, savings of corporations, direct taxes on corporations, and general government income from property and entrepreneurship. In short, many of these "other sources" include items that are a part of, or are closely related to, business income.

TABLE 129 Growth Rates per Annum
(%)

	1956–1963	1963–1975
GNP	4.9	9.6
Employee compensation	6.4	11.2
Agricultural income	3.8	5.1
Employee compensation + agricultural income	4.9	8.5

Source: These figures were derived from the national accounts tables in BOK, *Economic Statistics Yearbook, 1976.*

TABLE 130 Automobile Ownership

Year	Total	Government	Private	Commercial
1961	9,809	1,095	1,925	6,789
1965	13,001	1,619	5,507	5,875
1970	60,667	3,547	28,687	28,443
1975	84,212	5,023	50,093	29,096

Source: EPB, *Major Statistics of Korean Economy, 1977,* p. 111.

automobiles probably reflects a business-executive elite whose numbers and prosperity are increasing more rapidly than either GNP or the compensation of ordinary employees.

What has caused the rising income share of the business elite? No proof is possible, but the most likely explanations draw on the fact of the enormous acceleration in Korean growth in the context of an economy with a large, still fairly poor, and slow growing agricultural sector. Although the existence of a large reservoir of "surplus labor" in the countryside probably ceased to exist in a formal sense in the mid-1960s,[20] if in fact such "surplus labor" ever existed at all, as late as 1970 half of Korea's population still lived in rural areas. As already pointed out, the incomes of these rural people rose in the 1970s over the levels prevailing in the latter half of the 1960s, but at an average rate only about half that of the growth rate of GNP per capita.

Modern sector employers, therefore, could draw unskilled workers off the farm with wages that also rose at a rate that was well above the growth rate in agriculture, but still below the likely rate of increase in profits. Profits data are not sufficiently reliable for use here, but between 1965 and 1975 manufacturing value added rose at an annual rate of 20 percent a year in real terms, while manufacturing employment and real wages rose by 11.1 percent and 8.9 percent respectively. Thus profits were probably rising at a rate of nearly 20 percent a year or more than double the rate of increase in real wages.[21] Other possible explanations for what appears to have been a rising profits share include the lack of significant trade union power, and the fact that real wage increases of 8.9 percent a year would in and of itself have reduced organized pressure for even greater rises. Japan during its great growth spurt of the 1950s and 1960s, for example, was heavily unionized, but it is doubtful that unions had much influence on the wage level or that they were under much pressure from their membership for even larger real increases than they were in fact receiving.

If the share of profits and of the incomes of those in the upper tail of the distribution were rising as suggested above, it is important to note that the income of these wealthy started from a low base. The Korean War ensured that result. One estimate of wartime destruction suggests that by 1953 some 20 percent of the net capital stock of South Korea had been destroyed. Furthermore, there is little doubt that this loss fell disproportionately on those who owned urban property, that is, on those with the greatest wealth in pre-war Korea.[22] Thus although business income during the most recent decade of rapid growth may have contributed to a rise in inequality, one should not conclude that Korean business income groups commanded an unusually large share of total national income relative to what prevails in other developing economies. Many of these other economies also experienced an increasing share going to upper income groups, groups that often started with a much higher share than that prevailing in Korea in the first place.

EDUCATION AND DISTRIBUTION[23]

Education is widely believed to have a major impact on the distribution of income both within and between the various sectors of a society. Unfortunately, although there is ample reason for accepting a relationship between education and income distribution, there is much debate and little agreement about the precise nature of that relationship. At one extreme are those that argue that income differences reflect differences in "human capital" acquired for the most part through formal education. At the other extreme is the assertion that education is mainly a device for sorting out those who will be allowed to go on to better jobs and those who will not—the implication usually being that the best jobs are reserved in that way for the children of the elite. The latter position implies that income differentials are determined by power considerations having little to do with differences in skills and hence education, however distributed, has little impact on the distribution of income. The former position takes the opposing view that a greater degree of equality, not only in educational opportunity but in the actual amount of education received, will of itself go a long way towards eliminating income inequality.

Since this broader issue cannot be resolved here, the discussion will be confined to an analysis of the degree of inequality achieved in the amount of education that Koreans receive. On that score, there is little question that Korea even in 1953 had more children (relative to the numbers in each age group) in school than the great majority of other developing nations, and the percentages of eligible children enrolled rose steadily throughout the period (see Table 92). By 1965 primary education was nearly universal, and by 1975 middle school education was nearly so. Even a high school education was becoming the normal expectation at least for urban residents. The numbers going on to college, however, were only a small, albeit rising, fraction of the eligible age group. Thus to the degree that the educational level does determine an individual's productivity

434

and income, there is every reason to believe that the educational system was pushing Korea in the direction of less not more inequality. Even if one were able to take into account differences in the quality of education between schools at the same level, it is unlikely that this basic conclusion would be upset, given the pronounced nature of the trends.

So far this discussion of income distribution has concentrated on "equality of result" as the ultimate goal. But in many societies "equality of opportunity" may be of equal or greater importance than "equality of result." In the area of providing equality of opportunity the Korean education system also receives high marks by developing (and many developed) country standards. Children in Seoul are favored, and urban children generally have greater access to school at the higher levels than do rural children. There is discrimination against women, although it is declining, but there is little discrimination between regions of the country. Even where discrimination exists, however, it is generally much less pronounced than in countries at a comparable and often a much higher level of per capita income.[24]

Where access to higher schools is limited, academic merit, as measured by examinations given to all entrants, is the most common method of selection, although school fees (often quite heavy) also play a key role. Family status appears to play very little direct role in selection particularly in the best schools such as Seoul National University, although people from well-educated families have an advantage in taking examinations as they do in all other countries. In short, Korea's education system contributes both to less inequality in the size distribution of income and to a perception of those differentials that remain as being "fair" or at least more "fair" than they otherwise would be perceived. Unfortunately, we cannot accurately measure the quantitative significance of either aspect.

THE INCIDENCE OF GOVERNMENT TAX
AND EXPENDITURE POLICY

In the above discussion, areas where the Korean government has influenced the distribution of income have already been touched on. The government, for example, plays a major role in the determination of the rural-urban terms of trade and it also contributes, albeit not very generously, to investment in education. It is time, however, to turn to a broad-based consideration of the influence of the government on the distribution of income through its taxing and expenditure powers.

Government action through the budget can affect the level and distribution of income in many ways. An effective government economic development program, for example, will lead to higher future incomes, to changes in the supply and demand of factor inputs and hence in the distribution of income to those inputs. Here, however, we shall deal mainly with the more or less immediate impact or incidence of Korean government tax and expenditure efforts. The key question is whether, after taking into account how the government raises revenues and allocates expenditures, the resulting distribution of after-tax income plus benefits significantly differs from the before-government incidence results.

To accurately estimate tax and expenditure incidence, of course, one must have both accurate before-tax income distribution data plus a model of the economy that allows one to estimate how taxes and expenditures are shifted forward and backward. In the case of Korea, neither condition can be met at this stage, and we shall instead draw on a study by Roy Bahl which has filled the gaps in knowledge with a number of plausible but bold assumptions.[25] In ways similar to (but not identical with) the method used earlier in this chapter, Bahl allocates most property and business income to urban upper income groups. Bahl's results are presented in Tables 131 and 132.

As the results in Table 131 indicate, the Korean tax structure

TABLE 131 Distribution of the Government Revenue Burden

Income Group (% of families)	1965		1974	
	Percent of Income	Percent of Taxes	Percent of Income	Percent of Taxes
Urban				
Bottom 10%	2.4	1.7	2.7	3.9
2nd	3.5	4.1	3.4	4.9
3rd	2.4	4.7	4.2	4.8
4th	4.2	5.5	4.6	5.2
5th	5.2	6.5	5.2	5.9
6th	5.6	7.3	6.0	6.6
7th	6.7	9.0	6.4	7.1
8th	8.0	10.9	7.7	8.3
9th	18.1	18.4	14.2	14.2
Top 10%	44.9	31.9	45.6	39.1
Gini	.526	.415	.485	.406
Rural				
Bottom 10%	4.5	5.0	2.5	3.1
2nd	4.5	4.9	4.0	4.0
3rd	4.4	5.0	5.0	4.6
4th	6.3	6.1	5.1	4.6
5th	7.6	7.1	6.9	5.7
6th	7.6	7.1	7.4	5.9
7th	8.5	7.8	8.7	6.7
8th	10.6	9.7	10.1	7.4
9th	16.2	15.7	13.2	9.2
Top 10%	29.8	31.6	37.1	48.8
Gini	.347	.344	.413	.468

Source: Derived from Bahl, "The Distributional Effects of the Korean Budget."

TABLE 132 Distribution of Government Expenditure Benefits

Income Group (% of families)	1965		1974	
	Percent of Income	*Percent of Expenditures*	*Percent of Income*	*Percent of Expenditures*
		Urban		
Bottom 10%	2.4	5.1	2.7	6.0
2nd	3.5	6.6	3.4	6.9
3rd	2.4	6.8	4.2	7.4
4th	4.2	7.5	4.6	7.6
5th	5.2	8.4	5.2	8.1
6th	5.6	9.0	6.0	9.3
7th	6.7	10.1	6.4	10.0
8th	8.0	11.5	7.7	11.3
9th	18.1	15.0	14.2	13.8
Top 10%	44.9	20.0	45.6	19.6
Gini	.526	.225	.485	.199
		Rural		
Bottom 10%	4.5	6.6	2.5	5.1
2nd	4.5	6.6	4.0	6.3
3rd	4.4	6.6	5.0	7.2
4th	6.3	7.9	5.1	7.1
5th	7.6	9.0	6.9	8.6
6th	7.6	9.0	7.4	9.0
7th	8.5	9.7	8.7	10.0
8th	10.6	11.4	10.2	11.2
9th	16.2	14.2	13.2	13.5
Top 10%	29.8	19.0	37.1	22.0
Gini	.347	.195	.413	.232

Source: Derived from Bahl, "The Distributional Effects of the Korean Budget."

is slightly regressive particularly in the urban areas, and there has been no significant trend toward greater progressivity during the past decade of rapid growth. Actually, if estimates for intervening years were included, there may have been some increase in progressivity up to the early 1970s which was then followed by a reversal towards greater regressivity. This lack of progressivity would appear to reflect largely a tax system that still relies mainly on indirect taxes of various kinds. Direct taxes, including the income tax, have provided only about 30 percent of total government revenue for the past twenty years, and there has been no tendency for that percentage to rise over time.[26] As between sectors, there is an "undertaxation" of the rural sector which is in a sense a progressive element, since the rural sector is poorer than its urban counterpart. Again this result would seem to reflect the heavy reliance on indirect taxes. Farmers in Korea provide a large share of their consumption requirements themselves, while urban residents must purchase these same requirements.

In contrast to revenues, the incidence of government expenditure benefits is progressive, although estimates of expenditure benefits rest on even less solid foundations than do estimates of revenue incidence. The progressivity in expenditure benefits largely results from a growth in the budgeted share of economic and social services as contrasted to a decline in defense and general services. Within the economic services category, a relative shift away from expenditures on agriculture has created an urban bias in overall expenditure incidence.[27]

When the impact of the revenue and expenditure side is combined, the net effect is to make the budget a modest influence for reducing inequality in both the urban and rural sectors. Of greater significance is that the government budget causes important intersectoral transfers from the urban to the rural population and from present to future generations. The latter result is the product of a budget that has financed rapidly rising capital expenditures to a large degree out of borrowing and current account savings.

This limited impact of the government budget on Korea's income distribution should not come as a surprise. For example, using a large general equilibrium model based on Korean data, Irma Adelman and Sherman Robinson demonstrate that no single government intervention in the economy, with the possible exception of efforts to influence the rural-urban terms of trade, has much influence on the overall degree of inequality.[28] Even where a policy has an initially favorable impact on distribution, subsequent adjustments of the economy often offset much of that impact. Their "study reinforces the view that the distribution of income is firmly rooted in the structure of the economy, and that its path over time depends on the fundamental development strategy chosen by the society."[29] On the whole, Korea has picked a development strategy that has favored a comparatively low degree of inequality. Only a massive effort by the government involving a wide variety of interventions in the economy would be likely to move Korean society significantly further towards less inequality, at least in the short run.

THE IMPACT OF DISTRIBUTION ON GROWTH

Up to this point, interest has centered on what Korea's income distribution is, how it changed over the three decade period since 1945, and what were the major reasons for these changes or the lack thereof. An equally important question is how did Korea's income distribution and its changes over time influence Korean economic growth during this same period. In fact, it would not be far-fetched to suggest that how Korea's present income distribution impacts on the rate and nature of economic growth now and in the future will be the major determinant of the level of equality or inequality that will prevail in Korean society.

Unfortunately, we know even less about how income distribution affects growth than we do about how growth influences distribution. Econometric models have been developed for Korea to explain this interaction, but the results of these models depend heavily on the assumptions used in their construction, and what is assumed is often what it is most important to explain. The analysis here will not do any better and will in fact deal mainly with the nature of the problem rather than its solution.

The principal redistribution of income that has occurred in Korea resulted from the aftereffects of the removal of the Japanese when independence was regained. In assessing the impact of this redistribution, one must distinguish between short-run and long-run effects and between the agricultural and industrial sectors. In the short run in the agricultural sector, land reform led to some disruption mainly because landlords had been, and no longer were, a major source of rural capital, and they also played some managerial role. Over the longer run, alternative sources of rural capital were found, and the incentive effects of not having to share increases in productivity with a landlord probably outweighed by a substantial margin the benefits of landlord management. This latter effect must be taken largely on faith, however, because this writer, at least, has not been able to devise a test that would measure the change even in a crude way.

In the industrial sector, the short-run effect of losing Japanese capital and management was much more severe than in the rural sector. From a long-run view, getting rid of the Japanese, or at least removing their stranglehold on top jobs, was undoubtedly essential if the now clearly demonstrated entrepreneurial energies of the Koreans were ever to be released.

The relationship between income distribution and growth in the post-Korean War period is largely a question of whether, if the incomes of the richest 5 or 10 percent of all Korean families were greatly reduced, there would be a comparable reduction in either entrepreneurship or savings and investment levels. The unsatisfactory answer is that, given our poor knowledge of the determinants of Korean savings behavior[30] and our nonexistent knowledge of the relationship between income incentives and entrepreneurship, we simply do not know. We do know that, in a fully socialized economy producing mainly for a domestic market, the state can take over the savings and entrepreneurial functions and simultaneously reduce personal income differentials. But such information is of little help in understanding a dynamic manufactured-export-oriented economy where a major part of the entrepreneurial and savings function is left to the private sector. The highest incomes in Korea have, for the most part, gone to those who have led Korea's business boom. There are no maharajas in Korea or many others living off inherited wealth, nor have politicians and government bureaucrats been the main beneficiaries of high incomes. Whether Korean businessmen would have done just as well with lower incomes, due, say, to a vigorously progressive income tax, is an interesting question, but it cannot be answered.

CONCLUSION

Although much remains to be learned about the causes and effects of the distribution of income in Korea and elsewhere, a few tentative conclusions are possible. In the initial "asset redistribution phase," as the period of the late 1940s and early 1950s has been labeled,[31] Korea experienced a major redistribution of income towards the poor (or away from the rich). Because the people who held substantial wealth prior to 1945 were either Japanese or Koreans tarred by close association with the Japanese, a major redistribution was both politically feasible and had few negative effects on Korea's growth performance over the long term. To the contrary, it is likely that redistribution had a major positive impact on Korea's growth prospects, partly by eliminating sources of political tension and instability and partly by opening up opportunities for advancement for great numbers of able and ambitious Koreans.

Since the 1950s, there have not been major changes in Korea's

TABLE 133 Data Used in Calculating the Overall
Theil Statistic

$$\text{Theil Statistic} = \sum_{g=1}^{3} Y_g \ln \frac{Y_g}{N_g/N} + \sum_{g=1}^{3} Y_g \left[\sum_i \frac{y_i}{Y_g} \ln \frac{y_i/Y_g}{1/N_g} \right]$$

Between-Sector   Within-Sector Inequality
Inequality

where

1	=	farm household sector
2	=	urban household sector
3	=	business sector
Y_g	=	share of sector g in national income originating in the 3 sectors combined
N_g	=	the number of households in sector g
N	=	the total number of households obtained by adding the number of households in each sector. Urban households were assumed equal to all non-farm households which probably overstates their share.
y_i	=	income of the ith household.

Assumptions A and B: See notes to Table 117

		1963	1967	1970	1974	1975
A	Y_1	.465	.339	.312	.272	.286
	Y_2	.363	.450	.476	.437	.482
	Y_3	.172	.211	.212	.291	.252
B	Y_1	.577	.399	.359	.346	n.a.
	Y_2	.384	.529	.458	.556	n.a.
	Y_3	.309[a]	.072	.093	.099	n.a.
	N_1/N[b]	.486	.468	.387	.338	.324
	N_2/N[b]	.457	.455	.525	.579	.597
	N_3/N[b]	.057[a]	.078	.088	.083	.079
Theil Statistic 1[c]		.172	.172	.172	.172	.172
Theil Statistic 2[c]		.155	.155	.155	.155	.155
Theil Statistic 3[c]		1.120	1.120	1.120	1.120	1.120

TABLE 133 (continued)

---

^a1964 data

^bThe urban and rural household figures are those regularly published in the statistical handbooks. There are no reliable data on the number of business households, and the figures here are really only plausible guesses. In principle, business households located in urban areas should have been subtracted from the total number of urban households (and similarly in rural areas) but to simplify matters these households were added to the total figure and no subtraction took place. This latter simplification shouldn't introduce much distortion, but varying assumptions about the total number of business households in any given year could have a substantial impact on the overall estimate of inequality.

^cThese Theil Statistics are simply the average of those for the different years in Table 115. These figures were used for

$$[\sum_i \frac{y_i}{Y_g} \, ln \, \frac{y_i/Y_g}{1/N_g}]$$

rather than going back and recalculating each within-sector figure using samples normalized so that the size of each sample relative to the other two was equal to the share of that sector in the total number of households. The amount of distortion introduced by this simplification should not be significant.

distribution of income. There has been some reduction in differences in income between regions, and the rural-urban income gap has closed a bit in recent years, but overall distribution within rural areas and among urban wage earners has been quite stable. Only business incomes and the incomes of high level managers and professionals appear to be climbing more rapidly than that of the others, thus leading to a modest increase in the degree of inequality. Tax policy with its heavy reliance on indirect taxes and expenditure policy with the emphasis on growth related investment have together had little net impact on distribution, although a small amount of progressivity in the system does exist. For the most part, however, the higher incomes have gone to those in the private sector who have led the economic boom, not to rentiers and corrupt government officials. Korea has also remained a society with a high degree of equality of opportunity particularly by the standards prevailing in many other developing nations. Education is the major route to the top and access to education is becoming steadily wider, while progress up through the education system is largely a matter of academic achievement.

THIRTEEN

Summary and Conclusions

As we indicated in the introductory chapter, this study has two purposes: to throw light on the economic and social development of South Korea during the three decades since 1945 and to attempt to estimate the contributions, positive and negative, of American economic intervention. The historical setting for the second task began in 1945 when General Hodge and his assistants first set foot in Korea. With respect to the first task, however, the last three decades followed on a twelve-hundred-year existence of Korea as a single, unified, and independent state and a thirty-five-year period of colonial rule. Korea, when it was opened to foreign penetration in 1876, was not a haphazard collection of tribes arbitrarily enclosed by borders but was occupied by an unusually homogeneous population speaking a common language. This population was brought into the modern economic and administrative world by an occupation which, though exploitative in high degree, left a heritage of its own that significantly influenced the later course of Korean development. The Korean culture, the residue of Japanese penetration and occupation, and the division of what had been a unified country between north and south are the three principal antecedents on which any study of the development of the last three decades must build.

KOREAN DEVELOPMENT
BEFORE WORLD WAR II

The significance of Korean culture and the Japanese occupation on later development was discussed in Chapter 3. Although Korea's pre-modern experience differed from that of many developing nations, it was not unique. Korea, like Japan and Vietnam, was part of a broader East Asian culture centering on China. Confucianism, the state philosophy of Korea as well as of China, placed great emphasis on education and on a deference within the family, within the community, and within the society that tends to favor individual discipline and social stability. It has not gone unnoticed that everywhere in East Asia that Chinese influence has penetrated, Japan, Korea, Taiwan, Singapore, Indonesia, and Thailand, economic development has flourished. Such a widespread experience must have strong cultural roots.

It is tempting to hazard the guess that Korea has developed because it is occupied by Koreans, but this hypothesis hardly explains the relatively stagnant society that existed during the century preceding the opening of the country to external influences. It was these influences that began the process of modernization, but they acted on a society that obviously had the capacity for adaptation and growth. It was, in the latter part of the nineteenth century, a highly traditional and formal society which, during the five hundred year reign of the Yi dynasty, had suffered only two major and devastating military interventions from abroad, the latter one in 1594 from Japan. In 1876 when the ouside world began to intervene, Korea had had three centuries of peace during which its only external contacts were the loose relationships it maintained with China. It was a highly centralized society politically with no foci of power capable of contesting the government in Seoul. The tradition of extreme centralization has survived independence and everything that has occurred since 1945. But the concentration of power in Seoul did not mean concentration of power in the hands of the king. By the latter half of the Yi dynasty, Korean kings were hemmed in by a powerful bureaucracy vigorous in the preservation of its perquisites.

Already in the late nineteenth century, the growing population of Korea was pressing hard against the limited supply of arable land. By the time of the first Japanese land survey in 1918, Koreans on the average had only 0.12 hectares (about 1/3 of an acre) of arable land per capita. Only the Japanese had less arable acreage per capita. Intensive cultivation of the available land, however, yielded a high product per acre, high enough to feed an idle *yangban* population and, during the Japanese occupation, to permit large exports of foodstuffs to Japan. The tradition of intensive and productive cultivation of a limited amount of arable land has continued to be a characteristic of Korean agriculture.

In many ways, the most pervasive inheritance received by modern Korea from its East Asian heritage was the Confucian emphasis on education. To begin with, education in Korea was the major route to government office as it was in China. Without two decades or so of training in the Confucian classics a non-military man had little hope of obtaining the great prestige and substantial monetary awards of a government position. Unlike China, however, it was mainly hereditary aristocracy, the *yangban*, who were eligible for the examinations and hence for government office, but they constituted a sizable fraction of the population. Although the commoners below them rarely had an opportunity of acquiring a knowledge of Chinese classics, the invention of an excellent phonetic alphabet, Han'gŭl, made it possible for a considerable number to achieve literacy.

Korea in the late nineteenth century was an overwhelmingly agrarian society. Although Seoul had a population of perhaps 200,000, there was no other city as large as 100,000. The trade in foodstuffs and handicrafts between countryside and the cities had developed certain commercial channels and activities, but banking institutions were non-existent and there were no organized manufacturing operations. Superficially what post-war Korea inherited from traditional Korea was a predilection for highly centralized government, a high value placed on education, and an industrious and productive agricultural labor force. At a deeper level, the inheritance consisted of values and habits that have proved extraordinarily amenable to modernizing elements that have impinged from the outside.

The Japanese occupation of Korea was a regime of, by, and for Japan with as little participation of Koreans in leadership positions as could be accommodated. Nevertheless, their contribution to the modernization of Korea was undeniable, and this contribution was significant for later development. The influence of Japan on Korean society did not begin with colonial rule but had been growing continuously since the first contacts in 1876. For a period, Japan contested with other powers for influence, but victory over China in 1895 and Russia in 1904 disposed of the principal rivals. By 1910 there were 170,000 Japanese domiciled in Korea, and their activities permeated all sectors of the economy. By the end of the colonial period there were 770,000.

Korea was operated as a Japanese fief, and it was operated efficiently. The annual growth rate of net commodity product at nearly 4 percent a year was higher than the growth rate in Japan during the same period. During the first two decades of occupation, Korea was regarded as principally a supplier of foodstuffs and its exports of rice to Japan were large. Manufactures, however, also grew rapidly and when, in the 1930s, Japan turned towards war preparations the growth was accelerated with an increasing emphasis on heavy industry. There is no doubt that the colonial "enclave" character of Korean industrial development seriously lessened the spread effects of rapid economic growth. The impact was further reduced by the dominant role of Japanese ownership, management, and technical competence. By 1941, Japanese owned 59 percent of the existing manufacturing firms representing 91 percent of the total paid-in capital. Despite the fact that Japanese natives constituted only one-fifth of total manufacturing employment, they held some 80 percent of the technical and engineering positions in manufacturing.

Although the dominance of Japanese management and the enclave character, particularly of heavy industry, certainly limited the learning opportunities and the industrial experience for the Korean population, the influence of these decades of rapid growth and export expansion was far from negligible. Korean employment in manufacturing increased from 23,000 household heads in 1910 to 440,000 in 1940. By 1944 there were nearly 1,900 Korean engineers and technicians employed in manufacturing, another 1,300 in mining, and 2,000 in service industries. Altogether there were in 1944 some 7,000 Korean managers and 28,000 professional and technical workers. As early as 1937 there were some 2,000 Korean-owned factories and 100 of them each employed more than 50 workers. Nor was this industrial experience limited to Korea. By 1945 there were close to 2 million Koreans living in Japan, mostly in non-agricultural employment, and an additional million in Manchuria working in the cities and countryside of that Japanese-held territory. Most of these Koreans living abroad were repatriated after the war and brought their experience with them.

Furthermore the "demonstration effect" of exposure to modern technology and forms of organization, though less measurable, was important. When, in the 1960s, the Korean economy began to grow rapidly, it took the form of government-directed, export-led industrialization that had characterized the growth pattern during the colonial period.

Japanese colonial rule also added to the stock of human capital in the more conventional sense through expansion of the educational system. This system, assisted by Christian missionary efforts, was already much stronger than that in most premodern societies. After 1910, the Japanese expanded primary education vigorously as a major element in their program to integrate Korea into the Japanese Empire, and by 1945 there were over a million pupils in primary schools. The educational pyramid narrowed rapidly in higher grades but did not disappear altogether as it did under some colonial regimes (for example, the Dutch East Indies or the Belgian Congo). In the 1930s despite severe Japanese discrimination, there were tens of thousands of Koreans in high schools and thousands in universities. When independence came, such universities as the public Seoul National and the private Yonsei and Korea universities could draw on a long tradition of excellence.

Institutional development during the Japanese period was not confined to education. The finances of government were separated from those of the Korean Imperial Household and established on modern principles. The Japanese also introduced a modern monetary system to replace the chaotic non-system that existed during the Yi dynasty. A railway was constructed connecting Pusan and Seoul with Manchuria and Europe. In the rural areas, the Japanese established a high quality extension service designed to increase Korea's ability to supply Japan's requirements for rice.

Not all these institutional innovations survived the transition to independence, and those that did were subject to modification. The departure of Japanese administrators and technicians created a gap that took time to replace and made a substantial part of the industrial installations unusable. An even larger part was destroyed in the Korean War. The practical elimination of trade relations with Japan destroyed the export-orientation of Korean industry. Thus a substantial part of the Japanese economic inheritance was dissipated. But not all. Korea retained an impressive stock of human capital, a considerable complement of physical facilities, and an experience of how an efficient economy functioned that was to stand it in good stead later.

The experience of colonial rule inevitably created a hatred of the Japanese that continued to affect adversely political and economic relations with Japan until well into the 1960s. Perhaps the most damaging aspect of the colonial inheritance was the absolute exclusion of Koreans from political activity and from government. For thirty-five crucial years Korea was ruled almost exclusively by Japanese. No Koreans to speak of acquired any experience in the management of the public affairs of their own country. When Koreans finally regained control of their own government in 1948, they had numerous foreign political models to draw on, but their only direct experience was the discredited system of the Yi dynasty and with the autocratic rule of the hated Japanese. In a very real sense, therefore, the political instability that characterized the late 1940s and all of the 1950s was also part of the heritage of Japanese colonialism. At a crucial point in Korean history, Koreans had been deprived of the opportunity to develop effective political institutions of their own.

If the Japanese colonial heritage was a mixture of positive and negative elements from the point of view of economic growth, the division of the country at the 38th parallel in 1945 was an unmitigated disaster. The choice of the 38th parallel was a hastily considered decision by the U.S. State Department. If, however, it was recognized as a necessity that the Soviet Union and the United States be allotted separate areas to receive the surrender of Japanese troops, it is difficult to see that any other choice of boundary would have achieved better results. It was not the choice of the 38th parallel that created a permanent division between north and south but the rapidly developing postures of the cold war and the ideological divisions among Koreans aided and abetted by the occupying powers. General Hodge and his ill-prepared and hastily chosen staff entered Korea in 1945 to carry out an assigned mission, that is, to fulfill the promises that had been made at the Cairo and Potsdam

Conference (to establish an integrated and independent Korea), to make Korea strong enough to be a factor of stability in Asia, and to build up the new Republic as a display window of democracy for other Asiatic peoples to see and emulate. These were fair words.

When it became clear in 1947 that an integrated Korea could not be negotiated on terms acceptable either to the Americans or their Korean clients, the interests of the United States turned towards bringing into existence in the south a government strong enough to permit the withdrawal of American forces. What the obligations and responsibilities of the United States to this new government should be was unclear to Washington, but the invasion from the north in July 1950 and President Truman's decision for military intervention answered that question. South Korea was to become a client state into which the United States was to pour some $13 billion in military and economic assistance during the next twenty-five years. It created for South Korea a state of dependence, characterized in the early years by frequent intervention in its domestic affairs, from which it is only now emerging.

The division of a relatively integrated economy with the principal sources of electric power and heavy industry in the north and of light industry and the richest agricultural areas in the south, created economic difficulties, but these were not of lasting importance. The major impact was social and political. The kind of society and polity that has developed in South Korea has been powerfully shaped by the division of the peninsula and the ensuing war. The war and continued fears of attack from the north led to the creation and maintenance of the fifth largest army in the world and, as we saw in Chapter 2, the influence of the armed forces has permeated the society. The fear of intervention from the north also had a good deal to do with the failure of democratic stirrings in 1960, 1961, the military coup in the latter year, and the continuance of the strong and repressive government of President Park Chung Hee. It is useless to speculate on what the course of political and social development might have been in a united Korea, but there is no doubt that the military demarcation line has profoundly influenced the course of development in the south.

AMERICAN MILITARY AND ECONOMIC ASSISTANCE

Prior to the beginning of the Korean War in 1950, U.S. economic assistance, first under the U.S. Military Government and later under the Economic Cooperation Administration, was directed primarily to relief and rehabilitation. The main objective of U.S. policy was disengagement, indeed the failure of Congress to approve the modest development program proposed by ECA in 1949 together with Secretary of State Acheson's statement early in 1950 that Korea lay outside the American defense perimeter, may have triggered the invasion from the north, Imports during this period, distributed through various U.S. and United Nations agencies, consisted primarily of foodstuffs, clothing, petroleum products to keep wheels moving, and fertilizer to facilitate domestic rice production. American agencies, military and civilian, provided a certain amount of technical assistance, and the U.S. Military Government carried through the land distribution program discussed in Chapters 6 and 7. In general, American representatives, despite the existing political disorder and economic disruption, took a fairly rosy view of recovery prospects and anticipated an end of economic as well as military involvement within a few years.

The war changed all that. Not only was the South Korean economy devastated, but American intervention carried with it the responsibility, not only of defending the country against further attack, but of assisting reconstruction as well as political independence.

Although there was a certain economic spin-off from military assistance, its contribution to economic development, apart from economizing domestic military expenditures, could not have been large. It took the form mainly of installations—roads, bridges, and the like—of economic as well as military use, of the training of large numbers in the handling of machinery and equipment, and of officer-grade personnel in administrative techniques, and the provision of opportunities for earning foreign exchange over and above earnings from commercial exports. The maintenance of Korean armed forces of over 500,000 under a system of universal military service had produced by 1975 well over 2 million men who had undergone systematic training and had been released to the labor force. Retired officers were recruited in large numbers not only for government posts but as directors of many of the considerable number of public enterprises established since independence, with managerial results that are subject to question in informed circles. The supplying of American military installations with public utilities and other services and the sale of wŏn currency for military use yielded dollar earnings that amounted to about $100 million a year in the mid-1960s and approached $200 million a few years later. Korean military involvement in Vietnam not only yielded foreign exchange in troop pay but was accompanied by large scale construction projects and substantial exports for the use of American forces in the war zone. All these opportunities for earning dollars involved, of course, the commitment of Korean resources and are in no sense to be confused with concessional aid. Still, to the extent that shortage of foreign exchange was a limit to growth, the existence of these opportunities may have made some contribution to development. If one assumes that South Korea would, under any circumstances, have felt it necessary to maintain a strong military posture, by far the most important contribution of U.S. military assistance to development was the relief it offered to the budget and the economy.

The major impact on development obviously came from economic assistance. This impact took the form of the provision of commodity imports and productive projects, of technical assistance, and of influence on Korean development policies. The large inflow of U.S. assistance began immediately after the war and reached the high point in 1957. During the period 1953 through 1962, foreign aid, 95 percent of which came from the United States, amounted to some 8 percent of Korean GNP, 77 percent of fixed capital formation, and financed about 70 percent of imports. Until 1965 almost all U.S. economic assistance was in the form of grants which meant that when Korea later found it necessary to enter international capital markets to borrow it did so unencumbered with a serious burden of foreign debt.

By 1965 South Korea was well into the process of rapid economic growth, and U.S. economic assistance was not only declining but increasingly taking the form of loans rather than grants. If U.S. assistance is judged to have made a substantial contribution to Korean development, the contribution must have taken place predominantly in the period before 1965. We return to this question presently after summarizing certain other aspects of the aid program. Eighty percent of U.S. assistance in the period before 1965 took the form of program aid, that is, aid not related to specific projects. Nearly half of this was surplus agricultural commodities with other major components being fertilizer, petroleum, and materials for Korea's rapidly growing import-substituting manufactures. The sale of these imports yielded counterpart funds which constituted nearly 50 percent of government revenues during the 1950s and supported in large measure the salaries of the Korean military establishment. U.S. project aid was concentrated in the area of transportation, manufacturing, and electric power. Agriculture, education, health, and other social services received relatively minor allocations generally amounting in each case to less than 5 percent of total project assistance.

Any attempt to assess quantitatively the effect of U.S. material assistance on South Korean growth rates and the distribution of income runs up against the impossibility of knowing what would have happened to economic inputs, the structure of production, government policies, and even the government itself, in the absence of U.S. aid. One can only talk of probabilities, and an assessment must be essentially qualitative. Still, there *are* probabilities. It is difficult to see how a seriously war-damaged economy could have been reconstructed in a short period of time without massive foreign assistance. The heavy emphasis on fertilizer imports and later assistance to domestic fertilizer production was clearly a major factor in increasing farm production as noted in Chapter 7. The large imports of food-stuffs no doubt raised standards of living in the cities and served as an anti-inflationary device though, as in a number of other countries, U.S. surplus crop disposal policies had a negative effect on farm incentives, and this had to be corrected by the Korean government later. Aid-financed imports of raw material permitted a fairly rapid growth of import-substituting manufacturing enterprises and the development of entrepreneurs and managers who made their mark in the later period of rapid growth. What would have happened to domestic savings rates and export earnings, which were minimal during the 1950s, is impossible to say, but it is difficult for a student of the policies of Syngman Rhee to believe that his regime would have asked for, or received support for, the kind of austerity measures that would have been necessary to cope with the situation.

American economic assistance to Korea was not limited to the financing of programs and projects. The U.S. provided a considerable amount of technical assistance and, for a time, exercised a role in the shaping of economic policies. Thousands of American technical advisers have worked in Korea over the last three decades, in agriculture, education, as advisers on economic planning, and in other fields. And tens of thousands of Koreans have been sent abroad for training under USAID-financed programs. The early American efforts in education were directed towards restoring educational resources lost through the departure of all Japanese teachers and administrators, the deterioration of physical facilities, and shortages in educational supplies. Technical advice led to a temporary loosening and democratization of the extremely rigid and authoritative character of Japanese educational procedures, to increased emphasis on education for women, to the introduction of the standard American 6-3-3-4 year structure, and to a greater degree of local control. Later American activities in this field were pretty much limited to provision of physical facilities and many of the American-sponsored reforms were reversed. In agriculture, another major area of American technical assistance activity, a substantial contribution was made to the development of agricultural research and research institutions. Early American efforts to bring some order into the chaotic Korean financial situation led to the establishment of the Bank of Korea as a central bank and produced the General Banking Act of 1950. The most important USAID contribution in the field of planning was the technical assistance provided in the formulation of the Second Five-Year Economic Development Plan (1967–1971).

By far the most important American policy intervention in Korean economic activities took place during the period of U.S. Military Government with the distribution of Japanese-owned land. This distribution created an irresistible demand for land reform of all tenanted properties and led eventually to the Land Reform Act of June 1949 which established the Korean government as a mediator in the transfer of landlords to tenants. Between them, these measures succeeded in sharply increasing the rates of ownership to tenancy. While land reform may temporarily have reduced productivity per acre, this was far outweighed by the political and social consequences. As indicated in Chapter 7, the wealth of landlords was reduced and, over time, the earnings of small farmers substantially increased.

With the disappearance of U.S. Military Government and the coming into being of an independent government in 1948, the United States did not discontinue its efforts to influence domestic policy. Late in 1948 the first government-to-government assistance pact was signed. As a condition of receiving further assistance, it required the Korean government to follow certain stable economic policies, notably balancing the budget, regulating foreign exchange, effectively disposing of the formerly

Japanese-owned properties (now vested in the government), and establishing a "counterpart fund" in the Bank of Chosun into which the Korean government promised to deposit the wŏn equivalent of the dollar cost of U.S. grant aid and to use those funds only for purposes mutually agreed upon. In May 1952, an Agreement on Economic Coordination between the Republic of Korea and the Unified Command was signed creating a Combined Economic Board, composed of U.S. and Korean officials who met frequently on matters of economic policy. Disagreement within this board was also frequent. President Rhee's primary objective was to maximize receipts of foreign aid and to rehabilitate the economy with the smallest possible burden placed on Korean taxpayers. In pursuing these objectives, he exhibited great political dexterity. It was useful for his purpose to emphasize the poverty and unfilled requirements of Korea, and the government was not above underestimating agricultural output to this end. Inevitably this brought Rhee and his representatives into conflict with the Economic Cooperation Administration and its representatives on the Combined Economic Board.

The Americans pressed for a realistic exchange rate, but the Korean currency continued to be heavily overvalued during the Rhee regime. The Americans wanted less deficit financing and insisted, without noticeable effect, on higher taxes and reduced inflation which it was hoped would produce a larger volume of domestic savings. A turning point came in 1957 when the United States decided on a sharp reduction in economic assistance and more or less imposed a stabilization program on the Korean government. To take the period as a whole, however, it was Rhee who called the tune in economic policy. As so often happens, a weak regime confronting a strong power was able to use the very weakness to attain most of its ends. Rhee successfully pursued what might be called a policy of "coercive deficiency."

Since the Rhee Government pursued policies that were not conducive to economic growth, particularly its foreign exchange, interest rate, and tax policies, U.S. foreign assistance contributed substantially less than it might have contributed to Korean development. Alternatively, if the Korean government had in fact pursued sensible economic policies, the realized growth rate might have been achieved with substantially less foreign assistance. Still, the amount of foreign assistance during the 1950s constituted so large a fraction of economic inputs that its contribution to Korean development could not help but be substantial. It permitted rehabilitation after a devastating war; it maintained consumption standards at a higher level than could possibly have been sustained by Korean resources; and, by financing an expansion of public services and imports of materials for an expanding industry sector, it helped to create the preconditions for the rapid growth that took place after 1963. Without massive external assistance from 1945 to 1963, as we said in Chapter 6, Korean living standards would have been appreciably lower (perhaps 10 to 15 percent), post-war recovery and growth would have been slower, and it is possible that the country could not have survived as an independent entity in the face of North Korean pressures, and an economic performance that, through the 1950s, was much better in the north than in the south.

Before 1965, the United States was the source of well over 90 percent of the foreign assistance to Korea. This situation changed with the normalization of relations with Japan in 1965. Although the Korean government tends to treat concessionary contributions from Japan as reparations rather than assistance and, indeed, excludes from its conception of foreign assistance anything other than grants, if we adhere to accepted definitions of Official Development Assistance, U.S. bilateral assistance, including loans, amounted, in the 1970s to less than half of total ODA. But by that time the credit-worthiness of Korea was such that it was able to meet its major needs for foreign funds by borrowing on international capital markets. U.S. foreign assistance has made a negligible contribution to development since 1965 but, in the two decades after 1945, it was of crucial importance.

AMERICAN ASSISTANCE, 1953 TO 1963

As we saw in Chapter 2, the seven years that elapsed between the final settlement of the Korean War in 1953 and the overthrow of the Rhee Government in 1960 were distinguished by the highly personal, quasi-dictatorial regime of Syngman Rhee, by the support of the newly formed state by massive U.S. military and economic assistance, by quarrels between U.S. representatives and Rhee over questions of appropriate economic policy, and by a relatively slow growth of the economy. Rhee's political instrument was the Liberal Party which controlled the National Assembly and assured the passage of legislation drafted by the executive. Strong security forces policed elections and maintained a strict control over dissidents. Senior administrative positions were assigned to politically reliable colleagues who frequently feathered their nests in the course of allocating permits and licenses to the highest bidder. Corruption was also an important source of financing of the Liberal Party. Nearly half of government revenues were derived from counterpart funds from U.S. aid dollars and, since Rhee was reluctant to increase taxes, much of the remainder represented borrowing from the Central Bank. This inevitably produced a high rate of inflation. Between 1953 and 1957 the average rate of inflation was 40 percent. American insistence on a stabilization program brought the rate down to 20 percent and, assisted by two good harvests in 1958 and 1959, produced relative price stability in these years.

The cornerstone of the Rhee Government's economic relations with the United States was foreign exchange policy and, during the whole of this regime, Korea managed to negotiate an official rate that overvalued the wŏn and undervalued the dollar. U.S. pressure forced a devaluation from 6 to 18 wŏn in December 1953, and from 18 to 50 in August 1955. Other devaluations in January and February of 1961 brought the wŏn to 130 to the dollar. But during the whole of this period, persistent inflation assured a continued undervaluation of foreign exchange. Dollars were not, of course, available to business at the official rate, and the rates at which they were available were highly complex and frequently amenable to special deals.

Access to foreign exchange and to domestic credit were essential to business success and, since the Rhee Government encouraged a policy of low interest rates, access to bank credit was a valuable asset. The rationing of bank credit produced an active so-called curb market in which interest rates could rise to 4 or 5 times the cost of borrowing from the bank. The manner in which foreign exchange and domestic credit were allocated was an obvious invitation to corruption and the basis of a number of Korean fortunes was laid during this period. Some idea of how much "illicit" wealth was accumulated via business deals with corrupt politicians and government officials became evident after the student led revolution of April 1960 and the revelations of the subsequent Special Law for Dealing With Illicit Wealth Accumulation.

Despite internal dissention, less-than-sensible economic policies, and a good deal of corruption, the Korean GNP grew at a respectable average rate of about 5 percent between 1953 and 1957. This was a period of reconstruction, and growth proceeded from a relatively low base level. The stabilization program introduced in 1957 had the effect of reducing the rate of growth of GNP to about 3.8 percent between 1957 and 1960. But manufactured output grew much more rapidly averaging about 15 percent per annum in the earlier period and close to 10 percent in the latter. Manufactured output was to a considerable extent, import-replacing, encouraged by high protective tariffs and quantitative restrictions on imports. Commodity exports declined from 1953 to 1957 and, although an increase began in 1958, they did not regain their 1953 level until 1961. During the whole period, exports were a negligible component of total output ranging from 1 to a little over 2 percent of GNP.

Although the rate of economic growth during the 1953–1960 period could hardly be called satisfactory and, although the U.S.

government continued to view South Korea as a nearly hopeless case, in fact at least a few planks were being laid for a platform from which later rapid development could be launched. Entrepreneurial experience was accumulating in a sizable number of new enterprises. Education at all levels was expanding rapidly, indeed, university graduates were being turned out in numbers in excess of employment opportunities, a fact that had something to do with the student-led revolution in 1960. But these same graduates were, for the most part, to find useful employment during the ensuing period of rapid growth. South Korea by the early 1960s had a literacy rate difficult to match in the Third World. Land redistribution had been accomplished with relatively little disturbance to the rate of growth of agricultural output. And land reform plus the destruction of large private properties during the war had given the Korean population an unusually even distribution of assets and income. The large and well organized Korean army built up during and after the Korean War was maintained without serious financial burden to the economy, and it periodically inducted and, after training, returned to the work force sizable numbers of disciplined men familiar with the handling of mechanical equipment. What was needed was a strong and stable government willing to accept economic development as its first priority and able to put into effect the kind of policies needed to promote growth.

The revolution that swept President Rhee from power in April 1960 also disposed of his political instrument, the Liberal Party, which was unsuccessful in electing a single candidate in the elections of 1965 and 1967. It was replaced in power by a badly divided Democratic Party which, after a few months of interim government, chose, by a narrow margin, Chang Myon as Prime Minister. The forces that made the revolution, however, proved quite incapable of supporting the Democratic Government it had brought to power. The hated police and security forces were turned out of office and, with the army politically uncommitted, there was no force left to maintain order. The economic policy measures introduced by the Chang Myon

Government were those that had been ineffectually urged on the Rhee regime by American representatives. Politically difficult at any time, they were totally unacceptable to Chang Myon's constituency. As the regime limped along with popular forces out of control, fear of Communist penetration increased. Consequently, many Koreans breathed a sigh of relief when, on May 16, 1961, a small group of military officers with, perhaps 3,000 men overthrew the Chang Myon Government and assumed power.

The military group that seized power had little use for politics or politicians. The National Assembly was dissolved and a Supreme Council for National Reconstruction was formed to govern Korea. The constitutional reforms of the Chang Myon Government were ignored, and central control over local government was reestablished. Military officers were appointed as governors of the provinces and mayors of the chief cities. "Some 2,000 former politicians were arrested and about 17,000 civil servants and 2,000 military officers were either arrested, dismissed or retired."[1] The gangs that had flourished in the cities during the Chang Myon regime were rounded up and order was reestablished. Demonstrations were forbidden and the number of newspapers cut down drastically. The young colonels and lower-rank generals who had made the coup intended to establish a strong executive-type government unimpeded by politics and politicians or any such democratic nonsense.

The new Park Military Government sought to achieve a more rapid economic growth and to redress such wrongs as excessive indebtedness and low prices for farmers. Their expansionary fiscal and monetary policies inevitably led to rapid inflation and deterioration in the balance of payment. The economic situation was further worsened by a disastrous harvest in 1962 that necessitated a large increase in grain imports. The decline in foreign exchange holdings led to increased trade restrictions. From an economic point of view, the 1960s did not begin auspiciously. The Park Military Government had, however, made it clear that economic development and a lessening of dependence on the United States were to be its primary objectives. In 1961 the First Five-Year Economic Development Plan (1962–1966) was announced with a target growth rate of 7 percent per annum. In the light of the economic performance of the early 1960s this target seemed absurdly high but, in the event, it was exceeded. South Korea, in whose future American advisers had nearly abandoned hope, was on the verge of one of the most rapid sustained growth experiences known to economic history.

In the political arena, it soon became clear to the military junta that they could not continue to govern effectively without the support of a wider constituency. They were encouraged in this persuasion by threats from the United States to discontinue assistance unless there was a clear commitment to move toward civilian control. Consequently a new constitution was drafted and approved by a plebiscite in December 1962. It provided for a strong president, able to dismiss prime minister and cabinet without the consent of the legislature, and a weak national assembly. Central control of provincial and local government was maintained. The government announced the formation of a new party, the Democratic Republican Party, and authorized members of the Supreme Council for National Reconstruction to run for office. In the elections of October and November 1963, Park Chung Hee was elected President, though by a minority vote, and the government party obtained 110 of the 175 seats on the National Assembly.

THE ECONOMIC TAKEOFF IN KOREA

The beginning of the period of rapid economic growth is usually dated from 1963 when the increase in GNP in real terms was 8.8 percent as compared to an average of about 3 percent in the preceding three years. The shift was not quite as abrupt as the figures suggest. Recovery of agricultural production was largely responsible for the high growth rates in 1963 and 1964.

Stabilization measures imposed in 1963 and 1964 cut the

growth of manufacturing to only 6.5 percent in 1964 as the credit squeeze affected all businesses except those that were beginning to enter the export sphere. Still, when full account is taken of these vagaries, it remains a fact that from 1963 to date there has never been a year in which the growth of GNP in real terms has fallen below 6 percent; and in 1969 and 1976 it exceeded 15 percent. For the whole period 1963–1976, the average rate has been about 10 percent. This is a remarkable record by any standard.

Korean development has frequently been described as export-led industrialization and, indeed, the rate of growth of manu-factured output and export earnings has been phenomenal. It has changed the structure of the Korean economy drastically since 1960 as Table 134 indicates.

TABLE 134 Average Primary and Industrial Output Shares
at Factor Costs
(1970 prices)

	1960–1962	*1973–1975*
Agriculture, forestry, and fishing	.452	.246
Mining and quarrying	.015	.012
Primary total	.467	.258
Manufacturing	.094	.272
Construction	.027	.055
Utilities	.006	.020
Industry total	.127	.346

Source: Kim and Roemer, p. 61.

In the short space of a decade and a half South Korea became what is by Third World standards a highly industrialized economy. According to census figures, employment in agricul-ture and forestry as a percent of the labor force fell from 61.4 in 1960 to 48.5 in 1970, while employment in manufactures rose from 6.8 percent to 14.3 percent.

During this period high levels of investment were sustained by substantial increases in both domestic and foreign savings. The rates of return on investment were high, and a large share of profits was reinvested. Export earnings as a percent of GNP increased from an average of 3 percent in 1960–1962 to an average of 32 percent in 1974–1976; domestic savings from an average of 3.5 percent in 1960–1962 to an average of 17.5 percent in 1974–1976, and total investment from an average of 10.1 percent in the earlier period to 25 percent in the later. Foreign savings continued to be an important source of foreign exchange and investment, though its average share of total investment declined from 75.4 percent in 1960–1962 to 30 percent in 1974–1976.

While the labor force after 1960 grew at a rate of about 3 percent, the farm labor force remained relatively constant while, as farm workers moved to the cities, the non-farm labor force expanded at an average rate of about 6 percent. Unemployment fell from an average of 7.8 percent in 1960–1962 to 4.5 percent in 1970–1972. By the middle of the 1960s, South Korea had ceased to be a labor-surplus economy. Real wages in manufacturing, which had remained fairly constant from 1960 to 1965, more than doubled in the decade 1965 to 1975.

Although the growth of the Korean economy remained dependent on foreign savings during the whole of the period since 1960, both the trade balance and the balance of payments improved steadily. In 1977 Korea's trade balance was for the first time in surplus; export earnings exceeded payments for imports. Not only had the country achieved a high and sustained rate of growth, but it was no longer economically dependent on the United States or, indeed, any other country, for economic favors.

SOURCES OF GROWTH

Econometrically inclined, model-building economists are accustomed to explain, or at least attempt to explain, the growth of an economy in terms of an increase in inputs of capital, labor and land, and improvements in the productivity of these inputs. Productivity is considered to be increased by technological developments, increasing scale of output, an expanded rate of capital utilization, improvements in the health and education of workers, better allocation of resources, improvements in organization, and by other factors. Early in the development of this aggregative production-function type of analysis, the so-called "residual" left to be explained after account had been taken of the effect on output in increases in inputs of primary factors was considered to be large. In growing economies, productivity-increasing inputs (the residual) were sometimes found to outweigh the effect of primary inputs. Later, attempts have been made to measure the effects of some of these productivity-increasing inputs, particularly the education and training of workers, embodied and disembodied changes in technology, and the influence of changing scales of output. Insofar as plausible results have been achieved, they have had the effect of reducing the unexplained residual. Such attempts have been made to examine the sources of Korean growth with results to be considered presently.

Behind these changes in factor inputs and factor productivity lie changes in government policy affecting incentives and disincentives and changes in the institutional structures through which economic activities get organized. The program of economic liberalization introduced in Korea by policy changes in 1964 and 1965 is considered by many to be critical in the explanation of later growth. A sharp devaluation of the wŏn was accompanied by changes in trade, fiscal, and monetary policies that gave a new direction to Korean development. Along with these policy changes came institutional developments that significantly altered economic management. The First Five-Year Plan went into effect in 1962 and, in the years following, the Economic Planning Board developed an important role in the direction of resource use. The development of money and capital markets, the growth of an impressive group of business enterprises, the creation of a close and effective set of government-business relations, the growth of a large public enterprise sector, all affected the productivity of resource inputs.

Behind these policy and institutional changes was the emergence of a strong government capable of maintaining political stability thereby reducing uncertainty in business expectations, able to introduce policy changes difficult or impossible for a weaker and more fractionalized government, and capable of implementing these policy changes effectively; a government that embraced economic growth as a primary objective and as a principal legitimizer of its holding of power.

As we discussed in Chapter 3 and reemphasized at the beginning of this summary chapter, behind these sources of growth was a population with certain cultural characteristics and receptivity to foreign influences propitious to economic development. A common language and culture has facilitated a geographical and social mobility. The Confucian heritage has predisposed Koreans to value education highly and has favored the development of a disciplined and industrious labor force. Given the opportunity and assisted by powerful external influences emanating from Japan and the United States, the individual and social characteristics of the people have provided the proper seedbed for growth. To attain some insight into the development process, it is necessary to peel off these layers of explanation and consider their interrelationship.

In Chapter 4, we summarized a study of Korea's economic development in macroeconomic terms dealing with aggregate and sectorial growth rates of domestic and national product. The chapter dealt mainly with the period 1960–1973 when the average growth rate of gross domestic product at factor cost was 8.9 percent and the period 1963–1973 when GDP grew at 9.9 percent. An attempt was made to measure the sources of growth in the economy as a whole, of the private sector, the non-agricultural economy, of manufacturing, and of mining and manufacturing. Despite serious conceptual and statistical difficulties, the studies referred to throw considerable light on the relative importance of various inputs. During the period 1963–1973, reproducible capital grew very rapidly, at an annual rate of 8.3 percent for the economy as a whole and 10.4 percent in the manufacturing sector. These were the years in which foreign technology along with capital equipment was being imported, and consequently measures of the effect of capital inputs on output reflect the results of embodied technical change. The productivity of labor and capital was also increased by shifts in structure of production from lower to higher productivity employment. Christensen and Cummings estimate that for the private sector shifts of this sort produced a growth of 1.4 percent a year in the productivity of capital.[2] Of overriding importance in measuring the rate of growth of capital inputs, at least in manufactures, was an increase in the rate of utilization. Young Chin Kim and Jene K. Kwon found that, measured by increasing electric power consumption, the rate of capital utilization in manufacture increased by 80 percent between 1962 and 1971.[3]

Since it is the services of capital rather than physical availability that produce output, these figures lead Kim and Roemer to raise the rate of increase in capital inputs in manufacture from 10.4 to 18.7 percent for the period 1960–1973. Unfortunately no data on capital utilization are available outside the field of manufacture.

The labor force for the economy as a whole grew much more slowly than capital, although the rate was much higher in the non-agricultural sector and in manufactures. Measured in labor hours, the rate of increase during the period 1963–1973 was 4.6 for the economy as a whole, 7.7 percent in the non-agricultural economy, and 10.7 in mining and manufacturing. There have been several attempts to account for the effect of increases in the quality of labor on the rate of increase in output. A study by Chang Young Jeong, the results of which are used by Kim and Roemer in their calculations, attributes a 2.2 percent per annum growth rate in human capital per worker for the economy as a whole.[4]

Inputs of land in South Korea, in terms of acres, were relatively constant. The contribution of land enters to a small extent in various measures of capital inputs. But the effects of improvements in the productivity of agricultural land is not usually taken into account in these aggregative calculations. Yet there has been a substantial shift in land use in recent years towards more valuable crops and important changes in agricultural techniques. The value of land in South Korea has, moreover, risen rapidly.

The years 1960 to 1970 saw a substantial increase in the scale of plants and enterprises in Korean manufacture, but we are unaware of any attempt to measure the effects of those changes on the productivity of capital and labor. In a study of sources of economic growth in Japan between 1961 and 1971, Edward F. Denison and William K. Chung attribute as much as 20 percent to the effects on productivity of an increase in the scale of economic activity.[5] Nor do studies of Korean growth attempt to measure the effects of other changes such as improvements in management, better health of workers, and others that may well have affected productivity. Conceptual and statistical difficulties in these attempts at a quantitative assessment of sources of Korean growth inevitably leave a large unexplained residual. Still some impressions emerge with relative clarity, for example, the importance of rapidly increasing inputs of capital with embodied technical improvements, the effects of large changes in the rate of capital utilization, and the significance of improvements in the quality of labor inputs.

Behind these quantitative increases in inputs and outputs lay, as we have suggested, some significant changes in economic policy and in the institutional arrangements affecting the mobilization and allocation of resources. The basic policy changes that reoriented the Korean economy away from import-substitution toward export-led industrialization took place in the years 1964 through 1967. These are discussed in Chapter 5. In May 1964, the wŏn was devalued from 130 to 255 to the dollar, nearly a 100 percent devaluation. Shortly thereafter a

470

unitary rate took the place of the existing multiple rates. Interest rate reforms in 1965 approximately doubled bank rates for various types of loans. Other important reforms included a restructuring of the tariff system using the concept of effective protection and a thorough-going revision of the tax structure which, together with improvements in tax administration, produced a substantial increase in government revenue. In the eyes of some observers these policy changes constitute *the* explanation of Korea's subsequent rapid economic growth. According to Gilbert Brown, "The almost irresistible conclusion from Korean development experience is that with proper economic policies and a continuation of reasonable international aid levels most developing countries can achieve at least a 6 percent annual growth rate, and many countries could sustain growth rates as high as 10 percent."[6]

Although these policy changes were indeed of great importance there were other sources of growth as we have noted and shall summarize presently, and it is by no means true that any less-developed country by adopting a similar set of policies could achieve the Korean growth rate.

The policy changes of 1964–1967 have been described as a liberalization of the economy and to a certain extent this is correct. Devaluation and a doubling of interest rates brought the prices of foreign exchange and of money much closer to their equilibrium values and permitted the market to take over from administrative decision-making a greater role in shaping business decisions. These changes plus the revision of the tariff system brought the Korean price structure in closer touch with international prices and lessened many egregious price distortions. But they did not in one stroke produce a market-dominated economy. Korean industrialization and export expansion as well as other aspects of development have remained and continue to be very much a government-directed process. Over the next few years the price level increased 35–40 percent, while the exchange rate depreciated much more slowly. The result was a sharp increase in imports and a growing deficit in the balance of payments which led to a tightening of import limitations and an increase in some export incentives such as increased wastage allowances.

This alternation between periods of liberalization with the market assuming greater importance and periods of increased government intervention has been characteristic of Korean development, but at all stages it has been consistently a government direction of resource use. This direction has in general produced a trade pattern favorable to the exploitation of Korea's comparative advantage but a government-directed development nonetheless.

Nor has the government's promotion of export-oriented growth been limited to the manipulation of incentives. It has provided strong institutional support to exporters via the government-subsidized Korean Trade Promotion Corporation, and an authorization of the collection by the Korean Traders Association of one percent of the value of imports to be used as an export promotion fund. The government, furthermore, established in 1962 annual export targets detailed by commodity, markets to be penetrated, and by firms. An export situation room in the Ministry of Commerce and Industry carefully monitored the performance of individual firms with respect to these export targets. The government has also established industrial estates catering to the requirements of export-oriented enterprises. These estates are not only provided with a full range of utility services but are equipped with branch offices of central ministries and departments dealing with the import, export, and financial arrangements required to facilitate trade expansion.

In addition to change in the field of trade policy, the new government pursued an aggressive fiscal and monetary policy as indicated in Chapter 9. With the rapid decline in foreign grant assistance after 1965 it was necessary to mobilize both domestic and foreign savings to finance the growth of the economy. Although there have been substantial changes in the tax structure and tax rates since the mid-1960s, improvements in tax administration and the rapid growth of the tax base have been the principal contributors to the increase in government revenues. A determined effort to collect taxes was largely responsible for the increase in the ratio of tax receipts to GNP from 7.2 percent in 1964 to 14.4 percent in 1968. Over the years since 1968 indirect taxes, customs duties, and monopoly profits have accounted for from 60 to 75 percent of total national revenue, while personal income and corporate taxes have produced the remainder. The adoption by the government of realistic pricing policies for its government enterprises in the mid-1960s together with substantial improvements in their efficiency also significantly increased revenues. As a result of these developments, the ratio of tax yields to GNP increased from an average of about 9 percent in 1964–1966 to an average of about 17 percent in 1974–1976.

The increase in revenue together with repression of consumption expenditures permitted the government to move from a position of net dissaver to that of a net saver in 1964. From that point on, government savings increased rapidly to a high point of 7 percent of GNP in 1970, then dropped to 3 percent in the recession year of 1974 when large government expenditures were required to sustain output and employment but have since recovered. Government savings and business savings have been about equally important since 1960 with household savings showing large fluctuations while accounting, on the average, for not more than 20 percent of the total. Total domestic savings which averaged about 5 percent of GNP in the mid-1960s had grown to an average of about 16 percent in the late 1960s and early 1970s. It attained the unusually high figure of 22 percent in 1973, from which it since receded. On the whole, however, it is our judgment, expressed in Chapter 9, that considering the extremely rapid increase in GNP, marginal savings and tax ratios have not been impressive.

On the other hand, the success of the government in mobilizing foreign savings has permitted a rate of gross investment that has averaged well over 25 percent of GNP since 1968. Since

1964 foreign savings have averaged about 40 percent of total investment and have varied from a low point of 5.6 percent of GNP (in 1972) to a high point of 11.5 percent (in 1968). The fact that economic assistance had been on a grant basis until 1965, which permitted Korea to enter capital markets with a very low burden of foreign debt, was an initial inducement to foreign lenders, but the very high rate of growth of export earnings has provided the continuing incentive. Although relatively high rates of debt service charges to export earnings was a source of some alarm both in Korea and abroad in the early 1970s, the surge of exports since 1972 has alleviated those fears. By 1975 Korea was considered one of the safest repositories for foreign investment in the Third World.

On the expenditure side of the budget, the major shares have been accounted for by defense, economic services, and social services. Despite the maintenance of large armed forces, massive foreign military assistance has permitted the Korean government to hold defense spending to a modest 4 to 4.5 percent of GNP since 1965. This drain on the budget fell from 32.3 percent of general government expenditures in 1965 to 24.5 percent in 1975. This is an item, however, that has begun to increase and will probably increase further. Expenditures on economic services substantially increased from 24.9 percent of the budget in 1965 to 37.3 percent in 1975 with heavy emphasis in the later years on transportation and communications. Expenditures on education have accounted for over 60 percent of social services during the decade despite the fact that a very large percentage of the costs of education is borne by households. As indicated in Chapter 11, public expenditures on health, social security, welfare, and other community services have been minimal.

The Korean financial system closely coordinates the taxing and spending powers of the fisc and the borrowing and lending powers of financial institutions, and both fiscal and bank lending policies are powerful instruments in controlling the direction of economic development. The Bank of Korea, the main commercial banks, and all the special banks for agriculture, industry, foreign trade, and so on are publicly owned and are controlled by the Ministry of Finance. On the fiscal side, differential taxes and subsidies and, on the monetary side, preferential lending rates are used to influence business decisions. Early in the 1960s the introduction of a system of government loan guarantees was instrumental in opening the door for massive foreign borrowing by business. Approved enterprises were permitted to work out loan agreements with foreign leaders, often in the form of suppliers' credits. After approval by the Economic Planning Board these loans were guaranteed by government-designated banks. As we emphasized in Chapter 8, the use of preferential bank credit and the control of foreign borrowing were two of the most potent instruments through which government direction of economic development has been exercised. Whether an even more rapid growth might have been attained by allowing a greater role to the market, particularly in the determination of foreign exchange and interest rates, is an open question.

The Korean financial system appears to have been more influential in determining the direction of investment than in mobilizing domestic resources. On the whole, it is probably true to say that the financial system has, at least until recently, lagged somewhat behind other aspects of development. At various stages, money and capital markets have been unduly fractionated with financial intermediaries unable to perform effectively the task of equalizing the marginal costs of, and returns to, capital employed in different activities with similar risks. At the time of the interest rate reforms in 1965, an uncontrolled curb market provided perhaps a quarter of total business borrowing at rates that were a multiple of bank rates. The reforms led to a marked diminution of curb activities, but these subsequently recovered when low bank deposit rates led to tightened credit rationing. Government control of bank lending rates has had some influence on the direction of investment, but it has mainly served to handicap the mobilization of domestic savings and prevent financial intermediaries from an effective development of capital market services. Since 1972, however, the government has made a determined effort to promote financial institutions offering an alternative to private money lenders and has made some progress in establishing a securities market, but one that is still dominated by the Ministry of Finance.

The reforms of 1964–1967 were primarily concerned with trade, fiscal, and monetary policies, and the effects of changes in these on business incentives have been at the center of government attention since then. But export-led industrialization has been the result of the activities of a large number of enterprises, public and private, and the growth of business organization has been one of the remarkable aspects of Korean development. We attempted to deal with various aspects of this growth in Chapter 8. Although South Korea is thought of as one of the most capitalistically oriented countries in the Third World, the public enterprise sector is large. From 1963 to 1972, value added in this sector grew at the rate of 14.5 percent a year, while the whole economy was growing at 9.5 percent and the non-agricultural economy at 12.2 percent. During these years the public sector absorbed 30 percent of gross investments. In terms of value added it is comparable in share to the public enterprise sector in India.[7]

The fact is that the Korean government during the period of rapid growth has maintained a highly pragmatic attitude towards the issue of public versus private enterprise. It has not hesitated to ask a private firm to take over when public management has stumbled, as in the case of the Korean Air Lines. On the other hand, it has not hesitated to use public enterprise to avoid or overcome market imperfections.

Another sizable sector of manufacturing, as we noted in Chapter 6, is represented by foreign enterprise including joint ventures with Korean entrepreneurs. The first foreign direct investment project approved by the Korean government was a joint U.S.-Korea venture producing nylon filament in 1962. From then till the end of 1976, the Economic Planning Board estimates a total direct foreign investment of about $950 million.

From 1962 to 1968 foreign investments were predominantly American, directed mainly toward import-replacing activities. Since then they have been predominantly Japanese and concerned mainly with production for export. Over the whole period, Japan and the United States have accounted for 83 percent of total foreign direct investment.

The share of foreign firms and joint ventures in total output in mining and manufacturing was about 10 percent in 1974, but in certain industries such as petroleum, metal and metal products, and electric machinery and electronics it was much larger. Foreign investment in chemicals was also considerable, though its share of output was only 15 percent. Although foreign invested firms accounted for only 10 percent of manufactured output, their share of manufactured exports in 1974 was over 30 percent. In certain industries their share was very high, notably machinery and machine parts, (93.4 percent), electric and electronic components (88.6 percent), and metal products (84.2 percent).

Modern industrial technology in South Korea has until recently been almost entirely a foreign import. It has been acquired in connection with foreign direct investment and also through technological licensing agreements entered into by Korean firms. Foreign personnel have been employed in considerable numbers both by foreign firms and by Korean firms introducing these products or processes, particularly engineers, and specialists in financial management, overseas marketing and sources of raw materials supply. But these numbers have diminished rapidly as Koreans have been trained to take over.

Although the Korean government has been receptive to foreign private investment, most business firms, encouraged by government, have preferred to get their capital from abroad by borrowing rather than through joint ventures. It appears to be the view in the Economic Planning Board, and elsewhere in government circles, that the burden of repatriation is likely to be substantially less than in the case of direct investment. And most of the technology and technical expertise required to be imported can be effectively obtained via technological and management contracts. In the light of these preferences, and despite the fact that government policy does not place serious obstacles to direct investment, it seems likely that the share of foreign firms and joint ventures in manufacturing will decline rather than increase.

Although public enterprise and foreign firms account for a sizable fraction of output in mining and manufacture, more than three-quarters of output and of value added in these sectors is produced by wholly Korean-owned firms which account for nine-tenths of employment. The emergence of a large group of able entrepreneurs and managers is one of the important sources of Korean growth. In Chapter 8 we reported on a number of case studies of selected small enterprises and large conglomerates and on the results of an entrepreneurship and management survey by Jones and SaKong of a random sample of Korean enterprises.

AGRICULTURAL DEVELOPMENT

A shift of employment from agriculture to industry is characteristic of development in all countries, but in South Korea it has been extremely rapid. As we noted in Chapter 7, the share of farm population in the total was 61 percent in 1953, 55 percent in 1965, and was down to 38 percent in 1975. The farms have supplied the surplus labor that has fueled industrial expansion. Korea, in fact, ceased to be a labor-surplus economy some time in the middle 1960s. Real wages in urban areas began to rise rapidly around 1965, and the increasing scarcity of labor on the farms was one of the factors responsible for accelerated mechanization beginning in the late 1960s.

Although agriculture, with its average growth rate of output of about 3 percent per annum over the three decades since 1945, has not contributed a large share to the total growth rate, Korean agriculture is far from backward. Judged by productivity

478

per acre, indeed, it is one of the most advanced countries. Its rice yields nearly match those of heavily subsidized rice cultivation in Japan. The endowment of arable land is, on a per capita basis, one of the smallest in the world which explains the intensity of cultivation. Although extensive land reclamation projects have, in recent years, added something to total cultivable acreage, it has been hardly more than enough to compensate for the loss of farm land to the cities. This land shortage has forced Korea to continue to be a heavy importer of foodstuffs. Like Japan, South Korea, albeit unwillingly, has opted for emphasis on non-grain crops and has imported grain from abroad. Imports of agricultural and food products averaged $664.6 million in the years 1971 to 1975.

Since the total cultivated acreage is not much larger than in the 1930s, increases in agricultural output are almost wholly attributable to increased productivity per acre. And since labor inputs since 1960 have been relatively constant, the sources of productivity increases have to be sought elsewhere. They are to be found mainly in increased fertilizer inputs encouraged at first by AID-financed imports and later provided by domestic output, by improvements in seed varieties, and by the effect of rising urban demand in shifting cultivation away from grain production toward more highly valued crops. Until the late 1960s, government had very little to do with increasing the value of agricultural output; indeed for most of the period after the Korean War, government purchases of grain at low prices to alleviate the burden of inflation on city dwellers turned the terms of trade against agriculture. This policy changed beginning in 1969 partly as a result of the effect of a series of poor harvests on agricultural incomes, but partly also because government setbacks in the plebiscite of 1969 and the elections of 1971 suggested the need of cultivating the favors of the farm population. Grain prices were raised on the farms and continued to be maintained at a low level in the cities financed by outright government subsidy.

Serious government encouragement to agriculture has been

limited to the first few years after Independence and to the years after 1969. In the decade and a half between those periods government efforts were comparatively feeble, and those that were undertaken were heavily dependent on USAID. The land reforms of 1947 and 1948 did not increase productivity but transformed the distribution of agricultural assets and incomes in South Korea. The number of families owning all the land they farmed rose dramatically. The amount of rented land fell from 60 percent to less than 15 percent. The number of tenants fell to a miniscule 5–7 percent of the agriculture labor force. One reason why productivity did not increase as a result of land reform was because government made little effort to replace functions formerly performed by landlords.

Although the First Five-Year Plan (1962–1966) and the Second Five-Year Plan (1967–1971) announced significant agricultural programs, not much was done to implement them outside the areas of seed improvement and land reclamation. The Third Five-Year Plan (1972–1976), however, greatly increased the emphasis on rural development. Public investment in agriculture was four times that of the Second Five-Year Plan. Another notable government effort was the introduction of the Saemaul Undong (New Community Movement) in 1971. This program included income-generating projects based on cooperative work, with the government providing technical and financial assistance for improving facilities in education, health, housing, roads, electrification, communications, and other services.

The agricultural services provided by government are as heavily centralized as are all other South Korean government services. Agricultural extension services are provided by the Office of Rural Development with more than two thousand extension agents constituting a highly centralized bureaucracy with headquarters in Suwŏn.

The National Agricultural Cooperative Foundation is also a centrally directed bureaucracy operating through branch offices.

The members of the local organizations have little voice in determining either policies or operating procedures.

THE BENEFICIARIES OF KOREA'S GROWTH

As Chapter 12 argues persuasively, all major groups in Korean society have benefited from the extraordinarily rapid growth in national income since the early 1960s, though obviously some groups have benefited more than others. It has been generally recognized that Korea is a prime example of how growth can be achieved with equity and, if the Korean record is compared with that of most less-developed countries, there is no reason to question this proposition. A more complete understanding, however, of the relation of growth to income distribution in Korea can be achieved only by a disaggregation of the increase in income into its component parts. How is income distributed within the agricultural sector, within the urban sector, between the agricultural and urban sectors; and what has happened to business income?

The data that can be marshaled to answer these questions come from farm and urban household surveys, wage and salary surveys, and income tax returns. Though somewhat superior and more abundant than similar data in most less-developed countries, they are still insufficient in a number of aspects. In particular, they are weak in discerning the characteristics of the upper segment of the income scale. With respect to farm and urban household incomes, for most of the urban population, and for per capita incomes and the wage earnings of blue and white collar workers, they are adequate, at least since the early 1960s, to distinguish changes in income relationships. Chapter 12 applies to these data the various standard measures of income inequality.

With respect to income distribution within the rural sector the land reform measures of the late 1940s and early 1950s achieved a degree of equality that is rare in any country and that has not been lost in later development. Prior to land reform, about 4 percent of the rural population (the landlords) received about one-quarter of all farm income. After land reform, Japanese landlords had lost everything, and Korean landlords on the average had received compensation equivalent to perhaps one-sixth to one-fourth of their former land assets. The ultimate beneficiaries of this transfer of income were the former tenants. Since land reform was completed, there has been little in the way of trend in the distribution of income within the rural sector and only a very modest tendency for land ownership to become more concentrated. Although there was and is some difference in per capita and household farm incomes in different geographical areas, the cultural homogeneity and relatively small size of Korea has severely limited the degree of regional inequality.

Urban wage and salary differences are also not great, and there has been little discernable trend in these differences. Regional differences in wages are clearly on the decline as early market fragmentation has given way to increased mobility. There appears to be an increasing gap, however, between white and blue collar workers caused perhaps by the increasing size of the urban administrative class.

In Korea as in most countries there has been a substantial and persistent gap between urban and rural incomes though, at least in recent years, the gap is nowhere near as large as in most less-developed countries. The difference in rural and urban incomes has fluctuated rather widely as a result principally of variations in crop yields and changes in the government's grain price policies. Since 1969 the terms of trade have moved conspicuously in favor of agriculture and, in 1975, rural household incomes were 84 percent of household incomes in urban areas and per capita farm incomes 77 percent of urban per capita wage and salary incomes.

There are no really good data on business income and its

distribution in Korea or on the incomes of the upper tail of the income distribution. There are indications, however, that this income has been rising more rapidly for a number of years than has income in other sectors. Because of definitional differences, tax avoidance, and outright evasion, there is a very large difference between business income as reported in the national accounts and those indicated by the tax records, and there is reason to believe that the national accounts give a truer estimate of business income than the tax records. As we saw in Chapter 8, government encouragement to business and the very high ratio of debt to equity in Korean corporations has produced a high rate and a rapidly growing volume of profits. This is not adequately depicted in the data on income distribution. If it were adequately taken into account, Korea's income distribution would appear to be more unequal than some previous calculations have suggested. This does not mean, however, that Korea should be removed from the category of countries achieving growth with equity. Figures for other less-developed nations with which Korea is often compared are subject to the same kind of biases, often in more extreme form.

In Korea, as in other countries, there is a clear relation between the distribution of educational opportunities and the distribution of income. Those who leave school after a primary education receive lower incomes than graduates of secondary schools; secondary school dropouts receive less than graduates of high schools, and university graduates are among the highest of income receivers. There is, however, considerable debate on why this is so. Does superior education increase productivity or does it primarily signify membership in an elite group from which top governmental and business positions are filled? As we saw in Chapter 8, business leaders are, on the whole, not only highly educated but are drawn overwhelmingly from groups that were elite even before industrialization. On the other hand, there is ample evidence that superior education is a necessary ingredient to the performance of leadership functions.

One thing that is clear from the Korean experience is that educational opportunities are more evenly spread than in all but a small fraction of countries at similar income levels.

An examination of the impact of government tax and expenditure policies on income distribution leads to the rather tentative conclusion that the operation of the budget exerted a modest influence toward reducing inequality in both the rural and urban sectors.

In sum, rapid growth in Korea has been accompanied by a relatively equitable distribution of income despite the fact that, at the upper end of the scale, incomes have grown distinctly more rapidly than income as a whole. For the most part, these higher incomes have gone not to rentiers or to corrupt government officials but to a highly productive entrepreneurial class. Whether these business incomes were more than sufficient to induce the level of entrepreneurial activity Korea experienced was a question we raised in Chapter 8 but found impossible to answer. Whether the relative equity of income distribution has promoted political stability and thus contributed to economic growth is another interesting question equally impossible to answer.

THE ROLE OF GOVERNMENT
IN KOREAN ECONOMIC DEVELOPMENT

Behind the changes in policy and institutions that have characterized the period of rapid growth since 1963, there has existed an authoritarian and highly centralized government whose primary goal has been the acceleration of economic growth. It is a government that has maintained an extraordinary degree of political and social stability in the sense that its announced purposes and policies have not been subject to serious and organized efforts to oppose them. It has been able to initiate policy changes and to implement them in ways that would be difficult or impossible for a more democratic government to do. It is a government in which the decision-making process is in relatively few hands which has some developmental advantages and disadvantages but, in the short-run at least, the advantages probably outweigh the disadvantages. In South Korea a highly profitable and dynamic group of private enterprises operate under a comprehensive system of government direction but there is no question who calls the tune; it is the government. "Korea, Inc.," is undoubtedly a more apt description of the situation in Korea than is "Japan, Inc." of the situation in Japan.

As we saw in Chapter 2, South Korea since 1961 has moved away from a government with some of the trappings of democracy toward one with very few. The Constitution of 1962 established a government with a strong executive and a weak legislature and changes since then have strengthened the former and weakened the latter. The control of central government over provincial and local government were also reestablished in 1962. A plebiscite in 1969 authorized a third term for President Park, and the Yusin Constitution of 1972 not only authorized an indefinite term in office but greatly expanded presidential powers. Although the armed forces as such play little or no role in the shaping of developmental policies, retired army officers hold many government positions and manage a large percentage of public enterprises. South Korea does not have a military government but one that is strongly backed by the military.

It is a government that has shown itself capable of undertaking policy changes that, while in the national interest, have adversely affected the interests of sizable groups. Periodic devaluations have raised prices in an economy in which a large percent of total investment is imported and has increased the debt burden, in local currency, for enterprises that have borrowed abroad. Devaluation is a difficult step for a weak government to take. The Park regime has succeeded in raising government revenues substantially faster than current expenditures, thus producing a relatively high rate of government savings. For most governments increasing expenditures is politically more palatable than increasing taxation. The manner in which the government handled the oil crisis when the prices of imported oil quadrupled in 1973, by introducing conservation measures that quadrupled the price of gasoline and levied higher taxes on privately owned motor cars, would be difficult in a more democratic regime.

As we saw in Chapter 8, rapid industrialization in Korea has produced a group of large-scale, multi-firm enterprises representing a considerable degree of economic concentration. But these concentrations are in a decidedly weaker position vis-à-vis government than in most Asian countries partly because of public control of domestic credit and the necessity of securing government permission to borrow abroad. There is in Korea nothing like the zaibatsu groups of pre-war Japan whose ownership of banks was an element critical to their economic power. Since 1968, moreover, a series of measures under the heading of Law for Inducing Business Corporations to go Public have had considerable success in weakening the position of family groups while at the same time promoting the growth of security markets. Measures to enforce these laws have included unfavorable treatment in calculating corporate and personal income taxes and limitations on loans from public financial institutions. While large-scale enterprises are consulted by government in shaping economic policies and procedures, it is clearly government that has the whip hand.

The strength of the South Korean government is even more obvious in implementation than it is in the formulation of developing policies. In Myrdal's definition it is indeed a "hard state" capable of putting its policy measures into effect. As we noted in Chapter 9, the rapid increase in government revenues after 1965 was largely the result of improvements in tax administration under a newly established Office of National Tax Administration relatively free from political interference. Implementation of other policies has been as vigorous as that of taxation. If planning and policy-making are to be effective, there must be a set of mechanisms whereby individual and enterprise compliance is stimulated, forced, or cajoled. South Korea, in contrast to India and, indeed, to most less-developed countries, is even better at implementation than at planning. In Chapter 8, we discussed the various techniques used to "stimulate, force, and cajole" but crucial to the effectiveness of these techniques is a government capable of seeing that its programs are carried out.

The management of public enterprises is another area in which the impress of a hard state is visible. In many, if not most, less-developed countries, the public enterprise sector is subject to political interference and is commonly a major contributor to government deficits. This is not so in Korea. Although data are lacking to permit a comparison of the efficiency in the public and private enterprise in Korea, cases of serious inefficiency in the public sector are rapidly brought to the attention of the president. Public enterprise output in goods and services is priced close to social marginal costs, and the technical efficiency of production is demonstrably high. Far from being a source of deficits, the earnings of public sector enterprise make a sizable contribution to government revenue.

Government policy has deliberately kept labor organization weak, and the right to strike is unknown. Consequently South Korea has avoided the pressure from organized labor that in many Third World countries has maintained urban wages at artificially high levels, has led to the overstaffing of public enterprises, and has frequently seriously disrupted production. Wage rates have been determined by the market, and the rapid rise in wages since 1965 has been entirely a market phenomenon unassisted by government or union action. Since workers move relatively freely among various types of employment, there are few wage disparities to suggest an inefficient allocation. The maintenance of strict control over organized labor has undoubtedly been a factor favoring high profits and the reinvestment of earnings. The costs of such a policy have obviously been a serious repression of civil rights and, no doubt, in some cases an exploitation of workers by unscrupulous employers.

Policy decisions are made in South Korea by an extraordinarily small group of top officials. The President, in addition to receiving advice and information from individual ministries and the Council of Ministers has important independent sources in his strong secretariat and the Korean CIA. There is no doubt he is extraordinarily well informed on all aspects of economic development. He frequently takes a hand in initiating changes and, of course, all serious policy matters are referred to him. Minor changes in economic policy are made without consulting affected groups; others are "sold" to the public by carefully orchestrated publicity; it is relatively rare that a policy change becomes a matter of widespread public debate. The introduction of a value-added tax in 1976 and attempted introduction of a social security tax in 1975 are exceptions. The location in the Economic Planning Board of the Bureau of Budget assures that medium-term planning is closely articulated with annual budgeting and makes the head of the EPB, who is the Deputy Prime Minister, the principal officer for the coordination of economic policy.

We have been primarily concerned with the economic aspects of development and the sources of growth. Although the principal sources are evident, they are also numerous and it is impossible to give a quantitative estimate of their individual importance. The fact that all countries penetrated by the East Asian culture outside of China have shown similar rates of growth is a fact whose significance cannot be denied. In the eyes of some observers the macroeconomic policies espoused by the Park Government in the early 1960s and developed over time are an element of overriding importance and their relevance, indeed, is clear. But we do not feel that the adoption of similar policies could necessarily guarantee success to any less-developed country. Too many other factors were involved in the Korean case.

Massive foreign economic assistance particularly from the United States undoubtedly paved the way for an economic takeoff. Furthermore, if we assume that the maintenance of large military forces was necessary to South Korean security, the even more massive military assistance from the United States permitted these forces to be kept in being without an inordinant drain on the budget and on the economy. The modern technology which accelerated Korea's industrial growth came mainly from the United States and Japan financed in part by foreign assistance, and these two countries have provided the principal markets for the remarkable growth in exports and export earnings. The adaptability of the economy to external influences and the encouragement given by government to foreign investment and technological and managerial transfers have made their contribution.

The early accomplishment of comprehensive land reform, so difficult for most countries, and the expansion of educational facilities have helped to assure that the benefits of economic growth have been widely shared.

Finally and, in our view a factor of basic importance, has been the existence since 1963 of a government capable of maintaining political stability, of introducing policies that have been difficult for most less-developed countries to undertake, and of implementing those policies firmly and effectively. The economic record to date has been remarkable, but there remains the question whether Korea's exceptionally rapid growth is likely to be sustained.

FUTURE PROSPECTS

During the past fifteen years the South Korean economy has shown itself not only capable of rapid growth but of flexible adaptation to changing circumstances. The oil crisis of 1973, which dealt such a damaging blow to both industrial and less-developed countries around the world, reduced Korea's growth rate in 1974 and 1975 only slightly to the relatively acceptable figure of 8 percent. The industrial structure has exhibited a persistent adaptation to changes in factor proportions and market opportunities. Production has shifted away from labor-intensive output of textiles, footwear, and other soft goods towards iron and steel, chemicals, machinery, shipbuilding, and other heavy and more sophisticated products. The earlier concentration on export markets in the United States and Japan has been broadened by penetration of markets in Europe, the Middle East, and throughout the less developed world. The future development of the Korean economy depends very much on a continuation of this capacity for flexible adaptation.

The skepticism about economic growth that has become pervasive in the advanced countries has had little impact on economic planners, economists, and the general public in Korea. The consensus there appears to be that Korea can not only maintain its rapid growth but must continue to do so if it is to cope with the internal and external difficulties that need to be confronted over the next few years. The Long-Term Prospect for Economic and Social Development 1977–1991, formulated by the Korea Development Institute forecasts a growth of 10 percent per annum over the next decade and a half. This projection is generally accepted among planners and business groups as a feasible target.

Whether such a rate of growth is likely to be realized depends not only on the availability of necessary inputs but on changes in the structure of domestic requirements and on the receptivity of foreign markets for Korean exports. The necessary increase in inputs and sources of productivity gain are unlikely to impose serious limitations. There is no reason to think that Korea will not continue to enjoy the benefits of a highly motivated and industrious labor force. Although unemployment has decreased substantially over the last decade, there are still sizable pockets of unutilized and underutilized labor. While ample supplies of cheap labor are no longer available and skilled labor supplies have tightened noticeably, Korean labor costs are still highly competitive and educational and training facilities are rapidly adapting labor supplies to new requirements.

The increase in domestic savings, particularly in business

savings, has already brought the gross savings rate close to 25 percent of GNP. The fifteen-year forecast projects this savings rate to average over 30 percent in the 1980s and, although this implies an unusually high rate of marginal savings, the target is not out of the question. Since Korea now enjoys a high standing in foreign capital markets, any shortfall on domestic savings can, in all probability, be made good by foreign borrowing. Nor is there any reason to believe that capital investment will show a decline in productivity. Korea has made a bare beginning in the importation of advanced technology. Since the bulk of investment will be undertaken in relatively capital- and skill-intensive industries of heavy machinery, electronics, steel, shipbuilding and chemicals, technological progress may well accelerate.

The Korean economy is now led by an experienced group of entrepreneurs who have shown their capacity to move into new areas of production and to exploit new overseas markets in the Middle East and elsewhere. Their capabilities will be tested as Korea gradually loses, with increased wage costs, its comparative advantage in light manufactures to latecomers among less-developed countries. This process is already well under way.

The Korean economy now confronts significant changes in domestic requirements. The improvement in standards of living with substantial increases in income is bringing with it a shift in economic and social objectives the government can no longer ignore. Better housing, improved health care, a larger public contribution to education, urban transportation, and demands for pollution control and improvement in the quality of the environment, all represent pressing needs. Expenditure on these objectives cannot be expected to carry with it the increases in productivity that have accompanied investment in manufactures. The same can be said of the requirements for an increase in military expenditures. Gradual American troop withdrawals and, perhaps, some diminution in military assistance will inevitably place a larger burden on Korean shoulders. U.S. military assistance in the past has permitted Korea to maintain large military forces with domestic expenditure of no more than

4 to 4.5 percent of GNP. This rate is likely to increase to at least 6.5 to 7 percent and perhaps more in the near future.

The shifts in domestic requirements occasioned by increases in demands for social services and military expenditures can hardly fail to diminish to some extent the prospective rate of growth. There is, however, no reason to believe that the targets contemplated by the Long-term Prospect for Economic and Social Development cannot be attained provided world markets continue to remain open to Korean exports. It is true that limitations have been imposed on certain traditional exports, for example, limitation on footwear and clothing by the United States and silk by Japan. These limitations, however, have not been serious enough to prevent a 30 percent increase in Korean exports in 1977, fueling a 15 percent growth in GNP. The development of foreign markets in new products and new areas has more than compensated such losses as have occurred in others. In order to achieve 10 percent rate of growth over the next fifteen years, it is estimated that Korean exports will have to grow at an annual average rate of 18 percent during 1977–1981, and 14 percent for 1982–1986, and 12 percent 1987–1991. Much of this growth will have to come from exports of iron and steel, machinery, ships, and other heavy products, and from chemicals. Although the projected growth rates in total exports is substantially less than what has been and currently is being achieved, they still present, because of a large expansion in the base from which these rates are measured, a rather optimistic view of what can be accomplished.

The Korean economy can continue to flourish only in an open world, and it requires a high degree of temerity to express a judgment on how open the world is likely to be to trade and investment over the next fifteen years. South Korea is one of the most international trade-oriented countries in the world with exports, in 1977, amounting to 25 percent of GNP. It is, therefore, inevitably vulnerable to any serious damage to the channels of trade. On the other hand, despite the fact that in the next decade and a half it will acquire a population of 45 million and become one of the most highly industrialized countries of Asia, its exports still will account for not much more than one percent of total world trade. This gives it somewhat more room for maneuver than competing industrial giants, and the demonstrated flexibility of its government and business leaders holds promise for the exploitation of this room.

The increase in inputs, the introduction of new technologies, changes in the structure of production, and shifts in domestic and foreign demands will inevitably be accompanied by institutional changes, new policy requirements, variations in interest group alignments, and a changing socio-political environment. It is assumed in the fifteen-year projection that these adaptations will be forthcoming without injury to the highly productive socio-economic arrangements that have characterized the Korean economy in the recent past. It is impossible to foresee in detail what these changes are likely to be, but certain probable areas of adaptation can be envisaged.

As we have emphasized in this study, policy decisions in the Korean government are made by an extraordinarily small group of top officials. This close-knit group of decision-makers has assured great flexibility in the shaping of economic policies. In recent years, nevertheless, there has been a good deal of criticism, both within the government circles and outside, of the narrowness of the decision-making process. It seems probable that, as the economy becomes more complex and the number of affected interests expands, the government will find it increasingly necessary to cast a broader net and draw more participants into the formulation of economic policy. Whether this will involve loss in efficiency and flexibility is yet to be determined.

It seems probable that, as a broader range of interests is brought into the process of policy formulation this will be accompanied by a substantial decentralization of public decision-making. As we have emphasized, Korea is one of the most highly centralized governments in the non-Communist world with all the powers of appointment and levers of control located in Seoul. The concentration of decision-making is unlikely to prove effective in dealing with expanding social services in the fields of public health, community development, agricultural assistance, and local public works. It will be difficult to continue the development of a system of agricultural cooperation without a more extensive consultation of cooperators and, as the Saemaul experience has already shown, local interests have their own opinions on priorities in community development.

During the period of rapid economic growth, the relations of government to business have been unusually close with government clearly in the driver's seat. Government has strongly influenced the direction and rate of industrial expansion by controlling the allocation of domestic credit and access to foreign capital and through a complex network of incentives and disincentives and command decisions. In general, this industrial expansion has exploited effectively Korea's comparative advantage with timely adaptation to changes in factor proportions and changing market opportunities. In the process there has emerged a sizable number of efficient large-scale enterprises and a group of venturesome entrepreneurs. It is a question whether the business community in South Korea has not, by now, outgrown the period of detailed government direction, and whether it is not in the interest of continued growth in the economy that a greater reliance be placed on the market. The increasing complexity of industrial structure and the expansion of overseas markets would appear to argue for less government intervention and more freedom for business decision-making, and there are some signs that the course of government-business relations is already moving in this direction.

Finally, it seems improbable that trade-union activity and labor-management relations will continue indefinitely in their present state. The share of industrial wage labor in the total labor force is increasing rapidly, and it is heavily concentrated in large urban areas. The attachment of labor to particular firms, though real, has never been as significant as in Japan, and there is substantially more mobility geographically and among enterprises. It seems likely that the very weak trade-union movement in Korea will become stronger in the next decade and play a larger role in dealing with management regarding the terms and conditions of employment.

If and when these structural and institutional changes take place with a wider network of interests participating in policy decisions, with some degree of decentralization of a highly centralized government structure, with a movement away from planning and strong policy implementation towards a greater reliance on the market, and with a strengthening of labor organizations, it seems inevitable that significant social and political consequences will follow. New and stronger interest groups may well emerge representing additional centers of power and heralding a movement of South Korea towards a more pluralistic society. How such changes would affect the efficiency of economic processes we are not prepared to estimate. We have argued that, during the period of rapid economic growth, the existence of an authoritarian government accepting economic development as its first priority, able to maintain political stability, and capable of making difficult economic policy decisions, and implementing these decisions, has been a positive factor in promoting growth. Whether government could maintain a similar degree of authority in an increasingly complex economy and society, whether, if it did, it could still be a generator of growth, or whether, if authority is more broadly shared, the conditions of growth could still be maintained are not questions that we are prepared to answer.

If we assume that a high rate of economic growth, perhaps approaching 10 percent per annum over the next decade and a half, is sustained, who will benefit from this growth? The unusually equitable distribution of income in the early post-war period owed much to the two programs of land redistribution, the destruction of industrial assets during the Korean War, and the rapid expansion of access to education. This was the stage of preindustrialization in which, in most developing countries, standards of living in lower income segments of the population tend to lag behind. After industrial and commercial development is well underway, incomes in these segments tend to keep pace with the growth of national income. This has happened in South Korea during the period of rapid growth, and there is no reason to expect that it will not continue. Although there are still pockets of unemployment and under-employment, these will rather rapidly be mopped up at anything like a 10 percent rate of growth of GNP. A scarce rather than a surplus labor economy is what confronts Korea over the next decade. Since 1966 industrial wage incomes have increased as fast as national income, and there is no reason why this, or something better, should not continue even though government policy does little to augment wage incomes. Since it is public policy to limit the individual ownership of agricultural land, the distribution of farm assets and income is likely to continue to be relatively equitable and, with the rapid growth in the demand of farm products in Korea and a continued shift in land-use towards more valuable crops, the rate of increase in farm incomes should not fall far behind that of urban workers.

If any increase in the inequality of income distribution should occur, it is likely to come about because of an increased share going to large-scale business. As we have noted, the increase in this share has been rapid in recent years. On the other hand, government appears to be apprised of this possibility and prepared to do something about it. Speculative investment in land and other assets unconnected with particular business operations have been curtailed; attempts are being made to reduce the high debt leverage of corporations, which has been a source of high profits; and large firms are being compelled to distribute equities. Whether these steps will be sufficient to check the increase in income shares going to the *chaebŏl* is as yet unclear. On the whole, we are inclined to believe that a continued rapid income in GNP will be accompanied by no deterioration and possibly some improvement in Korea's distribution of income.

Early in the Park regime, the government announced as high

priority objectives not only an acceleration of economic growth but the attainment of economic and political independence. Important steps towards this end have been taken since the early 1960s, and the next decade and a half should see the emergence of South Korea as a fully independent member of the society of nations.

Relations with the United States are clearly in process of change. A sizable withdrawal of American troops occurred in the early 1970s, and it may be that, within the next five or six years, all U.S. ground forces will have been removed from Korea. Although air support and some continued military assistance will no doubt be provided for a longer period, the end of the military client relationship is in sight. Economic relationships have moved rapidly from the long continued donor-donee relations to one of trade partner, U.S. economic assistance has declined to a trickle, and its complete elimination would leave the Korean economy essentially untouched. Korea continues to export mainly labor-intensive manufactured goods to the United States and receives from it capital goods and technology. Limitations imposed by the United States on the imports of certain of these goods have occasioned difficulties for the Korean economy and have been the subject of hard bargaining. This is no more than to say that, in the trade area, the period of a favored relationship has ended, and from now on the United States and Korea can be expected to deal with each other in the usual arms length bargaining manner that characterizes the trade relationships between other countries.

In the area of trade and finance, Japan has become Korea's most important market and source of supply. In recent years Japan has accounted for about 25 percent of Korea's exports and 38 percent of total imports. Although Korea's balance of payments has improved markedly and may be in surplus in the next few years, its trade imbalance with Japan has not narrowed. In 1976, its trade deficit with Japan amounted to about $1.3 billion. One of the major factors underlying this lopsided trade relationship is the absence of complementary trade between the two countries. Korea imports mainly capital and intermediate goods from Japan; it sends in return mainly agricultural products and some labor-intensive manufactures including parts for Japan's consumer electronics exports, but most manufactures have difficulty in penetrating Japan's protective barriers.

In the future, these trade relations with Japan may well become even less complementary and increasingly competitive in the rest of the world. In recent years Korea has taken over some of Japan's export markets and can now compete with Japan in a growing number of export goods. As Korea steps up her export drive in the fields of heavy industry and chemicals, competition will no doubt intensify. In its trade relations with Japan, as well as with the United States, Korea is ceasing to be a dependent hanger-on and is becoming a fully independent trade rival and partner. During the next decade and a half, South Korea promises to become the third industrial country in non-Communist Asia, after Japan and India, and a country able to make its own way in the world.

———————

This evaluation of future prospects was written before the assassination of President Park. How are these prospects to be affected by the end of the Park regime and what can be said about the legacy of this regime? President Park was not only the dominant political figure in the Republic of Korea for eighteen years but was largely responsible for the program of rapid industrialization underlying Korea's phenomenal economic growth. He was outstandingly successful in evolving a set of economic policies that facilitated this growth and in transforming the Korean bureaucracy into an efficient instrument for implementing those policies. During this period he operated with continuously decreasing restraint on his authority.

The Constitution of 1962 which replaced the military regime of 1961 and 1962 gave large powers to the executive branch of government and concentrated administrative decision-making in Seoul. Under this constitution Park and his Democratic Republican Party came to power in relatively free elections in 1963 and again in 1967. Although the regime was described as "elite authoritarian rule," it could justly be claimed as representing the will of the majority. The shift to a more personal rule was foreshadowed in 1969 when the constitution was amended by plebiscite to permit a third term for Park, after which he promised to resign. This promise was conveniently forgotten, and a highly personal authoritarian rule was ushered in by the Yusin Constitution in 1972. On the political side, the legacy of President Park was movement away from a relatively democratic though highly centralized regime to an authoritarian government depending heavily on military support. The years during which the Republic of Korea might have gone on to strengthen democratic institutions and procedures had been lost.

On the economic side, the question is how the relatively optimistic forecast of the Long-Term Prospect for Economic and Social Development is likely to be affected by political change. We have advanced reasons for believing that rapid economic growth in Korea after 1963 was facilitated by a government capable of introducing unpopular changes in economic policies and assuring compliance with these policies. At the same time, there was some evidence that a broadening of participation in decision-making and a substantial shift in economic and social goals were clamoring for expression. President Park's contribution to economic development in Korea was great, and the benefits of this development were shared by all elements of the population. There is grave doubt, however, whether this economic contribution required the degree of repression for which he was responsible and whether the personal authoritarianism of his regime could have lasted much longer.

President Park was a purely Korean type shaped by his military environment and relatively impervious to Western cultural influence. He detested politics and politicians and was uninterested in relating the administrative structure of government to emerging political forces. He had two primary ambitions for his country, to make it strong and to decrease the dependence on foreign influence. His contribution to both of these goals was large. How the Korean economy will fare under other, possibly less-centralized authority is still to be tested.

Notes

Bibliography

Index

Notes

ONE   *Introduction*

1. Fred W. Riggs, *Administration in Developing Countries* (Boston, 1964), pp. 419–20.
2. David C. Cole and Princeton N. Lyman, *Korean Development: The Interplay of Politics and Economics* (Cambridge, Mass., 1971); Gilbert T. Brown, *Korean Pricing Policies and Economic Development in the 1960's* (Baltimore, 1973); Charles R. Frank, Jr., Kwang Suk Kim, and Larry Westphal, *Foreign Trade Regimes and Economic Development: South Korea* (NBER, New York, 1975), p. 216; Parvez Hasan, *Korea, Problems and Issues in a Rapidly Growing Economy* (Baltimore, 1976); Paul Kuznets, *Economic Growth and Structure in the Republic of Korea* (New Haven, 1977); Larry E. Westphal and Kwang Suk Kim, "Industrial Policy and Development in Korea" (Washington, 1977).
3. See also Westphal and Kim, "Industrial Policies and Development in Korea" in Bela Balassa, *Development Strategies in Semi-Industrialized Countries*, IBRD, and various essays in Wontack Hong and Anne O. Krueger, eds., *Trade and Development in Korea*.
4. Gunnar Myrdal, *Asian Drama* (New York, 1968), II, 895–896.
5. Chong Kee Park, *Social Security in Korea: An Approach to Socioeconomic Development* (Seoul, 1975), p. 2.

TWO   *Modernization: Third World and Korea*

1. S. N. Eisenstadt, *Modernization: Protest and Change* (Englewood Cliffs, N.J., 1966), p. 1.
2. Bernard Crick, *In Defence of Politics* (London, 1962), p. 21.
3. Lucian W. Pye, *Aspects of Political Democracy* (Boston, 1966), p. 71.
4. George Unwin, *Studies in Economic History* (London, 1927), p. 28.

5. U.S. Arms Control and Disarmament Agency, *World Military Expenditures and Arms Trade, 1964–1973* (Washington, G.P.O., 1974, pp. 1–3.

6. Morris Janowitz, "Military Institutions and Coercion in the Developing Nations " (Mimeo, Chicago, September 1975).

7. Ibid.

8. Riggs, p. 36.

A typically "modern" society is relatively industrialized, productive, and socially mobilized, with an effective government and system of public administration.

It need not be democratic. This may be a point of controversy, but I am assuming that we can ascribe the typically modern quality of life to a Communist dictatorship as well as to a pluralistic democracy. I shall suggest that the structures of a modern society are typically functionally specific, and hence they are also differentiated or diffracted, whether democratic or totalitarian.

9. Alex Inkeles, "Becoming Modern: Individual Changes in Six Developing Countries," *Ethos* 3.2:324 (Summer 1975).

10. Pye, p. 19.

11. Sungjoo Han, *The Failure of Democracy in South Korea* (Berkeley, 1974), p. 86. The author, who was a participant in the student uprising of 1960 says, "For those who witnessed and suffered from the abuses of Syngman Rhee's dictatorial rule and who helped bring about the eventual overthrow of the Rhee regime, *democracy* was the issue of primary concern. For the post-1961 generation, which has felt the apparent futility of liberal democracy in Korea, economic development has become the primary interest and goal," p. xi.

12. Richard C. Allen, *Korea's Syngman Rhee, an Unauthorized Portrait* (Rutland, Vermont, 1960), p. 12. Allen, who is not an admirer of Rhee, yet has this to say about him: "For all his shortcomings, however, Rhee was not merely a stubborn old tyrant in a position of power. He was an extremely astute political tactician, a fact that was on continuous display during his rise to the top of the cutthroat world of Korean politics. And on the international scene, Rhee parlayed Korea's status as a victim of Communist aggression with a degree of support from the United States which makes any new Communist attack unlikely."

13. Bae-Ho Hahn, "Korean Politics and Perspectives for Political Development," *Social Science Journal*, III, 1975.

14. Gregory Henderson, *Korea, The Politics of the Vortex* (Cambridge, Mass., 1968), p. 182.

15. Park Chung Hee, *The Country, the Revolution and I* (Seoul, 1963), pp. 19–20.

16. Cole and Lyman, p. 115.

17. Alexander Kim Youngman, "Korean Kundrehwa: The Military as Modernizer," *Journal of Comparative Administration* (November 1970), p. 355.

18. Kyung Cho Chung, *Korea, the Third Republic* (New York, 1972), p. 92.

19. Youngman, p. 358.

20. Ibid.

21. Bae-Ho Hahn, "Political Context of Economic Development in Korea" (typed, Korea University, 1974), p. 19.

22. Kyung Cho Chung, pp. 70 and 71.

23. *Far Eastern Economic Review* (May 16, 1975), p. 38.

THREE *Historical Foundations of Growth*

1. The story of these developments has been told in such works as Thomas C. Smith, *The Agrarian Origins of Modern Japan* (Stanford, 1959), and Ronald Dore, *Education in Tokugawa Japan* (Berkeley, 1965).

2. This basic point if not this precise figure will be made in a forthcoming book by Evelyn Rawski on popular education in traditional China.

3. Dwight H. Perkins, *Agricultural Development in China, 1368–1968* (Chicago, 1969).

4. Susan Shin, "Land Tenure and the Agrarian Economy in Yi Dynasty Korea: 1600–1800," (Harvard University, unpublished PhD dissertation, 1973), pp. 75–78.

5. This paragraph is based mainly on Susan Shin, pp. 98–109.

6. Yong-Ha Shin, "Yangban Land Reform and the Establishment of Private Landlordism in Early Yi Dynasty Korea, 1391–1470," (unpublished paper, 1970).

7. Susan Shin, Chapter 3.

8. Ki Hyuk Pak et al., *A Study of Land Tenure System in Korea* (Seoul, 1966), p. 48.

9. Henderson, *The Politics of the Vortex.*

10. James B. Palais, *Politics and Policy in Traditional Korea* (Cambridge, Mass., 1975), contains an excellent and lengthy discussion of this struggle.

11. Palais, p. 62.

12. For Japanese estimates, see E. Sydney Crawcour, "The Tokugawa Heritage," in W. W. Lockwood, ed., *The State and Economic Enterprise in*

Japan (Princeton, 1965), p. 31. The Chinese estimate is from D. H. Perkins, "Government as an Obstacle to Industrialization: The Case of Nineteenth-Century China," *The Journal of Economic History* (December 1967), p. 487 and is based on the tax estimates of Yeh-chien Wang, *Land Taxation in Imperial China, 1750–1911* (Cambridge, Mass., 1973).

13. More than 1,000 such markets have been recorded during and after the 18th century. Hochin Choi, *The Economic History of Korea* (Seoul, 1971), p. 175.

14. The history of money in Korea is much better researched than the history of commerce in general. A good discussion can be found in Palais.

15. This at least is the conclusion of Hae-jong Chun, "Sino-Korean Tributary Relations in the Ch'ing Period," in J. K. Fairbank, ed., *The Chinese World Order* (Cambridge, Mass., 1968), pp. 109–110.

16. Isabella Bird Bishop, *Korea and Her Neighbours* (first published in 1898, Seoul, 1970), p. 66.

17. Susan Shin, pp. 64–65. As a percentage of the total population these figures would be lower, since one would have to add landless laborers and the like who would, for the most part, not be *yangban*.

18. Government General of Chosen, *Annual Report on Reforms and Progress in Chosen, 1921–1922,* (Keijo, 1923), p. 273.

19. Chōsen Sōtokufu, Nōrin-Ryoru (Bureau of Agriculture and Forestry) *Nōka keizai gaikyō chōsa* (Seoul, 1940).

20. Bishop, p. 79.

21. The best discussion of the financial and intellectual millieu in which the Korean court at that time operated is in Palais.

22. Sung Hwan Ban, *The Growth of Korean Agriculture* (Seoul, 1974), p. 189.

23. Japan's growth rate during the same period was 3.4% per year for GNP, 2.1% per capita. Kazushi Ohkawa and Henry Rosovsky, *Japanese Economic Growth* (Stanford, 1973), p. 280.

24. Kwang Suk Kim and Michael Roemer, *Growth and Structural Transformation,* Studies in the Modernization of the Republic of Korea: 1945–1975 (Cambridge, Mass., 1979), p. 18.

25. Ibid. p. 26.

26. These estimates were made by Tai Hwan Kwon, "Population Change and Its Components in Korea," and are used by John Sloboda in his chapter in Edwin S. Mills and Byung-Nak Song, *Urbanization and Urban Problems,* Studies in the Modernization of the Republic of Korea: 1945–1975 (Cambridge, Mass., 1979).

27. Cornelius Osgood, *The Koreans and Their Culture* (Tokyo, 1951) p. 294.

28. Government General of Chosen, *Annual Report on Reforms,* p. 273.

29. David C. Cole and Y. C. Park, forthcoming study of finance in Korea.

30. This at least was the amount of land listed as "vested land" sold by the U.S. Military Government, and that land was supposed to include all land formerly owned by the Japanese and only that land.

31. The wholesale price index is referred to because there is no consumer price index for this period. See Kim and Roemer, p. 30.

32. Wontack Hong, "Trade and Subsidy Policy and Employment Growth in Korea" (Mimeo., Seoul, Korea Development Institute, 1976).

FOUR   *Economic Development, 1953–1976*

1. These shares in GNP are based on the current price series of national income accounts data. See BOK, *National Income Statistics Yearbook 1972*, pp. 62–64.

2. Because of foreign assistance, all major post-war economic policy decisions, including those not directly involving aid funds, had to be discussed with the U.S. Aid mission to Korea. It is therefore not clear whether the economic policies followed during this period reflected primarily the goals of the Korean government or those of the Aid authorities. See Kwang Suk Kim and Michael Roemer, "Macroeconomic Growth and Structural Change in Korea" (Seoul, KDI Working Paper 7705, 1977), p. 62.

3. BOK, *Economic Statistics Yearbook 1970*, pp. 322–327.

4. In addition to these reforms, the government took additional measures to increase incentives to exporters.

5. See Kim and Roemer, pp. 88–89.

6. Young Chin Kim and Jene K. Kwon, *Capital Utilization in Korean Manufacturing, 1962–71* (Seoul, Korea Industrial Development Institute, 1973).

7. Wontack Hong, *Factor Supply and Factor Intensity of Trade in Korea* (Seoul, 1976), p. 213.

8. In Korea, changes in grain inventories are largely determined by the size of the agricultural crop, particularly the rice crop, for the respective year and are unrelated to the voluntary savings decisions of individual economic units.

9. For the employment data based on the old surveys for 1957–1962, see EPB, *Korea Statistical Yearbook 1961* and *1963*. One may also use the 1960 census results, but the classification of labor force and employment data in the census report is not consistent with either the census results for 1970 and 1975 or the results of the labor force survey for the latter years.

10. Kim Kwang-sŏk, *Han'guk inp'ŭlleisyŏn ŭi wŏnin kwa yŏnghyang* (Seoul, 1973). For an English summary of this monograph, see K. S. Kim, "The Causes and Effects of Inflation" in C. K. Kim ed., *Planning and Macroeconomic Policy Issues* (Seoul, 1977).

11. M. Ishaq Nadiri, "Some Approaches to the Theory and Measurement of Total Factor Productivity: A Survey," *Journal of Economic Literature* 8.4:1137–1177 (December 1970).

12. See the mathematical derivation in Kim and Roemer, pp. 116–117.

13. These estimates are comparable with the sources-of-growth estimates for Korea's private sector GDP by L. R. Christensen and D. Cummings, "Korean Real Product, Real Factor Input and Productivity, 1960–1973" (Social Systems Research Institute No. 7507, University of Wisconsin, 1975).

14. The analysis in this section does not imply that similar rates of increase in factor inputs would produce the same results in another country. It is therefore emphasized that the results are only relevant to Korea and its rather special historical setting.

15. World Bank, *Atlas* (Washington D.C., 1976).

16. Hollis B. Chenery and Moises Syrquin, *Patterns of Development, 1950–1970* (London, 1975).

FIVE   *Industrialization and Foreign Trade*

1. The general principles underlying Korean differential tariffs are: 1) higher tariffs on commodities produced in Korea than on those not produced, 2) the escalation of tariffs according to the degree of processing from a low or zero rate on raw materials to the highest rate on finished goods, and 3) higher tariffs on non-essential or luxury goods than on essential goods. Charles R. Frank, Jr., Kwang Suk Kim, and Larry Westphal, *Foreign Trade Regimes and Economic Development: South Korea* (New York, 1975), pp. 36–37.

2. For the detailed description of each type of export incentive, see Frank, Kim, and Westphal, pp. 38–55, and for the effects of these incentives, Larry E. Westphal and Kwang Suk Kim, "Industrial Policy and Development in Korea" (World Bank Staff Working Paper No. 263, 1977), pp. I-10–I-25.

3. In addition to these actual devaluations, the U.S. dollar devaluations relative to the other major currencies during 1972–1973 and in 1977 resulted in the effective devaluation of the Korean wŏn, whose exchange rate has been tied to the U.S. dollar.

4. See Westphal and Kwang Suk Kim, pp. I-11.

5. Ibid., pp. I-24–25.

6. Anne O. Krueger, "The Role of the Foreign Sector and Aid in Korea's Development" (KDI Working Paper 7708, 1977), p. V-24.

7. These ratios are based on the national income accounts data at 1970 constant prices.

8. For the import statistics quoted in this section, see "Summary of Export and Imports" presented in BOK, *Economic Statistics Yearbook* relevant years.

9. The ratio of imports to GNP is estimated from the 1970 constant price data presented in the BOK, *National Income in Korea, 1975.*

10. The national income accounts data for 1976 are presented in the Bank of Korea's, *Monthly Economic Statistics* (September 1977).

11. Kwang Suk Kim, "Sources of Industrial Growth and Structural Change in Korea" (KDI Working Paper 7703, 1977).

12. Hollis B. Chenery and Lance Taylor, "Development Patterns: Among Countries and Over Time," *Review of Economics and Statistics,* 50.4 (November 1968).

13. Kwang Suk Kim and Michael Roemer, "Macroeconomic Growth and Structural Change in Korea" (KDI Working Paper 7705, 1977), pp. 193–197.

14. Moises Syrquin, "Sources of Industrial Growth and Change: An Alternative Measure" (World Bank, 1976).

For instance, Syrquin's total method of "source" decomposition in terms of absolute change (or first difference) can be expressed as the following:

$$\Delta X = R_1^d u_{f1} \Delta D \qquad \text{domestic demand expansion}$$

$$+ R_1^d \Delta E \qquad \text{export expansion}$$

$$+ R_1^d \Delta u_f D_2 \qquad \text{IS of final goods}$$

$$- R_1^d (A_2^m - \widetilde{A}_1^m) X_2 \qquad \text{IS of intermediate}$$

$$+ R_1^d [\Delta A - (A_1^m - \widetilde{A}_1^m)] X_2 m \qquad \text{technological change}$$

Effect on ΔX

Where X = production; $R^d = [I - A^d]^{-1}$ where A^d represents coefficients for domestically produced inputs; u_f = the proportion of total final demand satisfied by domestic production; D = final demand; E = exports; A^m = coefficients for imported inputs; $\widetilde{A}_1^m$ = a matrix consisting of elements, $\widetilde{a}_{ij1}^m = (a_{ij1}^m / a_{ij1}) a_{ij2}$: subscripts 1 and 2 represent two bench mark years; and Δ = the first difference operator. The above formula uses the first period IO coefficients and the second period production structure. This is a version of the Paasche index. Use of a Laspeyres type index is also possible.

15. Hollis B. Chenery, S. Shishido, and T. Watanabe, "The Patterns of Japanese Growth, 1914–1954," *Econometrica* 30.1 (January 1962).

16. Larry Westphal and Kyu Soo Kim, "KDI Input-Output Data Bank" (KDI, 1977, revised).

17. W. Arthur Lewis, "Economic Development with Unlimited Supplies of Labor," *The Manchester School* (May 1954), and G. R. Ranis and J. H. Fei, "A Theory of Economic Development," *American Economic Review* (September 1961). See also the discussion in Chapter 4 for Korea's labor market conditions in the early 1960s.

18. See Westphal and Kwang Suk Kim; Wontack Hong, *Factor Supply and Factor Intensity of Trade in Korea*; Wontack Hong, *Trade, Distortions and Employment Growth in Korea*; and Krueger, "The Role of the Foreign Sector."

19. Wontack Hong, *Factor Supply*, pp. 93–102, and Wontack Hong *Trade, Distortions and Employment Growth*, pp. 45–48.

20. David C. Cole, and Larry Westphal, "The Contribution of Exports to Employment in Korea" in Wontack Hong and A. Krueger eds., *Trade and Development in Korea* (Seoul, 1975).

21. Wontack Hong, *Trade, Distortions and Employment Growth* (Seoul, 1979), pp. 2–25.

22. Ibid. Hong estimated that the wage-rental ratio for all industries increased at an average annual rate of 25 percent between 1967 and 1973.

23. Westphal and Kwang Suk Kim, pp. 4–54.

24. Krueger "The Role of the Foreign Sector," V-10.

SIX   *Foreign Assistance*

1. Much of the material in this section is derived from Harold Koh, "The Early History of U.S. Economic Assistance to the Republic of Korea, 1945–1955," (Mimeo, HIID, September 1975).

2. William A. Brown and Redvers Opie, *American Foreign Assistance* (Washington, D.C., 1953), pp. 372–373.

3. Henderson, *The Politics of the Vortex*, Chapter 5.

4. Arthur I. Bloomfield and John P. Jensen, *Banking Reform in South Korea* (New York, March 1951), p. 15; prediction of self-sufficiency from George McCune and Arthur L. Grey, Jr., *Korea Today* (Cambridge, Mass., 1950), p. 115.

5. United States Senate, *Korea: Report to the President* Submitted by Lt. General A. C. Wedemeyer, September 1947. Committee Print for the use of the Committee on Armed Services (Washington, GPO, 1951), p. 6.

6. Krueger, *The Developmental Role of the Foreign Sector and Aid,* Studies in the Modernization of the Republic of Korea: 1945–1975 (Cambridge, Mass., 1979), p. 22.

7. Brown and Opie, p. 374.

8. Ibid., p. 373.

9. Bloomfield and Jensen, p. 19.

10. Paul Kuznets, *Economic Growth and Structure*, p. 36 ff.

11. U.S. House of Representative, *Korean Aid*, 81st Congress, 1st session Hearings before the Committee on Foreign Affairs on H.R. 5330 June 8–23, 1949 (Washington, D.C., GPO, 1949), p. 11.

12. Bloomfield and Jensen, p. 20.

13. Sung Cho Soon, *Korea in World Politics 1940–50: An Evaluation of American Responsibility* (Berkeley, 1967), p. 277.

14. Kuznets, p. 36.

15. Donald G. Tewksbury, *Source Material on Korean Politics and Ideologies* (New York, 1950), pp. 145–146.

16. Lewis writes, "Western agencies had trouble recruiting competent personnel for a wait-and-see effort, particularly UNKRA, which was uniquely addressed to the reconstruction problem. Under the circumstances, the U.N. agency had little success in soliciting funds for Korean reconstruction from the member countries, and the U.S. government's Korean economic policy became a compound of expediencies." John P. Lewis, *Reconstruction and Development in South Korea*, Planning Pamphlet No. 94, National Planning Association (Washington, D.C., December 1955), pp. 35–36.

17. Krueger, *The Foreign Sector and Aid*, pp. 76–77, notes that Congress passed an appropriation for $166 million, while the other nations' pledges fell far short of the $85 million which would have enabled the entire American contribution to be used.

18. Ibid., pp. 37–40.

19. Ibid.

20. Frank, Kim, and Westphal, p. 9.

21. Lewis, pp. 36–37.

22. Ibid.

23. Cole and Lyman, *Korean Development: The Interplay of Politics and Economics,* pp. 209–210.

24. U.S. Central Intelligence Agency, "Korea, the Economic Race Between the North and the South," National Foreign Assessment Center, January 1978.

25. Fixed capital formation rather than total investment is used because of the problem with inventory investment data discussed in Chapter 4.

26. Gustav F. Papanek, "The Effect of Aid and Other Resource Transfers on Savings and Growth in Less Developed Countries," *The Economic Journal*, September 1972, pp. 934–950.

27. K. B. Griffin and J. L. Enos, "Foreign Assistance: Objectives and Consequences," *Economic Development and Cultural Change,* April 1970.

28. Cole and Lyman, p. 170, and Krueger, *The Foreign Sector and Aid,* pp. 79–80.

29. Krueger, *The Foreign Sector and Aid*, p. 72.

30. Lewis, p. 78.

31. Cf. Wan Hyok Pu, "The History of American Aid to Korea," *Koreana Quarterly*, 3.1:77–96 (Summer 1969). Also, Joe Won Lee, "Planning Efforts for Economic Development," in T. S. Chung, ed., *Korea: Patterns of Economic Development,* (Kalamazoo, Korea Research and Publications, 1966), pp. 1–24.

32. Some of these plants eventually became successful export producers in the 1960s when relative prices and incentives were changed or they were expanded to realize scale economies.

33. Krueger, *The Foreign Sector and Aid*, pp. 44–46.

34. Byong Kuk Kim, *Central Banking Experiment in a Developing Country* (Seoul, 1965) and Gilbert T. Brown, *Korean Pricing Policies and Economic Development in the 1960's* (Baltimore, 1973).

35. Sock Kyun Chu, "Why American Aid Failed," *Koreana Quarterly*, 4.1:81–93 (Autumn 1962).

36. See Brown, pp. 52 and 138, and Byong Kuk Kim, pp. 47–48 for descriptions of the stabilization measures that largely ignore the application of U.S. leverage on the Korean government.

37. The Japanese agreement called for $300 million in grants, $200 million in "soft" loans and $300 million in commercial credits. See Cole and Lyman, p. 101.

38. Ibid., p. 90.

39. Sung-hwan Jo, "Direct Private Investment in South Korea: An Economic Survey," KDI Working Paper, 7707, 1977.

40. Ibid.

41. Cole and Lyman, Chapter 9.

SEVEN   *Rural Development*

1. This calculation, based on urban household surveys, is from S. H. Ban, P. Y. Moon, and D. H. Perkins, *Rural Development,* Studies in the Modernization of the Republic of Korea: 1945–1975 (Cambridge, Mass., 1980), Table 10.

2. Ibid., Chapter 3.

3. One of the best discussions of the nature of upland development can be found in Jin Hwan Park, *An Economic Analysis of Land Development Activities in Korea* (Department of Agricultural Economics, Seoul National University, 1969).

4. See United States Operations Mission to Korea, *Rural Development Program Evaluation Report: Korea 1967* and Ban, Moon, and Perkins, Chapter 4.

5. Korean Agricultural Sector Survey, *Analysis of New Land Development in Korea,* Special Report No. 3, pp. 13–14.

6. Yong Sam Cho, *"Disguised Unemployment," in Underdeveloped Areas With Special Reference to South Korean Agriculture* (Berkeley and Los Angeles, 1963), p. 76.

7. This statement is based on data from the farm household economic surveys. See Ban, Moon, and Perkins, Table 24.

8. Ban, Moon, and Perkins, Figures 11 and 12.

9. Chōsen Sōtokufu, Nōrin-Ryoru (Government General of Korea, Bureau of Agriculture and Forestry) *Chōsen no nōgyō* (Seoul, 1940), pp. 196–198.

10. Bureau of Agriculture and Forestry, Government General of Korea, *Nōka keizai gaikyō chōsa* (1940).

11. These figures from USOM/K, *Rural Development Program Evaluation,* p. 82 and Korean Traders Association, *Statistical Yearbook of Foreign Trade* as compiled in Ban, Moon, and Perkins, Table 39.

12. This discussion is based on Vincent Brandt, "Local Government and Rural Development" in Ban, Moon, and Perkins, Chapter 9.

13. See discussion in Jae Hong Cho, "Post-1945 Land Reforms and Their Consequences in South Korea" (unpublished doctoral dissertation, Indiana University, 1964). Another major source on Korean land reform is Ki Hyuk Pak et al., *A Study of Land Tenure System in Korea* (Seoul, 1966).

14. Ban, Moon, and Perkins, Chapter 7.

15. Ibid., Chapter 8.

16. Ibid., Chapter 10.

17. Jae Hong Cho, "Post-1945 Land Reforms," pp. 88–89.

18. Ban, Moon, and Perkins, Table 119 and Jae Hong Cho, "Post-1945 Land Reforms," p. 92.

EIGHT   *Government and Business*

1. E. Grant Meade, *American Military Government in Korea* (New York, 1951), p. 210.

2. Roy W. Shin, "The Politics of Korean Aid: A Study of the Impact of United States Aid in Korea from 1945 to 1966" (PhD dissertation, University of Minnesota, 1969), p. 51.

3. Kwang Suk Kim and Michael Roemer, "Growth and Macro Change in the Structure of National Product, 1945–1975," KDI Interim Report 7601, (Seoul, 1976).

4. Frank, Kim, and Westphal, pp. 96–97.

5. Park Chung Hee, *The Country, the Revolution and I* (Seoul, 1970), p. 26.

6. Park Chung Hee, *Our Nation's Path* (Seoul, 1970), pp. 39–40.

7. Irma Adelman and Cynthia Morris, *Society, Politics and Economic Development: A Quantitative Approach* (Baltimore, 1967), pp. 237–238.

8. Cole and Lyman, *Korean Development*, p. 27.

9. Hahn-Been Lee, *Korea: Time, Change and Public Administration* (Honolulu, 1968), p. 23.

10. David C. Cole and Young Woo Nam, "The Pattern and Significance of Economic Planning in Korea," in Adelman, ed., *Practical Approaches to Development Planning*. See also Charles R. Blitzer, Peter B. Clark, Lance Taylor, eds., *Economy-Wide Models and Development Planning* (London, 1975), p. 150.

11. Westphal and Adelman, p. 18.

12. Chitoshi Yanaga, *Big Business in Japanese Politics* (New Haven, 1968), p. 70.

13. For one version of the meeting, see "Memoirs of Kim Yong Wan," *Dong-A Ilbo,* May 12, 1976.

14. Myrdal, p. 903.

15. Frank, Kim, and Westphal, pp. 70–75.

16. These calculations are derived by Jones and SaKong from BOK, *Flow of Funds Accounts in Korea, 1963–1974* (Seoul, 1976).

17. Soon Chough, "The Economics of Price Supervision," *Seoul National University Economic Review* (December 1968), pp. 51–70.

18. Leroy P. Jones and Il SaKong, *Government, Business, and Entrepreneurship in Economic Development: The Korean Case,* Studies in the Modernization of the Republic of Korea, 1945–1975 (Cambridge, Mass., 1980).

19. J. A. Schumpeter, *The Theory of Economic Development* (Cambridge, Mass., 1934).

20. Yanaga, p. 38.

21. Johannes Hirschmeier and Tsunehiko Yui, *The Development of Japanese Business, 1600–1978* (Cambridge, Mass., 1975), p. 187.

22. Ibid., p. 264.

23. Richard E. Caves and Masu Uekusa, *Industrial Organization in Japan* (Washington, D. C., 1976).

24. Kyong-Dong Kim, "Political Factors in the Formation of the Entrepreneurial Elite in South Korea," *Asian Survey* (May 1976), p. 469.

25. Yŏng-nok Kim, "Han'guk kiŏpka chŏngsin ŭi pansŏng" (Reconsideration of the Korean entrepreneurial spirit), *Sasanggye* (August 1964), p. 38. (Translation by Il SaKong).

NINE   *Fiscal and Financial Development*

1. Isabella Bird Bishop, *Korea and Her Neighbors* (Reprint by Yonsei University Press, Seoul, 1970), p. 66.

2. The basis for conversion is that commodity output in the post-war period in South Korea has averaged 56% of GNP. If the same ratio is assumed for 1940, then the estimated GNP would have been 1.8 times the commodity output.

3. Chong Kee Park, *Development and Modernization of Korea's Tax System* (Seoul, 1977), pp. 17–18.

4. Arthur I. Bloomfield and John P. Jensen, *Banking Reform in South Korea* (New York, March 1951).

5. At the time, 1950, a struggle was being waged in the United States to free the Federal Reserve from Treasury control, and the Central Bank Act drafted for Korea embodied a number of features that the Federal Reserve would have liked to see in its own charter.

6. Arthur I. Bloomfield, *Report and Recommendations on Banking in South Korea* (Seoul, 1952), pp. 9–10, and Gene M. Lyons, *Military Policy and Economic Aid, the Korean Case, 1950–1953* (Columbus, Ohio, 1961), pp. 88 ff.

7. David C. Cole and Yung Chul Park, *Financial Development in Korea, 1945–1978* (Seoul, 1979), Chapter 4.

8. Chong Kee Park, *Development and Modernization*, p. 20.

9. Haskell Wald, "The Recent Experience of the Republic of Korea with Tax Collections in Kind," in Wald and Froomkin, eds., *Agricultural Taxation and Economic Development* (Cambridge, Mass., 1954).

10. In conventional macroeconomic symbols, the external or $M–X$ gap is equal to the internal $(I + G) – (S + R)$ gap, where M = imports, X = exports,

I = investment, G = government expenditures, S = domestic private saving, and R = government revenues. The Korean government sought to widen the internal gap as a justification for more aid to fill the necessary equal external gap, while the Americans tried to get them to reduce the internal gap.

11. As pointed out in Chapter 6 on foreign aid, military assistance to Korea from the United States has increased over the past decade, while economic assistance has declined.

12. Roy W. Bahl and Chuk Kyo Kim, "Modernization and the Long-Term Growth of Korean Government Expenditures" (Mimeo., Syracuse, New York), p. 46.

13. The attempt of the government to institute a social security program in 1975 generated vehement popular opposition, because it was perceived—correctly—as primarily a measure to increase government revenues. Chong Kee Park, *Social Security in Korea* (Seoul, 1975).

14. This tax was transformed into a value-added tax in 1977.

15. Chong Kee Park, *Development and Modernization,* p. 113.

16. This pattern of emphasizing the income tax was characteristic of the several papers on Korean tax reform written by Richard A. Musgrave and by Robert H. Johnson. For example, Musgrave, *Revenue Policy for Korea's Economic Development* (Seoul, 1965); and Musgrave, "Suggestions for the 1967 Tax Reform," (A report submitted to the Minister of Finance, March 1967).

17. Chong Kee Park, *Development and Modernization,* p. 75.

18. Gilbert T. Brown, pp. 63–68.

19. Chong Kee Park, *Development and Modernization,* p. 88.

20. Musgrave, *Revenue Policy.*

21. Chong Kee Park, *Development and Modernization,* p. 88.

22. Roy W. Bahl, "The Distributional Effects of the Korean Budget During the Modernization Process" (Mimeo., Syracuse, October 1977).

23. This approach may contain some bias in the direction of exaggerating the degree of inequality, but comparisons with Hakchung Choo's distribution estimates that combine household survey and income tax data indicate that Bahl's approach is more accurate than the unadjusted household survey data. (See Chapter 13 on distribution).

24. See Chapter 5 of this volume.

25. Edward S. Shaw, *Financial Deepening in Economic Development* (New York, 1973).

26. Byong Kuk Kim, *Central Banking Experiment in a Developing Country* (Seoul, 1965), p. 44–45.

27. Cole and Park, Chapter 4.

28. Ibid., Chapter 2.

29. The actors and events involved in this shift provide an interesting example of the interaction of Korean and American academics and government officials in the formulation of Korean economic policies. While there had been occasional discussion of interest rate policies over the years, and Arthur Bloomfield in a report in 1957 had expressed the opinion that raising interest rates would do little to stimulate the demand for deposits, it was Professor Lee Chang-Nyol of Korea University who first presented a strong case for interest rate changes in his study which was financed by U.S. Aid Trust Funds. Shortly thereafter three American Professors, John Gurley and Edward Shaw from Stanford, and Hugh Patrick from Yale, were brought to Korea by the U.S. Aid Mission to study the financial system and recommend improvements. Their report "The Financial Structure of Korea" (Seoul, United States Operations Mission to Korea, July, 1965, processed), taking off from Professor Lee's study, recommended raising interest rates on bank deposits and loans to levels approaching the unorganized money market rates. The report, and discussions with the powerful Deputy Prime Minister, Chang Key Young, and his monetary expert, Kim Young Hwan, opened the way to the government's presenting a bill to the National Assembly in August 1965, raising the legal ceilings on interest rates from 15% to 30%. Finally a provision had been included in the 1965 stabilization program that there would be an interest rate reform by the end of the third quarter of the year, and release of a portion of the AID program loan funds for the year was conditional upon implementation of a reform jointly agreed upon by the Korean and American governments. This mixture of national and foreign expertise plus aid incentives for self-help led to the monetary reform of September 20, 1965.

30. See Anand G. Chandavarkar, "Some Aspects of Interest Rate Policies in Less Developed Economies: The Experience of Selected Asian Countries," *International Monetary Fund Staff Papers*, Vol. 18 (March 1971), and Ronald I. McKinnon, *Money and Capital in Economic Development* (Washington, 1973), Chapter 4, for comparable data on Taiwan and Indonesia.

31. Gilbert T. Brown, Chapter 7.

32. Homer Jones, *Korean Financial Problems* (Seoul, June 1968) said that "the interest rate reform was in the right direction but . . . scarcely . . . satisfactory." (p. 42). He went on to say that "no free enterprise economy has ever prospered with such a distorted interest rate structure as prevails in Korea today (1968)," (p. 44), and that "deformed interest rate and price structures, arbitrary government decisions about investment forms, and distortions incident to the export campaign will provide obstacles to economic growth in the future," (p. 3). Williamson has argued that private savings in Korea have been adversely affected by the

large capital gains on real assets (which are not counted as either income or saving) and the displacement of domestic savings by foreign savings. Jeffrey Williamson, "Why Do Koreans Save 'So Little'?" *Journal of Development Economics* 5: 343–362 (1979).

33. There is strong evidence that both the foreign loans and domestic bank loans were used mainly to finance fixed investment. Inventory investment, at least for the corporate sector, has averaged only about one-tenth of fixed investment over the 1966–1975 decade. See Cole and Park, pp. 358–361. See also Sang Woo Nam, "Financial Structure, Corporate Investment and Financing Behavior in Korea" (PhD dissertation submitted to MIT, September 1977).

34. Larry E. Westphal and Kwang Suk Kim, "Industrial Policy and Development" (The World Bank Staff Working Paper No. 263, August 1977), pp. 3–39.

35. Gilbert T. Brown, p. 206; Edward S. Shaw, "Financial Patterns and Policies in Korea" (Processed, USOM/K, April 1967), p. 31.

36. Wontack Hong, "Trade and Subsidy Policy and Employment Growth in Korea" (KDI Interim report 7602).

37. See Cole and Park, Chapter 6 and BOK, *Report on Results of the August 3, 1972 Presidential Emergency Decree* (August 1973).

38. Cole and Park, p. 279.

39. Ibid., pp. 72–116.

TEN   *Education*

1. This chapter is a condensation by Donald Snodgrass and Noel McGinn of the study *Education and Development in Korea,* Studies in the Modernization of the Republic of Korea: 1945–1975 (Cambridge, Mass., 1980) by McGinn et al.

2. The graphs refer only to the earnings of regular, full-time industrial workers. This is a relatively homogeneous group; if data were available for a broader range of workers (including, say, government workers, farmers, and fishermen) the range of earnings associated with different levels of educational attainment probably would be wider still.

3. George Psacharopoulos and Keith Hinchliffe, *Returns to Education: An International Comparison* (Amsterdam and San Francisco, 1977).

4. James Coleman et al., *Equality of Educational Opportunity* (Washington, 1966); Torsten Husen, ed., *International Study of Achievement in Mathematics: A Comparison of 12 Countries* (Stockholm and New York, 1967); G. F. Peaker, *The Plowden Children Four Years Later* (Slough, 1971); Christopher Jencks et al., *Inequality* (New York, 1972); Alan C.

Purves and Daniel V. Levine, eds., *Educational Policy and International Assessment* (Berkeley, 1975).

5. And late-developing countries place even greater reliance on formal education as a credential device than did countries which developed earlier. Ronald Dore, *The Diploma Disease* (Berkeley and Los Angeles, 1976).

6. Previously access to these newly preferred forms of higher education was controlled largely through competition for admittance to a few prestigious high schools. Now the most important selection point is university admission; those who get into Seoul National University are particularly regarded as being tagged for success.

7. Lee and Whang report that by 1966 20% of the senior administrators in the Korean government were from the military; another 12% were university professors trained in public administration. Hahn Been Lee and In-joung Whang. "Development of Senior Administrators: The Korean Experience," *Koreana Quarterly* 13.3 (Autumn 1973).

8. Ross Harold Cole, "The Koreanization of Elementary Citizenship Education in South Korea, 1948–1974" (unpublished PhD dissertation, Arizona State University, 1975).

ELEVEN   *Population, Urbanization, and Health*

1. Robert Repetto, "Economic Development and Fertility Decline in the Republic of Korea," in Robert Repetto, Dae Young Kim, Tae Hwan Kwon, Peter Donaldson, and Son-Ung Kim, "Economic Development, Population Policy and the Demographic Transition in the Republic of Korea" (Draft manuscript, 1977), Chapter 4, pp. 81–82.

2. Edwin S. Mills and Byung-Nak Song, *Korea's Urbanization and Urban Problems* (KDI, September 1977), p. 8.

3. Tae Hwan Kwon, Hae Young Lee, Yunshik Chang, and Eui-Young Yu, *The Population of Korea* (Seoul, The Population and Development Studies Center, Seoul National University, 1975), p. 3.

4. Ibid., p. 20.

5. Kim and Roemer, p. 20.

6. Dae Young Kim, "Migration and Korean Development," in Repetto et al., Chapter 3, p. 4.

7. Peter Donaldson, "The Evolution of the Korean Family Planning Program," in Repetto et al., Chapter 6, p. 8.

8. Paul W. Kuznets, *Economic Growth and Structure in the Republic of Korea* (New Haven, 1977), p. 201.

9. See Donaldson, in Repetto et al. and references cited therein.

10. The total fertility rate (TFR) is the sum of the age-specific birth rates per thousand for all women of childbearing ages. Because it combines the fertility for all the childbearing ages for a given year, it represents the completed fertility of a synthetic cohort of women. A TFR of 3.9 indicates that the synthetic woman, representing all women of childbearing ages at that time, would have 3.9 live births.

11. Robert Repetto, Chapter 4, pp. 81–82.

12. Catherine S. Pierce, "Population Growth, Programs and Policies" in Parvez Hasan and D. C. Rao, coordinating authors, *Korea: Policy Issues for Long-Term Development* (Baltimore, 1979), p. 124.

13. This section draws heavily on Edwin S. Mills and Byung-Nak Song.

14. As pointed out by Williamson, capital gains on land are neither recorded as income nor as savings in the national income accounts, but they are a form of appreciation and accumulation for the landowners and substitute for other forms of saving. Williamson, "Why Do Koreans Save 'So Little'?"

15. Mills and Song, p. 218.

16. Ibid., p. 225.

17. Ibid., Chapter 9.

18. Ibid., p. 276.

19. Ibid., p. 278.

20. This section draws heavily on the paper by Hakchung Choo and James Jeffers, "Health and Economic and Social Development," prepared in connection with this Korea modernization study.

21. The World Bank, *Growth and Prospects of the Korean Economy, Annex C, Human Resources* (February 1977), pp. 77–78.

22. Choo and Jeffers, p. 21.

23. The World Bank, pp. 46–47.

24. Ibid.

25. Ibid.

26. Ibid.

27. Mills and Song, pp. 274–275.

28. Choo and Jeffers, p. 21

29. Chong Kee Park. *Financing Health Care Services in Korea* (KDI, July 1977), p. 15.

30. Ministry of Health and Social Affairs, *Yearbook of Public Health and Social Statistics, 1976,* Republic of Korea.

31. Choo and Jeffers, pp. 56–57.

TWELVE   *Income Distribution*

1. For a discussion of the properties of this measure, see Henri Theil, *Economics and Information Theory* (Amsterdam, 1967), Chapter 4.

2. Among the many efforts are Bertrand Renaud, "Economic Growth and Income Inequality in Korea," World Bank Staff Working Paper No. 240; Hakchung Choo, "Some Sources of Relative Equity in Korean Income Distribution: A Historical Perspective," in *Income Distribution, Employment and Economic Development in Southeast and East Asia* (Tokyo and Manila, July 1975) and the work on Korea of the Income and Assets Distribution Research Project of the Institute of Economic Research, Hitotsubashi University (Toshiyuki Mizoguchi et al.).

3. The upper limit cutoff in recent years was 200,000 wŏn per month until 1975 when it was raised to 350,000 per month. William I. Abraham, "Observations on Korea's Income Distribution and the Adequacy of the Statistical Base," (unpublished paper, April 1976).

4. Using 1973 data, for example, aggregating the "global income" figures (the upper tail of the distribution) reduces the Theil statistic from 1.287 to 1.167.

5. For a more systematic discussion of these issues see Simon Kuznets, "Demographic Aspects of the Size Distribution of Income: An Exploratory Essay," *Economic Development and Cultural Change*, October 1976, pp. 1–94.

6. Ministry of Agriculture and Fisheries, *Agricultural Census, 1970*, Volume 10, pp. 68–69.

7. For a discussion of Korean land reform, see Ban, Moon, and Perkins, Chapter 9.

8. This figure is from Ban, Moon, and Perkins and was derived according to a methodology first worked out by Jae Hong Cho, "Post-1945 Land Reforms and Their Consequences in South Korea," (unpublished PhD dissertation, Indiana University, 1964), p. 92.

9. This discussion is based on Ban, Moon, and Perkins, Chapter 9.

10. In the People's Republic of China, for example, collectivization has had little impact on differences among regions where the income of the richest 10% of the regions is on average four times that of the poorest 10%.

11. See discussion in Albert Keidel, "Regional Agricultural Production and Income," in Ban, Moon, and Perkins.

12. Ibid.

13. Ibid.

14. David Lindauer, "Labor Market Behavior in Developing Countries," (unpublished PhD dissertation, Harvard University, forthcoming).

15. This observation is made using data aggregated at the 5-digit (KSIC) industry level and relies on an assumption of stable intra-industry worker group income distribution.

16. Lindauer.

17. Shinichi Yoshioka, "A Study on Wage Distribution in Korea and Japan," Income and Assets Distribution Research Project, Hitotsubashi University, April 1976.

18. Young-Il Chung, "Over Time Changes in the Regional and Urban-Rural Income Differences in Korea," Income and Assets Distribution Reserach Project of Hitotsubashi University, p. 21.

19. Derived from data in Ban, Moon, and Perkins.

20. See paper by Roger Sedjo, "Korean Historical Experience and the Labor-Surplus Model," *The Journal of Developing Areas,* January 1976, pp. 213–222. Surplus labor as the term is used here refers to a situation where the marginal product of rural labor is below some institutionally set rural wage. The jury is still out on whether Korea ever had surplus labor in this formal sense.

21. These profits were, of course, being shared by a larger and larger number of businessmen, but it is likely that profits per recipient were still rising much faster than real wages.

22. Hakchung Choo, "Some Sources of Relative Equity," pp. 62–63.

23. The discussion in this section is based mainly on McGinn et al.

24. McGinn et al.

25. Roy Bahl, "The Distributional Effects of the Korean Budget During the Modernization Process."

26. Ibid.

27. Ibid.

28. Irma Adelman and Sherman Robinson, *Income Distribution Policy in Developing Countries: A Case Study of Korea* (Stanford University Press, 1978).

29. Adelman and Robinson, pp. 198–199.

30. For an analysis of Korean savings behavior, see Jeffrey Williamson, "Why Do Koreans Save 'So Little'?"

31. This phrase is from Irma Adelman, in Hollis Chenery et al., *Redistribution with Growth: The Case of Korea.*

THIRTEEN   *Summary and Conclusions*

1. Henderson, p. 182.

2. L. R. Christensen and D. Cummings, "Korean Real Product, Real

Factor Input and Productivity, 1960–1973," Social Research Institute, No. 7507 (Madison, University of Wisconsin, 1975).

3. Young Chin Kim and Jene K. Kwon, *Capital Utilization in Korean Manufacturing, 1962–1971,* Korea Industrial Development Research Institute, May 1973.

4. Chang Young Jeong, "Rates of Return on Investments in Education: the Case of Korea," K.D.I., W. P. 7408, September 1974.

5. Edward F. Denison and William K. Chung, *How Japan's Economy Grew So Fast: the Sources of Post-War Expansion* (Washington, D.C., 1976), p. 48.

6. Brown, p. 265.

7. Leroy P. Jones, "Public Enterprise and Economic Development: the Korea Case" (K.D.I., Seoul, 1975), p. 203.

Selected Bibliography

Principal Statistical Sources

Bank of Korea (Han'guk Ŭnhaeng). *Annual Economic Review of Korea: 1948*. Seoul. (Text in Korean, Statistics in both Korean and English.)

——. *Economic Review: 1949*. Seoul. (Text in Korean, Statistics in both Korean and English.)

——. *Monthly Statistical Review*, May 1947–May 1950. Seoul. (Text in Korean, Statistics in both Korean and English.)

——. *Annual Economic Review*, 1951–1959. Seoul. (Text in Korean, Statistics in both Korean and English.)

——. *Economic Statistics Yearbook*, 1960–1976. Seoul. (In both Korean and English.)

——. *Monthly Statistical Review*, March 1951–March 1969. (Text in Korean, Statistics in both Korean and English.)

——. *Monthly Economic Statistics*, April 1969–. Seoul. (Statistics in both Korean and English.)

——. *National Income Statistics Yearbook, 1972, 1973*. Seoul. (Text in Korean, Statistics in both Korean and English.)

——. *National Income in Korea, 1975*. Seoul. (Text in Korean, Statistics in both Korean and English.)

——. *Flow of Funds Account in Korea, 1971*. Seoul. (Text in Korean, Statistics in both Korean and English.)

——. *Input-output Tables, 1960, 1963, 1966, 1968, 1970, and 1973*. Seoul. (In both Korean and English.)

Chōsen Sōtokufu (Japanese Government General in Korea). *Chōsen Sōtokufu tōkei nenpō*. (Annual statistical report of the office of the Governor General of Korea.) Seoul.

Economic Planning Board, Bureau of Statistics. *Korea Statistical Yearbook 1952–1973*. Seoul. (In both Korean and English.)

——. *Annual Report on the Family Income and Expenditure Survey*, 1971, 1975. Seoul.

——. *Annual Report on Price Survey.*

——. *Annual Report on the Economically Active Population.*

——. *Economic Survey (Annual), 1966–1973.* Seoul.

Economic Planning Board, Korea Development Bank. *Report on Mining and Manufacturing Census, 1963, 1966, 1968.* Seoul.

——. *Report on Mining and Manufacturing Survey, 1967, 1969–72.*

Han'guk Ŭnhaeng (Bank of Korea). *Sanŏp yŏn'gwanp'yo chaksŏng pogo, 1960, 1963, 1966, 1968, 1970 and 1973.* (Report on input-output tables compiled in these years.)

International Monetary Fund. *International Financial Statistics Annual Report on Exchange Restrictions, 1966–1970.*

Keijō Nipposha (Keijō Newspaper Co.) *Chōsen nenkan* (Korean yearbook) 1942–1944. Seoul.

Korean Agricultural Bank. *Agricultural Yearbook.* Seoul.

Korean Electric Association. *The Electric Yearbook.* Seoul.

Korean Traders Association. *Statistical Yearbook of Foreign Trade.* Seoul.

Ministry of Agriculture and Forestry (Fisheries since 1973). *Agricultural Census 1960,* Seoul 1964; *1970,* Seoul 1973.

——. *Grain Statistics Yearbook.* Seoul.

——. *Report on the Results of Farm Household Economic Survey, 1965–1975.* Seoul.

——. *Yearbook of Agriculture and Forestry Statistics.*

Ministry of Commerce and Industry. Korea Reconstruction Bank. *Final Report, Census of Mining and Manufacturing, 1955, 1958, 1960.* Seoul.

Ministry of Construction. *Statistical Yearbook.* Seoul.

Ministry of Education. *Statistical Yearbook of Education.*

Ministry of Finance. *Summary of Financial Implementation.* Seoul.

Ministry of Health and Social Affairs. *Yearbook of Health and Social Statistics.*

Ministry of Home Affairs. *Land Registration Statistics, 1973.*

Ministry of Transportation. *Statistics Yearbook of Transportation.*

Taiwan: Economic Planning Council, Executive Yuan. *Taiwan Statistical Data Book 1975.* Taipei, 1975.

Taiwan: Directorate General of Budget, Accounting and Statistics, Executive Yuan. *National Income of the Republic of China.* Taipei, 1973.

The World Bank. *Atlas.* Washington D. C., 1976.

United Nations. *Yearbook of International Trade Statistics.*

Zenkoku Keizai Chōsa Kikan Rengōkai (National Economic Survey Federation). *Chōsen keizai nenpō.* (Korean economic yearbook). Seoul, 1942.

General

Adams, Donald K. "Education in Korea, 1945–1955." Unpublished PhD dissertation, University of Connecticut, 1956.

Adelman, Irma, ed. *Practical Approaches to Development Planning: Korea's Second Five-Year Plan.* Baltimore, Johns Hopkins University Press, 1969.

—— and Cynthia Taft Morris. *Society, Politics and Economic Development: A Quantitative Approach.* Baltimore, Johns Hopkins University Press, 1967.

—— and Sherman Robinson. *Income Distribution Policy in Developing Countries: A Case Study of Korea.* Stanford, Stanford University Press, 1978.

Allen, Richard C. *Korea's Syngman Rhee, An Unauthorized Portrait.* Rutland, Vermont, Charles E. Tuttle, 1960.

Bahl, Roy W. "The Distributional Effect of the Korean Budget During the Modernization Process." Mimeographed. Syracuse, New York, 1977.

—— and Chuk Kyo Kim. "Modernization and Long-Term Growth of Korean Government Expenditures." Mimeographed. Syracuse, New York, 1977.

Ban, Sung Hwan (Pan, Sŏng-hwan). *The Growth of Korean Agriculture 1968–1971.* Seoul, Korea Development Institute, 1974.

—— Pal Yong Moon (P'ar-Yong Mun), and Dwight H. Perkins. *Rural Development.* Studies in the Modernization of the Republic of Korea: 1945–1975. Cambridge, Mass., Council on East Asian Studies, Harvard University, 1980.

Becker, Garry S. *Human Capital: A Theoretical and Empirical Analysis with Particular Reference to Education.* New York, Columbia University Press, 1964.

Bishop, Isabella Bird. *Korea and Her Neighbors.* Seoul, Reprint. Yonsei University Press, 1970.

Bloomfield, Arthur I. and John P. Jensen. *Banking Reform in South Korea.* New York, Federal Reserve Bank of New York, 1951.

Brandt, Vincent. *A Korean Village Between Farm and Sea.* Cambridge, Mass., Harvard University Press, 1971.

Brown, Gilbert T. *Korean Pricing Policies and Economic Development in the 1960s.* Baltimore, Johns Hopkins University Press, 1973.

Brown, William A. and Redvers Opie. *American Foreign Assistance.* Washington, D.C., Brookings Institution, 1953.

Bureau of Agriculture and Forestry, Government General of Korea, *Nōka keizai gaikyō chōsa.* 1940.

Chenery, Hollis B. and Lance Taylor. "Development Patterns: Among Countries and Over Time." *Review of Economics and Statistics.* November 1968.

—— S. Shishido, and T. Wantanabe. "The Patterns of Japanese Growth, 1914–1954," *Econometrica.* January 1962.

—— and Moises Syrquin. *Patterns of Development 1950–1970*. London, Oxford University Press, 1975.

—— et al. *Redistribution with Growth*. London, Oxford University Press, 1974.

Chandavarkar, Anand G. "Some Aspects of Interest Rate Policies in Less Developed Economies: The Experience of Selected Asian Countries." *International Monetary Fund Staff Papers*, Vol. 18. March 1971.

Cho, Jae Hong. "Post-1945 Land Reforms and Their Consequences in South Korea." Unpublished PhD dissertation, Indiana University, 1964.

Cho, Yong Sam (Cho Yong-sam). *"Disguised Unemployment" in Underdeveloped Areas with Special Reference to South Korean Agriculture*. Berkeley, University of California Press, 1963.

Choi, Hochin. *The Economic History of Korea*. Seoul, The Freedom Library, 1971.

Choo, Hakchung (Chu, Hak-chung) and James Jeffers. "Health and Economic and Social Development." Mimeographed. Seoul, Korea Development Institute, 1978.

Chough, Soon (Cho Sun). "The Economics of Price Supervision." *Seoul National University Economic Review*, December 1968.

Christiensen, L. R. and D. Cummings. "Korean Real Product, Real Factor Input and Productivity, 1960–1973." Social Systems Research Institute No. 7507. Madison, University of Wisconsin, 1975.

Chung, Kyung Cho. *Korea, The Third Republic*. New York, Macmillan, 1972.

Cole, David C. and Princeton N. Lyman. *Korean Development: The Interplay of Politics and Economics*. Cambridge, Mass., Harvard University Press, 1971.

—— and Yung Chul Park. "Financial Development in Korea, 1945–1978." Seoul, KDI Working Paper 7904, 1979.

Coleman, James et al. *Equality of Educational Opportunity*. Washington, U.S. Office of Education, 1966.

Corden, N. M. *The Theory of Protection*. London, Oxford University Press, 1971.

Crick, Bernard. *In Defence of Politics*. London, Weidenfeld and Nicholson, 1962.

Dahl, Robert A. and Charles E. Lindblom. *Politics, Economics and Welfare: Planning and Politico-Economic Processes Resolved into Basic Social Processes*. New York, Harper, 1953.

Davis, Kingsley. *World Urbanization, 1950–1970*. Population Monograph Series No. 4. Berkeley, University of California Press, 1970.

Denison, Edward F. and William K. Chung. *How Japan's Economy Grew So Fast: The Sources of Post-War Expansion*. Washington, D.C., The Brookings Institution, 1976.

Dore, Ronald. *The Diploma Disease: Education, Qualification, and Development*. Berkeley, University of California Press, 1976.

——. *Education in Tokugawa Japan*. Berkeley, University of California Press, 1965.

Eckstein, Alexander. "Individualism and the Role of the State in Economic Growth." *Economic Development and Cultural Change*, Vol. 6 (1957/58).

Eisenstadt, S. N. *Modernization: Protest and Change*. Englewood Cliffs, New Jersey, Prentice-Hall, 1966.

Fairbank, J. K., ed. *The Chinese World Order*. Cambridge, Mass., Harvard University Press, 1968.

Frank, Charles R., Jr., Kwang Suk Kim (Kwang-sŏk Kim), and Larry Westphal. *Foreign Trade Regimes and Economic Development: South Korea*. New York, National Bureau of Economic Research, 1975.

Geertz, Clifford. *Peddlers and Princes*. Chicago, University of Chicago Press, 1965.

Gerschenkron, Alexander. "Ideology as a System Determinant," *Comparison of Economic Systems*. Edited by Alexander Eckstein. Berkeley, University of California Press, 1971.

Hagen, Everett. *The Economics of Development*. Homewood, Illinois, Richard D. Irwin, 1968.

Hahn, Bae-Ho (Han, Pae-ho). "Korean Politics and Perspectives for Political Development." *Social Science Journal*, III, Seoul, 1975.

——. "Political Context of Economic Development." Typed. Korea University, 1974.

Han, Sungjoo. *The Failure of Democracy in South Korea*. Berkeley, University of California Press, 1974.

Harbison, Frederick H. *Human Resources as the Wealth of Nations*. New York, Oxford University Press, 1973.

Hasan, Parvez. *Korea: Problems and Issues in a Rapidly Growing Economy*. Baltimore, Johns Hopkins University Press, 1976.

—— and D. C. Rao. *Korea, Policy Issues for Long-Term Development*. Baltimore, Johns Hopkins University Press, 1979.

Henderson, Gregory. *Korea: The Politics of the Vortex*. Cambridge, Mass., Harvard University Press, 1968.

Hirschman, Albert O. *The Strategy of Economic Development*. New Haven, Yale University Press, 1958.

Hirschmeier, Johannes and Tsunehiko Yui. *The Development of Japanese Business, 1600–1978*. Cambridge, Mass., Harvard University Press, 1975.

Hong, Wontack (Hong, Wŏn-t'aek). *Factor Supply and Factor Intensity of Trade in Korea*. Seoul, Korea Development Institute, 1976.

——. *Trade Distortions and Employment Growth in Korea*. Seoul, Korea Development Institute, 1979.

—— and Anne O. Krueger, eds. *Trade and Development in Korea*. Seoul, Korea Development Institue, 1975.

Husen, Torsten, ed. *International Study of Achievement in Mathematics: A Comparison of Twelve Countries.* Stockholm and New York, Wiley, 1967.

Indian Institute of Management at Bangalore. *Overview of Public Enterprise Sector in India.* Bangalore, 1976.

Inkeles, Alex. "Becoming Modern: Individual Changes in Six Developing Countries," *Ethos*, 3.2 (Summer 1975).

Janowitz, Morris. "Military Institutions and Coertion in the Developing Nations." Mimeographed. Chicago, September 1975.

Jencks, Christopher et al. *Inequality.* New York, Harper and Row, 1972.

Jeong, Chang Young (Chŏng, Ch'ang-yŏng). "Rates of Return on Investment in Education: The Case of Korea." Seoul, Korea Development Institute W.P. 7408, 1974.

Jo, Sung-hwan (Sŏng-hwan Cho). "Direct Private Investment in South Korea: An Economic Survey." Seoul, Korea Development Institute Working Paper 7707, 1977.

Johnson, E. A. G. *American Imperialism in the Image of Peer Gynt: Memoirs of a Professor-Bureaucrat.* Minneapolis, University of Minnesota Press, 1971.

Jones, Homer. *Korean Financial Problems,* Seoul, 1968.

Jones, Leroy P. *Public Enterprise and Economic Development: The Korean Case.* Seoul, Korea Development Institute Press, 1976.

—— and Il SaKong. *Government, Business, and Entrepreneurship in Economic Development: The Korean Case.* Studies in the Modernization of the Republic of Korea: 1945–1975. Cambridge, Mass., Council on East Asian Studies, Harvard University, 1980.

Kim, Byong Kuk. *Central Banking Experiment in a Developing Economy.* Seoul, 1965.

Kim, Joungwan Alexander. "Korean Kundrehwa: The Military as Modernizer," *Journal of Comparative Administration.* November 1970.

——. *Divided Korea: The Politics of Development, 1945–1972.* Cambridge, Mass., East Asian Research Center, Harvard University, 1975.

Kim, Kwang Suk (Kim, Kwang-sŏk). "Sources of Industrial Growth and Structural Change in Korea." Seoul, Korea Development Institute, W.P. 7703, 1977.

——. *Han'guk inp'ŭlleisyŏn ŭi wŏnin kwa yŏnghyang.* Seoul, 1973. For an English summary of this monograph see Kim, K. S., ed., *Planning and Economic Policy Issues,* Seoul, 1977.

Kim, Young Chin (Kim, Yŏng-jin), and Jene K. Kwon (Chin-gyun Kwŏn). *Capital Utilization in Korean Manufacturing, 1962–1971.* Seoul, Korea Development Institute, 1973.

Koh, Harold. "The Early History of U.S. Economic Assistance to the Republic of Korea." Mimeographed. Cambridge, Mass., September 1975.

Krueger, Anne O. *Foreign Trade Regimes and Economic Development: Liberalization Attempts and Consequences.* Cambridge, Mass., National Bureau of Economic Research, 1978.

——. *The Developmental Role of the Foreign Sector and Aid.* Studies in the Modernization of the Republic of Korea: 1945–1975. Cambridge, Mass., Council on East Asian Studies, Harvard University, 1979.

Kuznets, Paul W. *Economic Growth and Structure in the Republic of Korea.* New Haven, Yale University Press, 1977.

Kuznets, Simon. "Demographic Aspects of the Size Distribution of Income: An Exploratory Essay." *Economic Development and Cultural Change.* October 1976.

Kwon, Tai Hwan (Kwŏn T'ae-hwan), Hae Young Lee (Hae-yŏng Yi), Yunshik Chang (Yun-sik Chang), and Eui-Young Yu (Ŭi-yŏng Yu). *The Population of Korea.* Seoul, The Population and Development Studies Center, Seoul National University, 1975.

Lee, Hahn-Been (Yi, Han-bin). *Korea: Time, Change, and Public Administration.* Honolulu, University of Hawaii, 1968.

—— and In-jŏung Whang (In-jŏng Hwang). "Development of Senior Administrators: The Korean Experience." *Koreana Quarterly,* Autumn 1973.

Lewis, John P. *Reconstruction and Development in South Korea.* Planning Pamphlet No. 94. Washington, D. C., National Planning Association, 1955.

Lewis, W. Arthur. "Economic Development with Unlimited Supplies of Labour," *The Manchester School,* May 1954.

Lindauer, David. "Labor Market Behavior in Developing Countries." Unpublished PhD dissertation, Harvard University, 1980.

Lockwood, W. W., ed. *The State and Economic Enterprise in Japan.* Princeton, Princeton University Press, 1965.

Lyons, Gene M. *Military Policy and Economic Aid: The Korean Case, 1950–1953.* Columbus, Ohio State University Press, 1961.

McClelland, David C. *The Achieving Society.* Princeton, Princeton University Press, 1961.

McCune, George and Arthur L. Grey, Jr. *Korea Today.* Cambridge, Mass., Harvard University Press, 1950.

McGinn, Noel F. and Donald R. Snodgrass, Yung Bong Kim, Shin-Bok Kim and Quee-Young Kim. *Education and Development in Korea.* Studies in the Modernization of the Republic of Korea: 1945–1975. Cambridge, Mass., Council on East Asian Studies, Harvard University, 1980.

McKinnon, Ronald I. *Money and Capital in Economic Development.* Washington, D.C., The Brookings Institution, 1973.

Meade, E. Grant. *American Military Government in Korea.* New York, Columbia University Press, 1951.

Mills, Edwin S. and Byung-Nak Song. *Urbanization and Urban Problems.* Studies in the Modernization of the Republic of Korea: 1945–1975. Cambridge, Mass., Council on East Asian Studies, Harvard University, 1979.

Mitchell, Clyde. "Land Reform in Asia, a Case Study." Pamphlet No. 78, Washington, D.C., National Planning Association, 1952.

Myrdal, Gunnar. *Asian Drama.* 3 vols. New York, Twentieth Century Fund, 1968.

Nadiri, M. Ishaq. "Some Approaches to the Theory and Measurement of Total Factor Productivity: A Survey." *Journal of Economic Literature.* December 1970.

Nam, Sang Woo. "Financial Structure, Corporate Investment and Financing Behavior in Korea." Cambridge, Mass., PhD dissertation, Massachusetts Institute of Technology, 1977.

Osgood, Cornelius. *The Koreans and Their Culture.* Tokyo, Charles Tuttle, 1951.

Palais, James B. *Politics and Policy in Traditional Korea.* Cambridge, Mass. Harvard University Press, 1975.

Pak, Ki Hyuk (Pak, Ki-hyŏk) et al. *A Study of Land Tenure System in Korea.* Seoul, Korea Land Economics Research Center, 1966.

Papanek, Gustav F. "The Effect of Aid and Other Resource Transfers on Savings and Growth in Less Developed Countries." *The Economic Journal.* September 1972.

Park, Chung Hee. *Our Nation's Path.* Seoul, Hollym Corporation, 1970.

——. *The Country, the Revolution and I.* Seoul, Hollym Corporation, 1963.

Park, Chong Kee. *Development and Modernization of Korea's Tax System.* Seoul, Korea Development Institute, 1977.

——. *Social Security in Korea: An Approach to Socio-Economic Development.* Seoul, Korea Development Institute, 1975.

——. *Financing Health Care Services in Korea.* Seoul, Korea Development Institute, July 1977.

Peaker, G. F. *The Plowden Children Four Years Later.* Slough National Foundation for Educational Research in England and Wales, 1971.

Perkins, Dwight H. "Government as an Obstacle to Industrialization: The Case of Nineteenth-Century China," *The Journal of Economic History.* December 1967.

——. *Agricultural Development in China 1368–1968.* Chicago, Aldine Press, 1969.

Pierce, Catherine S. "Population Growth, Programs and Policies," in Parvez Hasan and D. C. Rao, coordinating authors, *Korea: Policy Issues for Long-Term Development.* Baltimore, Johns Hopkins Press, 1979.

Psacharopoulos, George and Keith Hinchliffe. *Returns to Education: An International Comparison.* Amsterdam, Elsevier Scientific, and San Francisco, Jossey-Bass, 1973.

Pu, Wan Hyok (Pu, Wan-hyŏk). "The History of American Aid to Korea." *Koreana Quarterly.* Summer 1969.

Pye, Lucien W. *Aspects of Political Democracy*, Boston, Little Brown, 1966.

Ranis, Gustav R. and J. H. Fei. "A Theory of Economic Development." *American Economic Review.* September 1968.

Renaud, Bertrand. "Economic Growth and Income Inequality in Korea." World Bank Staff Working Paper No. 240, Washington, D. C.

Repetto, Robert, Dae Young Kim, Tae Hwan Kwon, Peter Donaldson, and Son-Ung Kim. "Economic Development, Population Policy and the Demographic Transition in the Republic of Korea." Typed, Cambridge, 1977.

Riggs, Fred W. *Administration in Developing Countries.* Boston, Houghton Mifflin, 1964.

Robinson, E. A. G. and J. E. Vaizey, eds. *The Economics of Education.* New York, St. Martin's Press, 1966.

Schumpeter, Joseph A. *The Theory of Economic Development.* Cambridge, Mass., Harvard University Press, 1934.

Shaw, Edward S. *Financial Deepening in Economic Development.* New York, Oxford University Press, 1973.

Shin, Roy W. "The Politics of Foreign Aid: A Study of the Impact of United States Aid in Korea from 1945 to 1966." PhD dissertation, University of Minnesota, 1969.

Shin, Susan. "Land Tenure and the Agrarian Economy in Yi Dynasty Korea: 1600–1800." PhD dissertation, Harvard University, 1973.

Smith, Thomas C. *The Agrarian Origins of Modern Japan.* Stanford, Stanford University Press, 1959.

Soon, Sung Cho. *Korea in World Politics 1940–50: An Evaluation of American Responsibility.* Berkeley, University of California Press, 1967.

Syrquin, Moises. "Sources of Industrial Growth and Change: An Alternative Measure." World Bank, 1976.

Tewksbury, Donald G. *Source Materials on Korean Politics and Ideologies.* New York, Institute of Pacific Relations, 1950.

Theil, Henri. *Economics and Information Theory.* Amsterdam, North Holland Press, 1967.

Unwin, George. *Studies in Economic History.* London, Macmillan, 1927.

U. S. Arms Control and Disarmament Agency. *World Military Expenditures and Arms Trade, 1963–73.* Washington, G. P. O., 1974.

U. S. Central Intelligence Agency. "Korea, the Economic Race Between

North and South." Washington, National Foreign Assessment Center, January 1978.

U. S. House of Representatives. *Korean Aid.* 81st Congress. 1st Session. Hearings before the Committee on Foreign Affairs on H. R. 5330, June 8–23, 1949. Washington, G. P. O., 1949.

U. S. Operations Mission to Korea. *Rural Development Program Evaluation Report, Korea.* Seoul, 1967.

Vogel, Ezra F. "Kinship Structure, Migration to the City, and Modernization," in *Aspects of Social Change in Modern Japan.* Princeton, Princeton University Press, 1967.

Wald, Haskell. "The Recent Experience of the Republic of Korea with Tax Collections in Kind," in Wald and Froomkin, eds., *Agricultural Taxation and Economic Development.* Cambridge, Mass., Harvard University Press, 1954.

Wedemeyer, A. C. (Lt. General). *Korea: Report to the President.* Committee on Armed Services, U. S. Senate, Washington, G. P. O., 1951.

Westphal, Larry E. and Kwang Suk Kim. "Industrial Policy and Development in Korea." World Bank Staff Working Paper No. 263, Washington, August 1977.

—— and Kyu Soo Kim (Kyu-su Kim). "KDI Input-Output Data Bank." Seoul, Korea Development Institute, 1977.

Williamson, Jeffrey. "Why Do Koreans Save 'So Little'?" *Journal of Development Economics* 5: 343–362 (1979).

Yanaga, Chitoshi. *Big Business in Japanese Politics.* New Haven, Yale University Press, 1968.

Yoshioka, Shinichi. "A Study of Wage Distribution in Korea and Japan." Income and Assets Distribution Research Project, Hitotsubashi University, 1976.

Index

Abortion, 387, 389, 390, 391
Acheson, Dean, 174, 453
Adelman, Irma, 251, 440
Africa, 30, 31, 33, 61, 77
Agricultural Bank, 229, 232
Agricultural Cooperative Law, 232
Agricultural and Industrial Bank, 297
Agricultural services, 11, 12, 13, 81, 82, 90, 225, 228, 350, 450, 480
Agriculture: changes in, 9; mechanization of, 11, 221, 241, 478; under Japanese, 28, 75, 83–85, 90, 297; productivity in, 29, 97, 212, 479; reduced share of, 41, 99, 100, 211, 382, 465; pre-modern, 63–64; commodity product of (1910–1941), 76; at partition, 86, 88, 452; in 1953, 93, 180; in 1960s, 96–97; employment in, 108, 109, 110, 465; labor productivity in, 110, 111; output growth of, 152–153, 213, 258, 479; protection for, 156; and foreign aid, 168; supplies for, 170; and U.S. aid, 191–192, 455, 457; relation of to growth, 209–212, 478; production function for, 214–215, 218–225; government policies on, 11–12, 228–241; government expenditures on, 230–231, 312–313; terms of trade for, 11, 234, 236, 429; courses in, 345; in national income, 431
Aid, economic, foreign, 165–208; from Japan, 3, 165, 166, 181, 202, 206, 459, 480; grants vs. loans, 108, 358–359, 455; after Korean War, 123, 140; per capita, 165, 176; and social change, 204; under Rhee, 249, 305, 328; and chaebŏl, 288; decline in, 330; and education, 358–359; and GNP, 455; and imports, 455. See also Aid, economic, U.N.: Aid, economic, U.S.
Aid, economic, U.N., 3, 15, 93–94, 175–176, 179, 193, 453
Aid, economic, U.S., 165–208, 452, 453–455; and development, 2–3, 55, 166, 293; under Rhee, 7, 13, 15, 19, 29, 40, 77, 93–94, 140; in the 1960s, 14–16, 47; and education, 13, 23, 344–345, 358; reductions in, 46, 95, 108, 129, 141, 172, 174–175, 194, 205, 229, 296, 365, 455, 458–459, 497; grants vs. loans, 2, 190, 191, 197, 198, 199, 204, 206, 455; project vs. program aid, 190, 191, 193–194, 195, 455; disagreements on, 15, 192–193, 196–197, 305–306; and economic research, 179, 193, 194, 200, 202; and agriculture, 218, 228–229, 241; and inflation, 296
Aid, military, U.S., 55, 182–184, 326, 452, 454; under Rhee, 15, 40, 181; under Park, 46; in Vietnam War, 310, 454; effect of on budget, 489; decrease in, 491, 497
Armed forces: under Rhee, 43, 44, 45, 462; under Park, 46, 48–49, 485; size of, 49, 54–55, 452, 454; cost of, 88–89, 310, 491–492; and military assistance programs, 183–184; and financial aid, 197; and management skills, 254, 375, 454; personnel in Park Government, 310, 375, 463
Asia, 30, 31, 33, 36, 138–139, 291
Asian Development Bank, 166, 203
Australia, 43
Automobiles, 290, 317, 393–394, 395, 430, 432

Rhee and Park, 288, 289; education of, 372; incomes of, 442, 444, 484. *See also* Managers
Europe, Communist, 40
Europe, Western, 24, 30–31, 33, 90, 138–139, 490, 172
Exchange rates: 113, 126–130, 132–135; reform of, 1964, 128, 134; in 1968, 155; in 1974, 157; U.S.-Korean, 176–177; under Park, 196, 471; under Rhee, 249, in 1970s, 337. *See also* Foreign exchange
Export expansion (EE), 135–140; and output growth, 150–153; and employment, 161–162; vs. import substitution, 163; government and business in, 266–267; under Japanese, 448–449
Export-import link system, 127–129, 134, 135
Exports: and development, 4–6, 8, 103, 123–124, 126–132, 163, 330, 465; incentives for, 5, 8, 114, 126, 132, 135, 266, 335, 336, 472; expansion of, 4, 8, 14, 98, 103, 104–105, 123, 134–136, 138, 146, 150–151, 163, 309, 334; policy on, 5, 16, 95, 126; manufactured, 6, 8, 85, 87–88, 102, 121, 136, 143; of construction, 8, 124, 302; of rice to Japan, 10, 85, 448; to Japan, 55, 85, 138, 246, 447; to U.S., 55, 138; shifts in, 102, 136–138; and inflation, 113; purchasing-power-parity effective exchange rates for, 114, 132–135, 266; Chenery-Syrquin analysis of, 121, 122; (1953–1960), 126–127, 250, 461; (1961–1965), 127–129, 197; (1966–1977), 130–132; by commodity, 137, 143–146; by destination, 138–139; invisible, 141; and industrialization, 149, 151; protection for, 157; labor and capital in, 159–162, 163–164; and employment, 161, limits on, 162, 492, 497; earnings from, 201, 203, 466; financing of, 335–336; and GNP, 492; future of, 492
Expropriation: of land, 10, 238–239, 421; of Japanese enterprises, 247–248, 273, 288, 457–458. *See also* Land redistribution (reform)

Far Eastern Economic Review, 54

Families: of entrepreneurs, 18; planning for, 20–21, 370, 379, 381, 382, 386–387; size of, 21, 71, 415–418; nuclear vs. extended, 22, 28; and education, 24, 355–359, 360; and welfare, 311; structure of, 413, 415
Farms: output of, 9, 10–11, 13, 422, 429; size of, 421. *See also* Agriculture
Farmers: tenant, 9, 10, 73, 83–85, 419; owner-cultivator, 9, 13, 237–238, 419–421, 457, 480; incomes of, 9, 10, 13, 97, 209, 238–240, 418, 422, 457; and consumer price stabilization, 96; education of, 225, 344; debt cancellations for, 329; family sizes of, 415–416, 418
Federation of Korean Industries, 263, 286
Fei, J. H., 158
Fertility, 379, 381, 383, 387, 389, 391, 406
Fertilizers, chemical: increased use of, 8, 11; industry, 19, 173, 222–223, 229, 279; under Japanese, 82, 222; imports, 168, 222, 223, 228, 229, 436; aid-financed, 168, 172, 175, 180, 192, 202, 204, 222, 453, 455, 479; and agricultural output, 215, 222, 224; output of, 223, 250, 456, 479; distribution of, 224–225; prices of, 271; and public enterprise, 274
Finance companies, 338, 339, 340
Financial Associations, 232, 297
Financial system, 6, 19–20, 295–341; under Japanese, 81, 296, 297–300, 339; during 1950s, 94, 326–327; under Chang Myon, 127; under Park Military Government, 127, 202; mixed with fisc in Asia, 295–296; under U.S. Military Government, 296; fiscal/financial ratios, 300, 307, 340; during WW II, 300, 339; during Korean War, 302–304, 339; during reconstruction, 305–306; in 1960s, 327, 340; government control of, 327, 340, 474–475; reforms of 30 September 1965, 333–337; August 3rd (1972) Emergency Measures, 338; and aid, 339
First Five-Year Plan (FFYP, 1962–1966), 8, 17, 47, 95–96, 103, 255, 387, 464, 467 480

Harvard East Asian Monographs

STUDIES IN THE MODERNIZATION OF THE REPUBLIC OF KOREA: 1945-1975